This book may be kept

An Introduction to
Natural Theology

IMPRIMI POTEST:

Joseph P. Fisher, S.J.

Praep. Prov. Missourianae

IMPRIMATUR:

✠ Joseph E. Ritter

Archiepiscopus Sancti Ludovici

27 Februarii, 1959

An Introduction to Natural Theology

MAURICE R. HOLLOWAY, S.J.

Saint Louis University

New York

APPLETON-CENTURY-CROFTS, INC.

Test edition copyright © 1957
by Maurice R. Holloway

TO
Our Lady
Seat of Wisdom

Foreword

What is the God of the philosopher? Can the philosopher, that is to say, can human reason, unenlightened by the revealed word, come to a true and secure understanding of "He-Who-Is"? Is it possible for mere man, without the impact of a personal experience, intimate and intuitive, to arrive by means of an objective demonstration at an absolute affirmation that the Being we call God exists, or that He is Pure Act, Existence Itself, because without him the world of our experience is unintelligible, a complete contradiction?

And even if we admit, as all Christian philosophers must, that unaided reason is able by its own power to reach an objectively true and secure assent that God exists, is there any evidence, in the recorded history of our world, that man, without the directive knowledge of revelation, ever did secure by a metaphysical effort this absolute truth that the *Ipsum Esse* exists? Whatever be the answer to this difficult problem—and we do not pretend to know it—it is obvious that Father Holloway, in composing his philosophical approach to God, allowed himself to be guided by the knowledge of faith. Indeed, he must have prayed often for the enlightenment which the supernatural motion of divine grace brings even to the limited and imperfect intellect of a philosopher.

But there is another problem which has proved far more tormenting to the mind and heart of the Christian existentialists, men of the stamp of Blaise Pascal, Sören Kirkegaard, and Gabriel Marcel. This problem may be formulated thus: Is the God of the philosopher, whose existence is affirmed as the conclusion of an abstract reasoning process, the same reality which we call the God of religion, whom even an unlettered, ignorant child attains in the existential experience which is the act of faith?

vii

Let us note in passing that we shall not bother to present the pseudo-problem concerning the God of the theologian. For, if theology is a true speculative science, the theologian must found his search for true conclusions upon an act of faith in the revealed word. It would indeed not only be mildly irrational but sheer folly to search for true, scientific inferences when the premises from which the theologian infers these conclusions are themselves the subject of doubt. Our problem, then, regards solely the identity of the God of philosophy with the God of religion, and, if such identity is seen to be evident, since Pure Existence is necessarily unique, one may justly wonder whether any additional element of knowledge or of love is secured in the "connatural" knowledge of faith.

What is the God of religion? Does the acceptance of this God add anything to the content and to the intensity of the intellectual assent of truth attained by the philosopher in his rational search for the source of reality? What need, one may ask, is there in proposing a metaphysical approach, which is admittedly difficult, when, since the grace of God is always given to "him who does what he can" (*facienti quod est in se Deus non deneget gratiam*), anyone can come to the assent of faith, an assent which transcends the human intellect and rests upon the profound security of supernatural love. [1] For, while through a complex process of reasoning, the philosopher labors with rational data that is abstract and complicated, the existential act which we call faith, resulting as it does from an act of love, transforms here and now the life of the existing subject (man). In a manner, faith is the beginning of the vision of God (*inchoatio visionis*), and this vision is the existential end of man.

The knowledge of the philosopher is a knowledge of conclusions; the knowledge of the man of faith is an insight into the data of

----

[1] We are speaking, of course, of formed faith which accompanies justification: "Now the act of faith is an act of the intellect assenting to divine truth at the command of the will moved by the grace of God." (*Summa Theologiae*, II–II, 21, 9, c) "To believe does indeed depend on the will of the believer; but man's will needs to be prepared by God with grace, in order that he may be raised to things which are above his nature." (*Ibid.*, 6, 1, ad 3m) ". . . faith as regards the assent which is the chief act of faith is from God moving man inwardly by grace." (*Ibid.*, c)

revelation. The knowledge thus obtained by faith is not precisely a reasoned or a scientific knowledge. In a way, it is both a lesser and a greater knowledge than the knowledge of the philosopher. It is lesser since it does not possess the objectivity and evidence of philosophy. For the knowledge of faith is an obscure knowledge. "Faith is the evidence of things unseen," "*in speculo et in enigmate.*" On the other hand, it is a greater knowledge, for not only does it attain the intimate perfection of a personal existential experience, but it is an insight into the mystery of the life of God which God has revealed to man, and this insight is a knowledge of God which transcends the power of the human intellect.

When the learned philosopher, when the ignorant peasant speak of God, they declare the same reality, but their understanding of that identical reality differs enormously. The abstract and scientific approach of the philosopher necessarily gives him the certitude of evidence; in the act of faith, God is reached as the term of an intellectual judgment, not through a knowledge of objective evidence, but because of the causality of an act of the will [2] which moves the intellect to a free assent. For, in the act of faith the terms of the judgment are not understood in themselves, but accepted only because this judgment expresses God's revelation of himself to man.

In short: The knowledge of the God of philosophy is a scientific knowledge, a knowledge of conclusions which are derived from self-evident principles and factual experience. The knowledge of the God of religion is an obscure insight into the mysteries of God's life. This knowledge of the act of faith is not inferred from self-evident principles, but depends causally upon an act of love moving the intellect to accept the revealed word. The assent of the philosopher is necessitated by the evidence of a metaphysical

---

[2] ". . . the intellect is moved by the command of the will to assent to what is of faith." (*S.T.*, I–II, 56, 3, c) For, in the act of faith, "the intellect assents to something, not through being sufficiently moved by its proper object, but through an act of choice." (*Ibid.*, II–II, 1, 4, c) On the one hand, "the assent of science is not subject to free choice, because the knower is obliged to assent by the force of the demonstration, but the actual consideration . . . is subject to free choice. . . . On the other hand, in the case of faith, both these things are subject to free choice." (*Ibid.*, 2, 9, ad 2m)

demonstration. This assent is not a free act; in itself it is not a moral act. In the act of faith the knowledge of the revealed word does not necessitate an intellectual assent. This assent is a personal, subjective acceptance through an act of free choice. The act of (formed) faith is existential and meritorious; it is related to the last end.

From this parallel examination of the nature of the scientific study of the philosopher, and of the act of faith of the believer, we can infer the importance of a philosophical approach to God. Because the affirmation of the God of religion in the act of faith is an existential, personal experience, it is wholly *incommunicable*. Such an act would be an irrational affirmation if it did not suppose some rational, objective knowledge, some secure estimation of the fact of God's existence, an objective knowledge which can be communicated to all men. This objective, communicable, secure knowledge is provided by the philosopher. For the knowledge of the God of philosophy is a scientific, an objectively evident knowledge; consequently it is communicable. It will supply a rational, secure basis which man, any man, must require, if not in its entirety, at least indirectly, as a fundamental estimation of the existence of a Supreme Being. This rational basis, human reason must possess at least implicitly in the formation of the act of faith. While the act of faith need not actually depend upon a metaphysical process, the objective presentation of the philosopher in presenting a formal demonstration of the existence of God paves the way towards faith, for it proposes a necessary foundation for the acceptance of the God of religion, of the Triune God.

Today, with the confusion prevalent in the minds of many, and the despairing attitude that is not uncommon among thinkers, a clear, objective presentation of a knowledge of God attained through a metaphysical analysis of self-evident principles will help answer the anguished questioning of the existentialist-agnostic; it will do away with the uncertainties of the Neo-Kantian; it will dissipate the disturbing sadness, a sadness which is "unto death," of the materialists and logical-positivists.

This is the scope of the work Father Maurice Holloway proposed to achieve, and this endeavor he has fulfilled. Father Holloway's natural theology will be of value, not only in clarifying the young minds of university students, in communicating to them the security of a metaphysical foundation, and in forming in their thinking strong intellectual convictions, but this excellent book should also be a help to many others who are groping in their search for an absolute Truth to guide their lives.

It is always a source of profound satisfaction and heartfelt joy to one who has spent his life in the exciting work of teaching, of training the mind of the young to understand and love the great truths of philosophy, when he comes to the realization that one of his students has outdistanced his teacher. This realization in the evening of one's life is a very rewarding thought. May Father Holloway compose many books which will help men to find truth and to live accordingly, so that the day may come that these men, no longer hampered in their thinking by the limitations of the reasoning process of philosophy, nor by the obscurity of faith which is our lot in this life, may finally see God "as he is," *facie ad faciem.*

HENRI RENARD, S.J.

Preface

"The study of philosophy," writes St. Thomas Aquinas, "is not for the purpose of knowing what men have thought, but to know the truth of things." [1] It is the wise student that makes these words the ideal of his intellectual life. In natural theology, which is the crowning point and supreme moment in the science of metaphysics, we want to know what is the truth about God, insofar as that truth can be grasped by the human intellect reflecting upon the data of existing things. It may well be that the human intellect in its present condition cannot attain to an overwhelming knowledge of the first cause of things; it may be that this knowledge is highly imperfect, both in its content and mode. But it should be abundantly clear that such knowledge is supremely important. Natural theology is the queen and the crown of all natural sciences, and a little bit of a precious thing is of greater value than a lot of what is mediocre or inferior. Sacred theology, for example, teaches us that the least amount of sanctifying grace is of greater value than the whole material universe, than the whole natural order of things. For grace is of an essentially higher order than the natural order, since it is a real sharing in the inner life of the Blessed Trinity. So we could say, *mutatis mutandis*, that a little knowledge of the first cause is of more value than much knowledge about finite beings. For it is a knowledge of the Infinite, Necessary Being.

A Christian student is one who wishes to develop and to use his intelligence in the service of Christ the King. The fact that it is in this service that he is putting his intelligence demands an excellence and an effort that is as perfect as the student can make it. [2] But if anyone wants to be an intelligent Christian, he must acquire

[1] *Commentary on the Heavens*, Book One, lecture 22. Parma Edition, Vol. 19, p. 58.
[2] See Etiènne Gilson, *Christianity and Philosophy* (New York. Sheed & Ward, 1939), pp. 103–25.

truth for its own sake. If a person, for example, wants to practice medicine for God, he must first begin by learning the science of medicine, and this means that he must begin to learn the science of medicine *for itself,* since that is the only way a knowledge of a science can be acquired. No one can use anything unless he first possesses it; once we possess a thing we can always use it as an instrument. And that is why we must always begin by learning a science for its own sake. The end of a theoretical science, such as the science of natural theology, is to know and understand the truth of things.

Our supreme interest then in studying natural theology is to know the truth about God. It is not to engage in a dialogue with our contemporaries over the problems of a theistic philosophy. It is not to play the apologete, and answer the arguments, real and specious, of those who deny our positions. Our prime purpose and our supreme effort is to understand the truth. Apologetics and dialogues are by-products of the habit of science. They are important, and even necessary in their own order, but they are secondary to the acquirement of the truth. Again, there is no one who does not see this simple truth: only that person can safely and successfully engage in apologetics or in a dialogue who possesses the knowledge of the truth of things.

On the other hand, in our pursuit of knowledge we should be vitally aware of the real contemporary problems. It would be a mistake to consider the truths we wish to make our own concerning the existence and the nature of God as so many pieces of mental archaeology, stored in our memory and brought forth in ready-made answers as occasion requires. Knowledge is life, the life of the intelligence. And the student should try to get behind the fixed formula or the definition in which scientific thought is often expressed, and grasp the living truth embodied there. We should learn, by an effort of our intelligence, to think beyond words, and arrive at an understanding of things. Our intellect is a power of understanding, it is a vision. Our intellect is something that sees, and what it sees is reality as intelligible, as yielding up a certain meaning, as manifesting a certain transparency. And what reality yields up to the intellect is being itself, that can be shared in and

lived by the mind. Our intellect is a being that answers to being.
What we know is reality, relived in our intelligence. Unfortunately,
the expressions of the truth in words is often a faulty and mis-
leading affair. Words at times can hide more than they reveal. But
we must never forget that words signify things, not our ideas of
things, although they signify things by way of our ideas. [3]

So it is a knowledge of things that we want, not words; an understanding of being, not of formulas or mere definitions. One who
understands the truth of things, can read what a modern philosopher or scientist has to say about God, and can see where or why
they may be wrong in what they say, or in what sense they may
be perfectly right, even though that truth is expressed in terms
entirely different from the ones with which the reader is familiar;
or, as often happens, even though terms familiar enough to the
reader are used, terms like substance, relation, etc., but used with
entirely different meanings.

One more point. In the pages that follow we appeal rather continually to the works of St. Thomas Aquinas. This is for one reason
only. Because here we find the truth of things profoundly grasped,
clearly explained, and advanced with the greatest amount of evidence and certitude. This is our only reason for using these writings. There are certain modern problems concerning God that were
not envisioned by the Angelic Doctor, at least not in the precise
terms in which they are put by modern or contemporary thought.
But even in these cases, the student will find in St. Thomas the
principles of a solution, principles that are present implicitly, if not
formally and explicitly. Part of the habit of science is to draw new
conclusions from principles, and to see certain conclusions as principles for further solutions.

Method of Procedure

In the presentation of the positive matter of our science,
we shall adopt a certain set method, one we feel is best suited
to the normal inventive movement of the intellect and which
engenders most effectively within our intelligence the actual
existence of the science. In general, the method is as follows: first,

[3] See St. Thomas, *Summa Theologiae*, Pt. I, qu. 13, art. 1.

we shall present the problem as clearly and carefully as we can. Then, to see it precisely as a problem, we shall advance two or three difficulties it involves. After this, we shall appeal to evidence and reflect upon this evidence; or we shall appeal to previously understood knowledge. In this way we shall gain an understanding of the principles involved in a solution. When this solution is reached and understood, the difficulties originally advanced will be answered or distinguished. Then, by way of summary and synthesis, we shall formulate our findings in the form of a thesis.

Most of the historical matter has been put in appendixes. Appendix A (which treats of some famous, but invalid, philosophical proofs for the existence of God) could best be read after Chapter 2, and Appendix B (on the different agnostic philosophers) after Chapter 3. Appendices C, D, and E (on invalid proofs for God's existence from positive science, on Existentialism, and on Atheism, respectively) should be read after Chapter 4, which contains the five ways of St. Thomas. Finally, the last appendix (Appendix F, on man's natural desire to see God) should be read in connection with Chapter 5.

The author wishes to express his gratitude to all those who helped him in the writing of this book, especially to Fathers George P. Klubertanz, S.J., and Leo C. Sweeney, S.J., for their many suggestions and corrections; to Father John J. O'Brien, S.J., who will recognize here much that he taught me many years ago in natural theology; to Miss Margaret Flotte, for preparing the manuscript; and last but far from least, to Father Henri J. Renard, S.J., who has honored this book with a fine foreword and who has been over the years a constant source of help and inspiration to its author.

The following publishers have been kind enough to let me quote from the works mentioned: E. P. Dutton & Company, *A Discourse on Method and Selected Writings,* by René Descartes, translated by John Veitch; Desclée, *La Creation,* by A. D. Sertillanges; Philosophical Library, Inc., *A Short History of Existentialism,* by Jean Wahl; Random House, *The Basic Writings of St. Thomas,* translated by A. C. Pegis; Henry Regnery Company, *Truth,* by St. Thomas Aquinas, translated by Robert W. Mulligan, S. J.

St. Louis, Missouri

M. R. H., S. J.

Table of Contents

An Introduction to
Natural Theology

CHAPTER 1

The Nature and Characteristics
of Natural Theology

*Wisdom is an infinite treasure for men, by
which those who use it are made sharers of
the friendship of God.*
—*Book of Wisdom, 6/21*

Aristotle says that there is present in man a natural desire to
know. And this natural desire is never completely satisfied in this
life. Man never ceases to learn and man never ceases to have need
of learning. For example, the needs of practical life force us to
observe nature and to discover her laws. But much more than
this: man feels within himself an attraction to truth for its own
sake. There is a joy, often a profound joy, in acquiring and possessing knowledge that is purely theoretical. Down through the ages
men have passed on to each other, from generation to generation,
a knowledge of philosophy and of the various sciences. Such
knowledge is an invaluably precious heritage, and each age tries
to add, either in depth or in scope, to this heritage.

Man will never cease to ask profound questions about the world
in which he lives and about his own self. What is the origin of
this universe? What is reality? Why do things exist? Why is there
something rather than nothing? What are the principles that constitute all being? What does it mean to exist? These are questions
that arise from man's reflection upon the world and upon the
things that are.

1

1. Scientific Knowledge

The intelligence of man will never be content with a knowledge of mere facts. It wants to know the reason for these facts, it wants to know the *causes* of things. That is to say, man desires not mere knowledge, but scientific knowledge. To know the reason for a fact is to have scientific knowledge concerning that fact. Thus scientific knowledge is a knowledge of things through causes of one kind or another, or through something that can be considered as a cause. A simple example will bring out this difference between mere factual knowledge and scientific knowledge. If I fill a straw with water and hold my finger over the top end of the straw, the water will not fall out of the bottom end of the straw. This is a fact. And the wonder that it produces in the beholder incites his curiosity to find out why this is so. Knowledge, says Aristotle, begins with wonder. And so the mind investigates, and upon investigating comes to understand that the reason the water in the straw does not run out is that the pressure of the air below keeps the water in the straw. Now the mind knows the reason or cause of the fact, and its wonder ceases. That is why Aristotle says that while knowledge begins with wonder, it should not end there. It should end in scientific knowledge, in understanding the causes of things.

Upon reflection, the mind sees that to explain fully any given fact, a whole series of causes must come into play. Some of these causes will be more immediate and obvious, others more hidden and ultimate, until finally we come to that Being in reality that is the first cause and final end of all being. A simple example will make this clear. In visiting St. Peter's in Rome, I come across the beautiful "Pietà" of Michelangelo. If I ask myself who caused this marvelous statue, the obvious answer is the artist, Michelangelo. True enough; but he is now dead and the statue continues to remain in existence. Why does it continue to exist as a statue, why does it continue to keep the beautiful shape and lines of the "Pietà"? Again, the obvious answer is, because of the existence of the marble. But I can still ask myself, what are the causes of the marble, why is it existing here and now? What are the ultimate causes, the ultimate reasons for the existence of things?

Is there any science of beings in their ultimate causes, of being simply as *being*? Not merely a scientific knowledge of a given *kind* of being, for example, of man insofar as he is man, or of material beings insofar as they are material, or living beings insofar as they are living, but of all beings, man, material beings, living beings, but simply and precisely insofar as they are beings? And by being as being is meant something that exists insofar as it is, insofar as it exercises its act of existence, its *act* of being, which is *to be*. My friend John is different from a rose, and a rose is different from a skylark, but John and the rose and the skylark have this in common: they all are, they all exist. The skylark *is not* the rose, and John *is not* the skylark, and the rose *is not* John; all are different, they possess different natures, they are different *kinds* of beings. But each exercises its act of existence, each can be considered as *being*. And the science that deals with all beings, insofar as they are beings, insofar as they exercise an act of existence, is metaphysics.

2. The Meaning of Habit

In order to understand what the science of natural theology is, we must begin by understanding what metaphysics is; for as we shall see, natural theology is an essential part of metaphysics. When the student begins to study philosophy and hears that study called a "science," he is puzzled, because in his experience science has always been equated with the experimental sciences like physics or chemistry. Now physics and chemistry are special *kinds* of sciences, giving us a certain type of scientific knowledge. The word "science" itself has much broader meaning. Coming from the Latin word *scire*, "to know," science (*scientia*) means "knowledge"; not any kind of knowledge, however, but knowledge that is certain and necessary, and which the mind reasons to by way of conclusions.

The true and universal meaning of science will become much clearer when we see it for what it is: a certain kind of *habit* that the intellect acquires, a certain quality inhering in the intellect and which has been produced by acts, by an intellectual activity on our part. To put science in its proper context, then, we must begin by understanding the meaning of habit. In this discussion of habit we will presuppose from psychology the student's general familiarity with the different principles and powers that constitute man.

We have said that a habit can be defined as a certain quality that inheres in man, the presence of which makes a man well or ill disposed in his being or in his operations. If the habit makes one ill disposed, it is called a bad habit; if it makes one well disposed it is called a good habit. If the habit makes a person well or ill disposed in his *being,* it is called an *entitative habit,* a habit of being. Some examples of good entitative habits on the natural level would be health and beauty; examples of bad entitative habits would be sickness or ugliness. On the supernatural level an example of a good entitative habit would be sanctifying grace. A habit that makes a person well or ill disposed in his operations or human activity is called an *operative habit.* The purpose of such habits is to make easy and pleasant the different operations performed by man. Since science is an operative habit, making easy and pleasant for us a certain kind of intellectual activity, we will confine our discussion here to operative habits.

What powers or faculties of man are capable of possessing good operative habits? The answer becomes clear when we realize that in man there are two sets of powers or active potencies by which he is able to produce an act. One set will not need any habits in the production of their acts; the other will. The first set of powers are those that are limited to a *determined* action or passion. These are ordered by their very nature always to act in the same way. Such powers, since they are determined of themselves to only one kind of activity, do not need any habits. This is true, for example, of all man's vegetative functions, such as his power of nutrition, growth, and reproduction. It is also true of his external and internal senses, which have a determined way of acting and need no acquired habit in order to act well. Again, the will of man, insofar as it is naturally determined to the good in general or to its end which is happiness, needs no habit; nor does man's agent intellect, which has of itself a determined operation, namely, to make things actually intelligible as light makes things actually visible.

But man possesses another set of powers or active potencies, which are of a higher and less limited nature than the first. These are his rational powers. Not limited to one way of acting or to one object only, such powers can act in different ways and for different objects. They need, therefore, to be guided and ruled in their activity by something other than their own natures; they need the presence of good habits by which they can operate not only rightly, but with ease and with pleasure. For example, man's possible intellect, which is in potency to receive all intelligible forms, needs habits. For being of itself indetermined, our possible intellect needs habits that will rule and guide it in its activity, making that activity not only right or according to rule, but easy and pleasant as well. Also the will of man, insofar as it is free or indetermined as to particular goods, needs good habits which guide and facilitate good moral activity. Finally, man's sense *appetites*, both irascible and concupiscible, can possess habits insofar as these sense appetites share in right reason which rules and regulates these appetites.

To situate the operative habit of science more precisely, let us note that there are three different kinds of *operative* habits: those that are *given*, those that are *acquired*, and those that are *infused*. An example of a habit that is *given* would be the habit that the possible intellect possesses of immediately understanding certain truths, called the habit of first principles. By this habit the possible intellect through the light of the agent intellect, which is its rule, is naturally determined to this understanding.

An *acquired* operative habit is one that is gradually produced in our operative power through the proper activity of that power. Thus, for example, our will can acquire the habit of justice, our irascible appetite the habit of fortitude, or our concupiscible appetite the habit of temperance. Again, man's practical intellect, which orders knowledge to action, needs many habits: prudence, to guide it in its ethical activity; arts, skills, and sports, to make us act correctly and with ease in other activities. But the activity of man's possible intellect is not only practical but speculative, where knowledge is not ordered to operation, but simply to the understanding of the truth. Here in man's speculative intellect, or in the intellect as functioning speculatively, are placed the different habits of theoretical sciences—sciences like metaphysics, psychology, mathematics, physics, chemistry, and so forth. These are *acquired* operative habits.

An *infused* habit, as the name indicates, is one that is given to man from without; it is neither present in man by his very nature, like the habit of first principles, nor produced by repeated activity, like the acquired habit of metaphysics. It is infused into his nature by God. Thus every infused habit is supernatural.[1] Infused supernatural habits can be of two kinds: *entitative*, giving to man a second or "supernature," and an example of such a habit or quality is sanctifying grace; and *operative*, giving to man the operative powers to place supernatural acts. Examples of such supernatural infused operative habits would be the theological virtues of faith (infused by God into the intellect), hope and charity (infused by God into man's will). The entitative habit of sanctifying grace is infused into man's *soul*. Finally, while all infused habits are supernatural, not all supernatural habits are infused. One at least can be acquired, and that is the supernatural habit of sacred theology.[2] This is a true scientific knowledge, using the truths of faith as principles for the drawing of further conclusions.

[1] Unless, of course, God would infuse into someone's intellect the natural habit of metaphysics; in which case it would be natural as to its mode of being but miraculous as to its manner of reception.

[2] The truths of faith are the starting point for this science of sacred or revealed theology. When a person, attentively considering such truths and the relations that obtain among them, draws through reasoning further truths or "understands" more clearly and deeply these truths, defending them from error and attack, such a person generates within his intellect the supernatural operative habit of sacred theology. How sacred theology differs from the natural acquired operative habit of natural theology will be considered more in detail later on in this chapter.

Our final situation of the science of metaphysics, then, has been achieved. It is an acquired operative habit of the speculative intellect which enables its possessor to make with facility conclusions about being as being. Now we are ready to see more in detail how this habit of science differs from other scientific habits. [3]

3. A More Complete Definition of the Science of Metaphysics

We have seen that the science of metaphysics, of which natural theology is an essential part (as shall be discussed later), is a naturally acquired operative habit. But it is a special kind of operative habit, namely, a habit of knowledge—a habit by which man acquires new knowledge. But the knowledge gained through the habit of metaphysics is a special kind of knowledge, with traits and characteristics peculiar to it alone. It is to the kind of *knowledge* gained through this habit that we must now direct our attention, so that we will have a more complete understanding of the nature of metaphysics, and therefore of natural theology.

4. Metaphysical Knowledge Is Scientific Knowledge

The kind of knowledge gained through the habit of metaphysics is *scientific* knowledge. That is why the study of metaphysics is rightly called a *science*. But what is *scientific* knowledge? First of all, as we have seen, it is not mere factual knowledge, the kind of knowledge one would gain by reading a world almanac. In order to become scientific, knowledge must go beyond the fact to the reason or cause of the fact. I may know, for example, that men are mortal, because I have witnessed death many times. But this knowledge of man's mortality is factual, not scientific. When, however, I come to understand that there is within each man matter, which is a principle of corruption, my knowledge of man's mortality becomes scientific. For now I know not only that men die, but why they die. And so we can define scientific knowledge more explicitly as a *knowledge through causes*. But to know a thing through its

[3] For St. Thomas's teaching on habits, see *In III Sent.*, dist. 23, qu. 1, a. 1; *S.T.*, I–II, 57, 2.; 67, 1.

causes or principles is to draw a conclusion. The mind in actually drawing a conclusion, because of the evidence of the principles or causes, exercises a scientific act, an act of scientific knowledge. When through the exercise of many such acts the mind of man becomes facile and experienced in drawing conclusions, he is said to possess the *habit of science*. Thus a more strict definition of scientific knowledge is knowledge gained by the habit of drawing conclusions from principles, which principles are the cause or the reason why the mind draws the conclusion.

5. Causes That Give Scientific Knowledge Are Twofold

The causes or reasons why the mind may draw a conclusion are of two kinds. The first kind of cause is one that is both the ontological reason for the fact as well as the logical reason why the mind concludes to the fact. For example, when the mind concludes to the immortality of the soul because of its spirituality, the logical reason for the conclusion (because the soul is spiritual) is also the ontological reason, or cause in the being, why the soul is immortal.

The second kind of cause or reason for drawing a conclusion is one that is merely the logical cause, or necessitating reason, for the conclusion. For example, when upon the analysis of substantial change the mind realizes that such change is intelligible only if there exists within the essence of the thing primary matter, because of which a thing can become other than it is, and substantial form, because of which the thing is what it is, this fact of substantial change is the necessitating reason for positing or concluding to this twofold principle within material essence. But this substantial change is not the cause in the being for this twofold principle; rather, it is the other way around: this twofold principle is the reason why substantial change can take place in the being. But in both cases scientific knowledge is a knowledge gained through causes, which causes in the act of scientific knowledge are called premises.

6. Scientific Knowledge Is Knowledge Gained Through Reasoning

Since the act of scientific knowledge is arrived at through a knowledge of causes or premises, scientific knowledge is always *concluded to,* is inferred through other knowledge. Thus, strictly speaking, the act of scientific knowledge gained through the habit of *science* is had through reasoning. The drawing of a conclusion is an act of *reason.* An act of reason is opposed to an act of simple understanding, of "simple insight." Although the scientific act goes *from* simple insight and *ends* in simple insight, the drawing itself of the conclusion is an act of reason. For the truth of the conclusion is seen or grasped not simply because of itself, but because of the truths of the premises.

To see somewhat more in detail how the act of scientific knowledge differs from an act of simple understanding, we should recall that there are *two kinds* of first principles that the mind can know. There are first principles of *being,* things that cause or constitute being, like essence, *esse,* substance, accidents, and so forth. And these first principles of being themselves exist in reality, or better, because of them the complete being exists, or exists in such and such a fashion. For example, because of primary matter, which is an incomplete principle of being, mobile being exists in a corruptible manner; or because of quantity, again an incomplete principle of being, a thing exists as large or small, and so on.

Besides these incomplete principles of being, there are complete principles of being, that is to say, beings that are not *merely* principles of being, like *esse,* essence, and so forth, but complete natures or entities that subsist in their own right. For example, a father as the instrumental efficient cause of the existence of his son is a complete principle or cause of being.

Secondly, there are first principles that are not principles of *being,* but *first truths* about beings or statements about beings. And these principles exist only in the mind and are called logical principles or first principles of *knowledge.* They are first truths

about beings; they are indemonstrable first principles of knowledge. They exist only in the mind, but are caused by existing
things; whereas first principles of being exist in reality. An example of a first principle of knowledge or judgment about being
would be the principle of noncontradiction; namely, that something cannot be affirmed or denied at the same time. Another example would be the truth that the whole is greater than its part.

7. First Truths About Being Are Known by Simple Understanding

Now the first important difference between a principle of being,
whether complete or incomplete, and a first indemonstrable truth
about being is this: a first principle of being is something concluded to, something grasped as the result of a reasoning process
or an act of *science.* Whereas first truths or judgments about being
are not demonstrated, not concluded to, they are grasped immediately, and thus are known not by an act of science, but by an act
of simple understanding.

It is quite obvious that there must be some first indemonstrable
principles of knowledge which cannot be concluded to or demonstrated by any reasoning, by any science, but simply seen to be
true by an act of understanding. Why? Science is a movement
from principles or premises to conclusion. Science is concerned
with truths that can be *demonstrated,* that can be inferred through
and because of some other truth. Now the *first* truths about being
must themselves be indemonstrable. If there were no first indemonstrable truths in the order of knowledge, we would have to
proceed into infinity in the demonstration of our premises, and
since by definition we would never reach a *first,* neither would
we be able to establish any strict demonstration. Either there must
be some self-evident truths about being, or all science is impossible. Either some truths cannot be demonstrated, or nothing can
be demonstrated.

Thus the very first principles of scientific knowledge must be
self-evident; therefore, they cannot be known through the act or
habit of science, but through an act of simple understanding. This

act of simple understanding is achieved by the natural operative habit of our mind called the habit of first principles, whereby man through the light of his agent intellect naturally understands indemonstrable or self-evident truths.

8. The Habit of First Principles and the Habit of Science Contrasted

The human intellect, therefore, grasps the first indemonstrable truths about being through an act of simple understanding; it draws further truths or conclusions about being by an act of reasoning. The former is achieved through the habit of first principles, the latter through the habit of science. Let us now see in more detail the difference between these two operative habits of knowledge.

Indemonstrable truths are known *immediately*, once the intelligibility of the terms are understood. Let us be very clear here. When we talk about first indemonstrable truths, we are talking about logical truth, and hence about an act of judgment or an affirmation of being. For logical truth is found only in the judgment where the mind affirms or denies something about reality. It is not found in the simple apprehension of a nature or quiddity, although these first indemonstrable truths or affirmations about being are immediately placed by the mind once it understands the intelligibility of the terms.

Here in affirming this truth there is no middle term involved, as in the case of demonstration or scientific knowledge. For example, once the intellect understands the intelligibility or meaning of "whole" and the intelligibility or meaning of "part," it immediately understands the truth of the affirmation "the whole is greater than its part." This act is called *intellectus*, as opposed to *ratio* or reason, because one reads within (*intus legit*), by seeing (*intuendo*), the essence or quiddity of the thing. And since the proper object of the human intellect is the essence of material existents, the knowledge of first truths that become immediately known or evident to the mind once it understands the meaning or intelligibility of the terms is rightly called *intellectus,* or simple understanding. [4]

We are now in a position to see more clearly why metaphysics is a true science. For it reasons to or demonstrates the first principles or causes of being. [5] Moreover, it should be equally clear that metaphysics is also the *highest* natural science, since it demonstrates the very *first principles* of being as being. Because of this, metaphysics is not only a science, but also a wisdom, and wisdom *par excellence* in the natural order. A wise *doctor* is one who has attained the highest and most certain knowledge of medicine, or a *wise lawyer* is one who has done the same in law. But a *wise man,* or one who is simply and unqualifiedly wise, will be one who has attained the greatest certitude of the highest science. For such a one has attained not merely to the first principles of a given kind of being, but to the first principles of all being as being. And since it is by metaphysics that a man arrives at a scientific knowledge of the very first principle of all being, namely God, metaphysics is the highest natural wisdom for man.

9. The Material and Formal Subject of Metaphysics

How does the science of metaphysics differ from the other sciences? We best define a particular science by pointing out the subject matter with which it treats, and especially that particular aspect or point of view of the subject that differentiates it from other sciences that may happen to treat of the same general subject matter. In this way we arrive at a sort of definition, the general subject matter furnishing the material element or genus of the definition, and the particular aspect of that subject matter

[4] See St. Thomas, *In VI Ethicorum,* lesson 5.

[5] It should be noted, however, that although the proper act of the science of metaphysics is to draw conclusions about being as being, metaphysics uses the habit of first principles also. For the knowledge of a conclusion depends upon the knowledge of its premises, and ultimately upon the understanding of first indemonstrable truths, and these truths are understood by the habit of first principles.

furnishing the formal element or specific difference of the definition.

The material subject, then, of any science, is the thing we are studying and about which we will draw our conclusions. In metaphysics this material subject is being, that is, any thing which in any way possesses reality or shares in the perfection of existence. Our formal subject, or the aspect under which we study being, is precisely insofar as being is being, that is, insofar as a thing shares in existence. In metaphysics, everything about being is studied precisely insofar as it affects a being's *existence*.

10. The Material and Formal Object of Metaphysics

To define a science by its material and formal subject furnishes us with a working definition, but gives only an incomplete knowledge of the nature of that science. For further precision and clarification, we must consider the material and formal *object* of a science. The material object of a science is what I want to know about my subject. The object is, then, the *conclusion* that I draw about my subject.

What, finally, is the *formal* object? We have seen that scientific knowledge is not only a knowledge of the fact, but of the cause or reason or principle of this fact. A conclusion is not understood *scientifically* except in and through the knowledge or light of its principles or causes. It is these principles or causal premises which give rise to the conclusions of my science that constitute the *formal object* of that science.

Briefly, then, the material subject is *that which* I am studying in my science and *concerning which* I make my conclusions. In metaphysics, this is being. My formal subject is the point of view that interests me in my subject. In metaphysics it is the *existence* of being. My material objects are the conclusions themselves. In metaphysics these will be conclusions about being, for example, being is one, true, good, and so forth. My formal objects are the principles or causes of these conclusions. In metaphysics these will be certain metaphysical principles, like that of causality or finality, which are principles of demonstration. [6]

11. Metaphysics and Natural Theology Are the Same Science

The student may perhaps be wondering why we have begun by such a lengthy examination of the nature of metaphysics in a book professedly devoted to natural theology. The reason is a simple one. Metaphysics and natural theology are not two separate sciences, but constitute one and the same science. For natural theology is part and parcel of the science of metaphysics. A few simple considerations will bring out why this is so. The subject of metaphysics is being as being, and its object is to demonstrate whatever it can concerning being as being, especially the first and highest causes of being whether those causes be intrinsic and constitutive of being, like essence or existence; or extrinsic and productive of being, like its efficient or final causes.

Now as we shall see in the course of our study of natural theology, God is the first and only proper cause of being as being, and hence to conclude to the knowledge of the existence of God is the proper object of metaphysics. In fact, it is the principal and most important object of metaphysics. [7] Notice, God is not the subject

[6] At this point two things should be pointed out to avoid confusion in the mind of the student. What we have called the material and formal *subject* of a science, most authors call material and formal objects. Our doctrine is drawn from St. Thomas, *S.T.*, I, 1, 7. For Thomas's doctrine on the *objects* of a science, as we have used this term, see *S.T.*, II–II, 1, 1 and 2. The second point is more difficult. There are principles or causes of being, like essence, *esse*, matter, form, substance, accidents, which as constituting or causing the being itself, pertain to the subject of metaphysics. And there are also principles or causes of *knowledge*, such as the premises of an argument, which causes the knowledge of the conclusion. Such principles pertain to the formal object of a science. What we should be careful to note, however, is that being itself, the really existing thing, gives rise to or causes our principles of knowledge. When considered precisely in their role as productive of scientific knowledge, they are considered as principles of knowledge rather than principles of being. Thus, for example, such principles of being as the act of existence, essence, matter, form, etc., considered precisely as constituting or causing the existing being, belong to the science of metaphysics as subjects of that science; but considered precisely as constituting or causing further knowledge they are formal objects of the science of metaphysics.

[7] See *In Boethii de Trinitate*, qu. 5, a. 1, *resp.*

of metaphysics. For this is "being as being," about which the science draws its conclusions. And God cannot be directly grasped by the mind as a subject of predication. But God, in his existence and his nature, is the principal *object* or *term* toward which the whole science of metaphysics tends.

Another simple consideration will point up the fact that the study of God belongs *par excellence* to the metaphysician. We have seen that the metaphysician is interested in everything insofar as it exercises an act of existence. Now as we shall see, God not only shares in the perfection of existence, but is an act of existence. He is being not by participation but by essence, by his very nature. Not that we can know what this perfection of existence is *as in God*, as it is in itself, but only in reference or by analogy to its participation in creatures. As interested in existence, metaphysics is especially interested in God.

Natural theology belongs to metaphysics as a part belongs to a whole. Moreover, natural theology is the most important part of metaphysics, as the head is the most important part of the body. Just as metaphysical knowledge is the crown of all natural knowledge, so natural theology is the crown of all metaphysical knowledge. And that is why Aristotle, and St. Thomas after him, sometimes referred to metaphysics as the divine science or philosophical theology. [8]

12. The Definition of Natural Theology

With these considerations in mind, we are now in a position to give a more precise definition of natural theology. Once the metaphysician has proved that God exists, he can now use this term or object of his knowledge as a sort of subject matter about which he will draw certain scientific conclusions. In actually establishing

[8] *In Boethii de Trinitate,* qu. 5, a. 1, *resp.* Some authors refer to natural theology as an *integral* part of metaphysics. But this term must be correctly understood. For example, the hands and feet are integral parts of man; yet I can lose a hand or a foot, and still remain a man. But I cannot remove natural theology from metaphysics and still possess essentially the same science. Hence it may be better to call natural theology an essential part of metaphysics, as the soul is an essential part of man.

God's existence and in the further conclusions he will draw about the God whose existence he has established, the metaphysician becomes the natural theologian and moves within that part of metaphysics which is natural theology.

The material subject of natural theology, then, will be God. For it is concerning the existence and nature of God that the natural theologian wishes to draw his conclusions and make his predications. But what will be his formal subject, what will be the point of view from which he treats of God? It will be God insofar as he is knowable through the light of natural reason alone, apart from any revelation God may have made concerning himself. That is to say, it will be God as knowable through the being of creatures; in a word, God as the first principle and proper cause of being, as the pure act of subsistent existence. The material *object* of natural theology will be the conclusions or truths which we can learn of God as first cause of being, and the formal object will be those intelligible principles in being, and thus in our knowledge of being, because of which we can arrive at our material object, namely, those truths we can know about God through reason alone, such as his existence, his unity, his power, and so forth. [9]

13. The Difference Between Natural Theology and Sacred Theology

Natural theology, then, is the science of God as first cause of being, which knowledge is gained through the light of the un-

---

[9] At this point the student may be reasonably confused. On the one hand we say that natural theology and metaphysics are one and the same science, essentially; and on the other we proceed to define natural theology by a formal subject different from metaphysics, which would seem to differentiate them essentially as sciences. First of all, God as "First Cause of Being," "Pure Act of Subsistent Being" constitutes a formal subject only in very analogical, or as St. Thomas would say, *quasi* sense. For our mind does not grasp this subject in the same direct fashion that it does, for example, the subject "being as being" (the formal subject of metaphysics). Strictly speaking, there is no science of natural theology apart from metaphysics, for it is the term and principal object of metaphysics and so is reduced to metaphysics as any term is reduced to its genus. But there is a certain sense in which natural theology can be considered as a sort of science in its own right. Of course, it goes without saying that metaphysics as the science of being as being is incomplete as a science, does not obtain its full perfection and stature as a science, until it reaches its term in natural theology.

aided intellect working in the presence of an intelligibility [10] that is within created being itself, an intelligibility that is potentially present in the material sensible existents of our experience. But another question that must be settled before we can begin our study of natural theology is just how this highest of all natural sciences differs from the simply highest of all sciences—the science of *revealed* or *sacred* theology. The question is a most important one, but we can touch upon it only briefly and in its barest essentials. Perhaps the clearest and best way to bring out the difference between these two sciences is to show how they differ in their subjects and objects, and in the end and purpose one has in pursuing them.

The material subject of both natural and revealed theology is the same, namely, God. But their formal subjects are different. The formal subject of natural theology is God as first cause (efficient, exemplary, final) of being. Hence the light or intelligibility by which the natural theologian understands his subject is that furnished him by the intrinsic light or evidence of the beings of his experience, a light or intelligibility that flows from the natures themselves of these objects. In natural theology I study God according to what existing things can tell me about him, and my end or purpose in pursuing this science is truth itself, the possession

[10] Throughout these pages the word "intelligibility" will be constantly recurring. Just what is *intelligibility?* Perhaps a simple comparison will bring out its meaning. A man, through his eyes, is aware of an object *because it is colored;* through his ears, *because it is sounding;* through his touch, *because it is hard or soft,* and so forth. Now a man is aware of an object through his intellect *because it is intelligible.* Intelligibility, therefore, is that aspect or quality or *ratio* in the object − all such words are equally helpful and equally deficient − because of which the object can be grasped or understood by the intellect. An intelligible object is that which the intellect grasps when it knows, just as a colored object is that which the eye grasps when it knows, i.e., sees. Since the object of the intellect is being, intelligibility is simply the *ratio entis,* the aspect of being. It is being as transparent and open to knowledge. Now in knowing any object as being, our intellect grasps a twofold intelligibility, one differing entirely from the other. One is the intelligibility of *nature* or *essence* (SOMETHING); and this is simply apprehended. The other is the "intelligibility" of "to be," "to exist" (THAT IS); and this is affirmed. These two "intelligibilities" are entirely different, since existence is not a form or nature or essence, but an act, that act by which the being possesses existential actuality, by which it *is.*

of which is the good of the intellect. In this science I know God only as he is related to his effects. I know God only as a cause, albeit the first, most intimate and far-reaching of causes. The natural theologian does not and cannot study God independently of his effects, he cannot go beyond what creatures can tell him about God and what can be rightly inferred from such relative knowledge. The precious little that reason can tell us about the existence and nature of God always remains a relative knowledge, that is to say, a knowledge derived from the existence and nature of finite being and the intrinsic intelligibility of that being.

In sacred or revealed theology, however, things are entirely different. Here what lights up my knowledge about God are not created things "speaking to me about God," but rather what God himself has told me about himself and about other beings, or, finally, what God could tell me about himself or other things. What God has told me about himself and other things (as he has actually done in tradition and sacred scripture), or what he could reveal about himself and other things,—all these revealed or revealable truths—constitute the formal subjects of sacred theology. The material *object*, then, will be the conclusions or inferences that can be drawn from these principles or revealed truths.

But how can I know what God could have revealed about himself and finite being, a fact that brings these truths under the formal consideration of the sacred theologian and removes them from the formal consideration of the natural theologian? This question is easy to answer once we know why God has revealed what he has actually revealed to man. We know from sacred scripture that God has revealed to us certain things about himself and certain things about ourselves and other creatures for this purpose: to turn us to himself as our final end in order to help us save our souls. "This is eternal life, that they may know Thee, and Jesus Christ Whom Thou hast sent." [11] Hence, when we study any creature as it is ordered to God as our final end and eternal salvation, no matter what that creature may be, we are studying it according to what God could have revealed about it, we are studying it in the

[11] St. John's Gospel, Ch. 17, verse 3.

light of our eternal salvation. And such a study of creatures, says St. Thomas, belongs to sacred or revealed theology. [12] Thus we may conclude that sacred theology studies first of all God as our final end and salvation, and then creatures in their relationship to this end and salvation. Whereas the natural theologian studies first of all creatures insofar as by their intrinsic intelligibility they can lead him to a knowledge of the first cause; and then he studies the nature of this first cause, insofar as that nature is "revealed" through creatures. The scientific movement of the sacred theologian is, therefore, a descending one: from a consideration of God to a consideration of creatures in their relation to God; while the movement of the natural theologian is an ascending one: from a consideration of creatures to a consideration of God in his relationship to creatures.

Another very important difference between natural and sacred or revealed theology is this: in order to be a sacred theologian, in order to draw conclusions from what God has revealed to man, one must begin by accepting that revelation. The science of sacred theology presupposes faith in what God has revealed, for as we have seen these revealed truths constitute the principles or formal subject of this science. Now many of these truths, such as those concerning the Trinity and Incarnation, could never have been discovered by man's reason alone, since they are truths that essentially exceed his capacity to know. Thus they needed to be revealed by God himself. Since these truths are essentially supernatural, it follows that sacred theology is a supernatural science. It is supernatural both in its principles, which are the articles of faith, and in its end, which is eternal salvation. For salvation consists in seeing God face to face, which is a sight or knowledge essentially above our nature. Thus the knowledge gained through a study of sacred theology can be called supernatural, both in its principles that are above the capacity of the human intelligence to discover, and because it is knowledge that is ordered to the beatific vision, a vision that is supernatural.

On the contrary, knowledge gained through natural theology

[12] *C.G.*, Bk. II, Ch. 4. This whole chapter deserves careful reading.

is a completely natural knowledge, both because the first principles from which it flows are principles discoverable by reason
alone, and because the end of this science, namely the contemplation or possession of a philosophical knowledge of God as first
cause, is a natural end. [13]

Finally, how are these two knowledges, that of revealed theology and that of natural theology, related or ordered within the
Christian who possesses them both? In their own right and considered abstractly, that is, apart from the one possessing them,
both these knowledges are wisdoms, for as knowledge of the highest causes of things, these sciences can order everything in the
light of this highest cause. But the wisdom of natural theology is
ultimate only in the natural order, for in this science the ultimate
cause that orders everything is God as knowable through creatures.
And this is only, if it may be so expressed, a relative ultimacy, an
ultimacy based on a relationship to creatures. Whereas the wisdom
of revealed theology is simply ultimate, for what orders all things
here is God as known through himself and revealed to creatures.

Man, however, has only one final end, and that end is supernatural—the Beatific Vision. Hence, concretely, or within the
Christian possessing these two sciences, the knowledge of natural
theology is ordered to the knowledge of revealed theology. And
since it belongs to wisdom to order and not to be ordered, the
Christian possesses only one true wisdom, the wisdom of faith,
which orders all his other knowledge, including the natural science
of his philosophical knowledge of God. In a non-Christian who
possesses no science of revealed theology, his highest science, and
hence only wisdom, will be his philosophical knowledge of God.
But in the Christian, philosophical wisdom is subsumed under and
subordinated to his highest and thus only true wisdom, that of
sacred theology. And so when we speak of metaphysics or natural
theology as a wisdom, or as ordering all things through their highest cause, we must keep in mind that we are speaking of this

---

[13] For a good summary of these points, see St. Thomas, *In Boethii de
Trinitate*, qu. 2, a. 2, *resp*. This article should be read in its entirety.

science in the abstract, considering that knowledge in its own nature and apart from the person possessing it.

14. The Difference Between Natural Theology and Religion

We have defined natural theology as that science which investigates the existence and nature of God as he can be known by reason alone through his effects. We have further seen that revealed or sacred theology is a supernatural science that studies what God has revealed about himself and has been accepted by faith. To assert or to accept that a thing is true because of faith is not to see that it is true by an insight of the intellect, but to hold it as true for the extrinsic reason that someone has said that it is true. What moves one to believe is the authority of another, not the intrinsic evidence of the thing known. Thus faith plays no intrinsic or necessary part in the grasping either of the principles or conclusions of natural theology; whereas the very principles of revealed theology are accepted on faith.

But what is meant by *religion?* The word is susceptible of many meanings, but the general underlying meaning is always the same: the word "religion" expresses some relationship that obtains between God and man. If the relationship is one of knowledge, we can speak of religious knowledge; if it is one of some action or duty toward God, we have the more technical and exact use of the word "religion."

Now religious knowledge, or religion in the sense of knowledge of God, can take several forms. It could, for example, be simply synonymous with a knowledge of natural theology, as would be true in the case of a pagan philosopher whose whole knowledge of God had been obtained by his own personal insights and investigations, without relying on any authority whatsoever. Or again, apart from any revelation on the part of God, a man's religious knowledge could be a blend of personal insights and an acceptance on human faith of what other great philosophers have learned about God through their unaided reason. Thirdly, a man's religious knowledge could be co-extensive with the possession of both the sciences of natural and revealed theologies. And if these sci-

ences were possessed in their perfection, such a person would hold
on faith only those truths which exceed the capacity of the human
intellect to know and which would have to be revealed to man if
he were to know of their existence. For many truths that God has
seen fit to reveal, as for example the immortality of the human soul,
man can reach by unaided reason alone. Thus, in point of fact,
most Christians' religious knowledge is a blend of faith and reason,
many truths being held on faith which could be proved by reason
alone, and with both their natural and supernatural knowledges
of God more or less organized, more or less scientific. When a student in college says he is taking a course in "Religion," he is generally pursuing some such knowledge about God, with the em-
phasis placed on an organized knowledge of revealed truths about
God, trying to gain some little insight into them and the relationships that obtain among them—a sort of poor man's sacred theology. [14]

15. The Technical Meaning of "Religion"

But the word "religion" has an exact, technical sense, which
should be pointed out. In this sense religion is a moral virtue, a
species of the cardinal moral virtue of justice. Since man holds his
being essentially from God, he is subject to God according to his
whole being. Thus man owes God, as his Creator, both service and
adoration. Man is bound, *religatur*, to his creator. To recognize
this bond and to act according to its obligations is to practice *religion*. Religion, therefore, consists in that act by which man wor-
ships God, subjecting himself to him.

Now this must be an act that is befitting both the one who is
worshipped, and the worshipper. And since God, who is worshipped, is a pure spirit, we can unite ourselves to him by our
mind and will alone. Thus the worship of God principally consists
in those acts of intellect and will by which man is ordered to God.
And these are chiefly the acts of the theological virtues of faith,

[14] For a more thorough discussion of religious knowledge, see George P.
Klubertanz, S.J., *Introduction to the Philosophy of Being* (New York, Appleton-Century-Crofts, 1955), pp. 11–13.

hope, and charity. However, since we who worship God are material beings, and receive our knowledge through the senses, the worship of God requires on our part also bodily actions. And this for two reasons. First, because man is subject to God both in body and soul; and, secondly, because through such actions (as genuflections, prostrations, and so on) we excite both ourselves and others to spiritual acts ordered to God.

All those acts, therefore, by which man subjects himself to God, whether acts of the body or soul, pertain to the practice of the virtue of religion. Moreover, whatever service is done to our neighbor because of God, is considered as done to God. [15] It is clear, then, that such acts pertain to the same subjection to God, in which consists the virtue of religion. So that it follows that every good act pertains to the virtue of religion. To conclude: first and principally, the practice of religion consists in spiritual acts ordered to God; secondly, it consists in those bodily acts, like prostrations, that excite us to these spiritual acts, or like sacrifices, which signify these spiritual acts. Finally, the practice of religion consists in any act, interior or exterior, done for our neighbor because of God. [16]

16. The Characteristics of Natural Theology

At this point it may be helpful to sum up some of the characteristics of the science of natural theology. *First of all,* natural theology is a science, since it concludes to certain and necessary truths about the existence and nature of God as the first cause of being. *Secondly,* this science is also a wisdom, and the highest of natural wisdoms, since it orders all things and all knowledge through the first and highest cause, God. *Thirdly,* this science is a speculative and not a practical science. That is to say, of itself it is not ordered to the performance of any action or the production of any thing, but only to the contemplation of truth, and the highest Truth, God. Of course, the end or purpose of the one *learning* it may be practical; for example, to teach it to others and thus earn a living. Or a person may use this science in any number of ways;

---

[15] See St. Matthew, Ch. 25, verse 40.
[16] St. Thomas, *In Boethii de Trinitate,* qu. 3, a. 2, *resp.*

for example, to convince someone that there is a God. So that when we say that the end or purpose of natural theology is simply and only the contemplation of truth, of truth for its own sake, we must be careful to distinguish between two ends: the end of the science itself, and the end of the one learning the science. The end of the *science* is simply to give us truth for its own sake, just as the end or purpose of a watch is simply to tell the time of day. Furthermore, the end of the science and the end of the one learning the science may coincide: a student may study this science simply to possess the truth that it engenders in the mind, just as a person may acquire a watch simply to possess an instrument for telling the time. Again, as is obvious, these two ends, the end of the thing acquired and the end of the one acquiring it, may be different. I may buy a watch as a present for a friend, or simply as an ornament for my wrist. So, to conclude, when it is said that the end or purpose of natural theology is purely speculative, simply knowledge for its own sake, what is understood is the end of the science itself, leaving aside the end or purpose which a given individual may have in acquiring this science.

Fourthly, natural theology is the *most perfect and sublime* of all merely natural knowledge, for in this science the most perfect and highest of man's powers, his intellect, is functioning in reference to the most perfect and highest of all intelligible objects, God. For although the metaphysical movement begins with a consideration of creatures, or finite being, its term or goal is the first cause of these beings, God, and what creatures can tell us about God. *Fifthly,* natural theology is the *most satisfying and enjoyable* of all natural sciences, for while what this science can tell us about the existence and nature of God may be small in quantity, the little knowledge that it does tell us affords the intellect greater joy and satisfaction and contributes more to its perfection than all the knowledge we can find out about creatures through the other sciences.

Finally, the student would be entirely mistaken if he were to view the science of natural theology as a vague, abstract, highly notional sort of knowledge, miles removed from the concrete and the real. Part of our difficulty here is due to a false view of the science of metaphysics itself, a view that should be dispelled once and for all from the student's mind. For properly understood, metaphysics is the most real, the most concrete, and the most empirical of all the sciences.

It is most real because it alone professedly deals with that which makes the real to be real, that is, the act of existence. For existence is not only that which is most real in a thing, but it is precisely that which gives reality or actuality to all the elements or principles within a thing. In a word, metaphysics is the most real of all the sciences, because it deals not with this or that *kind* of reality, but with reality *as such*, with the real as real.

And metaphysics is the most *concrete* of all the sciences, because the act of existence which the metaphysician exploits in his science is the act of existence of the individual, extramental existent, whatever kind of being it may happen to be. Now the point is that this act of existence, this "to be," as exercised by the existent, can never be separated from that existent. We cannot abstract existence by our thought. Of course, the mind can formalize this non-abstractable perfection, as it does when it defines this act as that by which a thing is or exists, and gives this perfection a name: "existence." But this act as exercised by the thing can never be abstracted. As exercised, it can only be affirmed or asserted by the mind, it can be known only in and through a judgment. The act itself is the concrete act of this individual thing, just as the act of fighting or running is the concrete act of this individual fighter or runner. Thus the science of metaphysics, which deals with existence as exercised by things, is the most concrete of all the sciences.

Finally, and this may sound strange in the face of so much modern philosophy, metaphysics is the most *empirical* of all the sciences. "Empirical" comes from the Greek word for experience; and metaphysics is most bound up with experience. Not only because metaphysics takes its starting point from the immediate composite of sensible-intelligible experience—the immediate perception of existing sensible things—but also because metaphysics concerns itself with precisely that which is most immediate in our experience. And what is most immediate, absolutely first, in our human experience? The fact that things *are*, that they *exist*. [17] Only later, by further reflection, do we know in any distinct way *what* things are. Only later do we arrive at a knowledge of the nature of things. But *that they are* is immediately given, and since the fact that they are is due to their act of existence, metaphysics, which alone deals with that act as such, is the most empirical of all the sciences. In point of fact, existence is so immediately given in our experience of things that we often simply overlook it or take it for granted, and so fail to see the mysteries and the problems that existence holds for human understanding.

But can these characteristics of "real," "concrete," and "empirical" be applied to metaphysics in its term? Can they be applied to natural theology? The answer is a decided yes. God is, as we shall see, the first and only proper cause of the existence of things. And because of the greater perfection of cause over effect, because of their simultaneity, and the intimate presence of cause to effect, the study of God as first cause of being is anything but an abstract, universal, and remote approach to reality. St. Thomas has a statement in one of his works [18] that God is that which is most intimate in all creatures. Nor would it be a departure from simple metaphysical fact to add that God is more present to things than they are to themselves. If the actuality of things can fill the metaphysician with awe at the profound mysteries of being, the "metaphysics of God" can overwhelm the mind of the natural theologian.

It is true that in our present condition this metaphysics of God comes to us dispersed and scattered in the being of creatures, but it is easy to understand that we are dealing with something

[17] In the interests of clarity, the following remarks should be made. *That which* the intellect first understands, that which first "falls" into the intellect, is not existence, not essence, but being (ens), the composite *that which is*. However, that which first falls into the intellect from the aspect of *absolute actuality*, is not being (ens) but existence (*esse*): "esse (est) illud quod primo cadit in intellectu per modum actualitatis absolute." *In Peri Hermeneias*, Book One, lecture five, near end.

[18] *De Pot.*, qu. 3, a. 7.

more real and concrete than any creature of our immediate experience. It is likewise true that our knowledge of God is analogous and a mediate knowledge. But an analogous knowledge can be more real and full than univocal knowledge, and a mediate knowledge can be of something more perfect, more concrete, that is to say, more transcendently *one*, than our immediate knowledge of something. At present, these are only statements. Their full justification is the whole science of natural theology.

One final word. It would be unfair if it were not pointed out to the student from the very beginning that there is another characteristic of natural theology: it is the hardest to learn of all the sciences. There is nothing to be gained by minimizing the difficulties in learning a new science, and especially the science of God. There are no shortcuts to scientific knowledge. It is a hard affair and requires continual patience and concentration.

Why is metaphysics, and its crown, natural theology, so hard to really master? Because although this science begins with sensible intelligible experience, it seeks to penetrate into the ultimate causes of existing things. Now such causes cannot be sensed; they cannot even be imagined. They are transphysical, transimaginable. This does not mean that they are not real; they are very real indeed, since they are the very causes of reality. Supremely real in itself, the Being of God cannot be sensed or imagined by us in any way whatsoever. Nor can it be understood or intelligibly grasped by us in any direct or immediate way. It can only be understood by way of analogy and transcendence.

And the science of natural theology tries to penetrate into the reality of the suprasensible but very real Being that is God. Since we are so much creatures of sense and imagination, we find it very hard to go beyond the limits of, or at least to abstract from, the sensible and the imaginable. But this we must do if we are to master metaphysics. And it can be done, since our intellect is a power of spiritual vision and can transcend the vision of sight or imagination. But an intelligible, suprasensible grasping of reality takes effort, and it takes time. So that if at the end of our investigation of the first cause of being we have not attained a mastery of natural theology, we should have at least attained a healthy respect for it. [19]

17. The Man of Science and the Natural Theologian

Before we begin our actual study of the science of natural theology, it is extremely important that we note the difference between the way the man of positive science confronts the material and sensible existents of his experience, and the way those same existents are confronted by the natural theologian or the philosopher. [20] The scientist is not interested in things precisely as sources of intelligibility, but rather as sensible phenomena, as things offering themselves as observable or measurable in some way. His effort and purpose is not to explain the existential actuality of the things with which he deals, nor to penetrate with his concepts to the intelligible source of their unity and organization. The positive scientist wants to observe sensible phenomena, measure them, catalog them, interpret them, control them, and make predictions about their relations and operations. And for this his scientific method of experimentation, hypothesis, mathematical substitution, and noetic constructs are admirably fitted to the work he has to do.

[19] The extreme difficulty involved in acquiring the science of natural theology is intrinsic to the very nature of the science itself and to the human intellect. A simple observation will make this clear. The human soul is form of the body, and thus, as form, is essentially related to matter. Now the human intellect, while it is a power of the soul that uses no bodily organ, is nonetheless a power of the soul which is the form or act of the body. And therefore the human intellect is essentially ordered to know bodily or material things. Because the intellect is the power of a soul which is a form of a body, the intellect is not directly ordered or proportioned to the intelligibility of immaterial things, but can understand immaterial things only insofar as its knowledge of material things can lead it to such an understanding. And since there is no proportion in nature between a material essence and an immaterial essence, man in his present condition can never know any immaterial essence in itself. Immaterial things can be known only indirectly, and by way of analogy or comparison with material things. And since God is absolutely immaterial, any knowledge concerning him will be indirect, analogical, and very difficult for the intellect to attain. It will never be knowledge of God as he is in himself, but only as he is known in creatures.

[20] For a detailed discussion of this point, see Father Joseph Owens, "Our Knowledge of Nature," in *Proceedings of the American Catholic Philosophical Association*, Vol. 29 (1955), 63–86.

On the other hand, the natural theologian, or the philosopher, directs the eye of his intellect to another dimension within these same existents—the dimension of being itself. His purpose is precisely to explain the existence of things, to exploit the intelligible as intelligible. He is interested in the source, the cause, of a thing's unity, organization and operation, in grasping the intelligible nature that gives reason and meaning to the phenomena themselves. And his is the method of ontological insight and rational discourse.

It may be helpful here to point out some concrete differences between these two different and perfectly legitimate, and independent, confrontations that the mind of man can make to reality. The positive scientist always stays at the level of the (in some way) observable and measurable. One set of phenomena will be interpreted in terms of another, or one set of constructs or mathematical formulas in terms of another construct or another set of formulas. In such a procedure, the man of science will rightly either ignore or take for granted the ontological nature or intelligible essence that gives final meaning or possibility to these phenomena, for he is using the method of science, the method of observation and measurement. No matter how refined or how formulated, these remain his tools for his analysis of the real.

The philosopher, on the other hand, in the presence of existing material things, judges their existential actuality, and grasps within them the presence and the meaning of their potential intelligibility. And he does this by a natural and spontaneous movement of his intellect. He is interested in what these existing material things can reveal to his intelligence, not as sensible phenomena, but as being. And so the philosopher confronts a different sort of evidence than does the positive scientist—the evidence of intelligible being—whereas the scientist confronts the measurable evidence of observable phenomena.

From these different evidences, from the facts of measurable phenomena and the facts of intelligible being, the scientist is led to ask scientific questions about things, and the philosopher existential questions about being. What are these things, and how do they operate? asks the scientist. Why are these things and why are they the way they are? asks the philosopher.

The method of positive science, legitimate and eminently useful in itself and necessary to man's knowledge of nature, cannot tell us the whole story about things. For the method involves an incomplete, horizontal, and phenomenalized grasp of material things and their activities. There are other facts besides scientific facts; there is other evidence besides the evidence of positive science. The intellect of man possesses other ways of attaining to the truth of things besides the methods of science. Scientific experience is only part, and not the most important part, of the total human experience. But it not infrequently happens that a scientist, since he is also a human being, following the natural bent of his intelligence, asks himself some very unscientific questions. For example, why do these phenomena exist at all, or what is the reason for the unity and regularity of their activity, or the organization of their composition?

Now it should be obvious that no amount of observation or measurement, no amount of manipulation of concepts or of mathematical substitution, will ever reveal to the scientist why his scientific data *exist*, or why they exhibit the organization and unity they do. The *reasons* for these things are themselves simply incapable of scientific observation and measurement. But such reasons still remain facts, still remain real; just as real and just as factual as the scientific data themselves, and more so. But if a scientist does not understand the limitations of his method, if he thinks that the method of positive science is the *only* legitimate way to account for reality, he will dismiss all such questions about final causes or intelligible essences as unscientific and therefore meaningless. If his method is the only method of knowing reality, then such questions, since science cannot answer them, literally have no scientific meaning and should not even be asked.

Now the scientist is perfectly within his rights if he dismisses these questions as unscientific, but he is wrong if he dismisses them as meaningless. And should he persist in this view, he reads his own scientific effort right out of court. For if these questions are meaningless, then science itself is also meaningless. For the very method and purpose of positive science presuppose that there are unity and organization in the physical phenomena that positive science observes and measures. And to insist that the presuppositions of science have no meaning is to void and negate any scientific value of the conclusions of positive science based on such presuppositions.

Most of the great scientists of our day do realize the necessary limitations of the scientific method (they are not limitations on *science*, but limitations on human knowing) and recognize the legitimate claims of philosophy. They see that there are other facts besides those that can be observed and measured by their method; that there are other experiences in human living that open up vistas of knowledge besides the experience of mere sensible phenomena. They see that there can be no real conflict between science and philosophy, since each way of knowing moves at a different level of evidence and understanding. The movement of science is always horizontal, going from the measurable to the measurable, while the movement of philosophy is vertical, going from the sensible existent to being as being. There can only be apparent conflicts between scientists and philosophers, due to a confusion and misunderstanding of the method of science and the method of philosophy, the evidence of science and the evidence of philosophy.

When, therefore, a mathematician like Einstein tells us that there is no such thing as God, what he really means by this statement is that the existence of God is not capable of a mathematical formulation or demonstration—that the demonstration of God's existence lies outside the method of mathematics or of positive science. For God transcends whatever can be sensed or imagined, as do also the principles of efficient or final causality. What is caused, or that which causes, can be observed and measured, but causality itself is an evidence of being that can be neither observed nor measured; it can only be grasped by an act of intellectual understanding. So when an Einstein concludes apodictically that, therefore, there *can be* no God, he has simply gone beyond the limits of his mathematical method and is speaking, quite literally, nonsense.

We ought to remember, also, that competence in one field of learning is, of itself, no guarantee of competence in another field. Einstein was a genius at mathematics; he was an incompetent in theology. No one would dream of going to a theologian to learn his mathematics; and neither should one go to a mathematician to learn his theology. These statements seem obvious, but they need saying. For our thinking is often fuzzy, rather than critical, on this point. When a man achieves great prominence in some field he is considered an oracle of profound and universal wisdom. And this is especially true of our positive scientists. Science has accomplished such marvels in its own field that many are willing to pay it unlimited worship. And so we read all kinds of articles about what scientists think of God. Now it makes not one whit of difference to theology what a scientist thinks about God, just as it makes not one whit of difference to esthetics what a politician thinks about art. There is nothing wrong in worshipping science, provided we do so at the altar of science and the scientific method. But to say there are no other gods than those of science would be a most unscientific thing to say. [21]

18. Summary of the Chapter

"Natural theology, which is essentially the same science as metaphysics, treats of the existence and nature of God, insofar as these can be known through an understanding of created things."

a. State of the question

Before we begin our study of the existence and nature of God, it will be of great help to have some understanding of the nature of the science we want to acquire. What is natural theology? How does it differ from the other sciences? What are its peculiar charac-

---

[21] See Jacques Maritain, *Philosophy of Nature* (New York, The Philosophical Library, 1951), pp. 73–79; Etiènne Gilson, *God and Philosophy* (New Haven, Yale University Press, 1941), Chapter IV.

teristics? How, finally does it proceed in its investigation of God? These are the questions we have answered in this first chapter.

b. Explanation of terms

1) *"Natural theology . . ."* A "natural study of God" proceeds through the natural light of reason alone. In this science our un-aided reason, through the understanding of material and sensible things to which it is naturally ordered and proportioned, is led to the understanding of a Being that is immaterial and supra-sensible, that is, the Infinite Being of God. Thus, natural theology is different entirely from revealed or sacred theology, where God himself reveals himself to man. Natural theology, beginning with creatures and our understanding of creatures, *ascends* to some understanding of God insofar as God is revealed in creatures. Thus, in natural theology God is treated only as the first cause of things, so that our knowledge of him is relative to our knowledge of creatures. Whereas in sacred theology we begin with God, and from an understanding of God for his own sake, we then *descend* to creatures and study them insofar as they have some relationship to God. And so in sacred theology God is studied absolutely and for himself, and creatures are studied relatively, that is, as ordered to God.

2) *". . . is essentially the same science as metaphysics . . ."* This becomes clear once we realize that metaphysics, the science of being *as being*, can be considered in two ways. We can consider, for example, the *subject* of the science, which is *being as being*, and from this aspect of its subject matter, the science is properly called by its general name, *metaphysics*. Or this science can be considered from the point of view of the *principles or causes of its subject*. And from this point of view metaphysics has two names, since there are two kinds of principles or causes of its subject matter that are considered in this science: *incomplete* principles and *complete* principles. And insofar as metaphysics treats the incomplete principles of being, such as essence, *esse*, act, potency, substance, accident, and so forth, the science is aptly called *first*

philosophy, since these principles are first principles or causes of being.

But in this science we also demonstrate the first *complete* principle of being as being, whose causality extends to all beings. And this first complete principle, entirely perfect and completely in act, is something separate in itself and divine. And therefore metaphysics, insofar as it demonstrates the existence and nature of this first complete principle is aptly called a *divine* science, or natural *theology*. And we conclude that since it belongs to one and the same science to treat of its subject matter and the causes or principles of that subject matter, it must follow that metaphysics and natural theology are essentially one and the same science.

3) *"Natural theology . . . treats of the existence and nature of God . . ."* These words tell us not only the difference between natural and sacred theology, but also give us the *formal subject* of natural theology. In sacred or revealed theology *God himself* is the subject of the science, the material subject being *God* and the formal subject *"as revealing himself to man."* But God cannot be the subject matter of any natural science, that is, something that is *directly given in nature* to be investigated and known. For God is not directly offered to our intellect (as he is through faith in sacred theology) as an object of understanding about which we can make predications and draw conclusions. Rather in the natural order, God is offered to our intellect as some *term* whose existence must be demonstrated through reason. Thus he is offered to our intellect only indirectly and mediately, not through himself but through creatures. So strictly speaking, God cannot be the subject of any natural science, but only a principle or cause of the subject.

God, therefore, is the subject of supernatural or revealed theology inasmuch as he is immediately and directly offered to our intellect through faith; but the subject of metaphysics is *being as being*, and God as the first complete principle of being as being is a principle of the subject of metaphysics. Nevertheless, once we have demonstrated the existence of this first cause, seeing this cause as Pure Act and Subsistent Being, we can treat God so considered as a sort of subject for a part of metaphysics, namely, natural theology. About God so considered, as an intelligibility gained through creatures but properly refined by negation, analogy and eminence, we can make certain predications and further conclusions.

In this sense God is the material subject of our science of natural theology, and God as *first cause* is the formal subject of natural theology, that is, God insofar as he is revealed to us in his effects. The material *object* of natural theology are all those conclusions that our intellect is able to reach concerning such a cause. And, finally, the *formal* object are the premises or reasons why the intellect is able to make the conclusions; for example, such principles of demonstration as the principle of causality, finality, eminence, negation, analogy, and so forth; all of which principles arise from the evidence of being.

c. The proof

1) *First part: Natural theology is a science:* (*a*) Because it proceeds from principles or premises to conclusions known through these principles. For example, from the principle of causality or finality we can conclude to the existence of God; from principles of negation and eminence, we can conclude to the simplicity and eternity of God; from the principle of causality and analogy, we can conclude to the fact that God has an intellect, a will, and so forth. (*b*) Because natural theology gives *certain* and *necessary* knowledge of God, and not merely probable knowledge or contingent knowledge. And the reason for this is that natural theology proceeds from principles or premises that are themselves necessary and certain, and so because of them we can conclude to truths about God that are necessary and certain. Further, the reason why these principles or premises are themselves certain and necessary is that they arise from our consideration of being *as being*, and not from being as *this being* or *that being*, or as *sensible* or *material*, but simply insofar as something is or exists—as it shares

in the act of existence. Hence, insofar as these principles of demonstration abstract from all contingency and mobility in things, they can give rise to science or scientific knowledge, to knowledge that is certain and necessary.

2) *Second part: Natural theology is essentially the same science as metaphysics.* This is clear from the following argument: It is the nature of a science not only to treat of its subject matter but also of the causes or principles of its subject matter; because a science does not reach its perfection except through a knowledge of the causes or principles of its subject. For all scientific knowledge is a knowledge through causes. For example, the *philosophy of nature* does not merely treat of changeable being as changeable, which is the subject matter of the philosophy of nature. It also considers primary matter and substantial form, which are the causes or principles of changeable being. So, in like manner, *metaphysics* does not merely treat of being as being, which is its subject matter, but also of act and potency, substance and accidents, essence and *esse,* and so forth, which are the causes or principles of being as being.

But as we have seen, causes or principles of a subject may be of two kinds: some that are merely incomplete causes, like *esse,* essence, and so on, and others which are in themselves complete natures and beings subsisting in their own right and in their own proper natures. For example, a father is a complete being in his own right as well as the cause of the being of his son. And just as it belongs to a science to treat of the incomplete principles of its subject matter, so too it belongs to that same science to treat the complete principles of its subject matter. For example, the philosophy of nature does not merely treat of the primary matter and substantial form of bodies here on earth, which are the incomplete principles of its changeable being, but also of such complete causes as the sun or stars, insofar as these influence or cause change in bodies here on earth. So, in like manner, metaphysics does not only consider *esse,* essence, substance, accidents, and so forth, but also God himself, who is the first complete principle of being as being. Therefore it is clear that metaphysics and natural theology are essentially the same science.

But that natural theology and metaphysics are in a certain sense, or accidentally, different is also obvious. Because only the first *complete* principle of being as being is divine. And the reason for this is that this principle is the most complete and most perfect act, removed from all matter and separate from all motion. Therefore, it belongs to such an act that it can in no way exist in matter or in motion. But the incomplete principles of being are sometimes found in matter and motion and sometimes not. And therefore it does not belong to them that they *must be* in matter or motion. Thus in themselves they are not divine things. Whence it follows that only in its demonstration of the existence and nature of the first complete principle is metaphysics a truly divine science, and not in its demonstration of the first incomplete principles. Thus there is an accidental difference between metaphysics and natural theology, although natural theology is an *essential* part of metaphysics.

3) *Third part: Natural theology treats of God in his existence and nature insofar as these can be known from an understanding of created things.* Because this science is a natural science, it proceeds from the natural light alone of human reason. Our human intellect according to its nature is a power or faculty of our soul, and this soul is the *natural form of our body.* And therefore just as the soul itself is naturally ordered to the body, so this power of our soul—our intellect—is naturally ordered to the understanding of *bodily* or material things. And our intellect understands these material things by abstracting their essences from phantasms through the natural light of our agent intellect. Therefore our intellect cannot understand *immaterial* things, such as God, except insofar as its understanding of material things can lead it to such knowledge. So in natural theology God cannot be known except from our understanding of created things, by which understanding our intellect is led to a *mediate* and *analogous* knowledge of God.

19. Selected Passage from St. Thomas[22]

"Since the notion of science consists in this, that from certain things that are known other unknown things are understood, and since this takes place concerning divine things, it is clear that there can be a science concerning divine things. But the understanding of divine things can be considered in two ways. First, from our side, and in this way divine things are not knowable to us except through creatures, for we receive their understanding through the senses. The second way is from the nature of the divine things themselves. And thus taken in themselves they are the most knowable of all things. And although according to their own mode of being divine things are not known by us, nevertheless they are known by God and the blessed in heaven. Thus there is a twofold knowledge or science of divine things. One according to our way of knowing, which is to receive from sensible things principles with which to understand divine things, and in this way have the philosophers handed down to us the knowledge of divine things, calling first philosophy the divine science.

"The other is according to the manner of the divine things themselves, namely, that divine things themselves be grasped according to themselves; which indeed is impossible for us to do perfectly in this life. But there does take place in us in this life a certain participation in this knowledge, and a certain assimilation to God's knowledge, insofar, that is, as through faith that is infused in us, we adhere to the first truth itself for itself. And just as God, by the very fact that he knows himself, knows also other things in a manner peculiar to himself, that is, by a simple intuition and not by any discursive reasoning, so too, from the things which we know by faith by adhering to the first truth, we arrive at the knowledge of other things in a manner peculiar to ourselves, namely, by going from principles to conclusions. Whence those things which we hold by faith are for us as the first principles of this science, and the other things we know from them are as the conclusions of this science. From which it is clear that this science

22 From *Commentary on Boethius' De Trinitate*, qu. 2, a. 2.

is of a higher nature than that divine science which the philosophers have studied, since it proceeds from higher principles."

Suggested Readings

1. St. Thomas, *The Division and Method of the Sciences,* translated by Armand Maurer, O.S.B. (Toronto, Pontifical Institute of Medieval Studies, 1953), pp. 17–23, 46–66.
   On the Truth of the Catholic Faith, translated by A. C. Pegis (New York, Hanover House, 1955), Book One, pp. 59–78.

2. Etiènne Gilson, *God and Philosophy* (New Haven, Yale University Press, 1941), pp. 109–144.
   The Christian Philosophy of St. Thomas Aquinas (New York, Random House, 1956), pp. 7–25.

3. Jacques Maritain, *The Philosophy of Nature* (New York, The Philosophical Library, 1951), pp. 73-89.

4. Joseph Owens, C.Ss.R., "Theodicy, Natural Theology, and Metaphysics," *The Modern Schoolman,* 30 (1951), 126–137.

CHAPTER 2

Can God's Existence Be Demonstrated?

> *From the foundations of the world men have caught sight of his invisible nature, his eternal power and his divineness, as they are known through his creatures.*
> —St. Paul, *Letter to the Romans,* Ch. 1, verse 20

1. No Science Proves the Existence of Its Own Subject

From what we have seen so far concerning the nature and purpose of a science, a difficulty emerges at the very outset about the subject of natural theology. This difficulty can be put quite simply. No science is able to prove the existence of its subject. But natural theology is a science whose subject is God. Therefore, natural theology is not able to prove the existence of God. This is another way of saying that human reason is not able to give a scientific proof or demonstration of God's existence. Let us see the reason for this difficulty and whether or not it is susceptible of a solution.

First of all, the fact that no science can demonstrate the existence of its subject matter is quite easy to see. The subject of a science is some kind of being about which the science will draw certain and necessary conclusions through a process of demonstration or necessary inference. What is drawn is the conclusion; that about which it is drawn is the subject; and the reasons for drawing the conclusion are the principles or causes. These principles or causes of the conclusion are the formal object of the science, the conclusion itself being the material object.

Now a conclusion must be about something; hence, the conclusion itself *presupposes* the existence of the subject matter. Moreover, and this brings out the urgency of the difficulty, the principles that produce the conclusion must themselves arise from the subject matter concerning which they furnish us new knowledge. Hence both the conclusions of a science and its principles of proof presuppose the existence of the subject matter. For just as the conclusions arise from the principles, so do the principles themselves arise from the subject. If a science had no subject, neither would it have any proper principles or conclusions. The only possible way that a science could prove the existence of its subject would be either by principles that flowed from that subject, and this is impossible since the subject is not yet known to exist, or by principles drawn from a higher science, which is simply another way of saying that no science proves the existence of its own subject. The subjects of the different sciences are simply given or presupposed.

But what about the existence of God? God is not any being found or given in our sensible or intelligible experience of reality. Hence, his existence cannot be simply presupposed. Nor, on the other hand, can God's existence be demonstrated, for no science can demonstrate the existence of its subject matter. Moreover, natural theology is the highest of the natural sciences, and so there can be no appeal to a higher science for this demonstration. How do we solve this dilemma?

2. Natural Theology Is an Exception

If the principles by which we demonstrated the existence of God did indeed presuppose in the order of our knowledge the cognition of God's existence, then the circle would be a completely vicious one. But this is not the case. The principles by which we demonstrate God's existence, for example, the principle of efficient causality or the principle of finality, presuppose in the order of knowledge only the existence of being, not of a supreme being. Such principles arise in our intellect from the existence of material, sensible beings. And they arise from such beings, not precisely as material or sensible, but as *being*, as from something that *is*. Hence they are metaphysical principles, principles of being as being, the necessary and valid possession of anyone who reflects upon existing things. As such, they can be used in the order of knowledge, of science, to prove the existence of the first cause of being, as a necessary term in the real order.

Of course, once this term is seen as necessary, the mind also sees that in the order of being, the first principles of demonstration are ultimately founded in God, in the sense that God is the first cause of the existence of the beings from which these principles arise within our knowledge. Put briefly, we can say that our principles of demonstration presuppose *for us* only the existence and knowledge of finite sensible beings, although in themselves and ultimately they also presuppose the existence of God. With us, the order of knowledge and the order of being—the logical and ontological orders—are not the same. God is the first ontological principle of being. But for us, the first logical principle of being, the first judgment about being, is due to the beings of our experience. But since these principles of demonstration flow from being as being, from the fact that something *is*, rather than the fact that it is material or sensible, such principles of demonstration have the analogous and transcendent values of being itself. And so I can validly use such principles in my demonstration of God's existence.

Finally, let us remember that metaphysics and natural theology are the same science, not in the sense that they have the same subject, but in the sense that it belongs to the science of being to investigate the first cause of being. God is the principal object or term of first philosophy or metaphysics, not its subject. Metaphysics, therefore, like any other science, does not prove the existence of its subject genus, being as being, but it can and does prove the existence of the supreme Being.

3. Approaching the Problem

God is not found among the beings of our experience. If he does exist, that existence must somehow be inferred, be concluded to by a careful reflection upon the beings that do fall within our immediate experience. And when we speak of God here, in this first approach to the problem of his existence, we mean some higher being that is above man, upon whom man and the universe depend in some way for their existence and conservation. When the human mind first approaches this problem of God's existence, without any philosophical or scientific prejudices, it does not see any obvious or immediate reason why the existence of God cannot be demonstrated. For if God does exist, he has the perfection of being, and thus in some sense is capable of being grasped by the human intellect, which is the faculty of being. And so there seems no difficulty from the side of God. Furthermore, the mind knows that it must begin its proof with the evidence at hand, namely, the sensible and material existents of its experience. And since the mind can know these beings, there seems no difficulty from the side of these existents.

But to posit God as a necessary term of a demonstration there must be some evidence within being that moves the intellect to posit the term and to posit it necessarily. This evidence will be some knowledge that arises from material sensible being, in the light of which the mind sees the necessity of positing the existence of a supreme Being. It is at this point that our proof endeavors to become scientific, and it is also at this point that difficulties begin to arise. But if it can be shown that such knowledge, which can be used as a principle of true demonstration, has a validity beyond the material and sensible realms of being, then there is no reason on the side of our principles themselves why the existence of God cannot be demonstrated.

Reason must approach the problem of God's existence with the utmost care and caution. True, knowledge, and even conviction, of the existence of a supreme Being seems the natural and spontaneous possession of most of the human race, and this at any given period of its history. But there was also a time when men thought the earth was flat, or that it was the center of the universe —positions long since shown to be erroneous. So that while the philosopher may respect this common census of opinion and even investigate its origins, he will never base his demonstration upon its existence. The philosopher also knows that there have been and are atheists and agnostics in the history of thought, the former declaring that they can positively prove that there is no such thing as a supreme Being, and the latter maintaining that even if such a Being does exist, this existence cannot be demonstrated by any philosophical argument of which human reason is capable. Moreover, many of the arguments that have been brought forth to prove God's existence have been shown either to beg the question or to be inconclusive. And these false proofs have not been the products of average or mediocre intellects, but have come from men with the philosophical stature of a Descartes or a Leibniz or an Anselm. Even the five classic proofs of St. Thomas Aquinas have had their share of criticism.

In approaching this problem of proving God's existence, we will move according to the following steps. First, we will investigate the classic *objections* against demonstrating God's existence. Secondly, we will determine *what a valid demonstration would be,* and what elements must enter into it. Then we will be ready to try ourselves to prove the existence of God.

4. Classic Objections Against Demonstrating God's Existence

In the history of thought there have been two extremes regarding the impossibility of demonstrating the existence of God. Some thinkers have maintained that *any strict demonstration is quite superfluous,* since the existence of God is a self-evident fact. And since what is self-evident is incapable of demonstration, to demonstrate God's existence is impossible. At the other extreme are those thinkers who hold that *the existence of God is impervious to human reason.* If it is to be held at all, it must be held on faith.

Let us consider first the objections of those who say that the existence of God is a self-evident fact. Now, obviously, what is self-evident cannot be demonstrated. For to demonstrate means to go from the known to the unknown. That is to say, from the knowledge of term one and the knowledge of term two, the reason concludes to and understands a third term. Demonstration is strict reasoning, in the sense that the mind passes from term one to term three because of, and hence "through," term two. But in self-evident truths or self-evident propositions which express these truths, only two terms, and not three, are involved. Here once the meaning or intelligibility of the two terms is understood by the mind, the intellect *immediately* understands the truth of the proposition. The truth is not mediated by a middle term, but is seen immediately from the evidence or intelligibility of the two terms alone. Thus the proposition or truth is called *self-evident,* for to understand it we need not go beyond the proposition for any other evidence. Let us take a simple example to show what is meant by a self-evident proposition. When the intellect understands what a "whole" is and what a "part" is, it immediately understands what is affirmed by the proposition "a whole is greater than its part." Now some have maintained that the proposition "God exists" is just such a self-evident proposition. Let us see why.

1) Once the intellect understands what the name "God" means, and what it means "to exist," the mind immediately sees that God must exist. Why is this so? Because by the name "God" is meant a *supreme Being,* that is to say, something greater than which we cannot conceive or imagine. This notion or idea the intellect forms within itself when it hears and understands the name "God." So in this way God at least begins to exist in the intellect. But the point is that God, so understood, cannot exist only in the intellect, for that which exists both in the intellect and in reality is *greater* than that which exists merely in the intellect. But since God means *supreme Being,* than which there is no greater, it follows that God must exist also in reality. Thus the proposition "God exists" is self-evident, being made manifest from the very meaning of his name. [1] Hence his existence cannot be demonstrated.

[1] See St. Thomas, *Contra Gentiles,* Book I, Ch. 10, paragraph 2. This is the famous argument of St. Anselm.

2) Another way to understand the self-evidence of the proposition, "God exists," is to realize that the predicate, "exists," or "existence," belongs of necessity to the subject, "God." For God, as supreme and perfect Being, cannot be composed. His being must be absolutely simple. Hence in God there is no distinction between what he is, his nature, and the fact that he is, his existence. And, therefore, since existence belongs of necessity to the very nature of God, in the proposition "God exists," the intelligibility of the predicate is contained in the intelligibilty of the subject, so that it is obviously a self-evident proposition, and cannot be demonstrated.

3) The other classic objection of those thinkers who say that the existence of a supreme Being is a self-evident fact, is a most interesting one. Whatever is known naturally and spontaneously is known of itself, and thus needs no demonstration or investigation to acquire. But our knowledge of God must be of this kind. Why? Because man, by a natural desire, tends towards this supreme Being as towards the source of his happiness and his final end. And since man has this natural desire, he must also have a natural knowledge of God's existence, for there is no desire for the unknown. Thus the existence of God is known naturally and spontaneously, and cannot be demonstrated through creatures.

5. The Answers to These Objections

1) First of all, let us point out with St. Thomas [2] that this opinion that God's existence is a self-evident fact has a twofold origin. The first is habit or custom, the habit or custom that is built up from the very beginning in those who are used to listening to and invoking the name of God. For any habit, especially if it is contracted in childhood, acquires the force of a nature. Habits become a sort of second nature. It is a simple fact that those truths which we are taught as children, we hold as firmly and unquestionably as though they were self-evident and completely obvious truths.

The other origin of this opinion about God's existence as self-evident is a failure to distinguish between something that is self-

[2] *Contra Gentiles,* Bk. I, Ch. 11.

evident *in itself* and something that is self-evident *to us.* These
two are not always the same. For example, in itself God's existence
is "self-evident," in the sense that God in himself and of himself
is perfect actuality, since that which is God is his own "to be."
But that which is God, that is, God himself, cannot be conceived
by our mind, and so God remains unknown *to us.* Just as, for
example, the truth that every whole is greater than its part is
self-evident in itself. But if someone could not conceive or understand the meaning of "whole," that truth would remain unknown
to that person. With this in mind, let us now answer the objections
themselves.

Obviously, when a person hears the word "God" and forms some
idea or meaning for this word in his mind, it by no means follows
that therefore God must exist in reality. To begin with, even
among those who would grant that God exists, not all would say
that their concept of him is that of a being greater than which we
cannot imagine or conceive. The pagans, for example, who held
the existence of many gods, did not conceive of God in this way.
And some who have held one God thought that he was the world,
or nature, and so forth. So that it is simply not true that when a
person hears or thinks of the word "God," he thinks of something
greater than which cannot be conceived. So from this point of
view the objection has no validity.

But let us suppose, for the sake of argument, that all men did
understand by the name "God" a being greater than which could
not be conceived or thought. It still is not necessary that a being
greater than which cannot be thought exists in reality. Why? Because, as St. Thomas points out, a *thing* is posited or affirmed in
the same way that the meaning or intelligibility of its name is
posited or affirmed. [3] Now from the fact that the mind *conceives*
something when it says and thinks of the *name* "God," it follows
only that God exists *in the intellect,* that is, that there exists only
a *concept* of God. And, therefore, it also follows that that *thing*
greater than which cannot be thought, needs to exist *only* in the

[3] *Eodem enim modo necesse est poni rem, et nominis rationem.* C.G., Bk.
I, Ch. 11.

intellect. It does not follow that there must in reality, in existence outside my mind, a thing greater than which I cannot conceive.

And so there would be no contradiction if one affirmed that God did not exist. Only on the supposition that one would grant there did exist in reality a being greater than which could not be conceived, would it be contradictory to say that a being so conceived could exist only in the mind. Nor does it add any force to the argument to say, with Anselm, that if this being existed only in the mind, we could think of a greater being; namely, one that existed also in reality, so that a being greater than which cannot be thought must of necessity also exist in reality. For, as is obvious, it is still a question of something being *thought of* as existing also in reality; it is by no means a question of something actually existing there.

2) What is to be said about the second reason for alleging the self-evidence of the proposition "God exists," namely, that the perfection of existence belongs to the very nature of God? The answer to this objection is our distinction given above between a thing's being self-evident *in itself,* and self-evident *to us.* Just as the truth "the whole is greater than its part" is self-evident to us, so the truth that existence necessarily belongs to God is self-evident to those who see God, because in God essence and existence are one. But since in this life we cannot see the divine essence, neither can we arrive at a knowledge of God's existence through himself, but must arrive at this existence through creatures. Thus the truth of the proposition, "God exists," is not self-evident to us; rather, we must demonstrate its truth.

3) Does man have a natural desire for God, which would therefore presuppose a natural or spontaneous knowledge of his existence? It is true that men naturally desire God in the same way that they naturally know him. Now what all men naturally desire is happiness, and so they can be said to have a natural desire for God insofar as this happiness, which all naturally desire, is a certain participation in the goodness of God. Thus, just as God is not naturally desired as he is in himself, or according to himself, neither is he naturally known as he is in himself or according to

himself. He is naturally known only in his creatures, in his effects, from which we can reason to a knowledge of God.

It is abundantly clear that not all men place their happiness in God. Some desire riches as their happiness, others pleasure, power, and so forth. But all these things are desirable, all these things bring happiness, only because they are a certain participation in the goodness of God. So that just as in desiring these participations man may be said to be naturally desiring God, so in knowing these things and other creatures, man may be said to be naturally knowing God, not in himself, but in his effects. Just as a man who studies and examines the masterpieces of a certain artist, by that very fact automatically and necessarily gains much knowledge concerning the artist, for example, his peculiar technique of handling color, his special genius for line, perspective, and so on, so anyone who studies and examines creatures can be said to have some natural knowledge of God even though he is unaware or not conscious that this is really knowledge about God.

6. Objections That State God's Existence Must Be Held Only on Faith

Our first group of thinkers maintained that it is quite useless to try to demonstrate God's existence, since this truth is self-evident. Other thinkers have held the opinion directly contrary to this, stating that it is useless to try to demonstrate that God exists, since this truth is impervious to human reason and exceeds man's capacity to know it. It is a truth, therefore, that must be held on faith.

These thinkers have been especially influenced in their opinion by the weakness of the proofs that have been used to try to demonstrate God's existence. Seeing the fallacies and inconclusiveness of such proofs, and being unable to provide themselves with any better ones, many have simply concluded that it is quite impossible and useless to attempt to demonstrate that there is a God. Moreover, these men do have some positive objections against any demonstration of God's existence. It will suffice here to mention three of these, one drawn from the nature of God, one from the nature of demonstration, and one from the nature of human knowledge.

1) All philosophers who have dealt scientifically with the nature of the divine Being have shown that in God his essence or nature must be one with his existence. As regards this divine Being, it is the same question whether we ask *what* God is or *whether* God is. And since human reason cannot arrive at the knowledge of what God is, neither does it seem possible that human reason can demonstrate whether God is. To know the one is to know the other. But we cannot know the one (God's nature). Neither, therefore, can we know the other (his existence).

2) Furthermore, the very nature of demonstration precludes the possibility of proving the existence of God. For demonstration demands a middle term, in the light of which we can draw our new conclusion. Now as Aristotle points out, [4] the middle term of a demonstration is always the meaning or intelligibility of some name, which meaning or intelligibility we call a definition. For example, if one understands the meaning or definition of spiritual or immaterial as that which has no matter within its essence, then one can conclude in the light of this definition to the immortality of such an essence. For having within it no matter or principle of corruption, such an essence cannot corrupt, and so is naturally immortal. In this example, the middle term or *means* of demonstrating immortality is the intelligibility or definition of immateriality. A middle term must be some definition, otherwise strict demonstration is impossible. But since the human reason cannot form any definition or intelligibility about the nature of God, it possesses no middle term in the light of which it can conclude to God's existence.

3) Our third objection (a quite serious one) is drawn from the nature of human knowledge. All our principles of demonstration are known by human reason through the senses. [5] Therefore, it would seem to follow that anything which would exceed

---

[4] *Posterior Analytics*, Bk. II, Ch. 9 (93b21).
[5] See Aristotle, *Posterior Analytics*, Bk. I, Ch. 18 (81a38).

every sense faculty, and which is essentially higher than any sensible being, would be incapable of demonstration by such principles. But God exceeds every sense power and is essentially higher than any sensible being. Hence his existence cannot be demonstrated by principles known through the senses.

7. These Objections Answered

1) How are we to answer these three objections? By pointing to the error or misunderstanding from which each flows. For example, the first objection, which states that since in God existence and essence are the same perfection, and since the human reason cannot know what this essence is neither can it know of God's existence, flows from a misunderstanding of what it means to "know existence." Existence or "to be" can be taken in two senses. First, it can mean that intrinsic act or perfection of a being by which it exercises existential actuality—the intrinsic possession of the *act of existence*. Or, secondly, "to exist" or "to be" can refer to the mind's *affirmation* of existence. Here the mind asserts or affirms that something is or exists, because it is moved by evidence to make this assertion. For example, I may say "There is gold in them there hills." What the mind knows here is the truth of this proposition, the *fact* that there is gold. It does not know the gold itself. What exists here in my knowledge is the "to be" or reality of *the truth* of this proposition, which the mind has formed and affirmed, moved by the evidence. It is a knowledge of the *truth of a proposition*, not a knowledge of the existing gold, not a knowledge of the act of existing exercised by the gold.

Now let us apply this distinction to our objection. The *esse* or existence that is identical with the divine essence cannot be known by the human intellect in this life. For this is the Being that is God, the intrinsic possession of existence by which God is God. We simply do not know what this Being is. But the mind can form and affirm the proposition, "There is a God." And the mind is induced or moved to form this proposition because of the demonstrative evidence it has that points to God's existence. Thus God's *existence* can be demonstrated as a *fact;* it cannot be known as a *perfection*. What the mind actually knows is the truth, or being, of the proposition it has formed. But to the truth of this proposition there does correspond in reality an existing God.

2) The second objection flows from a failure to realize that there is more than one way to demonstrate a truth. The way mentioned in the objection is called demonstration *propter quid*. Here the middle term of the demonstration is a real definition or intelligibility of some nature or essence, which causes the mind to conclude to some other truth about this nature or essence. For example, when I understand that immateriality belongs to the nature or essence of the human soul, I am forced to conclude that this soul also has the property of immortality. The human soul is immaterial, *propter quid* (on account of which) it is also immortal. As is obvious, we cannot demonstrate God's existence by a *propter quid* demonstration, since this kind of demonstration presupposes some knowledge of the nature of God.

But there is another kind of demonstration, equally valid for the discovery of truth, which is called demonstration *quia*. For example, God exists *quia* (because) creatures exist. What is our middle term in this kind of demonstration? It is not some nature or definition of a nature. In place of such nature or definition we use here as a middle term some effect or fact *that is necessarily related* to the nature we are trying to establish. In such demonstration we can affirm the existence of something because of the necessary relationship that our middle term has to this something.

Thus in demonstrating that there is a God, the middle term of our demonstration will be some sensible existing being. But precisely as a middle term, as furnishing light for the reason to draw its conclusion that God exists, this sensible existing being will be seen *as an effect*, as a creature, and hence as having *a necessary relationship to God* as first cause. Demonstration *quia* can give the mind a valid proof for the fact that God exists, even though it can tell us nothing about the nature of his Being.

3) The third objection can be dealt with briefly here. Although God himself, in his own Being exceeds our senses and is essentially above every sensible being, his effects, his creatures, are

sensible beings. And it is from these beings that our demonstration takes its beginning. Moreover, as we shall see in greater detail later on, the principles of demonstration that arise from sensible beings, arise from these beings not insofar as they are *sensible*, that is to say, as they have this or that particular nature or essence, but insofar as they are *beings*, that is, insofar as they share in the act of existence. Hence such principles are perfectly valid to prove the existence of a Being which, while not sensible in its nature, does nevertheless possess existence. In a word, principles of demonstration which flow from being as being, are valid also for suprasensible being.

8. Conclusion

Now that we have answered the classic objections against the possibility of proving the existence of God, we are in a better position to see what a valid demonstration of God's existence must contain. [6] First of all, it must begin with the existence of extramental beings, for we want to prove that God exists, not that we think he exists. Secondly, it must begin with beings other than God, for to begin with some statement about God or some perfection of God is to beg the whole question. When we ask whether God exists, we cannot begin with something that in the order of *knowledge* already presupposes that existence. Thus our demonstration of God's existence, to be valid, must begin with the material and sensible beings of our experience.

Our whole proof will be to show that such beings are, as a matter of fact, not just beings, but effects; effects of some one supreme Being who alone could be here and now the proper cause of their act of existence. Thus our demonstration will be *a posteriori*, following and depending upon our experience of things, going from effect to the cause of the effect. So that any valid demonstration of God's existence has three steps: first, an existential fact; secondly, seeing this existential fact in a new light, namely, as an effect; thirdly, the concluding to, or inferring of, the existence of

---

[6] For a study and critique of some famous invalid proofs for the existence of God, see Appendix A.

what alone could have produced such an effect, the first cause of being, which we call God.

9. Summary of the Chapter

"There is no valid reason why we cannot know and truly demonstrate the existence of God. However, this demonstration cannot be made through any *a priori* or *a simultaneo* argument, but only through one that is truly *a posteriori*, that is to say, that begins with the existence of material, sensible beings."

a. State of the question

Having seen the nature and characteristics of natural theology, we now want to see whether we can demonstrate the existence of our subject, namely, God. But no science can prove the existence of its own subject, since the very principles of demonstration in any science arise from the existence of its subject matter. For example, the principles of demonstration used in the mathematical sciences arise from quantified being, which is the subject matter of these sciences. And the principles of demonstration used in the philosophy of nature arise from mobile being, which is the subject of this science.

Therefore, since both the conclusions of a science and the principles of demonstration by which these conclusions are reached presuppose the subject of the science, it follows that no science can prove the existence of its own subject. Hence, we must make the following distinction as regards the science of natural theology: Insofar as natural theology is essentially the same science as metaphysics, the existence of God is not demonstrated as the subject of this science, because the subject of metaphysics is being as being. Rather, in this sense, God is demonstrated as the ultimate *object* of metaphysics, or as the first cause of being as being. But insofar as natural theology is considered as a distinct part of metaphysics (as a sort of science within a science), and therefore as distinct from metaphysics as a part is distinct from the whole, we can speak of demonstrating the existence of God as the subject of this part of the science, for it is of this subject—as so demonstrated—that we make our conclusions.

In this second chapter we studied two points: first, that there is no valid reason why the existence of God cannot be demonstrated, and, secondly, that such a demonstration cannot be *a priori* or *a simultaneo*, but only *a posteriori*. In the next chapter we shall study the nature of an *a posteriori* demonstration.

b. Explanation of terms

1) *"There is no valid reason . . ."* That is to say, neither from the side of God, whose existence is to be demonstrated, nor from the side of our intellect, which performs the demonstration, nor from the side of the principles through which the demonstration is performed, does there appear any reason why God's existence cannot be known through a true demonstration.

2) *"However, this demonstration cannot be made through any a priori or a simultaneo argument."* By "demonstration" here is understood an act by which our reason arrives at the knowledge of some truth through its prior knowledge of some other truths. This new truth constitutes a *conclusion*, and is implicitly contained in the other truths, which are called the premises. For example, the truth of the immortality of the human soul is implicitly contained in our knowledge of its spirituality. Demonstration can be of two kinds:

(*a*) *a priori*, and this type is had when the logical reason that causes our knowledge of the conclusion is also the ontological cause of the existence of the thing concluded to. For example, our knowledge of the rationality of man is not only the logical reason why we *know* that all men have the power of laughter; it is also the ontological cause why men have this power. Therefore, this demonstration proceeds from cause to effect and is rightly called *a priori*; because the cause is always prior to the effect, at least in nature, if not in time.

It should be quite clear that the existence of God cannot be demonstrated in this way, because nothing is prior to God, and God has no cause. But some have held that the existence of God can be demonstrated through a "sort of" *a priori* argument, or as it is called, an argument *a simultaneo*. Such a demonstration takes its beginning from some perfection with which the existence of God is necessarily and *simultaneously* connected (hence the name, *a simultaneo*). For example, from the notion of an all *Perfect Being* there immediately and necessarily follows its existence, since existence itself is some perfection.

(*b*) *a posteriori*—a demonstration that proceeds from an effect to the cause of the effect. The nature of this type of demonstration, the only valid type for demonstrating the existence of God, will be studied in the next chapter.

c. The proof

1) "There is no valid reason why we cannot know and truly demonstrate the existence of God." This first part is easily established. For every impossibility for demonstrating the existence of God would have to come either from the side of God, or our human intellect, or from the evidence used in the demonstration. But from none of these is there any real impossibility. Therefore, *etc.*

(*a*) *Not from the side of God,* for if God exists, he is within the order of being and hence his existence is an intelligible fact. And so this existence can be known, if not as in God, at least as revealed through the existence of other beings. And so a knowledge of these other beings can lead us to the fact that God exists.

(*b*) *Not from the side of our intellect,* for our intellect can know, in some way or other, whatever has the intelligibility of being. This proposition is proved in the Philosophy of Man, where the intellect is shown to be the faculty of being.

(*c*) *Not from the side of the evidence used in our demonstration,* for although we begin our investigation with material and sensible existents, we study these existents not insofar as they are *material* and *sensible,* but insofar as they *are,* insofar as they possess the actuality of existence. Thus the principles of demonstration that we draw from such beings, as that of efficient causality or finality, have an application that transcends the material and sensible as such, and so can be used to establish the existence of a suprasensible being such as God.

2) "However, this demonstration cannot be made through *a priori* or *a simultaneo* argument."

(*a*) *Not through any a priori argument,* because in this kind of demonstration our middle term is some definition or intelligibility whose ontological correspondent is the real cause in the thing of what we conclude to in our demonstration of the thing. Just as the *knowledge* of man's rationality can give rise to our *knowledge* of his ability to laugh, so the fact that man *is* rational is the reason why he can laugh. But it is clear that God, if he exists, has no *cause* of his existence. Therefore, the existence of God cannot be established by any *a priori* argument, since such an argument goes from cause to the effect of the cause.

(*b*) *Nor through any "sort of" a priori argument,* that is, through an argument *a simultaneo.* Because in such an argument, the middle term is something that is immediately, necessarily, and simultaneously connected in the thing with what we want to demonstrate. It is, however, distinct in our knowledge of the thing, and so can be *considered as prior* to what we want to demonstrate. Therefore, upon the understanding of this thing, we understand what we want to demonstrate. For example, once we understand the immateriality of the human soul, we understand its immortality. In this way, through the immateriality of the soul is demonstrated its immortality. In the same way, some have held that through the knowledge of *some perfection of God* we can demonstrate his existence. But this is obviously impossible, for in such a demonstration we do not prove but rather presuppose that God exists. Any perfection of God presupposes his existence. And so it is impossible to prove that God exists through any *a simultaneo* argument.

3) "God's existence can be proved only by an *a posteriori* argument." The nature and validity of this kind of demonstration will be discussed in Chapter 3.

10. A Selected Passage from St. Thomas[7]

"Is God's existence self-evident to the human mind, just as first principles of demonstration, which cannot be thought not to exist?

"Reply: There are three opinions on this question. Some have said, as Rabbi Moses relates, that the fact that God exists is not self-evident, nor reached through demonstration, but only accepted on faith. The weakness of the reasons which many advance to prove that God exists prompted them to assert this.

"Others, as Avicenna, say that the fact that God exists is not self-evident, but is known through demonstration. Still others, as Anselm, are of the opinion that the fact that God exists is self-evident to this extent, that no one in his inner thoughts can think that God does not exist, although exteriorly he can express it and interiorly think the words with which he expresses it.

"The first opinion is obviously false. For we find that the existence of God has been proved by the philosophers with unimpeachable proofs, although trivial reasons have also been brought forth by some to show this.

"Each of the two following opinions has some truth. For something is immediately evident in two ways: in itself and to us. That God exists, therefore, is immediately evident in itself, but not to us. Therefore, to know this it is necessary in our case to have demonstrations proceeding from effects. This is clear from what follows.

"For a thing to be immediately evident in itself, all that is needed is that the predicate pertain to the nature of the subject. For then the subject cannot be considered without it appearing that the predicate is contained in it. But for something to be immediately evident with reference to us, we have to know the meaning of the subject in which the predicate is included. Hence it is that some things are immediately evident to everybody, as, for instance, when propositions of this sort have subjects which are such that their meaning is evident to everybody, as every whole is greater than its part. For anyone knows what a whole is and

[7] From *De Veritate*, qu. 10, a. 12. Translated by Robert W. Mulligan, S.J., in *Truth* (Chicago, Henry Regnery Co., 1952), Vol. 2, pp. 68-69.

what a part is. Some things, however, are immediately evident only to those with trained minds, who know the meaning of the terms, whereas ordinary prople do not know them.

"It is in this sense that Boethius says: 'There are two types of common notions. One is common to everybody, for example, if you take equal parts from things that are equal. . . . The other is found only in the more educated, for example, that non-bodily things are not in a place. Ordinary people cannot see the truth of this, but the educated can.' For the thought of ordinary people is unable to go beyond imagination to reach the nature of incorporeal things.

"Now, existence is not included perfectly in the essential nature of any creature, for the act of existence of every creature is something other than its quiddity. Hence, it cannot be said of any creature that its existence is immediately evident even in itself. But, in God, his existence is included in the nature of his quiddity, for in God *essence* and *existence* are the same, as Boethius says. And *that He is* and *what He is* are the same, as Avicenna says. Therefore, it is immediately evident in itself.

"But, since the essence of God is not evident to us, the fact of God's existence is not evident to us, but has to be demonstrated. In heaven, however, where we shall see his essence, the fact of God's existence will be immediately evident to us much more fully than the fact that affirmation and denial cannot both be true at the same time is immediately evident to us now."

Suggested Readings

1. St. Thomas, *Summa Contra Gentiles*, in *On the Truth of the Catholic Faith*, translated by A. Pegis (New York, Hanover House, 1955), Book One, Chapters 10, 11, and 12, Vol. I, pp. 79–85.
   Summa Theologiae, in *Basic Writings of St. Thomas*, by A. Pegis (New York, Random House, 1945), Vol. I, pp. 18–21.
2. Etiènne Gilson, *The Christian Philosophy of St. Thomas Aquinas* (New York, Random House, 1956), pp. 46–58.
   History of Christian Philosophy in the Middle Ages (New York, Random House, 1955), pp. 132–134.

CHAPTER 3

The Nature and Validity of *A Posteriori* Demonstration

Among those things that must be considered concerning God . . . there comes first, as the necessary foundation of the whole science, the consideration by which we demonstrate that God exists. For if this is not had, every consideration about divine things necessarily fails.

—St. Thomas, *Summa Contra Gentiles*, Book One, Ch. 9

So far in our study of natural theology we have seen and discussed the following points: first, the precise nature of the science itself, what it is and what it purports to do; secondly, the chief arguments that have been urged against the possibility of proving the existence of God, and their solution. Now we are ready to discuss our own *a posteriori* arguments for God's existence. The various arguments themselves will be studied in the next chapter. In this chapter we want to consider certain general truths concerning the demonstration of the existence of a cause from the existence of an effect, and how these truths have special application to the case of God's existence. In spite of the many invalid proofs offered for God's existence, and the different positions adopted by the agnostics, we must not think the case for such a demonstration by human reason a desperate one. Rather, we should focus our attention on the one valid way that remains, the way of effect to cause, and see why it is valid and what it entails.

1. The Notion of a Proper Cause

We will presuppose in this discussion the student's general knowledge of causes and effects that he has learned in metaphysics. Our precise interest here is to grasp the correct notion of a proper cause. A proper efficient cause is an agent that exercises its influence over the existence of some other being, the effect, through an activity that is properly its own, that is to say, through an activity that flows from its own nature, its own form—an activity that is proportioned to the nature of the agent.

For example, in the composition of this page, many causes have exercised their activity, but working together as a causal unit: the intelligence of the writer, his motor faculties or nerves, his fingers, the moved movement of the typewriter keys, and so on. And the complexity of this causal activity is nicely mirrored in the complexity of the effect produced: a written page that carries meaning. The various elements that constitute the unity of the effect, a meaningful written page, are proportioned to what in the agent has properly produced them. For example, the shape and configuration of the words are properly proportioned to the typewriter; whereas the meaning or intelligibilty that these words carry is properly proportioned to the intelligence of the typist. Hence, the proper cause of the meaning of the page has not been the typewriter, which has no intelligence, but the man behind the keys. Thus the first characteristic of a proper cause is this: it produces the effect by an activity that is proportioned to its own nature or being. Now in arguing from the existence of an effect to the existence of God, we will be arguing to the existence of God as the proper cause of the *existence* of the effect.

Another thing to remember about a cause, which never should be lost sight of in our demonstration of God's existence, is this: every true cause is simultaneous with its effect. This is true whether the causes are intrinsic, like matter and form, or extrinsic, like the agent and end, or whether the cause is principal or

instrumental. As long as the effect is here and now in existence
as an effect, the cause must be here and now influencing that existence. This will be seen much more in detail when the nature
of an ordered series of efficient causes is explained later on. Here
an example or two will suffice to show what we mean by saying
that cause and effect are always found "together"—that they must
have simultaneous existence. If I stop writing, the coming into
being of this page immediately stops; if I stop thinking, the coming into being of the intelligible content of the page immediately
stops. A cause is not a cause unless an effect is being produced;
and an effect is not an effect unless it is here and now being
caused, being influenced in some way in its existence by something else.

And so we can see how one set of causes may have been needed
to bring a certain effect into being, and another new set needed
to keep the effect in being, as, for example, in the case of our
written page. Once it is written, it *is* now no longer the effect of
the typist and typewriter; it *was* their effect, it was written. But
the page is not here and now any longer being caused by the typist or the typewriter. Yet the written page remains in existence,
it keeps on keeping the existence it received; and so it keeps on
depending on a series of causes that preserves it in being. The
existence of the paper conserves the existence of the words, and
the existence of the words conserves the existence of the meaning.
And all these things must exist simultaneously. This point of simultaneous existence of cause and effect is most important in our
demonstration of the existence of God. For once we see the need
of God as the only possible proper cause of the *existence* of any
being, we see that he must exist here and now if anything is to
exist at all.

Now we are beginning to see the possibility of proving God's
existence from the existence of things. Effects necessarily and immediately depend upon the existence of their proper cause, to
whose activity they are properly proportioned. So that given the
existence of the effect, the existence of its proper cause necessarily and immediately follows. Furthermore, material, sensible

existents are immediately known to us. Our knowledge of them is prior to our knowledge of God. Thus, if these existents can be shown to be effects, to be creatures, they can legitimately be used as a means of demonstrating the existence of God. As we shall see in our various proofs, these existents can be shown to be limited, imperfect, and contingent in their being. Thus they have the properties or characteristics of effects, of things that are produced, of things that have received their being. But to be an effect is to be here and now being caused, to be necessarily and immediately dependent upon the proper cause of being. This demonstration then would be valid and *a posteriori*.

2. These Observations Solve Many Seeming Difficulties

In any valid demonstration the conclusion cannot be present explicitly in the premises but only implicitly or potentially. If the conclusion is explicitly present in the premises, we have begged the question, for the premises are supposed to prove the conclusion, and the conclusion was already actually in the premises. But if the conclusion is only potentially or virtually present in the premises, then these premises do have the power or virtue to produce, to cause in us, the knowledge of the conclusion, and our demonstration is a valid one.

Now this is true in our demonstration of God's existence from the existence of sensible, material things. For these things are not considered at first by us in our demonstration explicitly and actually as effects. Rather, they are considered as certain things which when analyzed by the intellect, manifest certain characteristics (imperfection, contingency, limitation, and so forth). And from these characteristics the mind can conclude that they have a necessary relation or connection with some other being upon which they must here and now depend for their own being.

Secondly, in any valid demonstration the knowledge of the conclusion must be posterior to the knowledge of the premises. And since in *a posteriori* demonstration the order of knowledge is just the reverse of the order of being, nothing prevents the creatures from *being* posterior to God, even though our *knowledge* of the creatures precedes our knowledge of God. What the human intellect *knows* first is the being of sensible and material things; what it knows afterwards, or in the second place, is the existence of God. This is the order that obtains in our knowledge. But in the ontological order, or order of being, it is the existence of God that is first, and then the existence of sensible and material things, which depend upon God.

Thirdly, in any valid demonstration, the conclusion must follow with necessity from the premises. And this is true of our *a posteriori* demonstration of the existence of God, since this demonstration necessarily concludes to a necessary Being. And this is true, even though the demonstration proceeds from the contingent existence of some being. For because of this very contingency, the being is necessarily connected in its existence to a Being that is not and cannot be contingent. Hence the mind must necessarily conclude to the existence of a necessary Being, or to God.

Fourthly, this *a posteriori* demonstration, which proceeds from the existence of an effect to the existence of its proper cause, answers the objection that is sometimes put forward to show the impossibility of demonstrating that there is a God. If God exists, he is infinite in his Being. But the existents of our experience and the knowledge we have of them are only finite. Hence, as effects, these existents are not proportioned to any infinite cause, nor is our knowledge of them proportioned to any knowledge of an infinite God. There is no proportion between the finite and the infinite, either in being or in knowledge. So we cannot know God from our knowledge of creatures.

The answer to this objection is quite simple. That there is no univocal proportion or similarity between creatures and God, we admit. But we deny that there obtains no causal proportion or causal order between them, as we shall see when we discuss the nature of analogy. And this causal order or causal relationship is sufficient to tell us, not about the nature of God, but about the fact that he must exist.

Finally, one could not even ask the question, Is there a God? unless one had some knowledge, no matter how vague or no matter how obtained, of God. No one ever asks whether a "Goodoo" exists, because no one knows anything at all about a "Goodoo." The fact that we ask whether there is a God entails some knowledge of God. But this fact does not involve us in any begging of the question as regards God's existence. Because we do not base our demonstration for God's existence upon the existence of this knowledge of God, but upon the existence of things.

This vague and general knowledge of God, which seems to be the common possession of the human race may, upon reflection and examination, prove to be valid or invalid. This knowledge may even stimulate the mind to initiate a scientific investigation concerning God's existence; it may serve as an occasion for a demonstration. But the point is that such knowledge is not used in our premises when we demonstrate scientifically that God exists.

3. The Nature of This Demonstration

After we have actually gone through the various proofs for the existence of God, we will be in a much better position to understand the nature of the demonstration itself, and the precise movements made by the mind in reaching the conclusion that God exists. This process is one of going from the known to the unknown, from the being of the creature to the existence of God. Let us see how this process works.

The first step in our movement of knowledge toward God consists in the grasping of a fact of experience, for example, this thing is moving, the being of a man is more perfect that the being of a brute animal, and so on. We begin with a judgment of existence, and this judgment furnishes us with one of our premises. The second step or movement of the mind is an important one. Having made this judgment of existence, the intellect sees in the light or intelligibility of the being so judged a further consequence or inference. For example, this being that is moved is moved by another and not by itself. The evidence for this new knowledge, a knowledge that constitutes a conclusion for the intellect, is contained within the adequate intelligibility of moved being itself. The more detailed genesis of this second step we will have to establish in each of our proofs.

Now we have two premises: the fact of experience gained by a direct judgment of existence, and a universal judgment of being, which the intellect makes in the presence of the experiential fact and the light of the principle of non-contradiction. This second premise has been seen by the mind through an act of intellective induction. [1] It has been inferred and constitutes a conclusion for the mind. Our two judgments, or two premises, now stand as follows: "Something is moving. But this something is not moving

---

[1] The student should recall here what he has learned concerning induction and deduction. On the difference between these two kinds of inference, see A. H. Bachhuber, S.J., *Logic* (New York, Appleton-Century-Crofts, 1957), Ch. 4, especially pp. 41–44. For the difference between intellective and rational induction, see *ibid.*, Ch. 18, pp. 258–268. For induction, see also G. P. Klubertanz, S.J., *Philosophy of Human Nature* (New York, Appleton-Century-Crofts, 1953), Appendix K, especially pp. 388–393; also, *Introduction to Philosophy of Being* (New York, Appleton-Century-Crofts, 1955), pp. 257–264. Here we will recall only certain fundamental notions that bear upon the nature of our demonstration.

Inference: that process by which the mind proceeds from one to another, which other is seen to be implied in the former. Inference is of two kinds, *induction* or *deduction.*

(*a*) In *induction,* we proceed from sensible existents to general truths. This induction is *intellective* if we see the necessity of this general truth through insight into a particular case. Intellective induction itself is of two kinds: *direct,* when this "seeing" takes place immediately (as is the case with the propositions: "The whole is greater than its part," or "That which exists cannot at the same time not exist"), or after some little reflection. But in neither case is there question of using any middle term. The second kind of intellective induction is *indirect* or *reductive.* Here we see the necessity of a truth by an intellectual insight that is the result of *strict reasoning.* An example of such a truth will be our proposition: "God exists." On strict reasoning, see G. P. Klubertanz, S.J., *Introduction to Philosophy of Being, op. cit.,* pp. 260–261. Besides intellective induction, there is a second kind called *rational induction.* By this process we rise from a consideration of particular cases to a universal and necessary truth, although we do not intellectually *see* the underlying reason for that necessity and universality. An example of a truth gained by rational induction would be: "Unsupported heavy objects tend to fall toward the earth."

(*b*) In *deduction,* we proceed from a more general truth to a less general one.

itself, but is being moved by something *else*." With these two judgments in its possession, the intellect now moves to a further inference or conclusion, again placing this further judgment under the light or evidence of the first principle of being as judged; namely, the principle of non-contradiction. The intellect sees and judges that it is impossible to have an infinite regress, where one thing is always being moved by another. For this would involve the contradiction of not having a first and yet having something moved here and now. Again, this precise judgment will be established more carefully in the different proofs. Here we merely want to see the general movement in our knowledge.

Now we have three judgments, three premises: something is moving; it is being moved by another; but an infinite regress in moved movers is impossible. Each of these judgments has been inferred or concluded to by way of an intellectual induction. Now we are ready for a fourth and final judgment: Therefore, there must exist a first unmoved mover. No new evidence nor any new principle of knowledge is operative in making this judgment, but simply the premises themselves, so established. The further fact that we now give this first unmoved mover its common name, and call it God, is outside the actual movement of our knowledge toward the necessary term of contingent being. We simply label what we already have.

The above process has been gone through to show the student that a strict scientific demonstration of God's existence involves a rather complicated motion on the part of the mind. It is a demonstration achieved by indirect intellective induction or strict reasoning, where through the use of some middle term the mind has intellectual insight into the necessity of the truth that God exists.

In each of the five ways of St. Thomas that we will study, the mind goes through much the same noetic discursus. There will be minor differences, of course. For different kinds of causality are involved, different aspects of existents are considered, and different evidences are required for our judgments, and so forth. But the general pattern is essentially the same. We have examined the discursive pattern of the so-called "first way" of St. Thomas.

4. The Origin of First Principles

Since any *a posteriori* demonstration of God's existence depends upon the validity of the principle of causality, it is absolutely necessary that we understand just what this principle is, and how it arises in our mind from our judgment of being. First of all, what is a principle? In general, it is that from which something follows in some way or other. In this sense, fire is the principle of heat in a burning log, since it has caused or produced the heat in the log; or night is the principle of day, in the sense that day follows night, although there is no causal connection between the two. Every cause is a principle, since some effect always follows upon its causality; but not every principle is a cause, since something may follow upon something else without being caused by it. In this discussion of principles, we will consider principles only in the sense of *causal* principles.

What is a principle of being? Either it is something in the existent itself that influences or causes in some way its being, or it is something outside the existent, that causes or influences the being of the existent. An example of an intrinsic principle of being would be matter and form in the case of material existents, or the essence of a thing, or even the act of existence itself. Such principles of beings that belong to the existent itself are incomplete principles of being, principles or causes *by which* the existent is or by which it is what it is, or by which it is in such and such a way. An example of an extrinsic principle or cause of being would be the agent (as a father is the cause of the generation of his son) or the end or goal which influences the existent in its activity. Such principles of being that are extrinsic to the existent are complete principles of being, principles which cause the existence of other things. In this sense, as we shall see, God is the first complete principle of being as being.

Now that we know what a principle of being is, what is a principle of knowledge? It is something that gives rise to or causes knowledge. Thus a principle of knowledge can be a thing, for things are the causes of my knowledge of them, or it can be some knowledge, since the knowledge of one thing can lead to the knowledge of another, for example, my knowledge of the premises in a demonstration causes my knowledge of the conclusion. Thus premises are principles of knowledge.

What do we mean by a first principle of knowledge? Now there are different orders of knowledge. First of all, there is sense knowledge; secondly, there is the intellectual knowledge of natures or quiddities, which is had when the intellect understands, by an act of simple apprehension, what things are. And, thirdly, there is intellectual assent or judgment, when the intellect affirms or denies that things are, or are not, the way we know them. The intellect judges things when it asserts or affirms that things exist or that they exist in a certain way; for example, "John is," or "John is white." Now in each of these orders of knowledge there is something that is first; there is a first principle of that kind of knowledge.

Let us examine each of these three orders of knowledge carefully and see what its first principle or cause is. In that knowledge which is sensation, the first principle, or that which first causes sense knowledge, is the existing sensible object itself. The object as sensible first causes my knowledge of it as sensed.

In the case of the simple apprehension of what a thing is, the first principle or cause of this knoweldge is the essence or "whatness" of the existing material object. Hence, what first falls into the simple understanding of the intellect is an awareness or presence of "something." Now just as in the thing the actuality of the essence is due to the act of existence, so, too, in our knowledge of any essence it is the actuality of the essence that makes possible the actuality of our knowledge of it. Thus the intellect understands the essence *as of an existing thing*. That is to say, just as this "something" *is* because it is actuated by an act of existing, so it can be *known* (and hence can be a principle or cause of knowledge) because it can actuate the possible intellect. A thing acts insofar as it is in act, and the thing outside the mind is in act through its act of existing. That is why, our very first intellectual awareness of a thing is as of an *existing thing*.

What, finally, is the first principle or cause of judgmental knowledge? Again, it will be the thing outside the mind, but now precisely as existential rather than essential, that is to say, precisely as exercising an act of existing rather than possessing an essence actuated by that act. Therefore, the very first thing that the intellect affirms or assents is that this *is* something. Hence, the first principle or cause of our intellectual knowledge of being *is being itself*—the total existent, considered as "something that is"; understood by the intellect as something and asserted by the intellect as existing. [2]

Thus the first principle of sensible knowledge is the material sensible object as sensible; the first principle of the simple apprehension of what things are is the "total essence" of the existing material object; and the first principle of our judicial knowledge is the material existent, not only as existent, that is, not only as

[2] Or as existing in some way, e.g., as moving, as white, as big, etc. The very first thing that the intellect is aware of is an existing thing, something that is. This is an awareness of being. Psychologically, it is the awareness of a *totum*, a whole. But looked upon from the side of the simple understanding or simple consideration of what I know, the intellect does not assert its actual and explicit existence. Nevertheless, since it is the concrete sensible existent here and now present that has actuated both my external and internal sense faculties and is the reason why the form of the existing thing has actuated my possible intellect, the act of existence of the thing is causally, and in this sense really, present throughout the activity of sensation and simple apprehension. That is to say, there is a physical and causal continuity between the existent as existent and my knowledge of it. Yet the act of existence as such of the thing, that is to say, as an act known apart from the quiddity, can be grasped, can be known, only by a judgment. Thus in the order of knowledge, existence appears for the first time in our judgment of being. For it is only by an act of judgment that the intellect can explicitly know existence; i.e., by affirming or asserting it. For existence, as the actuation of essence, is formally incommunicable, and thus resistive to any abstractive activity of our intellect. Only forms are communicable; and the intellect, being itself a form, can only receive other forms. If, therefore, the intellect is to know existence, it must affirm it, posit it by an act. Here, in the judgment, act answers to act; just as in the simple apprehension of a nature, form or formation answers to the form of the existing thing. See *S.T.*, I, 85, 1; *In IV Metaph.*, lect. 6, No. 605; *De Verit.*, qu. 1, aa. 11 and 12.

exercising its act of existence, but also as having informed the intellect in the line of simple quiddity. [3]

The very first judgment that the intellect makes in the presence of sensible being is some affirmation concerning its existence; either simply that it is, or that it is such and such, is bright, is red, and so forth. When the mind affirms or assents that being is, it implies in this affirmation (and thus implicitly and concomitantly affirms) that being is not non-being. Thus in our very first judgment about being, the mind understands the principle of non-contradiction; namely, that it is impossible to affirm and deny being at the same time.

Now just as the sensible existent, actuating the senses through its sensible accidents and the intellect through its intelligible form or essence, is the first principle or cause of our judgments in the ontological order, or order of being, so, too, the principle of non-contradiction is the first principle of our judgments in the logical order, or order of knowledge. That is to say, all further judgments or affirmations about being can ultimately be judged for their rectitude in the light or evidence of this first principle. Notice what we are saying here. The principle of non-contradiction is not any evidence used as a formal premise in our demonstrations. Nor is it any "content" from which we deduce further truths about being. Rather, it is an ever-present norm that implicitly accompanies all our judgments about being. It is a logical principle, a light, that insures the rectitude of our conclusions.

To sum up: the first principle in the order of judicial knowledge, and which is implied and grasped in my first affirmation that this thing is or exists, is the principle of non-contradiction; and it is in the light of this principle that all further judgments about being are ultimately and reducibly seen to be valid. This principle itself is based upon the intelligibility of being, upon something that is.

[3] The intellect itself is, of course, a true principle or cause of knowledge, the agent intellect being the efficient cause, and the possible intellect being the "material" cause or subject from which knowledge is educed and in which it inheres. Also, the form of the thing understood, as that form is present in the phantasm and educed from the possible intellect, is a formal cause of my knowledge; it gives form and content to what I know.

Thus our first principles of knowledge are immediately grounded in the real, in the sensible existent.

5. The Principle of Causality

Let us now turn our attention to the principle of causality. What is this principle? It is an affirmation about being—a judgment. What does it affirm about being? It affirms that any finite being, in order to be, must have a source of its existence. This judgment or affirmation can be enunciated or formulated in different ways. As enunciated in the form of a proposition, it is called the principle of causality.

At this point we wish to do two things. First, to show how the intellect, confronted by the evidence of being, can conclude to the truth of the principle of causality; and, secondly, to show how this principle is seen to be valid in the light of the principle of non-contradiction. Thus in this way we shall see how the principle of causality is rooted in the intelligibility of being and hence in the actual existence of the real.

Notice that when we talk about the principle of causality here, we are referring to the principle of *efficient* causality, although *mutatis mutandis*, we can also formulate a principle for the other orders of causality. For example, "a being that is limited in its essential perfection, must have within itself the source of its limitation," would be a statement about material causality. Or, "a being that is of such and such a perfection, must contain within itself the source of this perfection," would be a statement about formal causality. Now how does the intellect arrive at the understanding of the principle of efficient causality?

6. The Evidence of Change

It is through the evidence of change that the intellect first comes to see the truth of the principle of causality. When we discuss the first way of St. Thomas for demonstrating the existence of God, in which he reasons from change in the existence of things to a necessary first cause of this change, we will see in some detail how the intellect concludes with absolute certainty to a universal principle of efficient causality that arises from the evidence of changing being. Here we will only indicate very briefly how this takes place.

When we watch a statue take shape under the deft touches of a sculptor, we see the potency that the marble possesses to be a statue gradually actuated to the actual possession of the perfection of being a statue. Or even in the case of substantial change, the potency that matter has to become, for example, a dog, is moved (through generation) to the actual perfection of being a dog.

Change, then, or coming into being, is a movement from potency to act. Thus every new perfection or every new being involves a movement from potency to act. Now this direct experience of change or production of being, and our affirmation about it, can be formulated in a proposition: "Nothing is moved from potency to act except by a being already in act." Why is this so? Because to act, or to move, means to be in act. Nothing gives what it does not have. If an agent is going to change something from cold to hot, the agent must itself be actually hot. It must be *in act* as regards the perfection of heat; otherwise it cannot cause heat in another. On the other hand, to be moved, to be acted upon, means to be in potency. For nothing receives something it already has. If water is to *become* hot, it must not already *be* hot; if so, it cannot become hot.

Thus it is absolutely impossible for any being to be in act and in potency at the same time as regards the same perfection. For this would be to affirm and deny the same thing at the same time; for example, that the water is actually cold and is not actually cold. And so we can conclude to the universal principle that nothing can move itself from potency to act, that nothing can be its own efficient cause. For the same being, at one and the same time, would have to actually have the perfection, in order to give it (as cause), and actually not have the perfection, in order to receive it (as effect). Thus whatever is caused, is caused by another. Or, as formulated above, "nothing is moved from potency to act except by a being already in act."

This principle of causality is absolutely universal. It applies to

every effect, every movement from potency to act. This principle
is also absolutely certain. To deny it is to deny the principle of
non-contradiction. That is to say, it cannot be denied by any real
assent of the intellect. We can deny it in words, but since the
words lack intelligible meaning, it is impossible for the intellect
to give real assent to such words.

Finally, we say that this principle of causality is *self-evident.*
Not in the sense that it is *a priori,* for this principle is derived from
sense experience, from the experience of changing things. Nor is
it self-evident in the sense that it in no way constitutes a conclusion
for the intellect. For the truth of the principle of causality is indeed
made known through another truth, for example, the truth that
things change. Rather, this principle of causality is self-evident
in this sense, that, as formulated, it carries within itself the intelligibility required in order to assent to its truth. We do not need any
new intelligibility, furnished by a third or middle term, in order
to see that the proposition is a true proposition. The terms of the
proposition carry with them their own intelligibility, which when
once understood, the intellect immediately assents to the truth of
the proposition. I have no need to bring in any further evidence
not already contained in the proposition. Put more explicitly, the
terms of the proposition, like *act* and *potency,* are understood by
the intellect in the light of the intelligibility of *being* ("that which
is"). Whereas what I *affirm* in the proposition, namely, that nothing is moved from potency to act except by a being already in
act (which is an *affirmation* of being), is seen to be true in the
light of the principle of non-contradiction.

7. Another Formulation of the Principle of Causality

The principle of causality as just stated reveals the need for
an efficient cause in every production of being. But it does not, as
so stated, explicitly point up the need for an efficient cause, here
and now, for those beings we already find actually existing around
us. In a word, while it adequately formulates the causal need from
the point of view of a thing's coming into being, it does not state

that causal need from the point of view of the very being of the thing.

Let us consider, therefore, another formulation of the principle of efficient causality that emphasizes more explicitly the need of a cause for a being that is in actual existence. Here is the way St. Thomas presents the proof to establish the necessity of such an efficient cause.

Whatever does not belong to the intelligibility of a thing, must come to that thing from without. But existence, "to be," does not belong to the intelligibility of any finite essence. For example, the essence of man, what man is, says nothing about his actual existence. The most exhaustive description of the essence of man will never reveal anything that necessitates its actual existence. Hence, the essence cannot be the efficient cause of the existence. Nothing gives what it does not have, and essence as such says only a capacity for existence. Essence is related to existence as potency to act. Thus, if any finite essence is going to exist, it must receive that existence from without. [4]

Now when existence is received from without, it follows that the being which receives it is contingent in the order of existence. And since contingency means a lack of necessity, we say that a contingent being in the order of existence is a being that may or may not exist. There is no necessary connection between what that being is and the fact that it exists. If such a being actually does exist, that existence cannot come from the essence itself, but from something outside that essence. And since existence cannot posit itself, cannot cause itself (for then it would have to be [as cause] and not be [as caused] at the same time), it follows that the existence of a finite being must come from some other being.

Once more it should be stressed that we are concerned here with the efficient cause of existence. For in a certain order, the essence is indeed a cause of existence. For essence receives and limits

[4] Of course, what exists is not the essence, but the being. The essence is a principle within being, namely, that by which the being is what it is; and existence is a principle *of* being, namely, that by which the being is. *What* exists is the being itself: "something that is."

existence. ⁵ But essence can in no way be an *efficient* cause of existence, since of itself it says only a certain capacity for existence. ⁶

Any essence, then, whose formal intelligibility says nothing about existence, is really distinct from its act of existing. Such is the case with all finite beings, for their essence does not include their existence. Since there is an actual distinction between what they are and the act by which they are, such beings are contingent in the order of existence. They may or may not exist. Hence, if we do find them existing, we know that their existence has been received from without. All finite beings are caused beings.

Of course, to say that finite beings are caused beings does not by that token prove that God exists. For one finite being could be caused by another finite being. The principle of causality simply points up the fact that a being does not cause itself. Therefore, to exist, it must be caused by another being. Our proof for the existence of God, which we are now ready to undertake, consists precisely in demonstrating that the only *proper* cause of the very existence of beings can be a Being whose existence belongs to its very essence—a Being whose very essence is To Be; whose existence and essence are identical. To prove the existence of God, one must prove the metaphysical necessity of positing a Being that has no cause but is the first and proper cause of the being of all other things.

8. Summary of the Chapter

"The only valid demonstration for the existence of God is one that proceeds by way of *a posteriori* reasoning, beginning with the actual existence of the things of our experience."

a. Statement of the question

In Chapter 2 it was shown how *a priori* or *a simultaneo* reasoning cannot validly be used to establish a scientific proof for the

⁵ See *C.G.*, Bk. II, Ch. 54, paragraph 4.
⁶ See St. Thomas, *Quaest. Disp. de Anima*, a. 14, ad 4m and 5m; *In Boeth. de Trinit.*, qu. 5, a. 4, ad 4m.

existence of God. Here in Chapter 3 we show how one must proceed if one would establish a valid proof for the existence of God. Only *a posteriori* reasoning is valid.

b. Explanation of terms

1) "... *a posteriori reasoning* ..." A valid argument for the existence of God must begin with the *existence* of things. The demonstration itself consists in showing, through an analysis of their nature and operations, that these things are so many *effects* which immediately and necessarily demand the existence of a supreme Being as the only proper cause of their existence. And because our knowledge of these things is *prior* to our knowledge of the existence of God, this knowledge of things can be a true means or *medium* for demonstrating the existence of God. Therefore, this demonstration is rightly called *a posteriori,* because our knowledge of God's existence is *posterior* to our knowledge of the existence of things. The demonstration proceeds from things in the world known *as effects,* to God as their necessary *cause.* Therefore, the first step in the demonstration consists in understanding things in the world precisely as effects, and the second step consists in understanding that only a necessary Being, one here and now existing through his essence, can be the proper cause of the existence of these effects.

In the following chapter, the different *a posteriori* arguments themselves will be studied in detail. Here we wish to give a general description of any *a posteriori* argument. When the things existing in the world are understood to be changeable, imperfect, limited, and contingent in their existence, at that moment they are precisely understood as effects. That is to say, they are understood as having received their existence from another. This other is their cause, and their proper cause. Through a power proportioned to its own nature, it necessarily and immediately produces existence as its proper effect.

2) "... *only a posteriori reasoning is valid* ..." (*a*) Because the conclusion is only virtually and not actually in the premises. For we do not begin with the things in the world *as effects,* but

only *as existing things.* They become known as effects through an analysis of their nature and operations. And once seen as effects, the intellect sees that they have a necessary relation to a cause.

(*b*) Because the knowledge of the conclusion follows the knowledge of the premises. Here the logical order, or order of demonstration, is just the reverse of the ontological order, or order of being. Ontologically, God is prior to creatures, since creatures receive their being from him. But in our demonstration, which takes place in the logical order, our knowledge of creatures is prior to our knowledge of God. Hence, our demonstration is valid, for God is *known* through creatures, and not through himself, although God *exists* through himself, and all creatures exist through God.

(*c*) Because we necessarily conclude to a necessary Being. Although we reason from contingent things (creatures), their very contingency necessarily relates them to a Being that is not contingent.

3) *The nature of this demonstration of God's existence.* The movement of our reason from the existence of the things in this world to the affirmation of the existence of God, is a complex one and demands at least some explanation.

First, the intellect grasps some self-evident fact, for example, "this thing is moving," or "this thing is more perfect than that." This self-evident fact constitutes the point of departure for further reasoning.

Secondly, the intellect understands something new about this thing it has grasped, for example, that "that which is moving is being moved by another," or that "the being which is more perfect than the other, is really 'approaching' a most perfect Being." This new knowledge constitutes a true *conclusion* for our intellect, and is grounded in evidence found in the "moving being itself," in the "more perfect being itself." This point will be made clearer when we study the different arguments.

Having made this second judgment (for example, whatever is moved is moved by another), the intellect now proceeds to a new conclusion (third step). This conclusion is made in the light of the principle of non-contradiction, as was also the second judgment. This new (third) conclusion is that one cannot proceed indefinitely (*ad infinitum*) in beings that are moved by another. For the intellect positively sees that such a procedure is self-contradicting. Because in such a procedure there is no *first* mover, and hence no intermediary movers (moved movers) that have received their motion. And in understanding that we cannot proceed "into infinity" in moved movers, the intellect sees that there must be a first unmoved mover. We see that God must exist.

This process of arriving at the existence of God can be called *intellective induction,* because the necessity of the truth so affirmed is really *seen* by the intellect. But also in the process *strict reasoning* is involved, since one or more middle terms are used in arriving at our conclusion. Finally, and obviously, this process is *inductive* throughout, for we do not proceed from a more universal truth to a less universal one (as is done in deduction), but rather from a particular existent to a necessary truth. [7]

Suggested Readings

1. Etiènne Gilson, *The Christian Philosophy of St. Thomas Aquinas* (New York, Random House, 1956), "Existence and Reality," pp. 29–45. These pages are practically indispensable for an understanding of St. Thomas's doctrine of being.
   Being and Some Philosophers (Toronto, Pontifical Institute of Mediaeval Studies, 1949), Chapter V, "Being and Existence," pp. 154–189.
2. Joseph Owens, "A Note on the Approach to Thomistic Metaphysics," *New Scholasticism,* 28 (1954), 454–476.
   "A Note on the Intelligibility of Being," *Gregorianum,* 36 (1955), 169–193.
3. Norris Clarke, "What Is the Really Real?" in *Progress in Philosophy* (Milwaukee, Bruce Publishing Company, 1955), pp. 61–90.

[7] Before proceeding to the actual proofs for the existence of God in Chapter 4, it is well to read the appendix on the agnostics (Appendix B).

CHAPTER 4

The Five Ways of St. Thomas

> *Who, therefore, is not enlightened by such
> splendors of created things, is blind; who is
> not awakened by such shouting, is deaf; who
> does not praise God in all these effects, is
> dumb; and who from such signs does not
> turn to the First Principle, is a fool.*
>
> —St. Bonaventure, *The Journey
> of the Mind to God,* Ch. One

A. THE FIRST WAY: PROOF FROM THE EXISTENCE OF MOTION

1. Statement of the Problem

In this first way we begin with an evident fact of both internal and external experience: the fact that there is motion in the world, that the things of our experience undergo change. For example, the youth becomes the man, the seed blossoms into flower and the flower into fruit; things change their size, their colors, their shape. Motion or change, the losing of one perfection and the gaining of another, is a simple, undeniable fact of human experience and knowledge. The problem of the First Way, therefore, can be stated as follows: Given this fact that here and now something is undergoing motion or change, can the human reason conclude to the existence of something that is here and now the first cause of this motion or change, but which itself undergoes no change whatsoever, a first unmoved mover that is God?

80

2. The Solution

The first step in our solution is to understand what we mean by motion. By motion or change we understand a transition from potency to act, the acquiring of any new perfection in any way. Hence we include the following kinds of motion or change. First of all, local motion. This is the most obvious of motions, but by no means the only kind. Secondly, we include here accidental changes in both qualities and quantity; for example, when an object becomes hotter or redder, or bigger or smaller. Thirdly, we include substantial change, the motion or mutation of one substance into another; for example, the changing of food into living human tissues. Fourthly, we include the immanent activities of cognition and appetition, like seeing, understanding, willing, and so forth. While the act of understanding or the act of willing are not in themselves motion, the intellect or the will cannot acquire these perfections without undergoing some change. In reaching their respective terms, the intellect in knowing truth and the will in desiring good go from potency to act. In this sense, these acts are real changes for man. But in themselves, as understanding and willing, they are the act of a being in act, and thus are not motion, which is the act of a being in potency insofar as it is in potency.

3. Whatever Is Changed Is Changed by Another

Granted the fact of change in the world, we are now ready to argue from this fact as follows: things change. But nothing changes itself. Therefore, whatever is changed must be changed by another. Let us see now why this is so.

Change or motion is a transition from potency to act. A piece of marble takes the shape of a statue beneath the strokes of the sculptor. My hand, which was cold, feels itself becoming warm beneath the rays of the sun. And so I say the sculptor produces the statue, the sun warms my hand. In the face of the myriad changes that take place around us, the intellect makes this affirmation concerning them: they are brought into being by an agent that is distinct from the change. Why? Because nothing is moved from potency to act except by a being already in act. And this is true because no being can give to another or to itself a perfection it does not possess.

Take a very simple example. I have a glass of cold water. It is actually cold, but potentially hot, since it can become hot. Now if the glass of water is heated, it must be heated by something besides itself, for it must be heated by something that actually possesses heat. To say that cold water can make itself hot is to deny the principle of contradiction. [1] For at one and the same time the water would have to be actually hot, since nothing gives what it does not have, and actually cold, since it is being moved from cold to hot. But to say that a glass of water is at one and the same time actually hot and actually cold is to say that it is cold and is not cold, that this perfection exists and does not exist at the same time. And this is an evident contradiction in being.

Therefore, we see that it is impossible for any being to move itself from potency to act. For this would mean that at one and the same time it has and has not the perfection involved. Thus anything that is moved from potency to act, as takes place in every change, must be moved or changed by another, by some being already in act.

We can formulate our direct experience of change into a proposition that has the force and validity of a universal principle: nothing is moved from potency to act except by a being already in act. To act means to be in act. To be acted upon (to be changed) means to be in potency. And since nothing can be in act and in potency at the same time, as regards the same perfection, it follows that nothing can move itself from potency to act. Nothing can be the cause of its own change. If it is changed, it is changed by another.

---

[1] Our example of hot and cold water is taken from St. Thomas who thought that cold, as well as heat, was a positive quality. We know that cold is only the absence of heat. Thus water can lose its heat (i.e., become cold) "of itself." But the point of the example is that water cannot heat itself.

4. In Things That Are Changed by Another an Infinite Regress Is Impossible

This brings us to our third step. In this step we argue as follows: If something is being moved here and now by something else, and this something else that moves is itself being moved by a third mover and the third by a fourth, and so on, either we must come to a first mover that is itself entirely unmoved, or the motion here and now existing is unintelligible. That is to say, there cannot be an infinite regress in an ordered series of moved movers. Why this is so is easy to understand. In such a series, each thing that is moved is moved by another. For example, the chisel is moved by the hand, the hand by the nerves, the nerves by the will, the will by the soul, the soul by that being from which it has received its nature, and which is keeping that nature in existence. Now in such an ordered series, if any one of the movers is removed, the motion of the chisel immediately stops. If the soul or the will or the nerves or the hand stop moving, the motion of the chisel ceases at once.

It is clear, then, that such a series cannot be infinite. For then, by supposition, there would be no first mover, and hence no motion here and now. An infinite series would render the existing motion unintelligible. All these infinite moved movers would have received their motion, but since there is no first mover, the *whole series* is one of received motion. And this is a contradiction. For such a motion would at one and the same time be received, since it has come from some other, and not received, since there is no first from which it originated. There would be no reason why any motion would be here and now existing. But since motion or change does so exist, we must conclude that there is a first unmoved mover, a mover that gives motion, but in no way receives it, a Being, therefore, that is in no way in potency to change, but is simply in act. Here is how St. Thomas puts the matter:

In movers and moved things that are ordered, where one, namely, is moved in order by another, it is necessary that if the first mover is removed or ceases from moving, none of the others will either move or be moved. And this is so because the first is the cause of the moving for all the others. But if there are ordered movers and moved things into infinity, there will not be any first mover, but all will be as intermediate movers. And so none of them will be able to be moved. And thus nothing will be moved in the world.[2]

And so we can conclude that in an ordered series of moved movers, that is to say, in a series where each mover receives its power to move from another, either the series must be finite, or if it is infinite, there must be some mover outside this series, upon which mover the movement of the whole series depends. An infinite series of movers, all of which have received their motion, is unintelligible without a first from whom they have received it.

5. This First Unmoved Mover Is Pure Act or God

Once the mind has seen the necessity of positing a first unmoved mover, it has already concluded to the existence of God. For such a mover must needs be a pure act of subsistent Being, a Being in which there is no potency whatsoever. For we have seen that in the order of being, something moves or acts insofar as it is in act, and something is moved or acted upon insofar as it is in potency. Now insofar as the first mover moves another, it is in act. But if this Being were any way in potency, to that extent it would not be in act, but able to receive act. Thus it would be movable, able to receive motion or perfection, and to that extent it would not be first, but would be ordered to something higher or more perfect than itself. Thus the first unmoved mover is in no way movable, exists in no way in potency, but is the pure actuality of subsistent Being. And this is God. In our proof we have considered motion as any change in being. In this unmoved mover there is, therefore, no potency for any change in being. Thus the Being of this first mover has not been received. It is by its very nature. Its nature is Being.

6. Answering the Objections

This "first way" of St. Thomas has been strongly objected to by philosophers of all kinds. It is to the answering of these objections

[2] *C.G.*, Bk. 1, Ch. 13.

that we must now turn our attention. First of all, living things move themselves, and so are the cause of their own motion. Thus a living thing would be itself a first unmoved mover. But since such things are obviously not God, the first way is clearly inconclusive. Again, according to modern physics, a moving body tends to remain in motion unless impeded by some other body. Thus such a body needs no cause of its motion, but rather of its cessation of motion. Finally, reciprocal causality would seem sufficient to explain the changes we experience. For example, I desire to paint a picture. The good of the object desired, that is, the picture to be painted, is enough to move my will. And my will, so moved, can move my hands to actually paint the picture. In none of these cases does it seem either necessary or possible to conclude to the existence of a first unmoved mover because of the existence of motion or change in the world.

To the objection that a living thing moves itself, we answer that it does so only because it is moved by another. A little reflection will make this clear. I get up and walk across the room. I am moving myself. Before "I exerted myself," I was not moving, I did not actually have the perfection I have now. Thus, even a living being cannot be in act and potency at the same time regarding the same perfection. A living being like man is a composite being, consisting of many principles or "parts" of being, so that one part can move another part, but no part can move itself, no part can give to itself a perfection it does not have.

And so I conclude that before I walked across the room, as a living being I had the active power or potency to walk across, not merely the passive potency to be moved across the room, like a stone. One part of me moved another. My will moved the nerves in my legs and they moved my legs, and my legs moved the rest of my body. But what moved my will? In the order of final causality, it was my desire to open the window and let in some fresh air. But in this first way we are interested in the adequate efficient causality of a given motion. And so I must repeat my question: Whence comes the efficacy of the will to move my locomotive faculties? From itself, in the sense that being a free will, it has power to "move itself"; but also from another, in the sense that this power to move itself it has received from another. And independently of this other it cannot move either itself or anything else. The will, being an accident, is immediately and directly dependent upon the substantial being of the soul, because of which being the will itself is and acts, and without which the will could neither inexist nor act.

But the soul of man itself has "come into being," it has received its existence from another. And just as the soul has received a share in being, it has also received a share in the activity that follows upon being. [3] Hence the soul has not of itself either the source of its being or of its activity; it has received its power to be and its power to act from another. So we conclude that, just as the soul itself must be here and now existing and "holding in being" its powers of will and intellect, so, too, there must be here and now existing in the soul and "holding it in being," the first unmoved mover, "moving" the soul to its being and to its being-a-mover. [4]

St. Thomas answers this objection about living beings moving themselves as follows:

When it is said that something moves itself, the same being is considered as both moving and moved. When, however, it is said that something is moved by another, one thing is considered as mover and another thing as being moved. Now it is clear that when something moves another, the fact that it is moving another does not mean that it is the first mover. Whence to say that something moves another does not exclude the fact that it itself may be moved by another and have from this other the fact that it is a mover. So, in like manner, when something moves itself, this does not exclude the fact that it may be moved by another and have from this other the power to move itself.[5]

[3] See St. Thomas, *S.T.*, I, 115, 1. "For according as something is participated, it is also necessary that that, too, is participated which is proper to this thing; for example, just as that which participates in light, also participates in the perfection of being visible. Now to act, which is nothing else than to put something in act, is *per se* proper to act as act."
[4] See St. Thomas, *In I Sent.*, d. 36, q. 1, a. 1; *C.G.*, Bk. III, Ch. 66 and 67; *De Pot.*, qu. 3, a. 7.
[5] *De Malo*, qu. 3, a. 2, ad 4m.

Our second objection concerned the principle of inertia and the First Newtonian Law of Motion: "Every body continues in a state of rest, or of uniform motion in a straight line, unless it is compelled to change that state by forces impressed upon it." And the objection was as follows: Since a body in motion, if unimpeded, remains indefinitely in motion, the philosophical principle that governs the first way, "Whatever is moved is moved by another," is false.

Our answer is that this law of inertia, even granted its complete validity as a principle of physics, in no way contravenes the metaphysical principle that whatever is moved from potency to act is moved by a being already in act. For physics is here treating motion and rest as two states. The body is considered as already in motion, or already at rest, and not as a body that begins to move or comes to a rest. Whereas the philosopher wants to know, why did this body begin to move? Whence came its power to move in the first place? And even while the body is in a state of motion, if that motion is accelerated, the law of inertia itself demands that this acceleration come from some extrinsic force. Thus our principle, "Whatever is moved is moved by another," remains a true assertion and is even, at the level of the phenomenon of local motion, verified in a certain sense by the law of inertia. [6]

Our third objection stated that the fact of reciprocal causality is sufficient to explain adequately the existence of any given motion. One object is the final cause of the motion, and then the mover, thus "finalized," exercises its efficient causality. Our answer to this is that in any transition from potency to act, final causes

[6] Notice, too, that the atomic theory which states that within the atom the particles called electrons are continually revolving around the nucleus, no matter how this theory is understood to express the mass-energy aspects of material reality, it in no way contradicts the philosophical truth that whatever is moved must be moved by another. Again, the scientist finds matter in motion; but it hardly follows from this that therefore matter puts itself in motion. No more than to find something existing means that this thing has caused its own existence. Matter needs to be conserved in motion just as much as it needs to be conserved in being. If matter is in motion it is because it has been created in motion and the first unmoved mover is here and now the ultimate cause of that motion. See Jacques Maritain, *Approaches to God* (New York, Harper & Brothers, 1954), pp. 26–29.

are indeed involved, and even material and formal causes. Moreover, as we shall see in the second way, there cannot be an infinite regress in these kinds of causality either. But the only cause of motion we are directly concerned with in the first way is the efficient cause. Even as inclined to act, even when I desire, for example, to kick a stone, I must exercise my power of moving. Whence comes this power? From myself or from another? That is the question. Our philosophical problem of moved movers here is explicitly one of a series of efficient causes alone. Final causes might indeed explain why the agent acts in this way rather than that, or even why the agent acts at all, rather than not acts. But a final cause cannot explain the efficiency itself of the agent.

7. Summary of the First Way

"From the existence of motion in the world, the existence of God can be demonstrated under the aspect of a first unmoved mover."

a. Prenote

This first way of St. Thomas proceeds from the following fact of both internal and external experience: that things are changing and moving in the world about us. For example, I see bodies moving from one place to another, I see living things growing, changing their color, their shapes, and so on. Now the intellect, understanding that things are being changed or moved, looks for the source of this motion. This source cannot be the being itself that is being moved. For then this being would be the mover and the thing moved at the same time and as regarding the same perfection. Thus this being that is moved must be moved by another. But what about this other? Is it the source of its own motion, or is it being moved by another in order to move something else? Reflecting on such a series of moved movers, the intellect sees that there must be a first unmoved mover, or else the efficiency of the moved movers and, therefore, the actuality of the motion itself, is unintelligible. In this way the intellect sees the necessity

of positing a first unmoved mover to explain the actuality of any
given motion it experiences. And this first unmoved mover is God.

b. Explanation of terms

1) *"From the existence of motion . . ."* Thus, in this first way,
we proceed from the existence, not the nature, of motion. We consider motion as a passage from one state of being to another, and
we consider that passage insofar as it shares in some way in the
actuality of existence. That is to say, we consider a being changing
(in some way) in its existence, and insofar as it is so changing.

2) *". . . motion . . ."* Any passage from being in potency to
being in act. Thus, motion here includes: (*a*) all accidental
changes: a change in a being according to place, or quantity, or
quality, and so forth; (*b*) all substantial changes, as when, for
example, non-living being becomes living being, and vice versa;
(*c*) the acquirement of any new perfection, like willing or understanding, even though these are not the act of a being in potency,
but the act of a being in act.

3) *". . . the existence of God is demonstrated . . ."* Insofar as
the very actuality of this change could not exist, unless there also
existed some first unmoved mover as the only adequate existential
source of the change, and from whom all moved movers receive
the power of moving others.

4) *". . . under the aspect of a first unmoved mover . . ."* In this
first way the existence of God is affirmed as a necessary term for
the understanding of the existence of motion in the world. Hence
God in this way is seen precisely as the first cause of change, as
a Being that can move others, but is himself incapable of undergoing any change.

c. Opinions denying our position

1) *The Eleatics*—for example, Parmenides and Zeno. This
school of philosophy denied the very reality of change, calling it an
illusion. The real was immobile, unchanging being. That change is
an illusion is easy to prove. For a being to change means that it
becomes other than it is. A man is ignorant; then he becomes a

philosopher. He is now other than he was before the change. But where does the change come from? Either the change was already there or it was not. If it was already there, there has been no change. If it was not there, then change has come from non-being. But from non-being, nothing comes. Hence the obvious conclusion: all change is impossible. Change is simply an illusion of the senses. The only thing that exists is being, unchanging and immobile.

The answer to the Eleatics and their dilemma was first given by Aristotle. What becomes does not become from non-being nor from being in act, but from being in potency. When water becomes hot, the change is not from hot water (for then there would be no change), nor from the water as cold, but from the water as capable of becoming hot—given, of course, the actual heat of an extrinsic agent.

2) *The Ionians*—for example, Heraclitus; also Bergson and others. This school goes to the opposite extreme and says that the only reality is motion or becoming itself. It is being that is the illusion. Reality is a mighty river of flux, and just as a man cannot step twice into the same river (for the waters have already passed downstream), so the mind cannot enter into the flux of becoming. For by the time it has grasped a thing in order to judge it, that thing has already changed. Being is the stabilizing and solidifying (and thus falsifying) work of the intellect. So there can be no first unmoved mover, since immobile being is an impossibility.

This position goes against our experience of motion. For man, with his senses and intellect, never grasps motion as such, but always something that moves. We do not experience change, we experience something changing. Motion is always the motion of something. A ball is moved; water is heated. Motion without a subject that is moved is as unintelligible as thought without someone who thinks, or existence without something that exists.

d. Proof

It is certain and evident to our senses, that in the world some things are in motion. Now whatever is moved is moved by another, for nothing can be moved except it is in potentiality to that towards which it is moved; whereas a thing moves inasmuch as it is in act. For motion is nothing else than the reduction of something from potentiality to actuality. But nothing can be reduced from potentiality to actuality, except by something in the state of actuality. Thus that which is actually hot, as fire, makes wood, which is potentially hot, to be actually hot, and thereby moves and changes it. Now it is not possible that the same thing should be at once in actuality and potentiality in the same respect, but only in different respects. For what is actually hot cannot simultaneously be potentially hot; but it is simultaneously potentially cold. It is therefore impossible that in the same respect and in the same way a thing should be both moved and mover, i.e., that it should move itself. Therefore, whatever is moved must be moved by another, and that by another again. But this cannot go on into infinity, because then there would be no first mover, and, consequently, no other mover, seeing that subsequent movers move only inasmuch as they are moved by the first mover, as the staff moves only because it is moved by the hand. Therefore it is necessary to arrive at a first mover, moved by no other; and this everyone understands to be God.[7]

B. THE SECOND WAY: PROOF FROM THE EXISTENCE OF EFFICIENT CAUSES

1. Statement of the Problem

The problem of the second way can be stated as follows. Granted that it is evident through internal and external experience that there does exist in the activity of beings ordered efficient causes, can the mind conclude from this fact to a first uncaused cause, which as first and as uncaused would be God?

2. The Solution

a. Step one: Efficient causes essentially and accidentally ordered

Having already established in Chapter 3 the nature and the origin of the principle of causality, the first step in our solution consists in knowing precisely what is meant by a series of *per se* sub-

---

[7] St. Thomas, S.T., I, 2, 3. Translated by A. Pegis, *The Basic Writings of St. Thomas* (New York, Random House, 1945), p. 22.

ordinated efficient causes, and how such a series differs from that of a *per accidens* ordered series. [8]

Causes can be ordered in two ways. One way is *per se*, or essentially, and the other *per accidens*, or accidentally. Causes are ordered *per se* whenever the virtue of the first cause influences the ultimate effect produced through the intermediary causes; when the causal influx of the first cause reaches to the ultimate effect through the other causes. For example, the art of a craftsman moves his hands, and his hands move the hammer, and the hammer moves the chisel, and the chisel moves (that is to say, forms) the statue, which is the ultimate effect. In this series of causes, the causal influx of the art-skill reaches the ultimate effect (the statue) through the other causes (the hands, the hammer, the chisel, and so forth). Here is the explanation of St. Thomas:

. . . two things may be considered in every agent, namely, the thing itself that acts, and the power whereby it acts. Thus fire by its heat makes a thing hot. Now the power of the lower agent depends upon the power of the higher agent, in so far as the higher agent gives the lower agent the power whereby it acts, or preserves that power, or applies it to action. Thus the craftsman applies the instrument to its proper effect, although sometimes he does not give the instrument the form whereby it acts, nor preserves that form, but merely puts it into motion. Consequently, the action of the lower agent must not only proceed from the lower agent through the agent's own power, but also through the power of all the higher agents, for it acts by the power of them all. Now just as the lowest agent is found to be immediately active, so the power of the first agent is found to be immediate in the production of the effect; because the power of the lowest agent does not of itself produce this effect, but by the power of the proximate higher agent, and this by the power of a yet higher agent, so that the power of the supreme agent is found to produce its effect of itself, as though it were the immediate cause.[9]

On the other hand, in a series of *per accidens* ordered causes, the causal influx reaches down not to the ultimate effect, but only to the proximate effect. The fact that this proximate effect

---

[8] Here we shall follow the doctrine of St. Thomas as set forth in his commentary on the *Liber de Causis*, lecture one.

[9] *C.G.*, Bk. III, Ch. 70.

itself causes some other effect is not due to the causal influx of the first cause in this series. As Thomas says, it is *praeter intentionem*, [10] outside the influence of the first efficient cause. Let us take a simple example of *per accidens* ordered causes to bring out this point. Suppose I light a candle with a match. The fact that this candle is then used to light another candle, and this second candle a third candle, and so on, is obviously outside the influx of the first efficient cause, that is, the match that lit the first candle. In this series of one candle lighting another, the influence of the first cause extends only to the proximate effect (the first candle as lit) but not to the ultimate effect (the last candle as lit). Since this last effect is outside the influence of the first cause, this series of causes is ordered only accidentally, for what is beyond the virtue of a cause is *per accidens*.

b. Step two: General characteristics of a per se ordered series of efficient causes

The essential note of a series of *per se* ordered efficient causes is that the influx of the first cause extends to the production of the ultimate effect, through the instrumentality of intermediate causes. Let us now reflect upon some of the other features of such a series of causes.

First of all, whenever a new effect is produced in the material universe, all four causes, material, formal, efficient, and final, are simultaneously and actually exercising their proper causality. For example, an agent of itself may be indifferently disposed to any number of particular effects. If it is to act, it must act in a particular way, which means that the action is directed toward a particular end or effect. Just as a final cause is not actually causing unless it is actually influencing the agent to a particular end, so the agent is not exercising its causality unless it is actually influenced by the final cause. There is no efficiency without finality, and there is no finality without efficiency. The final cause is not

[10] *"Intentio"* here is not the English "intention," but rather "influx" or "influence."

a cause in act unless it is actually being desired by the agent. Hence there is an essential ordering between these two causes, final and efficient, so that if the causality of the one ceases, the causality of the other also and simultaneously ceases.

What is true of final and efficient causes, holds also for formal and material causes. Every new production of being involves an eduction of some form, accidental or substantial. If any perfection is to be, it must be the perfection of something. Hence the activity of the agent consists directly in educing a form from matter. Obviously, the causality of form cannot be present without the simultaneous causality of matter; forms are educed from matter. [11] That both matter and form are simultaneously required for the existence of any finite material thing is evident from the fact that they constitute the very intrinsic composition of the effect itself. Hence, in any given production of an effect, in any new coming into being, these four causes are simultaneously, actually, and in a *per se* order, exercising their proper causality.

Another thing to notice in any essentially (*per se*) ordered causes is this: not only is the causality of the four causes properly and simultaneously exercised in the production of the effect, but it is also exercised in the conservation of the effect—in keeping the effect in existence. A being cannot remain in existence unless its matter and form be continually actualized, unless the *esse* of the form and of the matter perdures. But this *esse* itself was produced, either substantially or accidentally, through the eduction of a form from matter, and this eduction was achieved through the efficiency of the agent. The *esse* or existence of the effect is a produced or caused *esse*. As such it continually needs the presence and influx of its proper cause.

Let us take a simple example to bring out this important fact. A sculptor like Michelangelo, through his art, his hands, his hammer and chisel—a whole series of *per se* ordered efficient causes—brings into being the form of a statue, for example, the statue of Moses. But Michelangelo has been dead for four hun-

[11] Or, as is the case with the human soul, created in matter.

dred years and the statue continues in existence. Why? The existence of the accidental form of the statue (the figure of Moses) perdures because of the continued existence of the marble. And the existence of the marble perdures because of the continued existence of the ultimate constituents of marble, whatever they may be.

But what about these constituents themselves? They are not their own existence as we shall see in the third way. Their existence is limited by their form and their matter; hence it is a received and thus caused existence. Therefore, there must be continually present the proper efficient cause of their existence. Not just the material cause of their existence, which is prime matter; nor the limiting cause of their existence, which is their substantial form; but also the efficient cause of their existence, the continual influx of an activity that keeps outside nothingness the received "to be" that actuates the substantial principles of the being. There may indeed be instrumental conservative causes, even instrumental conservative efficient causes, of the existence of an effect, but these are all *per se* ordered to the all-pervading activity of the one unique proper cause of existence, namely, the activity of a Being who is its own existence and is the first efficient cause of all beings and the activity of beings.

c. Step three: Special characteristics of a series of per se ordered efficient causes

There are four special characteristics of such a series:

1) *From the very nature of the series,* all the efficient causes are required here and now, and in act, for the production of the effect. If any one of the causes is removed, the activity of the whole series immediately ceases. This follows from the fact that the causal influx of the first uncaused cause reaches down to the ultimate effect through all the intermediary causes, and not just through some of them. There is an essentially subordinated co-operation in the production of the effect; even the intermediary causes are subordinated one to another.

2) *The second special characteristic* flows from the first; namely, while all the causes involved are efficient causes, each one is of a different nature or species; for example, in writing, the chalk is a different nature from the hand. If these causes were of the same nature, one could do what the other does, and so we would not have to have many causes to produce the same effect. If the hand could do precisely what the chalk does, we would not have to use the chalk.

3) *The third characteristic is this:* Not only must all these causes be in act, but they must be in simultaneous act. There is no succession in time but only a subordination in causality. Here and now, at the instant the effect is being produced or maintained in existence, we have the first uncaused cause actually producing the effect through the instrumentality of all the intermediary causes. And these intermediary causes act as one single cause, since they all share in one single operation.

4) *This brings us to our fourth special trait:* In the activity of *per se* ordered efficient causes, there is question of only one single operation, one single causal influx in which all the efficient causes share according to their nature, forming therefore one causal principle from which this activity proceeds and which terminates in the same ultimate effect. There is, for example, only one operation by which God moves the will, the will moves the hand, the hand moves the chalk, and the chalk produces the lines on the blackboard. If there were many operations there would be many terms, and the effect would not be one but many. Of course, in the operation by which God operates, moving a nature, nature does not share; for the operation by which God operates is the divine substance. But the very operation of the nature is also the operation of the power of the first cause. Here is the way St. Thomas puts it:

. . . in the operation by which God operates, moving a nature, the nature itself does not operate; but the operation itself of the nature is also the operation of the divine power, just as the operation of an instrument is through the power of the principal agent. Nor is there any difficulty in God and nature producing the same effect, and this because of the order that exists between God and nature. [12]

To repeat: There is one single cause influx shared in or received by many agents, whether these agents are complete beings, or simply different potencies or powers of the same being. This influence is received from the higher cause by the lower and according to the nature of the lower. Two important facts follow from this: first, that the lower cause, for example, the piece of chalk, acts through the power of the higher cause, since it has received the action of the higher or principal cause; and secondly, the lower or instrumental cause gives something proper of its own in the production of the ultimate effect, since it receives the influence of the higher cause according to its (the instrument's) own nature, thus limiting and determining this influence according to its own nature. The writing of a piece of chalk is different, for example, from the writing of a pen. Here are two texts from St. Thomas explaining these points:

It is possible, however, for something to participate in the proper action of another, not by its own power, but instrumentally, inasmuch as it acts by the power of another; as air can heat and ignite by the power of fire. . . . (And) the secondary instrumental cause does not share in the action of the superior cause, except inasmuch as by something proper to itself it acts dispositively in relation to the effect of the principal agent. If therefore it produced nothing by means of what is

[12] *De Pot.*, qu. 3, a. 7, ad 3m. Later on, in our treatment of creation, we will discuss in detail the mysterious nature of divine causality. But here we can mention, briefly, three things: 1) the divine operation as formally immanent; 2) that same operation as virtually transient; and 3) the effect of this virtual transient operation of God. As formally immanent, the divine operation is identified with the divine substance. Hence, it is eternal, immutable, transcendent. As virtually transient, this same operation is *intentional*. It is a power or influx productive of effects. Under this aspect, the power of God looks outward, and is considered as a certain intention that produces an effect. Finally, the effect produced is the created being itself, or its operation, or the effect of its operation. St. Thomas (*De Pot.*, qu. 3, a. 7 ad 7m) gives an example to illustrate this divine causality. The colors that I see on the wall are also in the air, else I could not see them. I say the colors have formal existence in the wall and intentional existence in the air. So, in an analogous fashion, the divine power is formally in God (and is God), but intentionally (as an influx) in the creature. We should remember that this is only an example, and all examples are necessarily defective when applied to God.

proper to itself, it would be set to work in vain; nor would there be any need for us to use special instruments for special actions. Thus we see that a saw, in cutting wood, which it does by the property of its own form, produces the form of a bench, which is the proper effect of the principal agent.[13]

Every instrumental agent executes the action of the principal agent by some action proper and connatural to itself; just as the natural heat of the body generates flesh by dissolving and digesting, and a saw produces the perfection of the bench by cutting.[14]

d. Step four: Why there cannot be an infinite regress in per se ordered efficient causes

From the very nature of *per se* ordered efficient causes, it is easy to see why there cannot be an infinite regress in such a series. For an infinite regress means, by supposition, not to have a first cause. But if there is no first efficient cause, then neither can there be any ultimate effect. And the reason why there can be no ultimate effect is that there would be no causal influx which produced the effect. Why this is so becomes clear when we recall two facts about such a series. First, all the causes of the series are in act, in simultaneous act, and here and now actually producing the effect, either bringing it into being or keeping it in being. Secondly, each cause is essentially ordered to the cause above it, because it is here and now receiving from the cause above it the power by which it operates as cause. Now if we were to proceed infinitely in causes that receive their causality from another, we would always be dealing with causes that are intermediate, causes that are moved to their causality. Hence to say there is no first cause is to affirm and deny being at the same time. For on the one hand we affirm that all these intermediate causes have received an influence from another, and on the other hand we say they have not received it, since we deny there is a first from which they have received it. Since, *de facto,* the ultimate effect does exist, then *de iure,* there must exist a first cause which does not receive influence from another but is the cause of the influence received in

13 *S.T.,* I, 45, 5.
14 *C.G.,* Bk. II, Ch. 21, par. 7.

those intermediary causes. Hence the necessity of positing a first uncaused cause. [15]

3. Answering the Objections

First objection. It seems impossible to conclude to the existence of God as the first uncaused cause. This conclusion is based upon the principle of causality, and the principle of causality flows from a particular contingent sensible fact—for example, the sun is heating my hand. Now it is quite impossible, as well as quite illogical, to use a principle based upon a particular, contingent, sensible fact, to conclude to a universal, necessary suprasensible term. Contingency cannot give rise to necessity. A principle that flows from sensible phenomena is valid only when applied to sensible phenomena. Hence this second way of St. Thomas is quite impossible as well as completely illogical.

We answer: The principle of causality does not have its origin in sensible beings insofar as they are sensible, but insofar as they are or exist. Thus this principle is founded in being as such and its application is valid beyond mere sensible being. Moreover, although this principle originates from contingent beings, there is in these beings some necessity; namely, these contingent beings have a *necessary relation* to a cause. Therefore, by applying this principle of causality, we are able to posit God as a first cause.

Second objection. If the world is eternal, there is no reason why a series of efficient causes could not be infinite. But philosophy cannot prove with certitude that the world is not eternal. Therefore, neither can it prove with certitude that there exists a first efficient cause.

We answer that even if the world were eternal, an infinite series of essentially ordered efficient causes would still be a contradiction. Because in causes so ordered, the power of the first cause ex-

[15] The following texts from St. Thomas clearly demonstrate the point we are trying to make:
  (1) *In II Metaph.*, lect. 3, nos. 302, 303, 304.
  (2) *C.G.*, I, Ch. 13, second paragraph from end.
  (3) *S.T.*, I, 46, 2, ad 7m.

tends itself to the ultimate effect. And therefore without this power neither the ultimate effect can be produced, nor are the intermediary causes able to act. The question of the eternity or non-eternity of the world does not touch our argument, since it is not founded in any position concerning the duration of the world, but rather in the very nature of *per se* ordered efficient causes. However, as is clear, if the world were eternal, an infinite series of accidentally ordered causes (*ex parte ante*) would not be contradictory.

Third objection. Even in *per se* ordered causes, although a first cause might be required, it does not follow that this cause must be itself uncaused. For example, cause A could produce the power of causing in cause B, and cause B could produce the power of causing in cause C, and cause C could produce the power of causing in cause A. In this way, the first cause, cause A, would not be itself uncaused, and our proof would not conclude to the existence of God.

We answer that the mutual causality which this objection presupposes is not possible except among different kinds of causes; for example, between material and formal causes, or between efficient and final causes. But in our proof there is question of explaining the actuality of only one kind of series, namely of efficient causes. And, as is obvious, the same efficient cause could not at the same time both give and receive the power of causing.

Fourth objection. Finally, as Descartes has pointed out, all that this argument can conclude to is the imperfection of my intellect. I am not able to comprehend how an infinity of such causes could so proceed one from another from eternity without one of them being first:

I have not taken my argument (for the existence of God) from the fact that I see in sensible things a certain order or succession of efficient causes . . . because from such a succession of causes I do not see how I can conclude to any thing else except the imperfection of my intellect to understand; to understand, that is, how such a series of infinite causes could succeed one another from eternity without there being a first.[16]

16 *Primae Responsiones,* t. VII, pp. 106–107. Author's translation.

And a little later on Descartes gives an example of what he understands by such a series of ordered causes: "When I understand that
I was generated by my father, I also understand that my father was
generated by my grandfather; and since I cannot go on *ad infinitum* asking about the parents of parents, I simply and arbitrarily
make an end of the inquiry by saying that there was a first." In
other words, Descartes argues this way: from the fact that I cannot comprehend an infinite series of causes, it does not necessarily
follow that therefore there must be a first cause. And then he gives
us this example to prove his point: from the fact that I cannot comprehend the infinite divisions in a finite quantity, it does not follow
that there is an ultimate division beyond which I cannot divide.

We answer this objection of Descartes as follows: The reason
our intellect cannot go into infinity in such a series of *per se* ordered causes is that this series in its existence is finite. And our intellect positively sees that it must be finite, and thus it also sees,
from the very nature of the series, the necessity of positing a first
cause; for our intellect positively sees that an actual infinite series
of essentially ordered efficient causes would be a contradiction. [17]

Furthermore, the example that Descartes uses of an ordered
series of efficient causes shows that he essentially misunderstands
the second way of St. Thomas, which argues from a series of *per
se* ordered causes. Descartes gives an example of only accidentally
(*per accidens*) ordered causes, not essentially (*per se*) ordered
causes. As we have already noted, there is no repugnance in an
infinite regress of accidentally ordered causes, for they are not all
essentially ordered (are not here and now needed) for the ultimate effect. A man generates a son precisely as father, and not as
son of his own father, let alone as grandson of his grandfather.

Finally, when Descartes talks about the infinite divisibility of
quantity, he again misses the point. The divisibility of quantity is
potentially infinite; whereas in the second way, we argue from the
impossibility of an actually infinite series of *per se* ordered efficient causes.

[17] See St. Thomas, *S.T.*, I, 105, 5; *C.G.*, III, Ch. 67; *De Pot.*, qu. 3. a. 7.

4. Summary of the Second Way

"From the existence of subordinated causes, the existence of God can be demonstrated under the aspect of a first efficient cause."

a. Prenote

This second way of St. Thomas's proceeds from an evident fact of both internal and external experience; namely, the causality of things which we know through experience. I perceive, for example, that I am moving my hand, which moves the stick, which moves the stone. Now my intellect understands that such a series of efficient causes are so ordered among themselves that one cause essentially, that is, as a cause, depends upon the other, receiving from it the very power to cause. Thus the intellect understands the necessity of positing an efficient cause that is first and uncaused, in order to explain the very existence and actuality of the series. And this first cause, uncaused in its causality, is God.

b. Explanation of terms

1) *"From the existence . . ."* It is a question of causes actually in operation, whether as regards the coming into being of their effects or their conservation in being.

2) *". . . of subordinated causes . . ."* That is, this series of causes which are here and now, simultaneously and actually, required to produce one and the same effect, are so ordered that the causal influx of the first cause touches the ultimate effect. And therefore all the causes between the first cause and this ultimate effect have the character of an intermediary or *medium*. And since all these intermediate causes act in virtue of the first cause, participating as they do in one and the same power of causation, they can all be considered as only one intermediary cause. [18] Each, however, participates in this power according to its own proper nature and disposition.

3) *". . . the existence of God can be demonstrated . . ."*—in-

---

[18] See St. Thomas, *In Librum de Causis,* lect. 1; *C.G.,* Bk. III, Ch. 70.

asmuch as the very actuality of this series is impossible unless
there exists the virtue of the first cause, by whose power the intermediate causes operate. The mind sees that the existence of God
is the only explanation of this actuality which is received in these
inferior causes.

4) "... *under the aspect of a first efficient cause* . . ." God's
existence can be understood as a term, which term can take on
different aspects; for example, a first mover, causing movement
to other things. In this second way, this term, which is God, is
understood precisely as a first efficient cause, influencing the efficient causality in the causes ordered below it.

c. Opinions denying our position

1) *Kant and the Kantians.* All of these reject the proof of the
second way of St. Thomas because of their doctrine on being and
our knowledge of being. For the Kantians teach that the principle of causality upon which our proof depends is valid only for
the phenomena or manifestations of sensible things. Such a principle has no validity when applied to God. This position has been
criticized in our answer to the objections.

2) *Descartes and the Cartesians.* Descartes held that our argument concludes only to the imperfection of the human intellect
and does not positively nor necessarily conclude to the existence
of God. We have also answered this difficulty in answering the
objections.

d. The proof

Essentially ordered causes are found in reality. But it is impossible to proceed into infinity in essentially ordered causes without
destroying the actual effect. Therefore, there must be a first or
uncaused efficient cause, which is God.

Our first statement is simply a fact of experience, both internal
and external. Our second statement is demonstrated as follows:
First, it is impossible for a thing to be its own efficient cause, for
then it would have to exist before it existed, which is impossible.
Secondly, it is impossible to proceed into infinity in caused causes,

for in all essentially ordered efficient causes, the first cause is the cause of the intermediary, and the intermediary is the cause of the ultimate effect; and this is true whether the intermediary is one cause or many. But if the cause is removed, the effect is also removed. Therefore, if there were no "first" in efficient causes, there would be no first efficient cause, and thus there would be no ultimate effect, nor any intermediate efficient causes. Hence it is necessary to posit some first efficient cause, whom all call God. [19]

This same argument can be put a little differently as follows: If we proceed into infinity in *per se* ordered efficient causes, there would be no first efficient cause. And if there is no first, then all these ordered causes would have the characteristic of intermediate. But this is impossible; for at one and the same time they would be intermediate inasmuch as they have received their power to cause, and they would not be intermediate inasmuch as they have not received this power to cause from another. They would be and would not be causes, which is a contradiction. For since all intermediate causes participate in the same power of causing which they do not hold from themselves, they act as one single intermediate cause; thus they must receive this power from another that is not an intermediate cause, but the first cause. It is therefore clear that we must posit a first efficient cause. [20]

C. THE THIRD WAY: PROOF FROM THE EXISTENCE OF CORRUPTIBLE BEINGS

1. Prenote

Having seen how the existence of essentially ordered efficient causes leads the mind to the existence of a first uncaused efficient cause, we now wish to embark upon the third way that leads to God's existence. Besides our experience of the activity of existing things, there is another experience that calls for careful analysis and reflection: beings around us corrupt, "go out of" existence,

---

[19] See St. Thomas, *S.T.*, I, 2, 3.
[20] See St. Thomas, *C.G.*, Bk. I, Ch. 13, near end; *S.T.*, I, 46, 2, ad 7m; *In II Metaphy.*, lect. 3.

cease to be. Is it possible to show from the fact that things corrupt that there must exist an absolutely necessary Being?

2. Solution

1) *The fact of experience.* The fact from which our proof proceeds is that there are things around us that actually do corrupt; men, animals, plants die, and since they die or do corrupt, they are corruptible.

2) *This leads us to analyze the nature of corruptible beings.* Here the natural theologian takes the data of the philosopher of nature who proves that a being corrupts because it has within its essence the reason for its corruptibility, namely, primary matter. Thus when we speak of corruptible beings, we refer to those beings whose very essence is composed of matter and form, with matter being the source of the possibility of corruption. Notice, matter is the source of this corruptibility, it is not its cause. For, obviously, corruption as such has no cause. To corrupt means to go out of existence; corruption is non-being, and you do not need a cause to produce non-being. A new substantial form is educed from the primary matter, which eduction involves the simultaneous corruption of the old substantial form. But matter is the source of the corruption in this sense, that since it remains in potency to all substantial forms even while possessing one in act, new substantial forms can be educed from it, and this entails the corruption of the old form.

3) *The nature of incorruptible being.* This brings us to the consideration of the nature of beings that are incorruptible, that cannot cease to be by way of the corruption of their natures. That being is incorruptible which does not have within its essence the power to corrupt, whose essence has no potency for non-being. [21]

---

21 Strictly speaking, it is false to talk of a "potency for non-being," in the sense of a passive principle within the essence. For potency is always ordered to act, and there is no act of "non-being." Primary matter is a potency for form. Hence, when it is said that a composed essence has a potency for non-being, what is meant is that, since primary matter is a potency for all forms, a corruptible being can lose the form it actually has, thus corrupting, or ceasing to exist.

This would be true, for example, of any essence not composed of matter, as in the case of immaterial substances, like the angels. Form, or formal act, says of itself, only a possibility for being, a capacity for existence; it does not say, of itself, a possibility for non-being. Hence where we find in existence simple forms, we have a necessary being, possessing no possibility for non-being, and thus naturally incorruptible, immortal, sempiternal. Another case in point would be the rational soul. Once in existence, the rational soul is naturally immortal; when man corrupts the soul remains in existence, since existence or *esse* comes to the soul and is shared in by the body through the soul.

Finally, every form as such is incorruptible, because as form, it says only act in the order of essence, and potency for existence in the order of being. But in the case of non-spiritual forms, existence comes to the composite. Thus when such a composite corrupts, the form corrupts with it. Whereas a spiritual form, like the rational soul, can corrupt neither of itself nor by reason of the corruption of the composite. Not of itself, because it has in itself no potency for *non-esse;* nor by reason of the composite, since *esse* is given immediately to it and not to the composite.

4) *Whence comes the necessity of incorruptible beings?* Beings which necessarily exist may, or may not, have received this necessity from another. By supposition, beings that necessarily exist may hold this necessary existence from one of three sources: either from their essence, their act of existence, or from some other being. Notice that with this consideration we have left the plane of essence and are carrying on our analysis on the plane of existence. We are concerned now with the contingency of being, why these necessary beings are rather than are not.

If existence comes from the form or essence, then the being exists of its very essence. Its essence is existence. The being is pure act in the order of existence, subsistent existence, God. But if not, then the essence is actuated by something other than itself, by an act of existence that has come from without, and not from the essence itself.

Now we must direct our attention to this act of existence by which a necessary being exists. Whence comes this act of existence? Did it cause itself? But nothing can cause itself, for that would mean it existed before it existed, which is impossible. Is this act of existence its own reason for being? But then it would be an act of subsistent existence, not the actuation of an essence, but pure act, unreceived existence. And this, again, would be God. But if this existence is received, that is, if it comes neither from the essence nor itself, then it must be received from some other being. And since the necessary being is here and now existing, it follows that here and now it is receiving that existence from another. Hence that other must be here and now causing the existence, holding the necessary being in necessary existence.

Now we cannot go into infinity in necessary beings that receive their necessity from another. For if we did, there would be no first necessary Being. Thus we would be faced with the contradiction of beings that have received necessary existence from another, and yet no other (that is, a first) from which they have received it. For there is question here of essentially ordered effects—of beings that are here and now receiving, as from their efficient cause, their necessary existence. Hence, we must posit a first and absolutely necessary Being who holds its necessity from no one. It is the very nature of such a Being to exist. Such a Being contains no contingency whatsoever, neither in the order of essence nor existence, for its essence is to exist. Necessary beings which receive their necessity from another are necessary in the order of essence. For they are incorruptible and will never lose their being since they have no potency for non-being. Yet they are contingent in the order of being, since they have received their existence from another.

But have not these necessary beings also received their essences from God, and hence are not these essences also contingent? We answer that they have received from God necessary essences which are capacities only for existence, since they contain no matter and thus no potency for non-being. But they have not received from God subsistent existence, for this is impossible. Subsistent existence means unreceived existence: caused being cannot be infinite Being.

5) *Steps of our proof.* Let us look over the steps of our proof by which we have gone from the actual corruption of the beings of our experience to the existence of God.

(*a*) Beings corrupt; therefore they are corruptible.

(*b*) But if all beings were corruptible, there would be no beings in existence, not even corruptible beings. But this is obviously false.

(*c*) Therefore, there must exist some incorruptible, that is to say, necessary being.

(*d*) But this being will hold its necessity either from itself or from another.

(*e*) Since we cannot go into infinity in beings which hold their necessity from another, there must exist a necessary Being that has of itself its necessary existence.

(*f*) This Being is God.

6) *Proof of the steps.* (*a*) That corruptible beings need a cause of their being is easily seen. Corruptible beings are beings that are composed in their very essence. But a composed essence is one containing two distinct components or principles of being, matter and form. But components that are of themselves distinct do not come together in composition unless some extrinsic cause unites them, unless some agent educes the form from the potency of matter, by which eduction the composite begins to exist. As St. Thomas writes: "Every composite being has a cause; for those things which are distinct of themselves do not come together to form a unit unless through some cause that joins them." [22] "The existence of composite beings arises from the components." [23] "The existence of a thing that is composite results from the coming together of the principles (components) of that thing." [24]

(*b*) If all beings were corruptible, there would be no beings in existence. Therefore, it is impossible for all beings to be corrupti-

[22] *S.T.*, I, 3, 7.
[23] *In IX Metaphy.*, lect. 11, no. 1903 (Cathala ed.).
[24] *In Boeth. de Trinitate*, qu. 5, a. 3c.

ble. This is easy to see from the nature of a corruptible being. Even while such a being is existing it is possible for it not to be. Therefore, such a nature is of itself equally indifferent to *esse* or to *non-esse*. Thus if it is to exist and to remain in existence, it must receive this *esse* or existence from some cause. But we cannot go into infinity in corruptible beings that hold their existence from another cause, for reasons already studied in the second way. Hence we must place some being that is necessary. Here is the way St. Thomas states the matter:

We see in the world certain things that are possible to be or not to be, namely, things that can be generated and corrupted. But everything that is able to be has a cause; and since of itself it holds itself equally to two things, namely, to be and not to be, it is necessary that if it should come to be that this should happen because of some cause. But we cannot proceed into infinity in such causes, as was proved above through the argument of Aristotle. Therefore, we must posit some being that is necessary in its being. [25]

(c) Therefore, there must exist some necessary being, which holds its necessity either from itself or another. And we cannot go into infinity in necessary beings that receive their necessity from another. A consideration from St. Thomas will demonstrate very clearly the truth of this last statement. Existence is predicated of everything that is. Now when a common perfection is predicated of two beings, it is impossible that it be predicated of neither by way of causality. One must be the cause of the other, as fire is the cause of heat in another body, or some third being must be the cause of the perfection in both, as, for example, fire is the cause of the heat in two bodies. Hence it is impossible for two beings that are, that one of them should not have a cause of its existence: either both exist through a third cause or one is the cause of the other. Thus everything that is, to the extent that it is, must receive its being from that cause which has no cause of being. And this Being which has no cause of being is the absolutely necessary Being, God. [26]

25 *C.G.*, I, Ch. 15, par. 5.
26 *C.G.*, II, Ch. 15, par. 2.

There are other ways to show why we cannot go into infinity in beings that receive their necessity from another. The reason we use this proof is that it brings out a fact sometimes overlooked in the third way; namely, that there is no necessary connection between the existence of corruptible beings and beings which receive their necessity from another. The actual existence of the latter is not necessary to our proof. Even if there existed no simple substances, no spiritual beings like the angels, the existence of an absolutely necessary Being would be required for the existence of corruptible beings. The second step, however, is added to obviate an objection: perhaps a finite necessary being can adequately explain the existence of corruptible beings, and so from corruptible things we could not necessarily demonstrate the existence of God. But now we see that, as a matter of fact, since such necessary beings cannot explain the source of their own necessity, neither can they explain the source of the being of corruptible things. Since they are caused in their own being, they cannot be the first cause of the being of other things that are not necessary.

Thus we see that there are three kinds of beings:

(*a*) Those that are both intrinsically and extrinsically possible not to be; intrinsically, because they have within their essence a potency not to be, whose source is prime matter; and extrinsically, because they depend upon an extrinsic agent both for their coming into being, their generation, and for their duration in being. These are corruptible beings.

(*b*) Those that are intrinsically necessary, since they possess within their essence no potency from non-being. But extrinsically they are contingent or possible not to be, in the sense that they depend upon an extrinsic agent both for the reception of their existence and its conservation. And these are subsistent forms, like angelic essences, and the human soul. These forms can never cease to exist because they have no potency for *non-esse*. St. Thomas writes:

> For if there is some form which has existence, it is necessary that such a form be incorruptible. Because existence (esse) cannot be separated from something having existence, unless the form be separated from

this thing; and so if that which has existence is the form itself, it is quite impossible that existence be separated from this thing.[27]

Existence follows upon form, since form is the ultimate complement of substance, making substance a subject capable of receiving existence. If something is to be, it must be something. In beings that are composed in their essence, form can be separated from existence, because form can be separated from matter. But in beings where form is subsistent and where there is no matter in the essence, form can no more be separated from existence than it can be separated from itself. A subsistent form could no more lose its existence than the number two could cease being an even number. Of course, the existence is not the same as the form, no more than "even" is the same as the number two. But just as "to be even" inseparably follows the nature of "two," so does existence inseparably follow subsistent forms. Of course, the existence is a received existence, and hence is continually and extrinsically dependent upon an agent from which it has been received.

(c) A third kind of being would be one that is both intrinsically and extrinsically necessary; one that not only possesses in itself no potency for non-being, but whose existence itself is unreceived, and hence is not subsistent form but subsistent Being. Such a Being is infinite and necessary in the order of existence. God is such a Being.

There remains now only to mention how this third way of St. Thomas's differs from the preceding way. Here we are interested in the nature of the things around us rather than in their activity, although we arrive at a knowledge of these natures through a phenomenon produced through activity; namely, the generation and corruption of beings. The third way, then, is concerned with the intimate being of things. Since existence is an actuation of essences, existence is limited by the essence it actuates. Thus composed essences have a corruptible existence. Simple essences have an incorruptible, albeit a received, existence. The third way, then, is the way of contingent being. Through an analysis of beings that have received their existence from another, we necessarily arrive

[27] *Quaest. Disp. de Anima*, a. 14c.

at a term which is its own existence. The third way grasps its term, God, under the aspect of necessary Being, and thus more directly and more explicitly than the other ways sees this term as the necessary and proper cause of existence as such. [28]

3. Answering the Objections

Some philosophers have denied the validity of this third way of St. Thomas. Let us see what their objections are and whether we can answer them.

1) Kant rejects our argument for the following reason. When the mind is confronted with contingent beings, there is a natural tendency to conclude to a necessary Being. But this is due to the passion the human mind has for unity, and not to the existence of a necessary Being. For from the existence of contingent beings all we can legitimately conclude to is the existence of other contingent beings, unless we want to go beyond the evidence—a common fallacy of the human mind.

We answer that the human mind naturally tends toward its own proper perfection, which is to know truth. The reason the human mind demands the existence of a necessary Being from the analysis of contingent beings is due to the truth of the matter, insofar as the intelligibility of contingent being requires a Being completely necessary. Otherwise a contingent being is not intelligible. Our intellect in a positive way sees this necessity of positing a necessary Being.

2) But Kant insists that our argument makes the existence of an absolutely necessary Being quite impossible. A necessary Being who is the cause of the existence of contingent beings, is by that very fact related to the contingent beings it causes. For between cause and effect there must needs be a mutual and real relation, since the necessary Being is the real cause of the existence of the contingent beings. But a necessary Being possessing a relation to other beings, is by that very fact not absolutely necessary, but in some sense relative, since it has a real relation to other beings.

We reply that if the necessary Being causes the existence of con-

[28] See *De Pot.*, qu. 5, a. 3c.

tingent beings through some operation distinct from its substance, it would have a real relation to contingent being. But in God his operation is his Being, which is unchangeable. The whole change is in the creature. Therefore in the creature there is a real relation to God, but in God there is only a relation of reason to the creature. This point will be treated more thoroughly in the section on creation and the divine will.

3) There is a statement in St. Thomas regarding corruptible bodies that can be misunderstood and has caused some thinkers to reject this proof.

We find that some things are generated and corrupted, and consequently, are possible to be or not to be. But it is impossible that everything which is of such a nature would always be, for that which is able not to be at some time is not. If therefore all things were able not to be, at some time there would be nothing in existence. But if this is true, then there would be nothing in existence now . . . which is obviously false. [29]

To many these simple words contain a twofold fallacy. First, because a thing is possible not to be, it does not follow, as St. Thomas explicitly states here, that therefore it must at some time not be. Such a being may not be allowed to corrupt because of other causes. We answer that this is true: corruptible things need never corrupt. For example, as we know from revelation, this would have been the case with man's body had he not sinned originally, and it will be the case with his glorified body in heaven after the resurrection. But this requires something beyond the nature of the corruptible being, and we would have to analyze the cause of this incorruption and see whether this cause is a contingent being or not. The second alleged fallacy is this: To say that things that are possible not to be must some time not be, and therefore if only corruptible beings existed, there was a time when there were no beings in existence, and hence there would be no beings now, is not *prima facie* obvious. For maybe some of the corruptible beings that do exist have been around from the beginning; or if not, at least

[29] *S.T.*, I, 2, 3.

this statement of St. Thomas's would not be true when the world was still young and in its infancy.

What has happened is that these writers have missed the meaning of St. Thomas's statement. First of all, a corruptible being that is actually existing, must sooner or later cease to exist. For if, of itself, it never ceases to exist, never corrupts, that can only be because it is possible for it not to corrupt; but a being that is able not to corrupt is by that very fact incorruptible. Here are St. Thomas's words from his commentary on Aristotle's *De Coelo et Mundo:* "It is impossible that that which is corruptible should not at some time corrupt because if it at some time does not corrupt, it is able not to corrupt, and so it would be incorruptible." [30] Thus we can see how corruptible things must sooner or later of themselves cease to exist, else they are not corruptible. But what does St. Thomas mean by the second part of his statement; namely, that if only corruptible things existed, there would have been a time when no corruptible things existed?

His reasoning seems to be this: On the hypothesis that the world is eternal, generation and corruption have been taking place in an infinite duration of time. Now if all beings were corruptible, that is to say, if all of them have in their essence the potency to go out of existence, then this potency, if it has any intelligibility at all, if it is a real objective potency, must sooner or later be realized. Certainly it would be realized in the course of infinite time.

If this potency were not realized during the course of an infinite time, this could only be because the beings were able not to corrupt, that is to say, were *incorruptible*. Hence during the course of an *infinite* time, the potency to corrupt would be realized. And if it were realized in the case of one such corruptible being, it would *also* be realized in the case of all of them, for there is question here of an *infinite* duration of time. Thus by now all beings would have gone out of existence and there would be nothing. But there is something; hence, there must be in existence now some incorruptible being.

[30] Bk. I, lesson 29, paragraph 6.

Moses Maimonides, from whom St. Thomas borrows this proof, gives an example to prove his point. Supposing, he says, that we know that men have the power to write. If during an infinite duration of time, no man writes, we can only conclude that this is because there is no such potency in man. But we know from actual experience that some beings do corrupt and so possess the potency to do so. Thus this potency must sooner or later be realized.

If this is St. Thomas's reasoning, then it does seem inconclusive. A potency to write is one thing; a potency for non-being is quite another. For potency as such is always a relation or order to act. And apart from the act to which it is ordered, potency as such has no meaning, or intelligibility.

Now non-being is not act, but the denial of act. And so there can be no such thing as a real, objective potency for non-being. Matter is a real, objective potency for *form*. A being is generated *per se*, it corrupts *per accidens*. That is to say, it is because a new form is educed that the old form is reduced to the potency of matter. Corruption is not annihilation, it is only substantial change.

And so even on the supposition that the world is eternal, there would still be an eternal generation and corruption of individuals within a species and of individuals of different species. Thus beings would never go out of existence, since the potency that is in it for non-being is achieved only through the generation of another being. Of course, it is impossible (as we have seen) that there should be in existence only corruptible beings, but not, it would seem, for the reason given by Maimonides, and repeated here by St. Thomas. What St. Thomas may mean is that no corruptible things would be existing, not because they had all gone out of existence, but because they could never have existed in the first place. If we suppose a moment at which only corruptible things existed, at that very moment nothing would be existing. In other words, the supposition is quite impossible. For by supposition we would have beings which *qua* corruptible need a cause why they do not corrupt and at the same time do not have that cause, since by supposition only corruptible beings are existing. But since *de facto* corruptible beings do exist, it follows that here and now there must also be existing other beings that are incorruptible. [31]

4. Summary of the Third Way

"From corruptible and contingent beings, the existence of God as an absolutely necessary Being can be demonstrated."

a. Statement of the question

In the third way of St. Thomas, this is the problem: from the fact of experience that things in the world are generated and corrupted, is it possible to demonstrate the existence of an absolutely necessary Being? From an inspection of the innermost nature of contingent beings, is the existence of a Being in no way contingent demanded, as the only sufficient explanation of the act of existing in these contingent beings?

b. Explanation of terms

1) " . . *Corruptible Being* . . ."—That being whose essence is composed of matter and form. On account of its matter, such a being is intrinsically able not-to-be. Such a being can by its essence not-be.

2) *Incorruptible Being*—That being whose essence does not include matter, whether it is a simple subsisting form, like an angel, or the form of a body which has its own act of existing, like the human soul. (Text: *De Pot.*, qu. 5, a. 3c.)

3) ". . . *Contingent Being* . . ."—That which can not-be in the order in which it is contingent; for example, a corruptible being can not-be by reason of its essence; and *a fortiori* by an extrinsic reason, namely, by reason of an external agent. An incorruptible being can not-be only in the order of being; that is, it needs an external agent both for its beginning and duration in being.

4) *Necessary Being*—That which cannot not-be in the order in which it is necessary, for example:

> (a) necessary by a necessity of consequence: while he sits, Socrates necessarily sits.

[31] See *C.G.*, Bk. II, Ch. 30.

(*b*) necessary by a necessity of *matter:* if material things exist, they are necessarily corruptible.

(*c*) necessary by a necessity of form: forms which are not in matter, or which subsist in matter, *have a necessity of being.*

(*d*) necessary by a necessity of the *very act of existing:* what cannot not-be because it is the very act of Being. Such a Being does not *have* the necessity of being, it *is* the necessary Being itself. (Text: *C.G.*, Bk. II, Ch. 30.)

5) ". . . *existence of God can be demonstrated* . . ." From the fact of the corruptibility of material things, and from the fact of the contingency in the order of being of incorruptible things which have their necessity from another, we conclude to the existence of a Being which does not have its necessity of Being from another, but has it of itself. This Being is God.

6) ". . . *as a* . . . *necessary Being* . . ." That is, in this third way, God terminates our investigation not as the ultimate reason for the existence of motion, nor as the ultimate reason for causality in things, but as the ultimate reason for the act of existing in all things.

c. *Adversaries*

Kant rejected our argument for many reasons. (1) Because more is contained in the conclusion (necessary Being) than in the premises (contingent beings). (2) Because by applying the principle of causality to God (by saying that God is the cause of things), we make God a relative being (since a cause has a real relation to its effect). We have seen the answer to these difficulties.

Spinoza: Beings in the world only seem to be contingent; for contingency itself is a mode, and contingent beings are different appearances of the same necessary substance. Therefore there does not exist a necessary Being really distinct from contingent beings. Such a position as Spinoza's is Pantheism, "which is listed among those positions of philosophy that are fundamentally erroneous since not only is it contrary to faith, but it undermines all the principles of moral philosophy," destroying our freedom, and so on (See *De Malo*, qu. 6, a. *unic.*).

Geny, Chambat, Descoqs: What can be corrupted of itself may not corrupt accidentally, and therefore at least that part of the argument which says that if all things were corruptible, nothing would exist, is a fallacy. We have seen the answer to this also.

d. The proof

The argument begins with a fact: things corrupt and are generated; for example, men and animals die and are born. From this fact we argue thus:

1) *First step.* What corrupts can corrupt. But what can corrupt can either be or not-be. And what can either be or not-be is indifferent to both. But what is indifferent to existence and non-existence, if it actually exists, must exist through some cause. Now it is impossible to proceed to infinity in corruptible things that have their being from another. This impossibility is based on the notion of essentially ordered causes which we considered in the second way. Hence there must be some incorruptible or necessary being. (Text: *C.G.*, I, Ch. 15.)

Another argument that starts from corruptible things can be stated in this way: Diverse things because they are diverse, must have a cause of their union or composition. And corruptible things are composed of matter and form which are really diverse. Therefore they must have an extrinsic cause of their composition. But we cannot proceed to infinity in things having their composition from another. Therefore, there exists some uncomposed and incorruptible or necessary being. (Text: *S.T.*, I, 3, 7.)

2) *Second step.* This necessary being either has its necessity of being of itself or through another. But we cannot proceed to infinity in beings which have their necessity from another. The reason for this is that all beings which have their necessity of being from another, whether considered as many or as one caused being, do not have in themselves the explanation why they necessarily exist. Therefore there must be a Being necessary of itself. This is what men call God. (Text: *C.G.*, II, Ch. 15; *S.T.*, I, 2, 3)

D. THE FOURTH WAY: PROOF OF GOD'S EXISTENCE FROM GRADES OF PERFECTION IN BEINGS

1. Statement of the Problem

Having demonstrated the necessity for an absolutely necessary Being as the only complete explanation of the existence of contingent beings, we wish now to consider a new question. Is there yet another way that can lead the mind to the existence of God? St. Thomas tells us there is. Among the beings of our experience we find common perfections possessed by these beings in different degrees. Is it possible that these different degrees of perfections demand for their intelligibility as differing degrees the existence of a maximum degree of this perfection, and therefore the existence of a being who possesses this perfection in its maximum degree? This is the problem of the fourth way. We maintain that these different degrees of the same perfections do exist in beings; and, secondly, that they derive their intelligibility and their very existence from the maximum degree of the perfection. And this maximum is God. But in order to understand how this is so, an exact and careful understanding of the elements of our solution is required.

2. Solution

1) First of all, what do we mean here by "grades of perfection"? We mean that in several existing things the mind recognizes the presence of the same perfection, but sees it as belonging more to one being than to another. For example, men, animals, and plants all share in the perfection of life. All are living beings; but life is seen to be more perfect in man than in the animal and more perfect in the animal than in the plant. Again, we see that some beings are nobler than others; the being of man is more noble than the being of a dog; and the being of a dog is nobler (of greater ontological value) than the being of a rock, and so forth. Thus there are different grades or degrees of the same perfection, for

example, life, goodness, beauty, truth, nobility, in the different beings that exist around us.

2) Secondly, what kind of perfections are capable of existing in different degrees? Perfections which constitute the essences of things are incapable of different degrees. One cannot be more or less man, more or less dog. If the essence of man or the essence of dog changes, we have a different essence. We have non-man or non-dog. And this holds true for all essences, whether they be material essences like man or dog, or immaterial essences like the subsistent forms of the angels.

Two things about essential perfections are to be noted. Although incapable of existing according to different degrees (since "more or less essence" is a contradiction in terms: all men are equally men, else they are simply not men), an essence can exist in different individuals. But the fact that the perfection of man is found in Peter only "happens" (is incidental) to this perfection. That by which Peter is a man and that by which Paul is a man is the same specific or essential perfection: both possess a human soul and sensible matter. But that by which Peter is Peter and that by which Paul is Paul is different; namely, different individual sensible matters which are the principles of the individuation of the essence. Thus although all men are equally men, all men are not equal men, because of their accidental differences and their different individual sensible matters.

The second thing to be noted about material essences is that they cannot subsist. For an essential perfection to subsist means that it is able to exist apart from matter. But since matter belongs to the very essence of material perfections, such perfections can neither have existence nor intelligibility apart from matter. To be in matter means to be in individual sensible matter, for a universal as such cannot exist, since at one and the same time it would be common to many and yet be this existing thing—a clear contradiction. But this individual material essence can be considered by the intellect apart from its individual sensible matter, as happens when we abstract the universal from the particular. But the universal consideration of a material essence still includes common sensible matter.

To sum up: Essential perfections like humanity, rationality, animality, and so forth, since they cannot exist in varying degrees, are not numbered among those perfections considered in this fourth way. Moreover, these essential perfections if they are material cannot subsist. There is no subsistent man, no subsistent dog, since in order to exist, these perfections must exist in matter. What exists is this man or this dog, matter being the principle of thisness or individuation. Finally, since matter enters into their very essences, humanity, animality, rationality, and so forth, are not perfections of being as being but of being as limited being, for matter is the principle of limitation. Finally, even perfections of essence that are subsistent forms (such as the essence of an angel or the human soul), are limited perfections and not perfections of being as being. For any essence is potency in the order of being, since it receives and limits the act of being, which is existence.

3) There is a second class of perfections, which although capable of existing in different degrees in different beings, do not belong to that group of perfections by which the fourth way mounts up to God. These are the accidental perfections of material beings that depend upon matter both for their being and for their being intelligible. For example, the perfection of heat is found in fire, in hot water, in hot potatoes, and so on. This perfection can be found in material substances in different degrees, because this form can more or less intensely inform the substance. Now obviously there can be no such thing as subsistent heat; first of all, because heat as an accident cannot exist apart from substance. But even if heat were a substance, in order to be it would still have to be in matter, for sensible qualities demand sensible matter both for their being and for their being intelligible. Thus accidental perfections that depend upon matter also have no part in our proof; they are not perfections of being as being, but of material, limited being.

4) What kind of perfections then, when found existing in different beings in different degrees, demand for their being and

for their intelligibility the actual existence of this perfection in its highest and most perfect degree? It must be those perfections in whose intelligibility no note of imperfection or limitation is present. If limitation is present, it will be there not because of the perfection itself, but because of the being that possesses the perfection.

There are two principles of limitation in beings. In the order of essence, there is matter which limits form; and in the order of being, there is essence which limits existence. Material perfections as such are limited and hence can never exist as a maximum or unlimited perfection; and essences as such are not gradated and do not vary in beings. Hence neither can lead us to a maximum or unlimited perfection. Only those perfections that follow being as being, which follow being insofar as it exercises its act, which is "to be," demand a maximum for their intelligibility and for their existence. *Hence only those perfections that flow from the act of existing as such enter into the proof of the fourth way.*

5) Precisely what is meant by a perfection that flows from being *insofar as it is in act through its existence or "to be"*? We mean a perfection that is a perfection because of the *actuality* of the being and is a *limited* perfection not of itself, but because of the *limitation of this actuality* by reason of the essence that is actuated. A simple example will bring out our meaning. A flower, because it is a *flower*, possesses *vegetative* life; a dog, because it is a *dog*, possesses *sensitive* life; a man, because he is a *man*, possesses *rational* life. Thus in each instance, the *kind* of life the being possesses depends upon the *kind* of being it is, upon the being's essence. But the *actuality* of this perfection depends upon the actuality of the being. All are *living beings*. The perfection of life in each case is both actual and limited; but it is limited not because it is life, but because it is the life of a flower, or of a dog, or of a man. Hence, apart from the principle that limits it, life is an unlimited perfection of *being*. There can, therefore, exist a being that is unlimited life, for the limitation is not from the side of the perfection, but from the side of the particular essence that

receives the perfection. Of course, rational life is more perfect than animal life, and animal life is more perfect than plant life, because the essence of man is less limiting of the act of existence than is the essence of an animal, and that of an animal less limiting than that of a plant. But since essence is always potency in the order of existence, it will always exercise some limitation on the act of existing, and hence on those perfections given by the act of existing. If no limit is placed on the act of existing, it will be all-perfect and contain all the perfections of being.

The perfections of the fourth way, then, are perfections in whose notion and in whose being there is contained no imperfection. In creatures, such perfections can be perfections like being itself and the truth and goodness that are convertible with being; or like life, which is a perfection of being for living things, and so forth. These perfections are possessed by creatures by way of participation and not by way of essence. Or these perfections of the fourth way may be accidental perfections, like wisdom and knowledge, which are acquired habits or qualities inhering in the intellect. Hence their mode of being in the creature is both accidental, since these perfections inhere in a subject, and limited or participated, since it is human knowledge and human wisdom. But since "to know" and "to be wise" involve as such no imperfection, there can exist unlimited wisdom and unlimited knowledge.

A final characteristic of these perfections is implicit in what has already been said. These perfections are analogous and transcendent. First of all, to possess a perfection by way of participation and possess an analogous perfection do not always nor necessarily mean the same thing. For example, all existing men can be said to participate in the perfection of humanity, but they participate in this perfection univocally, for it is the same in all men. And this is so because humanity is a perfection of essence.

But to possess an analogous perfection is to possess a perfection that is found in greater or lesser degrees in different beings. And the reason why this participation is according to greater or lesser (that is, analogous participation) is that these perfections are due to the existence of the thing rather than to its essence. The act of existing, as actuating the whole being, is at once "different" for each being and absolutely incommunicable. It is possessed analogously by each being and it cannot be abstracted from the being the way a form is abstracted from matter. Existence cannot be abstracted from existing beings, or life cannot be abstracted from living beings, in the same sense that man can be abstracted from human beings and dog from canine beings. When we talk about existence and life, we formalize these perfections for purposes of communication and explanation, but they are not abstracted forms.

Such perfections are also transcendent. They transcend the predicaments and belong to none of them. Not in the sense that all beings possess these perfections (not all beings are living or have knowledge), but in the sense that in those beings that do possess them these perfections flow from the act of existing, which act transcends all the predicaments and belongs to none of them. And like the act of existing which they follow, these perfections cannot be abstracted in the way we abstract an essence or form. They are not common natures that we predicate univocally of existing things.

3. The Proof of the Fourth Way

Why does the intelligibility of "more or less" of the same perfection in different beings demand the existence of a maximum degree of that perfection? It seems clear that a rose possesses more being than a stone, and that a lion possesses more being than a rose, and that a man possesses more being than a lion. And by such a progression we would seem to be approaching a nature which possesses being in its highest perfection. But the point of the proof is to show that it is this highest perfection, unlimited being, that is the source of the intelligibility of the lesser degrees of the same perfection existing in these different natures. St. Thomas tells us that different degrees of the same perfection mean that these are participated perfections and hence are completely intelligible only on the supposition that there exists an unparticipated perfection, a highest degree. He demonstrates this fact in many places. We will analyze his proof from the *Summa Contra Gentiles*, Book II, Chapter 15.

The chapter itself is concerned with giving different reasons why God is the cause of being for all things. St. Thomas begins by saying that what belongs to a thing because of its own nature and not because of some other cause, cannot be found deficiently in that thing. For if something essential to a nature is subtracted from or added to that nature, it becomes a different nature. Just as, for example, when a number is added to or subtracted from, we have a different number. If on the other hand, while the nature remains unchanged, something in it is found lessened, then it is obvious that what is found lessened does not depend simply on the nature, but on something else. And its lessening is due to a greater removal from the thing upon which it depends.

Therefore what is shared in less by, or belongs less to, one thing than another, does not belong to this thing because of its nature only, but because of some other cause. And this cause will be responsible for these gradated perfections wherever they are found. Just as that which is hottest we see to be the cause of heat in all hot things, and that which is most perfectly light, the cause of light in all lighted things, so God is most perfect being and therefore the cause of all things of which we can predicate being.

Notice there are two phases here in the movement of St. Thomas's thought. The first consists in showing that degrees of more or less of the same perfection depend for their intelligibility upon the maximum degree of that perfection. The second makes more explicit what was only implicit in the first; namely, that the maximum grade is also the cause of the existence of the other grades of the perfections. The proof of the fourth way is formally complete with the end of the first phase, with the positing of the maximum degree as the only explanation of the intelligibility of the lesser degrees. Here we are concerned directly and explicitly with exemplary causality or the cause of the intelligibility of these degrees of perfection. The second step, which is outside the essential movement of the fourth way, consists in seeing explicitly what was present only implicitly in the first step; namely, that this maximum degree of the perfection is also the *efficient* cause of the very existence of the other degrees of this perfection.

Let us see whether we can grasp the cogency of the fourth way. [32] The fact from which we argue is the actual existence of different degrees of the same perfection. This existential experience is a composite and an intelligible one: the existence of many beings possessing the same perfection according to more and less. Reflecting upon this fact, we conclude that these grades would be unintelligible if there did not exist a maximum grade. Why is this so? Because perfections that are found in a deficient state are not in themselves adequately intelligible. They are intelligible only because they are more or less like that which is perfectly this perfection. Such perfections hold their intelligibility to the exact degree to which they approach or recede from the unlimited perfection in which they share. A thing is intelligible to the degree that it is and in the way that it is. We have seen that these perfections are not intelligible because of the nature in which they are found. For here the nature or essence is related to the perfection as receiver to thing received, as potency to act. And act neither is, nor is intelligible, through potency. It is the other way around: potency is and is intelligible through act. Hence, the intelligibility of the different degrees of the same perfection is not accounted for by the nature or essence that limits it. Rather, as act, the perfection renders intelligible the nature that limits it.

Nor can these more or less limited acts *of themselves* account for their intelligibility as limited. For of themselves *they should not be limited.* Here we are at the heart of the matter. Two things should be noted about each degree of the perfections. First, it is minorated (that is, it is not the highest degree since it is found in a limited condition), and, secondly, of itself it should not be limited (since, of itself, it says *only act* and in no way potency).

---

[32] Besides the basic text in the *Summa* (I, 2, 3), here are some other places where St. Thomas refers to and uses the argument from degrees of perfection to establish some truth about God: *S.T.*, I, 44, 1; *De Pot.*, qu. 3, a. 5c; *De Subst. Separ.*, Ch. 9 (explains how perfections like life, understanding, etc., are the act of *esse* for living, intellective, etc., beings); *Com. Theol.*, Ch. 68.

As act, it accounts for the intelligibility of its limiting potency, for apart from its act, or its intrinsic order to its act, potency has no intelligibility. But what accounts for the actuality of the limited perfection? Only the fact that all these degrees participate in the same unlimited degree of the perfection. The conclusion is a simple but necessary one: unless there exists here and now the unlimited degree of this perfection, the limited degrees have no reason for being, and hence have no intelligibility as limited degrees of the same perfection. The source of the intelligiblity of these minorated degrees of the same perfection cannot be the natures that limit them nor their own condition as act, but only the existence of the unlimited, unreceived, degree. This unlimited degree must, therefore, exist. In the fourth way we reach God under the aspect of unlimited Being.

Just as in the second way, the activity of finite beings is rendered intelligible only on the supposition that there exists an uncaused cause that is its own activity; and just as in the third way contingent beings are rendered intelligible only on the supposition that there exists an absolutely necessary Being who is its own necessary existence; so, here in the fourth way, the existence of different grades of perfection is rendered intelligible only on the supposition that there exists a Being who possesses these perfections in an ungraded or absolute degree. With the positing of this absolute degree the proof of the fourth way is completed.

But St. Thomas always goes on to show that this "Greatest Being" is the efficient cause of the participated perfections. God is not only the first exemplary cause why these grades of perfections are intelligible. He is also the first efficient cause why these grades of perfection exist. This addition to the proof is merely an explicitation in our knowledge of God's causality.

4. Some Added Considerations

a. How the different kinds of perfections in the creature pre-exist in God

In the course of our solution we analyzed three kinds of perfections: (1) perfections of essence, which do not allow of dif-

ferent grades; (2) accidental perfections which allow of grades
but cannot subsist because matter is intrinsic to their nature; (3)
substantial and accidental perfections which both allow of different degrees and in whose being and intelligibility there is no
note of limitation or imperfection. Only this third class is validly
used in our proof, because only these perfections allow of and
demand the unlimited (subsistent) existence of the perfection.
But God is not only the first cause of perfections that follow being
as being. He is also the cause of prime matter and of perfections
of essence. He is the cause of the existence of all perfections. Thus
all perfections must somehow exist in God.

Later on we shall see in detail how different perfections found
in creatures can be said to pre-exist in God as in their cause. It
suffices here to say that those perfections in creatures that contain
within themselves a necessary limitation, for example, humanity,
are said to pre-exist in God's essence only virtually. That is to
say, God possesses the power (*virtus*) to produce such perfections.
But what this perfection properly signifies can in no way be pre-
dicted of God, not even by way of analogy.

However, perfections that follow being as being, in which there
exists on the side of the perfection no limitation (like wisdom,
truth, life, and so forth) pre-exist in God *properly*. This means that
this perfection is in God not merely in the sense that he can cause
it, but also in the sense that it belongs to him by reason of the perfection itself. This perfection, however, is said to be in God analogously, since God possesses it in an infinitely higher degree and
according to an infinitely more perfect way than it is found in the
creature. In fact, as found in God this perfection is identified with
the divine Being, which is unreceived and subsistent, and thus
the perfections are subsistent, unparticipated, one with the divine
essence, which essence is subsistent existence.

b. How the fourth way differs from the third way

It remains now to be seen how this fourth way of St. Thomas's
differs from the third way, the way of contingent being. There are
several differences:

1) The third way began with the existential fact that beings corrupt and are generated, a consideration based on the nature or essence of beings.

The fourth way began with the fact that different grades of the same perfection are found in different things, a consideration based on beings as gradated in their being. Thus the points of departure of the two ways are entirely different.

2) Secondly, the third way mounted from corruptible beings to incorruptible beings, and from incorruptible beings to that Being which is absolutely necessary. But corruptibility and holding one's necessity of being from another are characteristics that point to a dependence upon an extrinsic agent. The third way concludes directly and explicitly to a necessary Being as to a Being who is such a cause or agent.

In the fourth way, on the other hand, we mounted from different grades of the same perfection to the supreme grade of this perfection. Here we grasped the perfection, not as contingent or as necessary, but precisely as gradated, as approaching a supreme grade, as pointing to a term which would make these different grades intelligible as grades. The fourth way concludes directly and explicitly to the existence of the supreme grade of the perfection as the cause of the intelligibility of the other grades, and hence to exemplary causality. Our approach was by way of the *intelligibility* of the grades.

5. Answering the Objections

First objection. If the different degrees of the same perfection depend upon the supreme degree of that perfection for their intelligibility, then the intellect must first know this supreme degree before it can know the lesser degrees. Hence, the fourth way does not prove, but supposes, the existence of God.

This objection is answered by a simple distinction. If one means that degrees of perfection are not intelligible to us unless we first know the supreme degree, this must be denied. But if one means that these degrees of perfection are not intelligible in themselves unless some supreme degree exists, the statement is true. It is a fact that we have knowledge of these degrees of perfection; hence, they are intelligible to us. And the intellect also understands that in themselves these degrees would not be intelligible unless there existed some supreme degree. Hence, for our intellect, the knowledge of this supreme degree constitutes a necessary *term*. But in itself this supreme degree is the first cause of the intelligibility of the other degrees and, indeed, of the very being of the graded perfections.

Second objection. The fourth way argues that the supreme degree is the cause of the perfections in which other beings participate. Thus the fourth way seems to be no different from the third, which argues from the contingency of beings.

Reply. Strictly speaking, the fourth way is formally complete once we have posited a supreme degree as cause of the intelligibility of the other degrees. What is then added, namely, that this supreme Being must be also the efficient cause of the perfections, is not essential to the proof.

Third objection. If this is true, then the fourth way does not seem to be based on the principle of causality. Hence the difficulty remains.

Reply. The fourth way is directly and explicitly based upon exemplary causality, but only implicitly on efficient causality. Efficient causality implicitly accompanies the whole of our proof, for from it flows the very existence of the perfections which are found in varying degrees in beings.

Fourth objection. Among things that are heated, we find various degrees of heat; hence there should exist some supreme degree of heat which is the cause of the heat in all hot things. And since this is clearly false, so is the parallel procedure of the fourth way of St. Thomas.

This objection is answered by showing that the perfection of heat is a perfection proper to being as material, not to being as being. And in the fourth way we do not argue from such perfections. St. Thomas's statement that fire is supremely hot and the cause of heat in all heated things, is used merely as a clarifying example. And he thought it was a good one, since in Aristotelian physics fire was considered (falsely) as one of the substantial elements. The error is in the faulty example, not in the principle exemplified.

Fifth objection. One does not understand a perfection as greater or less because it is approaching a maximum, but rather because of the order that is perceived to exist among the different things possessing this graded perfection. Thus "more and less" are intelligible independently of a maximum, and so the fourth way proves nothing.

We answer that this order itself, which is seen to exist among different things because of their greater or less participation in the same perfection of being, would not be intelligible unless there existed the supreme degree of this perfection. The very order itself, taken as a whole, implies reference to another; for *all* the degrees are minorated, since all the perfections are participated. And so our intellect sees that as such they are unintelligible without the existence of the maximum to which they are all ordered.

6. Summary of the Fourth Way

"The existence of God as the supreme and perfect Being can be demonstrated through the existence of degrees of perfection."

a. Statement of the problem

It is clear that there exist among beings different degrees of the same perfection. One being is better, nobler, truer than another. How is this fact to be explained? We maintain that the different grades of the same perfection among various beings would have no intelligibility as degrees unless there existed a supreme degree of this perfection; and this supreme degree is also supreme Being, or God.

b. Explanation of terms

1) ". . . *degree* . . ." This word of its nature means something that is relative, that is, more or less. Different beings participate in the same perfection in different degrees.

2) *". . . perfection . . ."*—that in a thing because of which it is or is said to be perfect (complete or finished) in some order of being.

(*a*) *Perfections of essence,* for example, the perfection of man, the perfection of animal, and so on: these perfections constitute the natures or essences of things and so are incapable of different degrees. There is no such thing as being more or less man; one is either a man or something else. Hence, there is no question of using this type of perfection in the fourth way.

(*b*) *Mixed perfections*—those in whose very perfection there is present some potentiality or limitation, and hence imperfection. Mixed perfections therefore do not follow from being as being, but from being as such a being. For example, in the perfection of reason there is necessarily some imperfection present; namely, a certain movement or passage from thought to thought. Furthermore, all perfections of essence are mixed perfections.

(*c*) *Perfections proper to a being as being.* These perfections contain no limitation or imperfection in their intelligibility. And if such a perfection is found limited, it is by reason of the subject which partakes of the perfection and not because of the perfection itself. For example, animality of itself is a limited perfection because it is material; but wisdom of itself is not limited, although human wisdom is. In the fourth way there is question only of these perfections. For all other perfections either do not admit of degrees, like the perfections of essence; or if they have degrees, these degrees are proper only to particular beings (for example, to material beings, like different degrees of heat in hot things). It is impossible that such perfections exist in a subsistent or unlimited degree. For to exist they must be in individual sensible matter. Perfections proper to beings as being follow upon the actuality of the act of existing itself. And for this reason they are perfections which are analogous and transcendent. Therefore, insofar as they are perfections actually being exercised, they cannot be known by any abstraction in the strict sense of the term.

3) *"The existence of God . . . can de demonstrated . . ."* By showing that the different degrees of the same perfection possess

no intelligibility unless there exists a supreme degree of this perfection, we show that God exists, since he is this supreme degree.

c. *The proof*

1) *General proof from the degrees of perfection in things.* (*a*) *The fact of experience:* in the existents of our experience different degrees of perfection are present. It is clear, for example, that a man is a more perfect being than a pig.

(*b*) *Metaphysical principle:* we do not predicate greater or less about different things except insofar as they approach some maximum.

(*c*) *Conclusion:* therefore, there must exist something that is the supreme good, supreme truth, supreme living being, and so on. And because that which is the supreme good, the supreme truth, and so on, is also the supreme Being, there must exist a supreme Being, or God himself.

(*d*) *Proof of the argument:* from the very notion of a graded perfection. Graded perfections, as graded, do not contain within themselves their complete intelligibility. Because there are many degrees of the same perfection, this perfection is participated and therefore incomplete and dependent upon something other than itself. Hence the very intelligibility of this order among these perfections which are participated in different degrees would have no meaning unless there exists at the same time a supreme degree of this perfection and unless that supreme perfection be in itself unparticipated, essentially such, and hence subsistent.

This supreme degree of perfection is both the cause of the intelligibility of the degrees and of the being of the perfections. In the fourth way it is the intelligibility of these perfections that is directly and explicitly considered. However, it is clear that the perfections hold their existence also from the supreme degree. But the formal and explicit argument of the fourth way is: Given the existence of the perfections, how explain the intelligibility or order of the differing degrees? That is why the fourth way is said to be grounded explicitly in exemplary causality and only implicitly in efficient causality, and why it is sometimes called a proof from truth rather than a proof from being. (Text: *Summa Contra Gentiles*, II, Ch. 15. Here the argument is expounded more completely.)

E. THE FIFTH WAY: THE PROOF OF THE EXISTENCE OF GOD FROM THE FINALIZED ACTIVITY OF NATURAL BEINGS

1. Prenote

The five ways of St. Thomas as they succeed one another become increasingly metaphysical. Each way exploits to a greater degree than the last the actuality of things. Motion, or an existent as changing, is for us the most obvious and manifest characteristic of sensible beings. Thus this evidence constitutes a good starting point; it is a good first way. But in itself such a characteristic of being is the least perfect and least stable manifestation of existential act. For here the very being of change is becoming, the reality of change consisting precisely in an ordering or movement to further being.

The second way is more actual than the first, for here our evidence is not the change itself that a being is undergoing in its existence, but the activity that is responsible for such a change.

The third way analyzes the natures from which such activity flows, which natures, as possessive of substantial being, are more perfect and stable than the accidental activity they exercise. But in the third way we analyzed these natures from the aspect of their corruptibility and contingency. We considered substantial being precisely as imperfect, namely, as corruptible and contingent.

In the fourth way our concern was an explicitly metaphysical one. For in this way we analyzed existents insofar as they manifested perfections that as such involved no imperfection, the minoration of these perfections being due to the limiting essence in which they were exercised. But the perfections themselves, as considered apart from their limiting principle, had nothing of contingency or imperfection about them.

The fifth way, the way of wisdom, is directly concerned with the existent as most actual. Here the transcendent property of being that this way considers is being as good, as perfect; hence, as desirable and therefore as finalizing the activity of natural agents. Thus the causality involved in the fifth way is final causality.

The student's knowledge of the general metaphysics of finality will be presupposed in our discussion of this fifth way. However, one or two statements about finality should be recalled here which bear more directly upon our demonstration. St. Thomas has described the final cause as the cause of causes and the cause of the causality in all causes. [33] It is both first and last; first in the order of intention and last in the order of execution. As actually exercising its causality, as actually "moving" or drawing the agent to its act, the end is in the intentional order, although what the agent desires because of this knowledge of the end is precisely the obtaining or effecting of the end in the real order.

A simple example will make these matters clear. If an artist desires to paint a picture, this desire must be founded in some knowledge, a knowledge of "a picture to be painted." Only if such knowledge is present can his efficiency be "finalized" toward its end. But what he wants to paint is a real picture. He desires the production of a real picture, but he is finalized to begin this production by his *knowledge* of a picture. The end as intended, as wanted, is the end as causing. This desire moves him to paint a picture; and the painted picture is the end as produced. Thus this end is last in the order of execution. For when the picture is finished, the desire of the artist is fulfilled, his efficiency ceases, and the total causal process comes to an end.

The importance of these considerations in the understanding of the fifth way will become clear as we proceed with the actual proof. But since the end as causing is the end as intended, and since the end as intended is the end as known, we can begin to understand how the presence of finality in the world demands the presence of an intellect that knows the ends for which things act and can thus direct such beings in their activity.

[33] See *S.T.*, I, 5, 4; I–II, 1, 2; *In V Metaphy.*, lect. 2, no. 775.

2. The Problem of the Fifth Way

In this fifth way, as in all the others, our starting point is an evident fact of experience; our everyday experience that natural beings act for definite and determined ends. We experience that the activity of fire, for example, always produces heat, ice always produces cold; a cat will always generate kittens and a dog puppies, and so forth. When the mind understands that natural beings always act in the same way, [34] it sees upon reflection that the end produced by this action of the natural being must be somehow intended. It sees that the action must be directed toward this end.

But what is directing the action, and hence the agent, toward this end? To direct something toward an end presupposes that the one so directing wants or intends that end, and so must know it. The bowman, for example, can direct the arrow toward the target only because the bowman knows the target is there and wants to hit it. But knowledge of the end to be attained presupposes an intellect that possesses this knowledge, that knows this end. Now natural things like fire and ice and dogs and cats do not have an intellect. So on the one hand we have natural beings that have no intellect, and on the other we see them always acting for the same end, and thus really directed toward an end that is forseen and desired. Therefore the presence of some intelligence is necessarily involved. We say that this must be ultimately a divine or subsistent intelligence—the intellect of God.

Thus from the fact that natural things act for an end we can demonstrate the existence of God. The problem of the fifth way can be stated as follows: From the regular and uniform actions of natural beings does it follow that these beings are acting for an end? And if they are acting for an end, does this fact presuppose an intellect that is directing them to their end? And from this intellect directing them to an end, does it follow that there must exist an intellect that is its own end, and therefore an infinite and subsistent intelligence, which is God?

[34] Or almost always; for if an action of an agent is interfered with, it may not produce its proper effect. Fire, for example, may not burn the log if the latter is soaking wet. The water interferes with the action of the fire and prevents it from producing in the log its usual heat.

3. Solution

a. The proof that there is finality in the universe

It is a fact of evident experience that the natural beings[35] around us always act in a uniform and regular fashion. We see that things always act in the same way and produce the same effects. They are never defective in their natural activity unless interfered with or impeded by some outside influence. Thus, for example, grape vines always produce grapes, and fig trees figs; when grapes ferment, we get wine, not beer; when wine is distilled, brandy is formed, not water, and so forth.

Thus we can conclude from this regular and uniform activity of natural agents that these agents are ordered to these ends, to the production of these determined effects. A determined way of acting manifests a determined order or relation between the agent, its activity and the effect produced by this activity. This definite order that obtains between the agent, its act, and the end or effect produced by the act we call finality. An agent is finalized or ordered to a certain act, and the act on its part is finalized or ordered to a certain term or effect that it produces.

Let us analyze this order a little more carefully. The determination that we find in the effect would not be present there unless that determination were already somehow contained in the action that produces the effect. Puppies would not be puppies unless they were produced by an action ordering to the production of puppies, and hence an action containing the determination that it produces in the effect. But let us go a step further: this action itself would not be ordered to the production of puppies (a determined effect) unless the agent in its turn was ordered to this kind of action. Thus the determination found in the effect is somehow pre-contained in the agent producing the effect. An agent can act in a determined manner only because the effect to be produced by the agent is already from the very beginning pre-contained in it.

[35] Natural beings are the products of nature. They are opposed here to artifacts, the products of man through art.

If this is so, then it follows that the agent received the determination of its activity from the effect or term that is to be produced. Thus the agent is ordered to its term. This is another way of saying that there is present a finality in the activity of natural things. If natural agents were not so finalized, the regularity and constancy of their activity would be unintelligible. If a natural agent were not determined to the production of a definite effect, there would be no reason why it should produce this effect rather than some other. If, for example, fire were not ordered to the production of heat, there would be no reason why fire should burn an object rather than cool it. If an agent produces a determined effect, it follows that it is ordered to that effect; the effect, therefore, has the aspect or characteristic of an end. [36]

The only explanation, therefore, of the constancy and regularity present in the activity of natural agents is the principle of finality. A determined effect would not be produced unless that effect was somehow already present in the agent before it acted. Now it is obvious that the effect to be produced is not pre-contained in its cause according to the *real* existence of that effect, since as an effect *to be produced* it has as yet *no* real existence. The effect to be produced must therefore pre-exist in the agent according to some *intentional existence,* and according to this existence it orders the agent to the production of a determined act, and thus influences or "moves" the agent. This influx or "motion" of the form of the term to be produced as influencing the production of the real or existential term is the causality of the end.

What we have said concerning the action of a single agent for a single end holds true also for the co-operation of many agents for a single end; for example, the constant recurrence of the seasons of the year, the action of the sun and the rain and the winds for the maintenance and growth of life upon the earth. It is also true of many actions of one agent acting for the good of the whole, as in the case of living beings. If all these agents, or if all these actions, work together for one determined end, that can only be because the end is somehow intended, somehow willed or desired of set

[36] See St. Thomas, *S.T.,* I–II, 1, 1.

purpose. Many different and diverse actions or agents cannot possibly act for a single determined and definite end unless they are ordered or directed toward that end. And they cannot be so ordered or directed toward that end unless the end be intended or willed of set purpose. But an end cannot be willed or desired unless it be somehow known. This brings us to the second step in our proof; namely, the fact that an agent acts for an end presupposes the existence of an intellect that knows that end.

b. Finality demands an intellect that is distinct from the world

Why finality or the ordering of something to an end demands an intellect is easy to understand. Between the agent, the action and the effect there is a certain proportion or relationship. The eye is made for seeing, and so it is constructed accordingly. It is not constructed like a hand or a foot, because its proper action is to see, not to walk or to hold things. An examination of the eye shows that it is correctly constructed for the reception of sense images or colored objects; and because of this knowledge man can make lenses and manufacture cameras to obtain somewhat the same result. In a hundred ways man can imitate nature, because he recognizes in natural things the presence of the correct means for the desired end.

But this proportion of means to end indicates that among the many possible means those were chosen that were apt and fitting for the end; therefore, this fittingness and proportion was known. This selection of means to end is the proper work of an intelligence. For to apprehend an object as an end is to know it as something to which other things are ordered, and this means to see the object under a certain universal aspect or condition. And this is to abstract the object from its concrete material condition and see it simply as something to which other things are ordered. But such abstraction from matter requires an intellect. It belongs then to an intellect to contain within itself the forms of things and their relations and proportions, even before the actual order of natural things comes into existence. Here is how St. Thomas explains this:

It belongs to the wise man to order. For the ordering of things is impossible unless there is known the relation and proportion that the things to be ordered have to one another and the order they have to the higher thing that is their end. [Just as in the case of the eye, there is an ordering or a proportion of the various parts among themselves and then the further ordering of the whole eye to the higher end, which is the act of vision.] For the order of things to one another is because of their order to the end. Now to know the relationships and proportions of things to one another can be done only by one having an intellect.[37]

Thus we see that to order either oneself to an end or to order something else to an end can be done only by an agent that possesses an intellect. Natural beings that have no intellect tend by a natural inclination toward their end. Some of these, like brute animals, tend naturally (that is to say, by the inclination or orientation of their very nature) toward an end that they apprehend. But a brute animal does not apprehend the end as end, but simply as this concrete sensible thing. Other natural beings, that have no cognition whatsoever, tend naturally toward an end they in no wise apprehend. In all these cases the end is either not known or not known as such. Therefore, such beings do not order either themselves nor any other thing to their end. Instead, they are ordered, they are directed to their end.

If, therefore, this determinate ordering of an agent to its end is to be rendered intelligible, if this order is to have any reason for existing, we must arrive at some agent that has within itself the idea of the term to be produced. We must arrive at an agent that knows the end as such. This agent will be really distinct from these natural things that are ordered to their end, as one having an intellect is really distinct from that which does not have an intellect, or as the one who orders is distinct from the one who is ordered. St. Thomas puts the matter clearly:

The end is determined for an agent by some other principal agent; as is clear, for example, in the motion of an arrow, which is moved indeed to a determined end, but to an end that has been determined for the arrow by the bowman. So, likewise, in the motion or operation of a

[37] *C.G.*, II, Ch. 24. Words in brackets added.

natural being; this, too, is toward a determined end; and this, too, pre-supposes an intellect, which establishes the end of the nature and orders the nature to that end.[38]

Natural things which are destitute of an intellect cannot possibly direct themselves to their end. These beings cannot establish for themselves their end since they do not know the end. Thus this end must be established for them by another; namely, by the one who has given them their natures. Nor could he establish this end for a nature unless he possessed understanding.

c. The supreme orderer is God

All that remains now is to show that this supreme orderer of the universe is God. To order or direct a nature to an end means that the end must be known and hence must pre-exist within an intellect. This intellect may either possess of itself this knowledge of the order, or it may have received this knowledge from another. If these ideas or forms of the ends to be produced are had by this intellect of itself, these ideas would be one with the nature of the intellect. As the first source of all order in other things, this intelligence would be its own end and ordered to nothing outside itself. And such an intellect would be infinite. But if this knowledge has been received from another, then such an intellect might know the order that is in the world, but it would not be the cause or source of this order. And that is why if the very order and finality that is in the material world is to be rendered intelligible, we must posit an intellect that is the very first cause and source of this order.

Here two things should be carefully noted. The first is that in going from an intellect that has received this knowledge of the order from another to that intellect that has this knowledge of it-self, we have not left the order of final causality and taken up a new argument on the plane of contingency and efficient causality. For we are still looking "in the same direction"; namely, for the ultimate source of order in our material world.

The second point to note is this: it is quite impossible for any finite intellect to be the cause of the order that exists in natural

[38] *De Veritate*, qu. 5, a. 1.

beings. It would be metaphysically impossible for God to be the first cause of the nature of a being and for some finite intelligence below God to be the first cause that orders this nature to its end. For what the nature of a being is, is determined by the end to which it is ordered. The nature and the end of that nature are inseparable in their being. It is because God wished to create beings that could think that he endowed them with rational natures and the power of understanding.

It must necessarily be the creator of this universe that pre-established the end of the universe, as well as the particular ends of all the natures that people this universe. It is impossible for God, say, to cause fire, and then for some finite intellect to direct this nature to its end, which is to exercise the act of heating and by so doing to produce heat in other bodies. For it is of the nature of fire to exercise the act of heating and thus to generate heat in other bodies. It is because the creator wanted to produce a being that could exercise this act, that he has caused such a nature as fire to exist.

4. Answering the Objections

1) *Materialists and determinists.* Our first objection against the fifth way comes from those philosophers who deny the very principle of finality in the activity of natural things. These are the materialists of all ages, from Epicurus and Democritus among the ancient Greeks, to Spencer, Darwin and Julian Huxley [39] among the moderns and contemporaries. The latter-named are also material evolutionists. All these deny that natural things act for an end or a purpose, and explain all the actions of beings by efficient causality alone. As summed up by Aristotle long ago, for these men, "rain does not fall from the sky that the grain might grow, but simply from necessity. For what is taken up to a great height must of necessity become cold, and becoming cold, it changes into

[39] For some references and texts of Darwin and Spencer, see Descoqs, *Praelectiones Theologiae naturalis* (Paris, 1935), Vol. 2, pp. 827–331. For Julian Huxley, see "Rationalism and the Idea of God," in *Essays of a Biologist* (London, Pelican Books, 1939), Ch. 6, and Etiènne Gilson's comments in *God and Philosophy* (New Haven, Yale University Press, 1941), pp. 128 ff.

water, and water being heavy must fall." [40] All of which proves for them that there is a necessity in the actions of natural things, not that there is any finality or purpose in these actions.

The trouble with these early materialists is that they did not go far enough in their analysis of this necessity. For a philosopher can still ask himself *why* fire *necessarily* burns and ice *necessarily* cools. Does not the very presence of necessary or determined actions presuppose the presence of finality in this activity? If fire burns rather than cools, it must be because the nature of fire is ordered to burning rather than to cooling. Fire is ordered to its act; if there were no ordering there would be no acting, for there would be no reason in the being why this effect should proceed from it rather than some other or opposite effect. Either these things are ordered to their acts or they do not act. But we see that they do act; therefore, they are ordered to their acts. And if they are ordered to their acts, they must be ordered by something that knows the end or term to which they are so ordered. These early materialists simply did not go far enough in their reflections upon the activity of natural beings.

The modern materialists and the materialistic evolutionists have tried to remedy this *lacuna* in the thought of their predecessors. For this purpose they appeal to two pseudo-scientific surrogates for philosophical causes. For the efficient cause of the philosopher they have substituted time, and for the final cause of the philosopher they have substituted chance. And so they argue as follows: given a sufficient length of time, the present order we find in the world could well have been, and in fact is, the result of chance.

We can explain their position by a simple example. The Bible as we have it today is made up of a certain order or sequence of different letters. The various possible combinations of these letters, while mathematically overwhelming, are still finite in number. Therefore, given a sufficient length of time and trying one combination after another, there is no contradiction to say that sooner or later you would come up with the combination of letters that is our present Bible. So, too, with the order in this world. The uni-

[40] *Physics,* Bk. II, Ch. 8 (198b18).

verse is made up of particles of matter or energy existing in a certain combination or order. This combination, or order, could be merely the result of chance and a considerable length of time. Thus these scientists see no need for any principle of finality or for a God who is ordering things to an end.

What is our answer to all this? First of all, as far as possibilities go, if you throw into the air all the letters of the Bible they might come down the very first time just as they are found in the King James Version, even with all the footnotes nicely in place. So, too, the very first coming together of atoms could have resulted in the present order that exists in the world. But in the very first combination of the simplest of elements or gases, or whatever we call the primordial material being, there was activity. And being existential activity, it was a determined kind of activity. Why did this first particle act this way rather than that? Why did it act at all? If it acted at all, it acted in a determined way, and if it acted in a determined way, it was ordered to this act. And if it was ordered in this act, this order was intended.

A philosopher sees that the very activity of natural things presupposes finality and hence an intellect, just as the philosopher sees that the existence of natural things presupposes an efficient cause who is infinite and subsistent Being. Now a scientist, as a scientist, may not be expected to follow this reasoning, since it is philosophical rather than scientific; but it is not for that reason any less real or legitimate. The scientist as a philosopher, or maybe even as man, should be able to see it, provided he is willing to exercise his intelligence outside the limits of a strictly positive scientific method.

But someone may say: things can happen by chance, can they not? To which we answer, yes. And chance means that the action produces an effect that was not intended by the agent? Perfectly correct. Therefore, the present order in the world could have come about by chance, and since it is the only order we know, we cannot use it to show there is finality and hence a God who knows the order? This time the answer is no.

First of all, chance is intelligible only on the supposition that order exists. For example, if all truths were doubtful, you would not know they were doubtful, since you would not know they were not certain. Just as doubt presupposes certitude, so chance presupposes order. For chance is a privation of order, just as doubt is a privation of certitude; and so chance is intelligible only in terms of the order which it lacks. Therefore, chance can no more give rise to order than blindness can give rise to sight or doubt can give rise to certitude. A perfection cannot be caused by the very privation of that perfection. A thousand blind men will never add up to one man who can see, and a thousand chances will never add up to one instance of real order.

Recall from metaphysics how chance arises. Being "A" acts according to its nature, that is, for a determined end; being "B" also acts according to its nature; again, for a determined end. The two actions intervene and an effect is produced which is not the end of either of these agents or of either of their actions. We say the effect took place by chance. This effect or term is not ordered, at least not from the viewpoints of the immediate agents involved. But this term does presuppose order. So the occasional presence of chance events in our world, like monsters and floods and earthquakes, far from disproving finality actually proves it, for it presupposes it. It presupposes an order which in this particular instance is lacking.

2) *Kant* [41] *and the Kantians* see in the fifth way of St. Thomas a simple and naive anthrophomorphism. Man sees that he acts for an end and has a purpose in what he does. He washes because he wants to clean his face; he studies because he wants to become a philosopher. And then man transfers this notion of purpose to non-human beings and asserts that they also, when they act, must be acting for an end or purpose. But it is highly arbitrary to transfer finality found in man to finality in the universe.

[41] The younger Kant, for example in his work *General Natural History and Theory of the Heavens* (1775), highly praised and commended the proof for God's existence from the order in the universe. But he criticizes this proof as anthropomorphic in the works of his maturity, for example, in both his *Critique of Pure Reason* (1781) and his *Critique of Judgment* (1790). He allowed to the principle of finality, at best, only a heuristic value for knowledge.

As is quite clear from our solution, St. Thomas in his fifth way makes no such transfer. We did not start with any analysis of human activity but with the regular and constant activity of things that have no intellect. And we did not conclude to the presence of an intellect ordering natural things by way of an analogy with our own human intellect, but by way of necessity, to explain the existence of the very order present in such activity. Furthermore, our own human intellect is itself a natural power that is ordered to its proper end. For man does not order his intellect to the truth; he finds that of its very nature it is already ordered to the truth. And man finds that his will is naturally finalized toward good. While man can order himself in many of his actions for ends that he sets up for himself, he nevertheless finds his powers initially finalized toward ends that he has not established, but toward which these powers tend of their very nature.

But if natural things are ordered by their very nature to their proper end, such ordering is intrinsic and from within, and so they need not be ordered from without by an intellect distinct from these natural beings. The answer to such an objection should be obvious. A natural being is ordered to its proper end both by its nature and by an intellect. Immediately and intrinsically, it is ordered by its nature, but ultimately and extrinsically, it is so ordered by the divine intellect who has established the end and created the nature.

Finally, we should be careful not to confuse the fifth way of St. Thomas Aquinas, which argues from the existence of order in the universe to the existence of an infinite intelligence, with Paley's argument from design. [42] In the latter's argument the universe is seen as a complicated and intricate machine. And just as one who sees a complicated and intricate watch reasons to the existence of a watchmaker, so man, seeing the vast machine that is this world reasons, by way of analogy, to the existence of a divine watchmaker, or supreme architect of the universe.

This argument from design, as given by Paley and unfortu-

[42] See William (Bishop) Paley, *Natural Theology* (New York, Harper and Brothers, 1855), Vol. 1, pp. 37 and following.

nately repeated in many books on Christian apologetics, does not prove the existence of God. An architect of the universe would have to be a very clever being, but he would not have to be God; no more than a maker of watches would have to be God. [43] Also, like many a watchmaker, he may well have ceased to exist, as far as this proof is concerned, and his machine would be running quite smoothly without him. Many of the objections directed against what some writers believe is the fifth way of St. Thomas are really directed against the watchmaker of Paley. St. Thomas's proof is entirely different. It is grounded in the metaphysics of finality, namely, in the existence of order. And this order, which is a kind of being, demands as its cause the here and now existence of a supreme intelligence which is also supreme Being.

3) *The Creative Evolutionists,* such as Bergson and Le Roy, do indeed admit finality, but it is not a pre-ordered or pre-determined finality. Things act for an end, but they do not find the end ready made for them; rather they create the end themselves. The end is immanent in the very thing that acts; it is nature in its most vital and existentially creative moment. What these philosophers want to avoid is a universe with a pre-ordained history. Finite being does not tend to some pre-existing exemplar or ideal which it strives to attain or imitate. If this were so, then the end of all things, at least in the intentional order, would already be a given fact. If the activity of natural things were governed by fixed and eternal laws, the future would simply be an endlessly repeated present. It is much more in keeping with the flux and rhythm of the universe to say that it progresses by creating its effects, which are not given beforehand as ends, let alone as foreseen and pre-ordained ends. To say otherwise would reduce the universe to a relative staticism; whereas it is a complete and perfect dynamism. So the end of the universe should not be considered as something foreseen and willed by a supreme and separate intellect. [44]

To this objection we answer: (1) to say that things create their

[43] See E. Gilson, *God and Philosophy, op. cit.,* p. 142.
[44] See Father Descoqs, *op. cit.,* II, pp. 332–342; H. Bergson, *Creative Evolution,* translated by Arthur Mitchell (London, Macmillan, 1911), pp. 57 ff.

own ends is to render all activity in the universe simply impossible; (2) the fact that the universe is governed by finality in no way subtracts either from its dynamism (which creative evolution destroys) or its history. The first point is easy to see. For something to create its own end is a contradiction, since the action which creates the end must itself be an action without an end, since the existence of the end depends upon the existence of the action. For Bergson, until the action is posited, no end exists, either in the real or intentional order. There is no reason, therefore, why the agent should act at all, or act in one way rather than another. On the supposition that agents create their own ends, all real activity is rendered impossible.

The second point deserves a fuller treatment than can be given here. We will have to content ourselves with two or three statements of fact. The Being of God is infinitely perfect and infinitely in act. The divine intellect knows the end of each being, the relations things have among themselves and their higher order to the good of the whole universe, whose end is God himself. The knowledge of this order by God constitutes, as we shall see later, divine providence. Now there is nothing static in a universe where things imitate and share in the being and activity of God. And since our universe is hierarchical, with one thing ordered to another, and all ordered to the good of the whole universe, there is room for endless progress and evolution in the universe.

And while God himself has no history, since his Being is measured by eternity and possessed by him wholly all at once, his universe unfolds in time and does have a history. The Being of God, since it is measured by eternity, physically and really co-exists with all times—past, present, and future. And when we recall that this divine Being is the proper cause of the being of all things, holding them in existence by his power and directing them by his providence, we see how God can bring things to ever higher and perfect ends, in a dynamic and evolutionary sweep that knows no bounds, since its source and its end is infinite and perfect Being.

4) A wise orderer does not destroy what he makes; for this is useless and against the notion of wisdom. One who is wise takes

care of what he has produced. But among things of nature some are contrary to others and destructive of others. There does not exist, therefore, a supreme orderer of the world.

We reply that a wise orderer not only attends to what is helpful for the individuals he has made but also to what is beneficial for the whole. Although the destruction of one thing in the universe is not good for that thing, it is, nevertheless, good for the perfection of the universe. By reason of the continual birth and destruction of individuals the perpetual being of the various species is preserved, in which the perfection of the universe necessarily consists.

5) At least moral evils, since they are especially repugnant to the divine orderer, must not be permitted in the world. Because moral evil is present in human acts, it seems that the supreme orderer of the world does not exist.

We reply that moral evil in no way comes from God, but solely from the free will of man; however, it is permitted by God on account of a greater good. St. Thomas writes:

God has a greater love for the greater good and therefore wishes the presence of the greater good than the absence of a lesser evil. Hence, for the purpose of bringing forth greater good, God permits some to do moral evil, which is in itself most repugnant, although one moral evil is more repugnant to God than another; thus to heal one evil he sometimes allows one to fall into another. [45]

It should be added, however, that the achieving by God of a greater good is not the final cause or reason for permitting the evil, but only the occasion for its being permitted. There will be more on this subject in the treatise on Divine Providence.

5. Summary of the Fifth Way

"From the presence of order or finality in the world the existence of God is demonstrated under the intelligibility of supreme orderer."

[45] *De Veritate*, qu. 5, a. 5 ad 3.

a. State of the question

In the fourth way the intellect, considering the various degrees of perfections, attained to God as the supreme degree of these perfections. This way has been aptly designated the way of contemplation. By contemplating these grades of beings, the intellect comes to understand that there is in the world a kind of splendor arising from its order. In the fifth way, we consider this order. What is order? Does it exist in the world? If it exists, what consequences does this fact hold? From the presence of order in the world we can demonstrate the existence of God as the ultimate source of this order, or as the supreme orderer of all things. And since it is the office of the wise man to order, this way is correctly named the way of wisdom. As we progress along this way we see how all things have been ordered by God.

b. Explanation of terms

1) "*. . . order . . .*"—some proportion or relationship between two or more things. These things which are ordered are either distinct as complete beings or as principles of being. Thus, for example, matter is ordered to form, substance to accidents, essence to the act of existing, nature to operation, operation to its object, and so forth.

2) "*end*"—that on account of which something acts or that toward which something is ordered; for example, form is the end of matter, operation the end of a nature, the completed work is the end of the operation, and so forth. The end, moreover, perfects the thing because it is its good and the cause of the thing's activity. Everything seeks after good. Therefore, the end always contains the intelligibility of good and the good that of end.

3) "*. . . finality . . .*"—the very order toward the end, or the ordination. This ordination is determined and definite for each nature.

4) *Final causality*—the influence of the end upon the operation of the agent. This influence, as such, is in the order of knowledge. For the end as the achieved effect does not yet exist in the real

order. The causality of end lies in the attraction the end has as something to be accomplished or attained. Therefore, the causality which the end exerts always presupposes an intellect in which the term to be produced intentionally exists.

5) ". . . *the existence of God is demonstrated* . . ."—that is, as supreme intellect in which there exists intentionally the term to be accomplished by each thing. We say the term exists in God intentionally because it exists there both as end and as thing known, or as an idea.

6) ". . . *supreme orderer* . . ."—insofar as God possessing knowledge of the end of all things can direct them to their end.

c. Adversaries

1) *The order in the world is the result of chance.* Epicurus, Democritus, Lucretius, and among the moderns, all the Materialistic Mechanists, most Positivists and many Evolutionists, deny that there is finality in the world: thus, for example, Buchner, Haeckel, Littre, Darwin, Spencer, the Marxists.

2) *The order in the world is the result of necessity,* that is, the result of blind fate and not of an intellect: Heraclitus, Empedocles, and others.

3) *Kant,* in his later years, having succumbed to the influence of Humean empiricism, said that this argument possessed no probative force, since the concept of finality was anthropomorphic and had sprung from an unwarranted application of the laws of human activity to the activities of the things of nature. However, even if it is invalid in metaphysics, Kant said that the principle of finality does lead us to *believe* in God.

4) *Many idealists,* although they do not deny the finality in the world, admit only an immanent finality; there is no ordering cause really distinct from the things which are ordered. Thus Hegel, Renan, Richet, Goblot, and others.

5) *Bergson, Le Roy,* and other adherents of the Philosophy of Becoming assert that natural things do not act like an architect who by the use of certain means attains an end which he had previously set up for himself, but rather like an inventor, who con-

tinually searches and experiments until he finds an end. Therefore for these philosophers the end is more of a force which pushes rather than one which attracts; it is more a push from behind than an attraction from the front. Natural things give rise to their end by their own spontaneous activity.

d. The argument: The fact of experience with which this proof begins

The things of nature always or almost always act in the same manner; therefore, their actions are determined and definite; for example, fire heats things, animals give birth to offspring of the same species, and so on. From this fact we argue in the following manner:

1) From the regularity of actions, there follows that there is an order between the agent, its operation and the effect.

2) From this order it follows that all agents act for an end.

3) From the fact that the things of nature act for an end, it follows that this end must be foreknown.

4) But knowledge of an end presupposes an intellect which knows the end.

5) But natural things which act for a known end lack an intellect.

6) Therefore there must exist an intellect distinct from these things, in the manner that a thing not possessing an intellect is distinct from one having an intellect.

7) Moreover, this intellect which has knowledge of the ordination of things toward their end either has this knowledge of itself or from another.

8) But there cannot be an infinite regress in intellects having this knowledge from another. Therefore, there must exist a supreme intellect which is the first cause of all things in the order of finality and which guides them to their proper ends. And this is God.

e. The proof for each step of the argument

1) That which regularly and constantly produces the same effect is determined to that effect. For if the agent is not determined

to this effect, there is no reason why it should produce this effect rather than some other. An agent which is not determined to some effect would not attain any effect. But, as a matter of fact, it does. Therefore, it is determined to an effect; and this is to act for an end. (Conclusion of No. 2.)

3) That this end must pre-exist in the agent is clear. For the end determines the agent in its action and, therefore, must be in the agent in some way. But the end as effect does not yet exist. Thus it must be intentionally present in the agent before it exists as effect.

4) That which is intended must be known because nothing is desired unless it is known. But the end which is intended is an object of desire. Therefore, it must be known.

5) That many natural things have no intellect is clear. Brutes act for an end apprehended in sense knowledge; therefore, the end is not known as end but as something concretely pleasant or harmful. Plants and other natural things in no way apprehend an end. But the end must be known as end; otherwise the thing cannot be directed to it. Now the things of nature are directed to an end; therefore, there must exist an intellect distinct from these things. (Conclusion of No. 6.)

7) For an intellect to have this knowledge of itself or from another is a complete disjunction. If knowledge of the end is from another, it is apparent that the intellect knows the order in our world, but it cannot cause this order, because this knowledge is from another.

8) If there were an infinite regress, the order in this world would not be rendered intelligible because there would not be a first cause to order things towards their end. There must exist an intellect which possesses of itself and by itself the knowledge of the order in this world. In this intellect the ideas, or the forms of the terms to be produced, have not been received from another. Hence they are of the same nature as the intellect itself. Therefore this intellect is first truth, the establisher of natures and the ordainer of their ends. And this is God.

F. APPENDIX TO FIFTH WAY: CAN THE EXISTENCE OF GOD, UNDER THE TERM OF A SUPREME LAWGIVER, BE PROVED FROM THE EXISTENCE OF MORAL OBLIGATION?

A proof from moral obligation can be made, but it is really only a special instance of the fifth way. For to be obligated to an end is simply a special way of being ordered to an end. This obligation to an end is not something subjective. It is an objective fact of man's nature, based on that nature as intellectual and free. Thus man does not oblige himself; he *is obliged,* and hence he is obliged *by another.* And that which obliges another to act in a certain fashion is a lawgiver. Thus we can conclude that if the obligation man finds in his own nature is to be rendered completely and adequately intelligible, it can be done so only on the supposition that there exists a supreme lawgiver, which, while respecting the freedom of the rational creature, obliges or binds this creature to do good and to avoid evil.

Our proof, therefore, consists first in showing that moral obligation does exist. This is a fact of experience to which man's conscience bears witness. Man knows that he is physically free to kill, cheat, lie, and so forth. But he knows that he is not morally free to do so; that is to say, he sees that he is obliged by his nature to avoid these things. If he does not, he goes contrary to his nature and commits moral evil. Thus man sees at one and the same time that he is lord of his actions, in the sense that he can do good or evil; and that he is subject to the law of his nature: to do evil is morally wrong and goes contrary to his nature. Thus by his nature, a law is imposed upon man to do good and avoid evil.

The reality of moral obligation is not something merely subjective. Obligation belongs by necessity to man's nature and cannot be violated without weakening and destroying that nature. As we have already seen, a nature that is not ordered to a determined end, could not exist; it would be nothing. For what a nature is, is determined by the end to which it is ordered. Otherwise it could not act, and hence could not exist. Therefore, human nature, as endowed with intelligence and freedom, if it were not obliged to do good and avoid evil, would be a contradiction in terms. It would be and not be a nature endowed with intelligence and free will. Thus obligation is as objective a fact as human nature itself. Moral obligation is simply a special case of the principle of finality. To be obliged is to be ordered to act in a certain fashion. The judgment or proposition, "good must be done and evil must be avoided," is as immediately evident to the practical intellect as the judgment "every agent acts for an end" is to the speculative intellect. [46]

Whence flows this obligation upon the will to do good and avoid evil? From man's nature? Obviously, but only proximately from his nature. Since man's nature does not oblige itself, but rather finds itself obliged, the nature of man is not itself the ultimate source of this obligation. The ultimate source of obligation must be a Being who is its own end, and therefore the first norm of morality for all other free beings. Otherwise obligation is not completely intelligible and has no adequate cause for being. There must exist a supreme lawgiver. And this lawgiver is God. For God alone has dominion over human nature, directing an intelligent and free nature to its proper moral end, that is, obliging it to do good and avoid evil.

G. CAN THE EXISTENCE OF GOD BE DEMONSTRATED FROM THE EXISTENCE OF A GENERAL CONSENSUS OF MANKIND?

Is the following argument a genuine demonstration of the existence of God? It is a fact that, considering the history of the human race as a whole, all nations at all times and in all places have generally believed in the existence of a superior being deserving of worship and upon whom man depends in many ways. Now the only sufficient reason for the existence of such a continuing and universal consent among men must be the objective fact that there is a God. No other fact could adequately explain the existence of

[46] On this point, read S.T., I-II, 94, 2.

this general conviction of mankind. Therefore God exists as the only sufficient reason for the existence of this conviction.

A little reflection should make it clear that such an argument is not a valid demonstration for the existence of God. The proof has a certain suasive value, but of itself it does not constitute a demonstration. And this for many reasons. First of all, the gods of the Gentiles were usually false gods; secondly, the cause of the conviction that a god or gods existed was often simple human faith, or human fear, or superstition and not the objective evidence of being. Where such objective evidence is the motive for this conviction, the validity of the conviction is not founded upon the general consent itself, but upon the evidence. And this evidence will be one or other of the five ways. Independently of such evidence, the argument from common consent is not conclusive. In a word, the existence of this common conviction *as such* does not constitute a separate valid demonstration for the existence of God, since such consent, to be valid and objective, must itself be grounded in one of the *a posteriori* proofs already considered. [47]

H. A GENERAL PROOF FOR GOD'S EXISTENCE

Having studied in detail the five ways of St. Thomas for establishing God's existence, let us turn our attention to a more general proof that underlies any Thomistic demonstration that proceeds from the being of our experience to the Being of God. Such a proof is drawn from a consideration of the act of existing and the proper cause of such an act. We will present this proof in a rather summary form, but with sufficient development so that it can be grasped by the student, provided he recalls carefully to mind what he learned in general metaphysics concerning the act of existing and the principles governing proper causality.

Our proof begins with a reflection upon the existing things around us. The purpose of this reflection is to see, in a general fashion, that within a being there is a difference between what the being is and the act of existing by which it is. Let us consider sev-

[47] See Appendix C for some invalid proofs from positive science for the existence of God.

eral different existing things: this red rose, this white horse, this newborn babe. Obviously, these are different kinds of being; a rose is not a horse, nor a horse a baby. And yet while they are different kinds of being, all these beings have something in common: they all are, they all exist. Therefore, at one and the same time they have something in common and they are different.

Why do they differ? Because each has a different essence, each is different in what it is. And what do they share in common? Existence; each one is, each possesses an act of existing proportioned to its essence. If I ask what each of these beings is, I get three different answers. But if I ask whether each being is, I get the same answer. Now, as is evident, when two beings differ and are alike at the same time, that principle in the being by which they are different, namely their essence, cannot at the same time be that by which they are alike, namely, their act of existing, which all have in common, although in varying degrees.

To the answer to the question, what a thing is, corresponds the essence of that existing thing. To the answer to the question, whether the thing is, corresponds the existence of the thing. And since we have seen that these two principles cannot be the same in the thing, it follows that there is a real distinction in the thing between the essence and the act of that essence—existence. Or to put it positively, there is in the thing an actual composition between essence and existence. [48]

Second step of proof. This step of the proof consists in showing that only a Being whose proper nature or essence is "to exist" can be the proper cause of the existence of other beings. Or to put it another way, the perfection of existence can never be the proper effect of any being in which there is an actual composition between its essence and its act of existing.

[48] Notice, we are not saying here, in this general Thomistic proof for the existence of God, that any and every philosophical proof for God's existence is based on the actual distinction within a finite being of its essence and act of existing. But what we are saying is this: in our opinion every proof for the existence of God based upon *St. Thomas's* notion of being either presupposes this actual distinction or establishes it in the course of the demonstration. That the nature of such a distinction can be easily misunderstood goes without saying.

Existence (*esse*) is the common effect of all finite causes, for every cause influences in some way the existence of its effect, either substantially or accidentally. And since existence is the common effect of all finite causes, it can be the proper effect of no finite cause. But every effect must have its proper cause, something that produces the effect through an activity of its own nature, through an activity proper to itself. And since no finite being is the proper cause of existence, since existence is not the proper nature of any finite thing, the proper cause of existence will be infinite Being.

That uncreated Being is the first and only proper cause of existence (*esse*) is one of the most frequently established themes in the writings of St. Thomas. [49] To him nothing seemed more obvious or easier to prove than this fact. Where we have different causes producing many different effects, the diversity of these effects can only be due to the diversity of the natures involved: every agent acts similar to the way it is. But if there is present in these different effects an element that is common to all of them, this common element cannot be reduced to anything that is proper to these natures. And since existence (*esse*) is the common element produced by every finite nature, existence cannot be the proper effect of any finite nature.

Let us take a simple example to prove this point. A builder causes a house to exist. Fire causes fire to exist. What is proper in the one case is the house, and in the other, the fire. Hence the builder is the proper cause of the *house* and fire is the proper cause of *fire*. But both made their effects exist. Hence, since existence is common to both effects, it is proper neither to the builder nor to the fire. [50]

Two important facts follow from this simple consideration. The first is this: if we are to find the proper cause of existence, we will not find it until we arrive at an agent whose own proper form is an act of existing. Causality is activity; to cause is to educe from potency to act. But eduction from potency to act can only be accom-

---

[49] See, for example, *S.T.*, I, 45, 5, ad 1m; *C.G.*, II, Ch. 15, par. 2; *De Pot.*, qu. 7, a. 2, *resp.*
[50] *De Pot.*, qu. 7, a. 2c.

plished by a being in act. Every agent acts insofar as it is in act. And an agent is in act through its form. Now when we say that an agent is in act through its form, we do not mean to imply that it is the form that actuates a being. Form is act only in the essential order. What form actuates is matter, thereby giving to substance its final complement in the order of essence, rendering substance immediately capable of existential actuality. Through form, substance becomes a fit subject of existence. But it is existence that actuates substance in the order of being. Therefore, a being as being is in act through existence. But a being as agent, as producing this rather than that determinate effect, is in act through its form.

When we say, then, that every agent acts insofar as it is in act, and it is in act through its form, what precisely do we mean? We mean that the form, say the form of man or of fire, limits the existence to the existence of a given particular nature. Hence, when a particular being acts, it will be limited in its activity by what it is, that is, by its form. When it acts, it must, therefore, produce effects that are proportioned to this form. Its proper activity is confined to its proper nature.

Our conclusion, then, becomes clear. Existence as an effect can be proportioned or proper only to that being whose very nature is existence, where, therefore, existence is limited by nothing but itself, that is to say, where it has no limits whatsoever. Such a Being must be pure act, subsistent existence. And this Being we call God.

If only an agent whose very nature is existence can be the proper cause of created existence, then our second important fact becomes obvious. All other agents, insofar as they do produce existence, will do so only as instruments of this proper cause. All created beings do produce existence, because all created beings do participate in "the nature" of existence; [51] but the effect thus produced is not proper to them nor proportioned to them, but only to the Being whose nature is unparticipated, subsistent existence.

If God alone is the only proper cause of existence, then all created effects can remain in existence, only so long as God is con-

[51] *C.G.*, II, Ch. 66, par. 7; *S.T.*, I, 45, 5, ad 1m; *S.T.*, I, 104, 1.

tinually present, causing and preserving this existence. For the removal of a proper cause automatically and immediately results in the removal of what it is properly causing. Thus if any creatures are even conservative causes of existence (*esse*), they will be so only as instruments of the first cause. [52]

Our general proof, then, for the existence of God can be summed up as follows: Every effect must have its own proper cause. A proper cause is one that produces its effect through an activity that is proportioned to its own proper nature. Fire is the proper cause of fire, man is the proper cause of man, since "fire" and "man" are the proper natures of these causes. The proper cause of existence, then, can only be a being whose proper nature is "to exist," where there is no distinction between what that being is and its existence. Hence, from a consideration of beings that share in existence, the mind is led to affirm a Being who is unparticipated existence, a Being who is by reason of his very essence, and who is, therefore, the proper cause of the existence of all other beings. And this necessary Being we call God. [53]

Suggested Readings

1. Etiénne Gilson, *The Christian Philosophy of St. Thomas Aquinas* (New York, Random House, 1956), Chapter III, "The Proofs for the Existence of God," pp. 59–83. Brief clear summaries of each of the five ways.
2. Jacques Maritain, *Approaches to God* (New York, Harper & Brothers, 1954), pp. 16–71. Discussion of some modern objections against the five ways.
3. Joseph Owens, "The Conclusion of the prima via," *The Modern Schoolman* (1952–1953), pp. 33–53.

[52] See *S.T.*, I, 104, 2.

[53] Before going on to the second part of the book (which treats of God's nature), the student should read Appendix D (on Existentialism) and Appendix E (on Atheism).

CHAPTER 5

Man's Knowledge of the Divine Nature

> *Wisdom does not consist merely in knowing that God exists, but in approaching a knowledge of what he is; which indeed we are not able to do in this life except insofar as we know what God is not. For he who knows a thing as it is distinct from all other things, approaches a knowledge of what that thing is.*
>
> —St. Thomas, *On Truth,*
> qu. 10. a. 12, ad 7

A. HOW THE NATURE OF GOD CANNOT BE KNOWN

1. The Problem of Knowing the Nature of God

Having seen that the existence of God can be demonstrated, we are now ready to investigate a new and a different problem, for a philosopher is not only interested in the existence of things but also in investigating their nature or essence. Hence it is quite natural and in accordance with reason that having established the existence of the first cause of being as being, we should now want to understand the *nature* or essence of this first cause. [1] The essence of a thing is that by which a thing is what it is. Can the human mind know *what* this first cause of being is? Or can the mind of man simply arrive at the bare and unqualified fact that there *is* such a cause and no more? That is the precise problem we want to investigate in this present chapter.

[1] See *S.T.*, I, 12, 1.

One fact may be noted at the outset. It is quite impossible to have knowledge that something exists without by that very fact possessing some vague and confused knowledge of what that thing is. [2] And this is so because the very causes that lead me to affirm the existence of this thing lead me also to affirm that existence in some qualified or determined way. Each of the five ways posited the same existing term, but each did so under a slightly different formality. I know that this term is immutable, necessary, unlimited, intelligent, and so forth. In other words, the five ways themselves give the mind some vague knowledge of the nature or essence of the term to which they lead. [3] Thus we have already achieved by means of these very investigations into God's existence more than simple unqualified knowledge that when I say "God exists," all I know is that this proposition is a true proposition. The very truth of this proposition must include some other truths. If this proposition told me *absolutely nothing* about the subject "God" except *mere existence* it could not even tell me this; for I would have no way of distinguishing the existence of God from the existence of any other being. To know that God exists is to know that an unchangeable, necessary, unlimited, intelligent Being exists. And this is already some knowledge "about God's nature."

2. Division of the Problem

We will divide our problem into two parts. First, is God's nature or essence knowable in itself—can it *be known?* Secondly, can it be known by us? Is that essence intelligible for us? This second part, whether God is intelligible for us, will be divided into two questions: first, in what way is God not intelligible for us, and secondly and more importantly, in what way is the divine essence or nature intelligible for us? The solution to this problem is the

[2] See St. Thomas, *De Trin.*, qu. 6, a. 3. " . . . concerning no thing is it possible to know that it is, without having some knowledge of what it is, either a perfect knowledge or a confused kind of knowledge."

[3] In this chapter and throughout the rest of the book, the terms *essence* and *nature* will be used interchangeably. Strictly speaking, there is a difference: the essence of God is that by which God is God, and his nature is this essence considered as the source of his operations.

answer to the all-important question: What knowledge can the human mind have in its present condition of the nature or essence of God?

3. Is the Divine Nature Intelligible in Itself?

Nothing is easier to prove than the fact that the essence of God is knowable or intelligible in itself. Each of the five ways proves that God is intelligible in himself. The first way concluded to the existence of an immobile Being. But that which is immobile is without matter, and that which is without matter is intelligible. Forms when abstracted from matter become actually intelligible. Forms that can exist without matter are actually intelligible. Immateriality is the root of intelligibility. Therefore, God, as the supremely immaterial Being is also the supremely intelligible Being.

The second way concluded to a term that was the first uncaused efficient cause. Since this cause is in no way caused by another, it is no way in potency. Thus it is supremely in act; it is pure act. Now every being is intelligible insofar as it is in act; for a thing acts insofar as it is in act, not insofar as it is in potency. Things, because they are in act, cause our knowledge of them. To be in act is to be intelligible. Thus God as pure act is supremely intelligible.

From the third and fourth ways we can argue the same: God is infinitely intelligible because he possesses the actuality of Being in an absolute and supreme way. In the fifth way we saw that God must exist in the sense that there must be in reality an intelligence that not only knows the order that is in our world but has actually established that order. Since God intends this order, he knows it; and since he actually does know it, the order is intelligible. Finally, since this idea or the order is not received from another, it is one with the nature of God. Hence our conclusion that God must be intelligible by his very nature.

4. Is the Divine Nature Intelligible for Us?

God's nature is supremely intelligible in itself. But can we know that nature? Is it intelligible for us? Before the question, *"What*

can we know about God," can be answered, we must first answer
the more fundamental question: "Is it *possible* for us to have
knowledge of God's essence?" The only factors we have with which
to answer this question are: (1) the nature of man's intellect; (2)
the manner or way in which that intellect knows; and (3) the
nature of the things that the intellect knows. By an examination
of these facts we shall come to understand, first of all, in what sense
it is impossible for the human intellect to know the divine essence.
With this negative part out of the way, we shall be in a better position to see in what sense we can have some knowledge of what
God is.

5. Statement of the Problem

Man, a composite of body and soul, of sense and intellect, can
have three kinds of knowledge of things.

First, he can have through his senses an immediate intuition of
sensible things; the senses immediately intuit their proper object.
Such cognition is not called immediate because there is no *medium*
between the faculty and the external existing sensible object, for
all man's knowledge is had by an intentional union with the thing
known. And this union is effected by the presence in the faculty
of the species of the object. In sensible knowledge there is needed
a sensible species. Rather, this knowledge is called immediate because there is no *medium* that has to be *known first* before I know
the object. Moreover, this cognition is called *intuition* because I
grasp the object precisely as it is here and now exercising its being,
namely, in a sensible fashion. Here intuitive knowledge is opposed
to abstractive knowledge. [4]

Secondly, man through his intellect knows the nature of existing
things by abstracting their quiddities from the phantasm. This intellectual knowledge of the nature of existing things is immediate
in the same sense used above concerning sensible knowledge. That
is to say, there is no *medium* that first has to be known before we
know the existing thing. For the *species* by which I know the thing
has been received from the thing. However, this knowledge is not

[4] See St. Thomas, S.T., I, 12, 4.

intuitive in the same sense that sensible cognition is. This intellectual cognition is abstractive. It does not give us knowledge of the nature according to the mode of being that the nature is here and now exercising. For the nature as existing is actually sensible and only potentially intelligible; whereas the nature as known is actually intelligible, for it is considered apart from its individual sensible matter. *What* I know is, immediately and directly, the actually existing thing. But the *way* or *manner* I know it is different from the way or manner it actually exists. I grasp intelligibly that which exists sensibly, and in this sense there is no intuition of the nature, but there is an immediate knowledge of the nature. [5]

Thirdly, man through his intellect can know the nature or essence of a thing *mediately*. For example, when the intellect comes to understand that man is a rational animal, it knows something about the animality that is present in the nature of irrational animals. Through a knowledge of the animality in Paul, I know something about the animality in a dog. Now, as is clear, such knowledge of the dog is not knowledge of it through its own proper form, but knowledge through another thing or, more precisely, through the knowledge of another thing. Thus this kind of intellectual knowledge is called mediate, since I know one thing through my knowledge of some other thing. This mediate knowledge is the only kind of knowledge the human intellect can have of the nature of God. We shall analyze and consider more in detail this knowledge when we come to our specific problem of applying it to our knowledge of God's nature.

At this point we want to establish the following: it is impossible for the human intellect to have the first two kinds of knowledge about God's nature; that is, either an immediate intuition, as we

---

[5] *Ibid.* The word "intuition" has many different meanings in different authors. It is sometimes used simply as a synonym for "insight," "simple understanding," etc. The definition of intuition given here, namely, knowing an object both according to what it is and the way it is, is a good, workable definition. However, we should note that "sense intuition" limps from the side of "intuition," since the senses as such grasp only accidental manifestations of the object. On the other hand, "intellectual intuition," is for man a contradiction in terms, since the intellect as such never grasps its object according to the sensible mode of being it actually exercises.

have in sense knowledge, or an immediate abstractive knowledge, as we have when the intellect abstracts the proper form from the thing.

6. Intuition of the Divine Nature Impossible for Man

Why is it that the human mind in its present condition cannot have an immediate intuition of God's essence comparable to our knowledge of sensible objects? It is not obvious that this kind of knowledge should not be ours, as the three following considerations show.

1) Aristotle tells us that in a certain sense the soul of man is all things, for through cognition it can become all things. The senses can cognitively become all sensible objects and the intellect can cognitively become all intelligible objects. Now since the divine essence is actually and supremely intelligible, it should follow that the intellect should know the divine essence in the same way the senses know the sensible object.

2) Moreover, there is another philosophical principle that seems to demand an immediate and intuitive knowledge of God's essence. What is received in another is received according to the manner of the one receiving it. Now God is in all things by his essence, his power, and his presence, as we shall see later on when studying the divine attributes. Therefore God is in our intellect by his essence. But when something is in our intellect, it is received according to the nature of the intellect, and the nature of the intellect is to know. Thus the divine essence would seem to be present in our intellect as an intelligible form and hence as immediately and intuitively known.

3) Finally, truth of its very nature is knowable; but God's essence is truth itself. And since our intellect is made to know truth, it should follow that it can know the divine essence itself. Does it not seem strange that that which is in itself supremely intelligible and which is intimately present in our intellect should not be immediately known and grasped by our intellect?

7. The Solution to This Problem

Let us now try to solve this problem. We shall find that its solution lies in the very nature of man.

To know is to act in a certain way. And all activity is limited and regulated by the nature of the being that is acting. Every agent acts according to the way it exists. Applying this metaphysical principle to that area of activity which is cognition, we say that the way one knows is determined by the way one is or exists. And the way one is or exists is determined by his nature or essence. As long as we remain in this life, our human soul has its existence in matter. This is its natural mode of being, upon which its natural mode of knowing follows. Hence the intellect naturally can know things that have their existence in matter, and whatever else can be known through the knowledge of *such things*.

Now it is quite clear that the nature of material things cannot give our intellect a knowledge of the divine essence or nature of God. In each one of its natural acts of cognition, our intellect has the phantasm as that object from which it abstracts the intelligible species of the material existent. Whatever the human intellect understands in this life, it understands through species abstracted from the phantasm. And since the divine essence is not a material existent, it is not one of those proper objects concerning which our intellect can have immediate knowledge in this life. Moreover, since the divine essence is in no way sensible, man in this life can in no way intuit the divine essence. Hence our conclusion: Since the divine essence is in no way sensible and in no way has existence in corporeal matter, it cannot be grasped by our intellect either by an immediate intuition or by immediate abstractive knowledge.

This last statement brings us to our second problem. The intellect cannot know the divine essence through any form that represents that essence. No created form, no matter what its source, could ever give us a knowledge of the divine essence, whether that form be abstracted from matter, or whether it be immediately infused into our intellect by God. Why this is so is easy to see. We have just seen that everything the human mind understands in this

life is understood through species (intelligible forms) abstracted
from phantasms. Now none of these forms is able to represent the
divine essence nor, for that matter, the essence of any immaterial
being. The reason is a simple one: The essences of sensible and
material things, whose likenesses are the intelligible species abstracted from the phantasms, are of a different order from the essences of immaterial substances and the divine essence. For example, the intelligible species of "man" abstracted from the phantasm
is simply unable to represent the essence of an angel or of God.
So we must conclude that according to the natural cognition that
our mind has in this life, we can know the essence neither of God
nor of angels.

In the *Summa Theologiae*, [6] St. Thomas lists three reasons why
no created intellect can see the essence of God by means of any
created likeness or similitude. Two of these will serve to summarize
and complete what we have been saying.

To see anything, whether by sensible or intellectual vision, two
things are required: first, a visual power, and secondly, a union of
the thing seen with this power. For there is no seeing in act unless
the thing seen is somehow present in the one seeing it. In the case
of corporeal vision, the thing seen cannot exist through its own
substance in the one seeing it, but only through its likeness. The
likeness of the stone is in the eye, not the substance of the stone.
And through the presence of this likeness or sensible form the actual vision of the stone takes place.

On the part, therefore, of the thing seen, which in some way
must be united to the one seeing, we argue that through no created
form or likeness can the essence of God be known. The first reason
St. Thomas gives for this we have already seen. Forms taken from
a lower order of beings can in no way lead us to know the essence
of higher things. For example, through the form of a body, we cannot understand the essence of an incorporeal thing. And therefore
much less through the likeness of any created thing could we know
the uncreated essence of God.

Secondly, the divine essence is identical with the divine Being,

[6] I, 12, 2.

which is not true of any created form. Thus no created form can be a likeness that represents the divine essence as it is in itself. The only form that would enable us to see that essence in itself would have to be the divine uncreated essence itself.

Hence our conclusion: Although in order to see God there is required some likeness on the part of the power that sees, which in the next world will be the light of glory that strengthens the intellect to see God, [7] this divine essence is not able to be seen by any likeness which would represent this essence as it is in itself. The form by which we will see God's essence in the beatific vision will be the divine essence itself.

8. Summary

In this life it is impossible to see the divine essence by any immediate intuition, because of the very nature of man. For man is a material being, whose soul has its existence in a body and hence whose power of understanding is limited in its natural knowledge to the abstracting of forms from sensible existents. And God, as pure spirit, in no way falls beneath the senses and is in no way abstractable. [8]

Secondly, none of the forms that man can abstract represent that divine essence as it is in itself. The human soul, as form of the body, can know the truth about something immaterial only insofar as it can be carried beyond itself by those things which it understands through the intellect's abstracting from the phantasm. Now these abstractions made from sensible things can never raise the intellect of man to the understanding of the essences of immaterial things, for there is no proportion between the essence of sensible things and the essence of immaterial things.

Thus it is quite impossible for the human soul united to the body to understand the natures of any immaterial being. [9] Moreover, even in the next life, the essence of God will not be seen by any created form or representation, but by its very self. For that which

[7] *Ibid.*
[8] See *S.T.*, I, 12, 3.
[9] See St. Thomas, *In I Metaphy.*, lect. 2, No. 295.

is created cannot represent the uncreated, nor that which is finite the infinite.

9. Answering the Objections

With these principles in mind, let us now attempt to answer the objections placed at the beginning of our investigation. The first objection was this: As the senses through sensible cognition can become and know all sense objects, so the intellect through intellection can become and know all intelligible objects. But God is supremely intelligible. Therefore, the intellect can know the essence of God.

We answer that all this objection proves is that the human intellect even in this life can have *some knowledge* of the divine essence. It does not prove that the intellect can know the divine essence in itself, nor in the same way that it can know the essence of material things.

The second objection stated that what is received by another is received according to the being of the one receiving. And since the being of the intellect is intelligible and God is present in the intellect by his essence, he is in the intellect as known and therefore as immediately and intuitively known.

A simple distinction suffices to answer this difficulty. Although God is in the intellect, he is not present there as an intelligible form but as one giving existence to the intellect, just as he is present in all other creatures. God gives all creatures existence, but he gives it to each according to its proper nature. And so by his essence he is present in the human intellect as an efficient cause giving it the existence that is proper to a faculty of knowledge. In this sense God is in the intellect after the manner of the intellect, and not in the sense that he is there after the manner of an intelligible form known by the intellect. [10]

Our third objection stated that since the intellect was made for truth and God is truth by his very essence, it should follow that man's intellect was made to know the essence of God. All this objection concludes to is: (1) God is supremely intelligible; (2)

[10] See St. Thomas, *De Verit.*, qu. 10, a. 11, ad 8m.

man in some sense can know God. In what sense he can be known by us depends upon the nature of our intellect. And as we have seen in our solution, since our intellect is a power of a form that has its existence in matter, our intellect can only know the essences of material things with immediate knowledge. To what extent our intellect can have some mediate, non-quidditative knowledge of the essences of immaterial things will depend on how far, and in what way, the forms or species of material things can give knowledge of immaterial essences.

The intellect of man, therefore, in this present state of union with the body cannot know the divine essence (1) by way of a *sensible intuition,* since God is in no way sensible and thus in no way proportioned to our sense faculties; or (2) by way of *intellectual intuition,* for, although God is indeed immediately intelligible in himself, the intellect, as united to the body, can only know the intelligible by abstracting it from material things; (3) nor can God's essence be known by an *immediate abstractive knowledge,* by a form that would represent the divine essence. And this for two reasons: first, because God is not material and hence our intellect could not abstract the proper form of God and, secondly, a form other than God's, whether abstracted or immediately infused into the intellect, could not represent the divine essence, for God's essence is infinite and the form would be finite.

10. The Natural Knowledge of the Separated Soul

Before going on to our next problem of how the intellect of man in this life can know something about God, let us ask this question: Could man, in any condition of his nature, see or know the divine essence by immediate knowledge? When man dies, and his soul's power of understanding no longer has its existence in matter, will the intellect then be able *naturally* to grasp the essence of God immediately, as it is in itself? The answer is no.

The separated soul, according to St. Thomas, will have some knowledge that is connatural to it. [11] The separated soul will know naturally its own substance and through that knowledge it will

11 On this point, see S.T., I, 89, 2.

also know the substances of other separated souls and will even have some natural but deficient knowledge of the substances of the angels. But in no connatural way will the separated soul be able to see the divine essence immediately.

And the same holds true for the natural knowledge of an angel. By knowing his own substance, an angel can know the substances of all angels below him in being. And through the infused species that are connatural with his nature, an angel can know the substances of higher angels. Moreover, an angel has some connatural knowledge of God, insofar as the angelic nature is a likeness of God, and the angel knows this likeness. But no angel can know naturally the divine essence immediately and as it is in itself. For no angelic nature, nor any infused species, is sufficient to represent the divine essence.

Hence our conclusion: No created intellect can naturally, that is to say, because of a power or a cognition proper to its own nature and mode of being, see the divine essence immediately as it is in itself. This is possible only insofar as God, through a gift higher than nature, namely through grace, joins himself to the created intellect so that he becomes intelligible for that intellect. [12]

B. HOW THE NATURE OF GOD CAN BE KNOWN

The important question that we want to consider here is this: Can the human mind know anything more about God than the simple, unqualified fact that he exists? When I say that there is a God, does that statement constitute the sum and substance of my knowledge about God? To understand the exact import of this problem and better to grasp the answer given it, let us discuss the difficulties involved and then work out a solution.

1. Question: Can the Human Mind Achieve Any Knowledge About God?

It seems that the human mind cannot know anything at all about God, and this for two simple reasons. First, the human intellect al-

[12] If the student wishes to see more in detail the metaphysical principles controlling these conclusions, he should read the following two articles from St. Thomas's *Summa Theologiae:* I, 12, 4; I, 56, 3.

ways knows a thing through some form. But since God eludes every form of our intellect, he can in no way be known by us. Secondly, if something is to be known, there must be some proportion between the one who knows and the thing known; there must be some proportion between the knowing faculty and its object. But between the human intellect and God there exists no proportion, just as there exists no proportion between the finite and the infinite. Therefore, the intellect can in no way know God.

2. Solution

Let us begin by saying that the intellect can know a thing in two ways. First of all, it can know a thing through its own proper form as, for example, the intellect understands what a stone is through the form (species) of the stone. Secondly, a thing may be known through the form of some other thing that is similar to it as, for example, a cause may be known through its effect or one may know a man through his picture.

Furthermore, a thing can be known through its own proper form in one of two ways. The form can be the thing itself that is known. For example, God knows himself through his own divine essence. Here the form by which God knows and what God knows are identical: the divine essence itself. Or another example is had in the self-knowledge of an angel: an angel knows its substance through the very intelligibility of that substance.

The second way a thing can be known through its own proper form is had when that form is different from the thing known. For example, the species of a stone, by which I see the stone, is different from the physical substance of the stone. Sometimes these proper forms will be abstracted from the thing known, as in the case of our natural human knowledge: the form of the stone is abstracted from the stone. Or these forms of the thing known may not be abstracted from the thing but infused into the intellect. For example, an angelic intellect naturally knows the material things of this world, not by forms abstracted from these things, but by forms or species infused into its intellect by God.

As we have seen, the intellect of man in this life is in potency only for those forms or species that it can abstract from the senses. The intellect of man, as the act of a form in matter, is related to the phantasm as the eye is related to color. Just as the faculty of corporeal vision can see an object only if it is colored, so the faculty of intellectual vision can understand a thing only if it can abstract it from the phantasm. Since God in this life cannot be known by the form that is his divine essence, and since no likeness or species of God, whether abstracted naturally from things or infused by a miracle into our intellect, can represent the divine essence as it is in itself, we have the two following conclusions. First, in no way can we know what God is in himself. Secondly, if we are to have any natural knowledge at all about God, it must be through forms abstracted from his effects existing around us, since to know by infused forms is not natural to the human intellect. Whatever knowledge we have about God we gain through a knowledge of his effects in this world.

3. Univocal Effects

Effects are of two kinds. First, there are those effects that equal the power of their cause. An effect produced by a univocal cause is in the same species, or has the same essential perfection, as the cause that produced it. Hence through the knowledge of such effects the intellect can understand the very nature or essence of the cause. For the effect equals the power and, hence, the nature of the cause. In such cases we have mediate knowledge or knowledge through the effects of the thing known and not through the proper form of the thing known. But it is mediate knowledge that is quidditative, that tells us what the cause is in itself. This type of cognition, then, yields mediate but quidditative knowledge of the thing. [13]

---

[13] By *quidditative knowledge* of a thing we mean a knowledge of the essence of that thing, as that essence is in itself. By *non-quidditative knowledge* of a thing we mean a knowledge of the essence, not as it is in itself, but as it is deficiently manifested in another, or has some relationship to another. Thus man has a quidditative knowledge only of the essences of material things. He has only non-quidditative knowledge of the essence of God and spiritual substances.

For example, the essence of animality is adequately expressed in such beings as dogs and cats. The intelligibility of dog or cat gives me quidditative knowledge of the animality in other species of animals. Or if I know what it means for John to be a man, I have quidditative knowledge of the humanity in Peter or in Paul. Such mediate knowledge is really knowledge of the essence in its own proper and ontological nature. That is why we can predicate individuals univocally of the same species and species univocally of the same genus. In the order of nature, the order of generation and corruption, beings are produced by univocal causes. Thus the effect equals the virtue or power of the proper cause.

4. Analogous Effects

Secondly, there are those effects that lack this equality with their causes. This is the case with analogous causes. Through such effects we cannot understand the power of the cause, and so we cannot understand its essence or quiddity. Here the only thing we can know through such non-univocal effects is that the cause exists. Thus in such knowledge the effect is a principle for understanding the existence of the cause, just as the effects of univocal causes are principles for understanding the essence or quiddity of the cause.

Concerning our knowledge of God, every effect is of that nature which can tell us only about the existence of God and not about his essence. The reason is not hard to see. The sensible effects of God that are known by us do not sufficiently express the divine essence or, for that matter, the essence of any supra-sensible or immaterial being. God and these other immaterial beings are in a different genus of being entirely. In fact, God is in no genus of being, and so these effects can give us no knowledge of the divine essence or of any immaterial essence, even in a generic fashion.

And what is true of the sensible effects of God is also true of his immaterial effects, like the human soul in man. Since the soul is of a generically different nature from the divine substance, it can give us no quidditative knowledge of God's nature. Thus neither by way of similitude, that is, considering the perfections found in creatures as likenesses of the divine essence, nor by way of causality, that is, considering creatures as effects of the divine essence, can the intellect of man gain any quidditative knowledge of the divine essence. For in the one case these likenesses do not sufficiently express the divine essence, and in the other case these effects do not equal the power of the cause. In this life the intellect of man can never know what the nature of God is in itself.

Moreover, this is true not only of the purely natural knowledge we have of God, but also of that knowledge gained through supernatural revelation. Knowledge of God's nature gained through revelation is no more *quidditative knowledge,* no more knowledge of the divine essence *as it is in itself,* than knowledge of God's nature gained through the unaided use of reason. Divine revelation comes to us according to our mode of knowledge. And, therefore, although by this revealed knowledge our intellect is elevated to know something about God that otherwise it would have been ignorant of, revelation does not elevate us to know in any other way except through sensible things. On this point, St. Thomas quotes the following statement from the Pseudo-Denis with approval: "It is impossible for the divine light to illumine us from above unless it be hidden within the covering of many sacred veils." Whatever these veils may be, metaphor, simple analogies, parables and so forth, they are sensible things. "Now," continues St. Thomas, "knowledge by way of the sensible is inadequate to enable us to know the essence of immaterial substances. So we conclude that we do not know *what* immaterial forms are, but only *that* they are, whether by natural reason based upon created effects or even by revelation by means of likenesses taken from sensible things." [14]

But at this point we must be very clear on what we mean by our knowledge *that God exists.* For, as St. Thomas says, of those who know *that a thing is,* one may know this *more perfectly* than another. Causes are known from their effects, and a given cause

[14] *In Boethii de Trinitate,* qu. 6, a. 3.

is known more perfectly from its effects the more one understands, through a study of the effects, the *relationship* that obtains between the cause and the effect. [15] The order or relation between an analogous cause and its effect, can be considered by the mind in three ways. First, I can consider the way or manner that the effect proceeds from this cause. Secondly, I can consider the effect insofar as it has a certain likeness to its analogous cause. Finally, I can consider the unlikeness that obtains between cause and effect, how the effect lacks the perfection of the cause. And according as the mind grows in its knowledge of this threefold consideration of the effect to its cause, the more it grows in its knowledge that God exists, or how God exists, or how God does not exist, always remembering that this knowledge and this growth in knowledge of God is in the line of *that* he is, and never of *what* he is.

To know what God is in himself would be to know the quiddity or essence of God in the Aristotelian sense of that word: to know in itself that by which God is God. Such a knowledge, in any degree, is impossible for man in this life either through natural or revealed theology. But man will have this knowledge in heaven through the beatific vision. In this life we cannot have even "just a little bit" of such quidditative knowledge, a sort of generic and confused knowledge of God's essence in itself, as we can have, for example, in the case of material essences. When I first know man as corporeal or as animal, I have a real, albeit imperfect and generic, knowledge of man's essence in itself. But with God even this imperfect type of quidditative knowledge of his nature is absolutely impossible.

This is a distinction too often lost sight of, or too often misleadingly stated, when discussing the human intellect's knowledge of God. His effects gives us no knowledge of his essence in itself, even in a very vague or highly potential way. They do indeed tell us something about God and in this sense something about the nature of God. But they tell us absolutely nothing about the nature of God

[15] *Ibid.*

as it is in itself. For example, if all I know about man is that he walks upright on two legs, this is still knowledge of man's nature in itself, although it is a very incomplete and potential kind of knowledge. Nevertheless, it does in some imperfect sense define what man is: I have grasped man's nature in one of its activities, and to that extent I know what man is. But concerning what the essence of God is in itself, the human intellect, in grasping the divine effects has no such knowledge. For here we have an essentially different relationship to the cause. That is to say, the most generic activities of man, by which I achieve some knowledge of what he is, such as walking or eating, are still the activities of man, whereas the activities and perfections by which I try to come to understand God always remain the activities and perfections of creatures.

But just as the human mind can grow more and more in its knowledge of a nature through the knowledge of more and more perfect acts of this nature, so the human mind can grow more and more in its knowledge that God exists through more and more profound considerations of the relationships that obtain between the divine effects and their cause. We grow in such knowledge of God, for example, (1) the more perfectly the mind understands the production of these effects and the efficacy of this production; (2) the more the mind understands the causes of nobler effects, for these causes will bear in a higher manner a likeness to God, and thus will comend more to us the eminence and majesty of God; (3) the more one comes to know that God is further and further removed from all those things that appear in his effects.

Let us give some simple instances of growth in such knowledge. When we understand that effects proceed from God by way of creation, that God can create and not merely make, then while we do not know what God is, we know from this fact that he exists in a much more perfect way than does any creature. Secondly, when through the positive sciences we come to learn the unbelievable number and distances of the stellar galaxies, or when we begin to understand the almost infinite energy locked up within a single atom, again these wonders may not tell us what God is, but

they do give the mind a new insight into the power and the majesty of the creator. And, finally, the more we can understand how
God exceeds his effects and is removed in nature from those effects,
the greater becomes our knowledge that God exists. [16]

C. A THREEFOLD WAY OF KNOWING ABOUT GOD

St. Thomas speaks often of a threefold way of knowing God. In
different places he gives the members of this triple way different
names and explains them in slightly different terms. We shall call
the threefold way the way of causality, negation, and transcendence. In explaining the nature of this threefold way of coming
to know more about God, and the kind of knowledge it gives us of
God, we shall follow what St. Thomas has to say on this matter in
his *Commentary of Boethius' On the Trinity*, question 6, article 3.

After having told us that neither through natural knowledge nor
knowledge gained by revelation can the intellect of man know
what God is, but only that he is, St. Thomas continues:

It should be noticed, however, that we cannot know *that* a thing is
without knowing in some way what it is, either perfectly or at least confusedly, as the Philosopher says we know things defined before we
know the parts of the definition. [17]

The analogy is clear enough. Just as some knowledge of the thing
defined is presupposed and included in my knowledge of the
parts of the definition (as man is present in understanding the parts
of his definition, animal and rational), so in arriving at the knowledge that there is a God, the mind already has some vague and
imperfect knowledge of God.

Let us see why this is so. If someone, for example, knows that
man exists and desires to know what is man, he must learn the
definition or meaning expressed by this term "man." But he could
not ask himself the question, "What is the nature of this man that
I know exists?" unless he had already conceived man as a certain
"something," whose existence he knows but whose definition he

---

[16] See St. Thomas, *In Boeth, de Trinitate*, qu. 1, a. 2.
[17] This reference to the Philosopher, who is Aristotle, is found in *Physics*
I, 1, 184 (a24–b12).

does not know. Man has already been conceived according to some remote generic knowledge, as material or as living. Or he has been conceived according to some accident that he manifests, for example, he is of large stature or white color. A knowledge of definitions, like that of demonstrations, has its beginning in some already existing knowledge.

Now the same is true about our knowledge of God and other immaterial substances. We cannot know that they are unless we also know in some confused way what they are. The analogy holds, but there is a great difference between the confused, imperfect, generic knowledge we have of a material thing like man and the confused, imperfect knowledge we have of God or of some other immaterial substance. For this confused knowledge we have of God is in the line of non-quidditative cognition, while that we have of man is in the line of true but imperfect quidditative knowledge.

Another difference to be noted is this: Since God is in no genus, I cannot know what God is even by the most imperfect and confused generic knowledge of his essence. God is not in a genus because his essence is in no way distinct from his act of existing. Only those beings whose essence is different from their act of existing can be put in a genus. Something that is in a genus shares some essential perfection with some other being, although the act of existing of each thing is absolutely proper to it and incommunicable. And since God's essence is one with his act of existing, God can be in no genus of being. [18]

As regards material beings, we know them in the beginning by some remote generic perfection, for example, as a body or a material substance. Then we make this knowledge more and more perfect by adding affirmative differences which make the genus more and more proximate, which contract or limit the genus to a certain species, etc. After knowing a thing as a body, we can know it as living and then as sensitive, and so on, gaining a more perfect and proper knowledge of the thing.

[18] On this point, see St. Thomas, *On Being and Essence*, translated by A. Maurer (Toronto, 1949), Ch. 5; *De Pot.*, 7, 3c; *C.G.*, Bk. I, Ch. 25.

In the case of God, instead of knowing him by way of remote genus, since he is in no genus, we know the divine substance by way of negations. We say God is *immaterial, incorporeal, without* accidents, *without* shape, and so forth. In the case of material beings, we begin with remote genus and by the additions of affirmative differences make our knowledge of the being more and more proper, distinguishing it from all other beings. So, too, in the case of God, each subsequent negation limits and determines the previous one, so that we come more and more to see what God is not, achieving a proper knowledge of God in the sense that through these negations we can distinguish God from all other beings. [19]

We see then that corresponding to our knowledge of material substance by way of less and less remote genera, we have in our knowledge of the divine substance the way of removal, adding one negation to another to distinguish the divine substance from all other beings.

But there is also a way of coming to know God analogous to the way we know material substance through its accidents. In God there are no accidents. And this for many reasons. Accidents form a composition with their substance, and in God there is no composition. Substance is related to its accidents as potency to act, and in God there is no potency. [20] What type of knowledge can we have of the divine substance that corresponds, analogically speaking, to our knowledge of material substance through a knowledge of its accidents? Since substance causes its accidents, there exists between a substance and its accidents a proportion of cause to effect. Also, a substance is more perfect and of a higher order of being than the accidents it causes. Thus, while God has no accidents, we can say that there are certain things that manifest God, and these are his effects. In the place of accidents, we have these sensible effects produced by God which tell us something about him by way of causality (for these effects are related to the divine substance as effects to cause) and by way of *transcendence* (for God

---

[19] On this point, See *C.G.*, Bk. I, Ch. 14.
[20] To see why there can be no accidents in God, it will suffice to read *C.G.*, Bk. I, Ch. 23.

completely transcends all his effects, inasmuch as his essence is identified with his own Being). "We conclude then," says St. Thomas, "that with regard to immaterial forms we know *that* they exist, and instead of knowing *what* they are we have knowledge of them by way of negation, by way of causality and by way of transcendence." [21]

1. Man's Knowledge of Angels

What we have said about our knowledge of God also holds true for our knowledge of any immaterial substance, for example, our knowledge of angels. For while St. Thomas will say that immaterial substances may be in a "genus," in the sense that their quiddities are distinct from their act of existing, [22] we can in no way know what this generic perfection is in itself. Thus knowledge of angelic substances is had by way of negation also: angels are non-material, non-sensible, non-corporeal, and so on. Furthermore, although these substances do possess accidents, we in no way know what these accidents are in themselves, for they are proportioned to a substance of which we have no knowledge. Thus while in the case of material substances we can have some confused and imperfect knowledge of what they are through a knowledge of their most generic perfections and of certain accidents they possess, this is simply impossible in the case of immaterial substances and the divine essence. Here through many and successive negations, and through the way of likeness accompanied by unlikeness and transcendence, we arrive at a more and more proper and a more and more perfect knowledge of God (and angels), but never of *what* God is, but only of *what he is not* and how he differs from and *transcends* all the effects of which he is the source.

2. Conclusion

Let us conclude these considerations with a quotation from the Angelic Doctor, found in his *Commentary on the Epistle of St. Paul to the Romans*, where the Apostle to the Gentiles reveals to

[21] *In Boeth. de Trin.*, qu. 6, a. 3.
[22] *Ibid.* "Created immaterial substances, however, are indeed in a genus."

us that the pagans were inexcusable for not reaching the true God, since from the visible things of creation they should have arrived at the power, the divinity, and the eternity of the creator. That is, they should have arrived at the knowledge of the one true God. In commenting on this, St. Thomas writes:

There is something with regard to God which is entirely unknown to man in this life, namely, what God is ("quid est Deus"). . . . And this is so because man's knowledge begins with those things which are connatural to him, namely, sensible things, which are not adequate to represent the divine essence. Nevertheless man can know God from creatures of this sort in three ways, as Dionysius says in the *Divine Names: First,* through causality. For since such creatures are imperfect and changeable, they must be reduced to some unchangeable and perfect principle. And from this we know that God exists (*de Deo an est*). *Secondly,* by way of excellence (*per viam excellentiae*). For all things are reduced to a first principle, not as to a proper and univocal cause, as man begets man, but as to a universal and transcendent cause. And from this we know that he is above all things. *Thirdly,* by way of negation, because if he is a transcendent cause, nothing which is in creatures can belong to him. . . .[23]

3. Answering the Objections

Many pages ago we began our investigation by a reflection upon two objections which seem to preclude any knowledge whatsoever of God except the mere fact of his existence. Let us now recall these objections and discuss their solution.

The first objection stated that the intellect always knows a thing through some form, and since every form of God escapes the human intellect, it follows that our intellect can have no knowledge of God. We reply that what this objection proves is that man can have no knowledge of God through a form that would represent him. We can have no knowledge of what God is in himself. But although all forms escape God, we still can know the forms of his effects, and through the knowledge of these effects we can know something about God, who is their cause.

[23] Chapter One, lecture 6. On the *via similitudinis,* see *C.G.,* Bk. I, Ch. 29. For an excellent treatment of the *triplex via,* see Gilson, *The Christian Philosophy of St. Thomas Aquinas* (New York, Random House, 1956), pp. 97–110.

The second objection stated that between the knowing subject and the thing known, there must exist some proportion as between a knowing faculty and its object. But since there is no proportion between the human intellect and God, the one being finite and the other infinite, neither can there be any knowledge of God by the human intellect.

To answer this objection we must understand the nature of a proportion. A proportion is a relation of likeness or of order between two things. This proportion may be of two kinds. First, insofar as that by which the two things are alike is in the same genus. For example, two things may possess the same color, or possessing two different colors, are alike in this, that they are both colored. Two things may be alike in that they both have the same degree of heat or, having different degrees of heat, are alike in that they are both hot, etc. In this way there can be *no proportion* between God and any creature, since God is not in any genus of being, and so cannot be like his creature by any effect that is in a genus.

But the other proportion that can exist between two things is a proportion of simple order. One thing is ordered to the other. For example, such a proportion exists between matter and form, cause and effect, and so on. It is this kind of proportion that is required between the thing knowing and the thing known or knowable. This order is required since the knowable is the act of the knowing faculty. And this is the proportion of the creature to God, of the knower to the knowable.

But because of the infinite manner in which the creator excels his creature, the proportion here is not such that the creature receives the creator's influence according to the latter's full power, but only deficiently, so that the creature cannot know the first cause perfectly. God, as a knowable Being, is proportioned to the human intellect in this life only in and through his effects. That is to say, God as a knowable Being is proportioned to the human intellect in this life not in and through himself (perfectly) but only in and through his effects (deficiently). God is indeed the act of our intellect and hence known by that intellect, not in himself and immediately, but only as that act has been received in the effects and known through them. God is knowable mediately through creatures.

But one might press the objection a little further. Must not a potency and its act be reducible to the same genus of being? For example, matter and form are reducible to the genus of substance, and the one knowing and the knowable object are reducible to the genus of intelligible beings. And since God as knowable is the act (through creatures) of the knowing potency, have we really solved the difficulty? God is not reducible to any genus whatsoever, so that it would seem that there cannot be between the creature and God even the proportion of order or of potency and act.

We answer by saying that the intellect and the intelligible are indeed *of the same genus*, as potency and act. But God, as an intelligible, is not *in any genus*. That is to say, as an intelligible, God does not belong to any genus by participating or sharing in the nature of the genus. But God does *pertain* to the genus of intelligible things, in this sense that he is the principle and cause of this genus. His effects, moreover, are not outside the genus or class of intelligible things. Therefore, here below God can be known through these effects, just as in heaven he will be known through his essence.

D. SUMMARY OF THE CHAPTER

"Although God is supremely intelligible in himself, the human mind in its present condition is unable to know what God is, either through any intuition or through any abstracted form that could represent the divine essence. However, through God's effects in the world we are able to have some non-quidditative knowledge of God, by way of causality, excellence, and negation."

a. State of the question

Having established the existence of a Being completely immobile, wholly uncaused, absolutely necessary, supremely perfect and the orderer of all things, we now wish to investigate a new problem. For the human intellect not only naturally desires to know the causes of things—even the ultimate causes—but it also

desires to know the essences and natures of these causes. It therefore seeks to ascertain the essence of the first cause. [24] (*S.T.*, I, 12,
1)

An essence is that principle in a being by which it is what it is.
Is it possible to know the essence of God? Or can the human mind
in this life only ascertain the *fact*—and nothing further—of God's
existence? In our position we see that the truth is found between
two extremes. Although in this life the intellect can have no
knowledge whatever of *what God is in himself*, it can, however,
grasp more than the mere *fact* that God exists. And this knowledge
of God (through the threefold way of causality, excellence and
negation) can become for man more and more perfect. (*In Librum
Boethii de Trinitate*, qu. 1, a. 2c.)

b. Explanation of terms

1) ". . . *intelligible* . . ."—that which can be known in some
way by the intellect.

2) ". . . *in its present condition* . . ."—in this life, where our
intellect is a power of the soul united to a body as the proper act
of that body.

3) ". . . *what God is* . . ."—the divine essence or quiddity as
seen or known in itself; that by which God is God.

4) ". . . *intuition* . . ."—that is, not merely immediate cognition, but knowledge of a thing according to that thing's mode of
being, whether this intuition is effected without a *species* distinct
from the thing known (as is the case in the beatific vision), or by
means of such a distinct *species* (as in sense intuition). (*S.T.*, I,
12, 2)

5) ". . . *through any abstracted form* . . ." Although the intellect grasps, through a form or species an existing thing, it does
not understand the nature according to its material mode of being.
The material thing exists as sensible and individual, but it is understood as intelligible and universal. We say the nature is understood
by abstraction, since it is considered apart from its individual sen-

[24] For a discussion of the much controverted point of whether man has a
natural desire for the vision of God, see Appendix F.

sible matter. Abstractive knowledge, moreover, may be had in two ways (*S.T.*, I, 12, 4):

(*a*) *immediately*—when a thing is known through its own proper form;

(*b*) *mediately*—when a thing is known through the form of another thing. (*S.T.*, I, 56, 3) Here, in this context of knowledge, form and species are simply synonyms. Hence form here does *not* mean the substantial form of the thing, but rather it means that which the intellect abstracts from the thing. It is that because of which the thing is known. This form, as abstracted, is in the intellect; as known it is "in" the thing, that is to say, it *is* the thing as known.

6) ". . . *representing the divine essence* . . ."—that is, giving us knowledge of *what God is* in himself.

7) ". . . *some non-quidditative knowledge of God* . . ." This knowledge is:

(*a*) *proper*—that is, it is knowledge of God alone as distinct from every other being.

(*b*) But it is a proper knowledge obtained through other things; from the forms of God's effects and not from the divine form itself. In this sense the knowledge of God is opposed to proper knowledge derived from proper forms.

(*c*) *analogous knowledge*, that is, non-univocal, since the effects of God neither equal the power of their cause, nor are they in the same species or genus as this cause. Therefore, insofar as such knowledge that is gained about God can be applied only to him, it is called *proper*; insofar as it is based on other forms, it is *analogical*; and insofar as it is a knowledge from effects which do not adequate their cause, it is termed *analogous*.

8) ". . . *non-quidditative* . . ." In no way either perfectly or imperfectly, distinctly or confusedly, do we have any knowledge of the essence of God in itself. For in no way do the forms of his effects represent the divine essence as it is in itself. This non-quidditative knowledge *signifies* or points out God, but it does not *represent* his essence.

9) ". . . *through causality* . . ."—insofar as every cause, even

an analogous one, produces effects similar to itself. The effects in the world are in some way similar to God. (*C.G.*, Bk. I, Ch. 29)

". . . *through . . . excellence* . . ."—insofar as the divine agent, because he is his own act of existing, infinitely exceeds whatever is to be found in his effects. (*In Epistolam ad Romanos,* Ch. I, lect. 6)

". . . *through negation* . . ." "Since God is a cause that exceeds its effects, nothing found in creatures can be compared to (the creator)." (*Ibid.*, cf. *C.G.*, Bk. I, Ch. 14) Through this "threefold way," which is not three independent ways, but rather one complete and adequate explication of the way of divine causality, the human mind more and more perfectly attains to knowledge of God. But this knowledge never tells us what God is, but only what he is not, or how he is, or how he is infinitely removed in his Being from creatures and infinitely transcends them.

c. Adversaries

1) *Those who err through excess* say that God is the first thing known, or that the intellect in this life is able to have some sort of direct intuition of the divine essence. This is the position of the *Ontologists* and *Illuminati.* For pertinent passages in St. Thomas, see *In Librum Boethii de Trinitate,* qu. 1, a. 1, and 3; *S.T.*, I, 88, 3.

2) *Those who err by defect.* (*a*) *Agnostics of ancient and medieval times:* as, for example, *Plotinus,* who taught that God was above being and therefore completely unknowable, and that men were united with God through love and not through knowledge. *Moses Maimonides,* who taught that men were unable to have any *positive* or *proper* knowledge of God. For example, when we say that God is wise, all we mean is that God causes wisdom, or that God is not stupid. As we shall see later, according to Maimonides names are predicated of God *equivocally.*

(*b*) *Modern agnostics:* such as *Kant,* who taught that God, as supra-sensible, in no way could be known through metaphysical principles. The existence of God is a postulate of the will, and his nature is entirely unknowable. The intellect can affirm nothing of God without contradiction. Others with the same views would include *Hamilton* and *Mansel*. *Modernists*, as *Loisy* and *Tyrrel*, hold that our knowledge of God has only an emotional and subjective value. It helps one to live a religious life if he thinks of God as personal, intelligent, and so forth. But such knowledge tells us nothing of God. The *Positivist* and *Empirical* view as put forth by *Hume, Mill, Spencer, Comte,* and others, has its philosophic foundation in the Kantian system: the principle of causality has no validity outside sensible things.

d. Proofs for our position

1) *God in himself is supremely intelligible.* (*a*) A thing is intelligible insofar as it is separated from matter, for matter, as pure potency, is the root of unintelligibility.

But God, as completely immobile, is separated from all matter. Therefore, in himself, he is supremely intelligible.

(*b*) A thing is knowable insofar as it is in act, for as in potency it can not act on the knowing subject.

But God is supremely *in act* (as first uncaused cause, completely necessary Being, perfect Being). Therefore, God is supremely knowable.

2) *The divine essence is not able to be known through sensible intuition.* God cannot be sensed, for there is no proportion between an actually intelligible object (God) and our sense power. (See *S.T.*, I, 12, 3)

3) *The divine essence is not able to be known through intellectual intuition.* In this life the human intellect has no knowledge of essences unless they are abstracted from the phantasm. For the proper object of the intellect, as the power of a form in matter, is a quiddity which has existence in matter. But the essence of God does not exist in matter. Therefore, in no way can the divine essence be apprehended by the human intellect. (See *S.T.*, I, 12, 4; 11)

4) *The divine essence cannot be known through any form representing it.* No created form can represent this essence, whether this form be abstracted from things or infused into the intellect by God. For any created form, since it is created, is not

its own act of existing. But the divine essence is its own act of existing. Therefore, the created form cannot represent the divine essence as it is in itself. Note that the question here is about immediate (although abstract) knowledge. (See *S.T.*, I, 12, 2)

5) *However, we are able to have some knowledge about God through his created effects in the world.* (*a*) Every agent produces effects that are in some way like to itself; therefore, the effects of God in the world are in some way like God. (*C.G.*, Bk. I. Ch. 29)

(*b*) But God is not a *univocal* agent, and so the effects he produces are not of the same nature or essence as God. His effects do not equal the fullness of his power. Therefore, they are not adequate to give us a knowledge of God's essence in itself.

(*c*) Moreover, because the divine essence is its own act of existing, God cannot be put into any *genus*; and so we are unable, through his effects, to have any knowledge of his essence in itself, even the most generic and imperfect knowledge.

6) *By way of (a) causality, (b) excellence, and (c) negation:* (*a*) ". . . according as his power in producing things is more perfectly known; . . . because a cause is more perfectly known through its effect in proportion as the relation of cause to effect is more and more perfectly seen in the effect." *In Lib. Boeth. de Trin.*, qu. I, a. 2.

(*b*) ". . . according as the cause of effects that are of higher degrees is known, for—since these effects bear a certain resemblance to their cause—they more effectively manifest the superior perfection of the cause." *Ibid.* Moreover, since God is his own act of existing and whatever is in God *is* God, it follows that all the perfections of being are in God in an unsurpassed and eminently perfect way.

(*c*) "Thirdly, insofar as God (the first cause) comes to be known as more and more removed from all the qualities which are manifest in the effects." *Ibid.*

Although St. Thomas does not always use the same terminology in describing this threefold way, the following remarks can be made concerning it.

(*a*) Since God can be put into no genus, we are unable, in our advance toward a knowledge of God, to begin with a remote genus and then add further differences. Instead of knowledge by way of genus and difference, we must use the way of removal, saying that God is not a body, not finite, and so forth. One negation added to another makes more perfect our knowledge about God, until it becomes a distinct and proper knowledge; that is, it can be said *only* of God and *distinguishes* him from every other being.

(*b*) The material sensible beings of our experience are manifested to us chiefly through their accidents. God, of course, has no accidents. But just as accidents are an external manifestation of the inner nature of things, so God's effects (creatures) are in some way an external manifestation of the divine nature. And so we can use these effects to gain some knowledge of God. This is done, *first*, by noting that these perfections in creatures are in some way similar to God; *secondly*, by denying that these perfections are in God as they are in creatures. Since God is his own act of existing, and since whatever is in God is God, these perfections as in God are identified with his own act of existing. And so they are present in him in an infinitely more perfect manner. *Finally*, since God infinitely exceeds and transcends all creatures, none of the perfections in creatures are comparable to God. Our investigation of God is always concluded by the use of the way of negation. On this matter St. Thomas writes: "Whatever knowledge our intellect can have of God fails adequately to represent him; and so the nature of God always remains hidden from us. This, then, is the best knowledge we can have of God in this life: that he is above any thought we can have concerning him." (*De Verit.*, qu. 2, a. 1, ad 9m)

And again: "It is because human intelligence is not equal to the divine essence that this same divine essence surpasses our intelligence and is unknown to us; wherefore, man reaches the highest point of his knowledge about God when he knows that he knows him not, inasmuch as he knows that that which is God transcends whatsoever he conceives of him." (*De Pot.*, qu. 7, a. 5, ad 14m)

(c) For a better understanding of how our knowledge about God proceeds by means of this threefold way, let us consider how it works in the concrete, using as an example the perfection of "wisdom." We observe that some creatures are wise, and that wisdom is a perfection of being as being. So we affirm that God also is wise because he is the cause of wisdom in creatures (way of causality). We begin by affirming something of God.

But we see that wisdom in man is an accident and limited; so we deny that wisdom is in God as an accident or as limited. Here we deny something about God (way of negation). Finally, since wisdom in God is the same as his Being, we affirm that wisdom in God is infinitely more excellent than wisdom in creatures (way of excellence). By reason of the excellence that this perfection has in God, we end our investigation by stating that wisdom in God is infinitely removed from the wisdom of the creature, and that *what* this perfection is as in God is completely unknowable to the human intellect.

Even in its purified state this knowledge in no way represents the divine essence as it is in itself; neither as regards *that which* is affirmed about God, nor the *manner in which* it is affirmed. However, a more thorough treatment of this matter will be had later on, when we consider how this purified knowledge we have of God is predicated of him. For the present, we can say with St. Thomas:

There is a threefold application of terms to God. First, affirmatively: for instance, I can say *God is wise,* since there is in him a likeness to the wisdom that derives from him. But since that wisdom is not in God *as* we understand it and name it, we can truly deny this wisdom of God, and say: *God is not wise.* Again, since wisdom is not denied of God as though he were lacking in wisdom, but because in him it transcends the wisdom we know and name, we must say that *God is super-wise.* Accordingly, Dionysius explains perfectly by these three ways of ascribing wisdom to God, how these expressions are to be applied to God. [25]

[25] From *De Pot.*, qu. 7, a. 5, ad 2m.

Suggested Readings

1. St. Thomas, *Summa Theologiae*, in *Basic Writings of St. Thomas*, by A. Pegis (New York, Random House, 1945), Vol. 1, pp. 91–111. *The Division and Method of the Sciences*, translated by A. Maurer, C.S.B. (Toronto, Pontifical Institute of Mediaeval Studies, 1953), pp. 66–78.
2. Etiènne Gilson, *The Christian Philosophy of St. Thomas Aquinas* (New York, Random House, 1956), Chapter IV, "Haec Sublimis Veritas," pp. 84–95, 97–110. Excellent pages on the way of Negation and Analogy.

CHAPTER 6

The Problem of Naming God

> *But Moses pleaded with God: How if I ap-*
> *pear before the Israelites with the message*
> *that the God of their fathers has sent me to*
> *them, and they ask me, What is his name?*
> *What answer shall I make? And God said to*
> *Moses, I am the God who IS; thou shalt tell*
> *the Israelites, THE GOD WHO IS has sent*
> *me to you.*
>
> —*Exodus*, Ch. 3, verses 13–14

1. Can God Be Named?

Having seen how the human intellect in this life can attain to some knowledge of God, let us now consider how this knowledge can be predicated of God. This is the problem of naming God. For each thing is named according as it is known. What we say about a thing depends upon what we know about it. Predication is our use of knowledge. Through the triple way of causality, negation and excellence we can possess a knowledge of God. Now we want to know whether this knowledge can be put into meaningful words that can be predicated of the divine essence? Are such words predicated in a metaphorical or proper sense, a univocal or an analogous sense?

In this chapter we will consider three problems. First, can God be named? Secondly, what name best signifies the divine essence? Thirdly, and most importantly, in what sense are the different names that we attribute to God predicated of the divine essence?

194

2. Objections Against the Possibility of Naming God

There are two main objections against using names to refer to God. The first objection is drawn from the general characteristic of all nouns, and the second from the particular nature of different classes of words. By "name" here we mean any part of speech, any word or combination of words that is capable of expressing a thought or idea about God.

First objection. Every noun that we know either signifies something concrete or abstract. A concrete noun always signifies something that is composed. For example, "man" signifies someone having humanity. In the sentence, "Peter is a man," "man" signifies a composite, namely, a being whose nature is a rational animal. But the divine essence is completely simple and uncomposed. Hence it cannot be signified by any concrete noun. On the other hand, an abstract noun does not signify *that which* exists but rather that *by which* something exists in a certain way. For example, "whiteness" signifies that by which something is white. But God subsists. Hence he cannot be signified by any abstract noun. I cannot say, "God is holy," for that implies composition; namely, something possessing holiness. But neither can I say, "God is holiness," for holiness is that by which something is holy. Hence no noun (or adjective) can be applied to God.

Second objection. The second objection considers each kind of word and shows how none of them can be applied to God. We have just seen how no noun (or adjective) can be said of God. Adjectives, furthermore, always signify the subject plus a quality. Hence they cannot be used to signify God, who is not composed. Verbs and participles always imply time in their meaning. But in God there is no time. Thus verbs and participles cannot properly signify God. Pronouns labor under the same difficulties that attend nouns, besides the fact that demonstrative pronouns imply matter,—something I can point to or point out. Hence it follows that for expressing our knowledge about God all words are equally useless. God in no way can be named by us.

3. Principles That Govern Our Naming of God

These principles flow from our previous section on how the intellect in this life knows God.

1) Just as God is known through his effects, so in like manner he is named with words signifying his effects. The names we attribute to God are names that were first imposed upon creatures and used to signify creatures. [1]

2) Just as no knowledge we have of God in this life represents the divine essence in itself, so no name that we give to God signifies this essence in itself.

The reason for this second statement flows from the very nature of words. Words are the vocal expressions of our thoughts. They express our concepts, and our concepts are the intentional likenesses of things. What we know are things, not our concepts, but we know things through our concepts. Hence, what words signify are things, not concepts, although they signify things *by way of the concept*. [2] And just as no concept that we can have of God in this life represents the divine essence as it is in itself, so no name that we use to signify God signifies the divine essence as it is in itself.

A simple example will bring out our meaning. The word "man" signifies by way of my concept the very essence of man, shared in by Peter and Paul and all individual men. And this word "man" signifies that essence as it is in itself. Therefore, we say that the name "man" not only signifies the essence of man, but it expresses that essence, for it is the sign of a concept in which the essence of Peter and Paul and all individuals is intellectually grasped and known. On the other hand, the word "God," while it may signify properly and distinctly only the divine essence, in no way signifies that essence in itself, and in no way expresses that essence. For the concept corresponding to the name "God" does not intellectually grasp the divine essence in itself.

4. Solution

Thus the answer to our problem "Can God be named?" is quite simple. *First*, God can be named because God can be known.

[1] See St. Thomas, *S.T.*, I, 13, 1.
[2] *Ibid.*

Words are merely the signs or vocal expression of our knowledge of things. *Secondly,* God must be named in the same way that he is known. The way we know a thing is also the way we name it. And since we can never know what God is in himself, no name can signify the divine essence in itself. *We simply have no name for what God is,* for we have no concept of what God is. *Thirdly,* just as a purifying process has to take place in our knowledge before it becomes proper and distinct knowledge of God, so a like purifying process must be made of the names we take from creatures before they can be properly and distinctly used to express this knowledge. Purified and refined, they may then be predicated of God. The exact nature of this refinement we will see when we compare the way the same word is said of the creature and of God. This will be done when we discuss predication by way of analogy.

5. Answering the Objections

Our first objection stated that all nouns are either concrete or abstract. Those that are concrete signify composite things, and those that are abstract signify some non-subsistent form by which a thing exists. But God is neither composed nor non-subsistent; he is simple and subsistent. Hence no noun can be used of God.

We answer that just as all our cognition about God is derived from our cognition of creatures, so all the names we use were originally imposed to signify creatures, and creatures moreover whose knowledge is connatural to us, namely, material creatures. And material creatures that are complete, perfect and subsistent, are composite beings, while the substantial and accidental forms by which they subsist are incomplete beings.

Therefore, we use two kinds of names to signify these two kinds of perfections. Names imposed by us to signify things that are complete and subsistent must signify these in the concrete, for it is in the concrete that they exist. And concrete material things are always composed. Thus concrete names as derived from creatures always signify what is composed.

On the other hand, names that are imposed to signify simple forms, do not signify any thing that exists, but rather a form by which something exists according to some perfection. For example, whiteness is that by which something is white. In a creature, therefore, what is simple, is incomplete and non-subsistent; what is subsistent and complete is composed. However, God is both simple and subsistent. Thus the mode or way of signifying as pertaining to creatures cannot be the same as pertaining to God.

Yet these names retain *one aspect* of their signification when used to name God. Abstract names will signify God as simple, and concrete names as subsistent, with the abstract name losing its aspect of incompleteness and the concrete name its aspect of composition. Usually the signification is rendered clear by use of the concrete reflexive pronoun "itself." For example, we say God is "goodness itself," "goodness" emphasizing the simplicity of this perfection and "itself" its concrete subsistence. But even as thus corrected and purified, such names as "goodness itself," "truth itself," although they properly and positively name God, do not tell us what this goodness is as it exists in God. We can no more know what divine goodness is than we can know what the divine essence is, since these are identical in God. Our naming of God has all the limitations of our knowledge of God. [3]

The answer to the second objection becomes clear from our answer to the first. As imposed to signify material things, the mode of signification that a word has is that proper to a material being. Therefore, while *what* is signified by the name can in some sense be said of God, the *way* the name signifies can in no sense be said of God. [4] In creatures adjectives signify the substance according to a certain quality; in God they signify the quality as identical with the substance. Verbs and participles, as applied to creatures, always consignify time; in God they consignify his eternity, which includes all time.

Just as we cannot understand nor signify simple subsistents except after the manner of composite beings, so neither can we understand and ex-

---

[3] See St. Thomas, S.T., I, 13, 1.

[4] *What* a word means is one thing, and its mode of signification or *way* of expressing that meaning is another. For example, a word may express a meaning abstractly or concretely, simply or composedly, etc. These are its modes of signification. This distinction between the meaning of a word and the way a word can express that meaning will be seen more in detail presently.

press in words simple eternity except after the manner of temporal things. And this is due to the connaturality that our intellect has for composite and temporal things. [5]

Demonstrative pronouns point out God not insofar as he can be sensed, but insofar as he can be understood. For it is according to intellect that God is demonstrable. [6]

6. A Final Observation

In names that are imposed to signify material things because of our knowledge of them, we have seen that we can make a distinction between that which is signified through the name and the manner of signifying that the name has. This distinction in a name is analogous to the distinction in the concept between what is known by the concept and the way it is known. What is known by the concept and expressed by the word is in the thing, but the *way* it is known in the concept (immaterially, universally, and so on), and the way it is expressed in the word (abstractly, simply, and so on) is not in the thing. According to its manner of signifying, no word is ever said of God, for God is in no way either composite or abstract. But what is signified by the word can *in some sense* be said of God. However, even this signification, purified of all the conditions and imperfections that attend its origin from creatures and its signification of creatures, does not express the divine essence in itself. That which a word signifies, even when divested of all imperfection or limitation of meaning, does not, even confusedly or generically, name God as he is in himself.

There is only one infinite word that expresses the divine essence in itself, and that is the Word of God, the Second Person of the Blessed Trinity. Since our words can never signify the manner of being of the divine essence, neither can they ever signify that Being in itself. Since God is his own Being, not only is his essence absolutely unknowable by us but also absolutely unnamable. Just as no created form can represent that essence in itself, no name which expresses this created form can signify that essence in it-

[5] *S.T.*, I, 13, 1, ad 3.
[6] *Ibid.*

self. The names we apply to God, like "infinite Being" or "infinite goodness," do indeed apply only and properly to God, and tell us something about God. But they do not name that essence in its proper mode of being.

7. What Name Most Aptly Signifies the Divine Essence?

Although God cannot be named in himself, he can be named in the same way he can be known, that is, through names borrowed from creatures. Our next problem is this: of all the names that can be applied to God, which one most aptly designates the divine essence? Obviously, certain names will be better than others to bring out certain relationships between the creature and God. But all things being considered, what name best designates God?

Philosophy has been helped in this problem through revelation. For in *Exodus* the name of God is revealed to Moses. When Moses says to God, "When they (the Israelites) shall say to me: What is His Name? What shall I answer them? And the Lord said to him: This you shall tell them: Who Is has sent me to you. (*Qui est misit me ad vos.*)" [7] The name of God that he has revealed to us is: *Who Is.*

If we reflect upon this name, we shall see that there are three reasons why of all names it most aptly signifies the divine essence. First, because it does not signify any form, but a simple act: *to be*. Moreover, it signifies this act as a name and, therefore, as the very essence of God. And since God's act of existing is his essence, *Qui Est*, "Who Is," best signifies that essence. Names are imposed because of the nature of the thing, and God's nature is one with his Being.

The second reason why *Who Is* best signifies God is that this name is in no way determined. All other names, like "wisdom," "love," "goodness," "truth," imply some determination. Even though names like *The One, The True, The Good* ("God") are convertible with being, they at least add a relation of reason to being, and thus are more determinate and less absolute than being. As St. Thomas points out, although our intellect in this life

[7] *Exodus*, Ch. 3, verse 13.

can never know the essence of God in itself, yet any name that determines what we do understand about God falls short of the way God is in himself. [8] Therefore, the less determined and the more absolute a name is, the more aptly it can be said of God. As St. John Damascene writes: "Of all the names that can be said of God the best is: He is who is, for it comprehends everything within itself as within an infinite and indeterminate ocean of substance." [9] "He Who Is" in no way determines the mode of God's Being, which is not true of any other name. Finally, this name most aptly applies to the divine essence because of what is consignifies; namely, existence in the present. And this is most true of God, whose Being knows neither past nor future.

8. "He Who Is" and Subsistent Being Itself

"He Who Is" is sometimes written as a noun with two modifiers: Subsistent Being Itself. The "Itself" indicates that God's being, while concrete, is not composed, and "Subsistent" emphasizes the fact that God is, and does not have, existence. "Subsistent Being Itself" is simply "He Who Is" made more substantive or namelike. It is a more stylized and technical way of saying "He Who Is." But the name "Who Is" brings out better the fact that God is existential act and that this act is eternal and completely indetermined. "Who Is" is the name God told us to call him and it is the name St. Thomas chooses as most proper. It best represents God as we know him, but it in no way represents God as he is in himself. It names the divine essence as knowable by us; it does not name what that divine essence is in itself.

9. "Who Is" or Subsistent Being Signifies God's Essence as Known by Us

In the case of material beings, that name which is most proper to them signifies their definition; and their definition declares what the essence of the thing is. The essence of a thing known fulfills three functions: first, it tells us to what order of beings the

[8] *S.T.*, I, 13, 12.
[9] *De Fide Orthodoxa*, Bk. I, Ch. 9 (PG 94, 836).

thing belongs, since the essence makes a being what it is. What a thing is as known is called its quiddity; what the thing is as existing is its essence. That is why essence is something relative, something ordered: ordered to *esse*, as the very word essence implies. Essence always consignifies *esse*.

Secondly, essence as known distinguishes a being from all other beings. The essence of man, for example, distinguishes him from all other animals. This is so because the essence of man is what is properly his own, whereas he shares animality with other animals and existence with other beings. Finally, the essence as known furnishes the mind with the cause or reason why certain properties can be demonstrated about that essence. In this sense we say that the definition or quiddity is a means of demonstration. The essence is the source and cause of these properties and activities. As such a source and cause, the essence of the thing is called nature.

With these facts in mind, we can understand why "Who Is" or "Subsistent Being Itself" names and constitutes our knowledge of the essence of God, [10] just as, analogically speaking, "rational animal" names and constitutes our knowledge of the real essence of man. First, this quasi-essence puts God in his proper order of being, that of existential act, since God's essence is one with his existence. Secondly, this quasi-essence distinguishes God from all other beings, since the essence of no other being is identical with its existence. Finally, it furnishes the mind with a means of demonstrating the properties and attributes of God. Because God is subsistent Being, he must be also subsistent truth, and so on.

We come now to the third and most important part of our prob-

[10] Some authors distinguish between God's physical and metaphysical essence, his physical essence being the divine essence as it is in itself, and his metaphysical essence being the divine essence as knowable by us. The word "metaphysical" is a much abused word, and its use in this context constitutes another abuse. Metaphysics is the science of the real as real, of being as being; hence if used at all, it should always point out what is most actual and real in the thing itself. For this reason we have not followed these authors who call "Who Is" or "Subsistent Being Itself" the name of God's metaphysical essence. Rather we say this names his essence-as-known-by-us (quasi-essence).

lem of naming God. How are the names derived from creatures applied to God? This part contains a twofold consideration. The first we will call the *absolute* application of a name to God. Are names that are derived from perfections found in creatures applied to God properly or merely metaphorically? The second consideration concerns the *relative* application of a name. Are names derived from perfections found in creatures applied to God *and to creatures* in the same sense, in an entirely different sense, or in an analogous sense?

10. First Consideration: Proper and Metaphorical Use of Names

A name is applied to something in a proper sense if what the name signifies is found in the thing as an intrinsic property and perfection. A name is used metaphorically when the thing named manifests an activity or nature that is found properly only in some other thing. Two simple examples will bring out the difference between proper and metaphorical use of terms. In the predication, *John is wise,* wisdom belongs intrinsically and properly to John. When, however, we say, *John is a pig,* "pigness," which is the proper nature of pigs only, is said of John's nature insofar as that nature manifests an activity normally associated with pigs and which makes us think of pigs. [11]

Can names derived from creatures be said properly of God, or must they be applied to the divine essence only by way of metaphor? It would seem that no name can be applied properly to God.

The first reason is this: When I say that God is wise or good or beautiful, I know what these things signify in creatures. But God is infinitely removed from the wisdom, goodness, or beauty of creatures. So I remove such perfections from God rather than predicate them of him. And the wisdom, goodness and beauty found in creatures is the only kind I know. Such words seem, there-

[11] The statements, *John eats like a pig* and *John is a pig* (or *John runs like a deer* and *John is a fleet-footed deer*), by no means express the same idea. Simile and metaphor are two irreducible modes of expression. Simile expresses likeness, metaphor expresses identity. John *is* a pig. But the identification of John with the foreign nature of pig is due to an activity observed in John that is proper to pigs.

fore, to be said metaphorically rather than properly of the divine essence.

Furthermore, names of *material things* are said of God only metaphorically and not properly, as for example when I say God is a strong fortress or a loving mother. But all names derived from creatures are of this nature, since all of them—even names like "being" and "truth" and "wisdom"—imply matter. For they consignify time, composition, and other conditions of material things. Therefore, all names are said of God by way of metaphor and not properly.

11. The Solution

The solution to this problem is simple enough if we keep in mind the following facts:

1) We know God because of perfections which are in creatures, but which have proceeded from God by way of causality.

2) These perfections are in God according to a more perfect mode of being than they are in creatures.

3) The intellect of man understands these perfections as they are found in creatures.

4) The *way* the intellect understands these perfections is the way it signifies them by names.

5) Therefore in every name two things must be considered: (*a*) the perfection itself signified by the name: like goodness, life, or wisdom; (*b*) the way or manner in which this perfection is signified by the name.

6) If the perfection signified by the name is a perfection of being as being, that is, a perfection in whose meaning there is contained no imperfection, then the name is applied properly to God. God possesses the perfection intrinsically and by reason of the perfection. In fact, the perfection is said more properly of God than of the creature, since God possesses it essentially or as identified with his essence; whereas the creature possesses it only by way of participation and as distinct from its essence. Moreover, the perfection belongs primarily to God (*per prius*) and only secondarily (*per posterius*) to the creature, since God is the cause of the per-

fection in the creature. But although the perfection signified by the name belongs properly and primarily to God and is intrinsically and essentially in God, it is not signified as it exists in God. For this would give us a knowledge of the divine essence in itself, which we cannot have in this life. Finally, the manner or way in which this perfection is signified is never properly applied to God. In fact it is not applied to God at all. For names signify perfections the way they are found in creatures, that is, according to some limitation or imperfection. [12]

Our first conclusion, then, is this: The name in its mode of signification is never applied to God, but only the perfection signified by the name. Secondly, the perfection signified by a name may be of two kinds: a perfection in whose meaning is contained an imperfection, for example, "man," "stone," or "lion"; and perfection in whose meaning is contained no imperfection, for example, "good," "wise," or "holy." The former are perfections that do not follow being as being, but being as limited or material. Hence in the case of such perfections, not only is imperfection found in the way the name signifies, but in the very signification of the name. Thus names that signify such perfections are applied only metaphorically to God, even according to what they signify. But the latter names signify perfections of being as being, and so contain no imperfection. Thus what these names signify is applied properly to God, but not their manner of signification.

12. Answering the Objections

Since the wisdom of God is infinitely removed from the wisdom of creatures, what the name "wisdom" signifies is found *more perfectly* in God than in the creature. What I remove from God is not wisdom, but created wisdom. Because God is uncreated wisdom, I can even say that God is above wisdom, that is, above human wisdom.

As far as the second objection is concerned, we admit that all names that imply limitation or imperfection *in what they signify* are said only metaphorically of God. But names like "goodness,"

[12] See St. Thomas, *S.T.*, 1, 13, 3.

"beauty," "truth," or "being" are said properly of God, even though they include limitation and material conditions in their *mode of signification.* For this latter is not predicated of God, but only *what* these names signify.

13. Summary

All names that signify a perfection of being as being, and therefore in whose signification there is implied no imperfection, are applied to God properly as regards what they signify. The manner of signification cannot be applied to God. On the other hand, all names that signify a perfection that is not one of being as being but as such a being, and therefore in whose signification is implied some imperfection, are said of God only metaphorically, even according to what the name signifies. Their mode of signification can in no way be applied to God. Finally, even when a name that signifies a perfection of being as being is applied to God, this name in no way signifies this perfection *as it is in God.* The name "wisdom" when said of God leaves the thing signified (that is, God) uncomprehended and exceeding the signification of the name. [13]

14. Relative Application of Names to God and Creatures

We now wish to consider the relative application of a name. Are names when applied to God and to a creature applied in the same sense, in two completely different senses, or in some analogous sense? There is question here only of those names that signify a perfection of being as being, for these are the only names that are applied properly to God. Secondly, there is question here only of what is signified by the name, for again that is the only thing about a name that is said of God. Specifically, then, the question to be answered is this: Does that which a name signifies change completely when applied to the creature and to God? or does it remain the same? or is there a third possibility? For example, what happened to the meaning of wisdom when said of man and of God?

Before we begin our solution, let us recall that in every name there are three things to be considered:

[13] *S.T.,* 1, 13, 5.

1) The reason why the name was imposed. This reason will always be some effect or aspect about the thing so named. For example, St. Thomas says a stone is called *lapis* in Latin because *laedit pedem*, "it hurts the foot." [14] Obviously, a name used according to the reason for its origin is said properly and primarily only of the creature.

2) Secondly, there is the manner in which the perfection is named. For example, wisdom is signified after the manner of an accident, that is, a habit or disposition. Or goodness is signified after the manner of an incomplete or non-subsistent (abstract) perfection. The manner of signification of all names, since it follows the perfection as found in creatures, is never applied to God.

3) *The signification of the name itself.* This is concerned merely with the perfection signified, abstracting both from its mode of signifying and the reason for its imposition. Here, if what is signified is a perfection of being as being, the name is properly said of God and more properly of God than of creatures; moreover, it is said primarily of God and only secondarily of creatures. If, on the other hand, what is signified is a perfection of being as limited, the name is said metaphorically of God and properly only of that creature which actually possesses the perfection. With these distinctions in mind we are ready to consider our problem.

15. Names Signifying Perfections of Being as Being Are Not Said of God and Creatures Univocally

First of all, we say that the meaning does not remain the same. The perfection signified by the name is not predicated *univocally* of the creature and of God. No perfection is found in God and in the creature according to the same essential degree or specific formality. All the perfections that are in God are God. They are identified with the divine essence and this essence is identified with the existence of God. Now the act of existing of each thing is completely proper to the thing and thus absolutely incommunicable. A being could no more share its act of existing with another than it

[14] *S.T.*, I, 13, 2 ad 2.

could cease to be itself. The existence of a thing cannot be communicated to another; and since God's perfections are identified with his existence, no perfection can be found in any creature the way it exists in God. It is as impossible for any creature to have a perfection in the same degree God possesses it as it would be for that creature to be God. For God has all the perfections of being as being essentially, whereas these perfections are possessed by creatures only by way of participation. Moreover, univocal predication is immediately seen to be impossible between creatures and God when we recall that even among creatures no perfection of being as being is ever predicated univocally. Only perfections of essence (of being as limited) are ever predicated univocally of two or more things. [15]

16. Names Signifying Perfections of Being as Being Are Not Said of God and Creatures Equivocally

The problem of equivocity between divine and created perfections deserves careful attention. Equivocal words are words that have the same sound but completely different meanings. Aristotle correctly calls these words *aequivoca a casu*. That is to say, they are simply two different significations which happen (*a casu*) to have the same sound (*aequivoca*). Equivocal predication is the use of the same sounding words according to their different meanings. Notice that there is no such thing as an equivocal concept. There are only equivocal words. The word "pen" is an equivocal word, for it can signify an instrument for writing or an enclosure for animals. But two concepts, not one, are involved. The term "man" expresses a univocal concept. The term "being" expresses an analogous concept. The term "pen" expresses two completely different concepts, each being univocal as applied to its inferiors. Hence when we predicate an equivocal word, the word remains the same, but the concept and the signification of the word changes completely. Thus we can put our question as follows: When I say God is wise and man is wise, is the sound of the word the only thing

---

[15] For further reading on this point, see *S.T.*, I, 13, 5; *De Verit.*, qu. 2, a. 11; *C.G.*, Bk. I, Ch. 32; *De Pot.*, qu. 7, a. 7.

these predications have in common, their significations being entirely different?

It should be quite clear that no perfection of being as being can be predicated of God and the creature with a completely different meaning, that is, equivocally. And this for many reasons.

1) Between things that merely happen to have the same name, there exists no order or relationship. For example, an instrument of writing is not called a pen because it has some order or relationship to an enclosure for pigs. But this is not true of the names that are said of God and creatures, because in such community of names we consider the order of effect to cause that is found between the creature and God. Thus nothing is said of the creature and God by way of pure equivocation.

2) Where there is pure equivocation, there exists no likeness between the things named, but only a unity of the external word. But between the creature and God there must exist some likeness, since God has caused the creature, and everything causes according to its nature. Thus it is quite impossible that a perfection found in the creature and said of God, can be said by way of pure equivocation.

3) When something is said of two things by way of equivocation, it is impossible that the knowledge of one can lead to a knowledge of the other. Our knowledge of things does not depend upon the external *word*, but upon the concept or meaning of the word. Now as we have already seen in the five ways, from a knowledge of perfections found in creatures, we are led to a knowledge of God. Thus predication by way of pure equivocation between God and creatures is impossible.

4) It would be quite futile to predicate names of a subject, unless through those names we gained some knowledge of that subject. But if names were said of creatures and of God equivocally, we would learn nothing about God through such names, since the meaning of these names are known to us only according as they are said of creatures. Thus all efforts to demonstrate God's existence from creatures, or to demonstrate anything else about God, would be completely useless. It would be equally meaningless to

say of God that he exists or does not exist, that he is good or that he is evil, and so on. All of which is false. But someone may say: through such words we simply learn what God is not. For example, when I say God is living, I simply mean that he does not belong to that class of beings that have no life. We answer: but then the word "living" is not applied to God in a purely equivocal sense, since through this predication of "living," the creature and God are alike in this, that we deny non-living being to both of them.

To conclude, then, we say that if names were applied to creatures and to God equivocally, no knowledge of God would be possible, and it would make no difference what name we applied to God, for all names would be equally meaningless. God would be and would not be the cause of creatures, for he would not cause them according to any likeness to himself. All of which are so many impossibilities and contradictions. [16]

17. Names Signifying Perfections of Being as Being Are Said of God and Creatures Analogously

Since the meaning of a word like "wisdom" or "being" does not remain the same when predicated of a creature and of God, and since for reasons just seen the meaning cannot change completely, it must follow that just as there is some likeness between perfections in creatures and in God, so also there must be some likeness between the meaning of the word as applied to God and to the creature. Notice that we are talking about the meaning of the word, for this is what is applied, and it is applied to both analogously, that is, according to some proportion or proportionality of meaning, which is due to the proportion or proportionality of the perfection between God and the creature.

18. Difference Between a Univocal and Analogous Concept

A concept represents extra-mental reality. Hence, a concept deals with things insofar as these have some order to our knowledge. A concept is univocal if it contains only one meaning equally participated in by all the things represented by the concept and

[16] See C.G., Bk. I, Ch. 33; S.T., I, 13, 5.

signified by the name which orally expresses the concept. Let us take two examples of univocal concepts to illustrate what we mean. The concept of animal represents one formal perfection equally shared in by all animals—dogs, cats, men, and so forth. The concept of man represents one formal perfection equally shared in by all men—Paul, John, or James. Notice that univocal concepts are always and only concepts of perfections of essence, and never of being as being. The word ("animal," "man," or "flower") that corresponds to such a concept is called a univocal word and is used in exactly the same sense when applied to all the things it signifies.

An analogous concept, on the other hand, is one that does not contain only one meaning that is equally shared in by the different things represented by the concept. Such, for example, is our concept of wisdom. We know that there is created wisdom and that there is uncreated wisdom. But there is not one meaning of wisdom that *abstracts* from both created and uncreated, and thus includes neither in its meaning. For this would be no meaning of wisdom at all. Whereas, in the case of the univocal concept of animal, this does abstract from both rational and irrational (for example, from man and dog) and actually includes neither. And the same is true of all univocal concepts as regards their inferiors. But the concept of wisdom does not abstract from wisdom as created or wisdom as uncreated. It actually includes both kinds of wisdom in one meaning, not explicitly, but only implicitly. And this is true of all analogous concepts. Hence the unity of an analogous concept is an imperfect unity.

In a word, wisdom is not equally shared in by men and by God. Wisdom in God is essential wisdom, and so includes all wisdom. Wisdom in man is participated wisdom, and hence only a partial wisdom. So it is quite impossible that from created wisdom and uncreated wisdom the mind can abstract that which is common to both but which actually includes neither. There is one concept that includes both wisdoms actually but implicitly. Whereas a univocal concept includes its inferiors only potentially and not actually.

19. The Problem of Analogy

The difficulty of predicating anything analogously of God and creatures is, essentially, the difficulty of there existing any proportion between divine and created perfections, of their being any proportion between the Being of God and the being of the creature. The problem of predication is the problem of our use of knowledge. And the problem of knowledge is ultimately the problem of things, since things cause and measure our knowledge of them. And the basic problem of things concerns their act of existing and their relationship to that act.

For example, I can predicate my concept "being" analogously of two existing beings because I *know* that they exist analogously. And I can know that they exist analogously because they *do exist* analogously. Different beings, independently of my knowledge of them, exercise their act of existing in such a way that there is an analogy among them. For each being not only exercises an act of existing, but exercises that act according to what it is. An analogy between beings arises because of the way each thing exercises its existence. Our present problem is to see how this analogy is to be understood when applied to our naming of God.

To understand this problem let us recall some definitions from metaphysics concerning analogy.

1) *analogy:* the proportion or likeness that exists between two (or more) things.

2) *the analogates:* the things that possess this analogy or likeness.

3) *prime analogate:* the thing that principally, or more perfectly, possesses the analogous perfection.

4) *attributed analogy or analogy of attribution:* the analogous perfection is intrinsic to only one of the analogates, but is attributed to the others because of some relation these have to this perfection.

5) *proper analogy:* one analogate is like or proportioned to another by something that is intrinsic (proper) to each analogate. Proper analogy can be of two kinds:

(*a*) *analogy of proportion:* a direct likeness of one analogate to the other.

(*b*) *analogy of proportionality:* an indirect likeness of one analogate to the other. Each analogate has within itself an intrinsic proportion, and this gives rise to a proportion of proportions, or a proportionality, between the analogates.

Now let us see some examples of predication by way of analogy.

(*a*) By way of an analogy of attribution: "The man is healthy" (since he possesses health as an *intrinsic perfection*).

"The medicine is healthy" [17] (for it can *cause health* in man).

"This diet is healthy" (for it can *preserve health* in man).

"His complexion is healthy" (for it *manifests the health* in man).

In this example, the perfection "health" is attributed to the medicine, the diet and the complexion because of some relationship (cause, sign, and so on) that medicine, diet, and complexion have to the intrinsic health in man.

(*b*) By way of an analogy of proper proportion:

> "Substance is being."
> "Accidents are being."

The perfection of being is intrinsically participated in by both substance and accidents, but the being of the accident is caused by the being of the substance. Hence there is a direct order or proportion of the one to the other. Thus between incomplete principles of being there is an analogy of proper proportion. This analogy is sometimes called analogy of participation, since (in the example given) each principle participates, in its own way, in the act of existing, because of which participation each principle is analogously alike.

(*c*) By way of an analogy of proper proportionality:

> "Paul is being."
> "Man of War is being."

Between Paul and Man of War, considered as beings, there is an indirect proportion or a proportion of proportions. The being

---

[17] In some of these examples, correct English usage would demand "healthful." We have kept the word "healthy" to avoid verbal confusion.

that Paul is, is due to the unique proportion that obtains between his essence and his act of existing. The being that Man of War is, is due to the unique proportion that obtains between his essence and act of existing. And between the two there is a proportion or relation of these two intrinsic proportions. This proportion of proportions we call proportionality. There is a *proportionality*, therefore, in their *being*. The analogy between complete beings is an analogy of proper proportionality.

With these principles in mind, let us ask ourselves this question: Can there exist any analogy between the being of creatures and the Being of God? It would seem not. And this for two reasons. First, there can be no proportion, that is to say, direct likeness between the creature and God. Secondly, there can be no indirect likeness or proportionality between the creature and God. And since these are the only two proper analogies, it seems impossible that there be any analogous predication of the perfections possessed by God and the creature.

20. No Direct Likeness Between Creatures and God Seems Possible

When one analogate is directly proportioned to another, there must exist between the two beings a measurable distance. Ontologically measurable, of course, not spatially. And this is so because the existence of the direct likeness constitutes a direct order or relation between the two beings. This order puts some determination or limitation on the beings so ordered. And since the Being of God can have no limit or determination, neither can it have any direct order or proportion to the creature. On the other hand, if this distance is not ontologically measurable between the creature and God, the creature can hardly be said to be like God. Hence, it seems impossible that there should exist an analogy of proportion between the creature and God. And St. Thomas seems to say the same thing:

There is a certain agreement between two things having a proportion to each other from the fact that they have a determinate distance be-

tween each other or some other relation to each other, like the proportion which the number two has to unity in as far as it is the double of
unity. . . . (And because) in those terms predicated according to
(this) type of analogy, there must be some definite relation between the
things having something in common analogously, nothing can be predicated analogously of God and creature according to this type of analogy;
for no creature has such a relation to God that it could determine the
divine perfection.[18]

21. No Indirect Likeness Seems Possible

But what about the analogy of proportionality? This analogy
would in no way determine the divine Being, because the likeness
would not exist directly between the Being of God and the being
of the creature, but would be only indirect, that is to say, it would
be a likeness of proportions because of what God is and what the
creature is. St. Thomas explains the analogy as follows:

Again . . . agreement is occasionally noted not between two things
which have a proportion between them, but rather between two related proportions—for example, six has something in common with
four because six is two times three, just as four is two times two. (And
this) is the agreement of proportionality. . . . (And in this) type of
analogy, no definite relation is involved between the things which
have something in common analogously, so there is no reason why some
name cannot be predicated analogously of God and creature in this
manner. [19]

That such proportionality would in no way contract the ontological distance that must obtain between the Being of God and
that of the creature, St. Thomas more clearly attests in his answer
to the fourth objection of this same article.

A likeness that is found because two things share something in common
or because one has such a determinate relation to the other that from
the one the other can be grasped by the intellect—such a likeness dimin-
ishes the distance. A likeness according to an agreement of proportion
does not; for such a likeness is also found between far or little distant.
Indeed, there is no greater likeness or proportionality between two to

[18] *De Veritate*, qu. 2, a. 11, *resp.* Translation by Robert W. Mulligan, S.J.,
in *Truth* (Chicago, Henry Regnery Company, 1952), p. 113. Words in parentheses added.
[19] *Ibid.* Words in parentheses added.

one and six to three than there is between two to one and one hundred to fifty. Consequently, the infinite distance between a creature and God does not take away the likeness mentioned above. [20]

Now, while admitting with the Angelic Doctor that a proportion between two proportions would in no way lessen the distance between the two analogates, since the likeness is not direct but only indirect, we must still answer this question: Is such a proportionality possible in the case of God? St. Thomas merely asserts that such an analogy is possible, while the very nature of proportionality as he describes it seems to render its existence impossible in the case of God. The reason is a simple one. Proportionality is a proportion between proportions. Hence within each analogate there must exist a proportion as the foundation for the proportionality. But a proportion must be between two terms that are distinct in some way. In the creature, there is a real distinction between its essence and act of existing, and because of this real distinction there can be a proportion between the essence and act of existing. Because of this proportion within the creature, the creature is what it is and hence can be *proportional* to other created beings. But in God essence is identical with existence. Hence there are not two terms, but only one, and so there is no proportion within the Being of God, and therefore no foundation for a proportionality with the creature.

So we conclude: an analogy of proper proportion seems impossible between the creature and God, since it lessens the ontological distance between them. And this is impossible, for God is infinite and the creature finite. And an analogy of proper proportionality seems impossible between the creature and God since there is no proportion or order within the being of God. There seems then absolutely no analogy, either direct or indirect, between the creature and God.

22. The Solution to This Problem

How solve this problem? A solution would include the answers to these three questions: First, what kind of analogies cannot

[20] *Ibid.*, p. 114.

exist between the creature and God? Secondly, what kind do exist and what are the reasons why they do? Thirdly, and finally, how can we answer the objections given above?

First of all, what kind of analogous predication does not obtain between the creature and God? Names that are said of many because the perfection signified by the name is intrinsic to only one of the analogates and merely attributed to the other analogates, cannot be predicated of God. As we have seen, names are predicated of God properly and not merely by way of extrinsic denomination. Thus the analogy that obtains between medicine, food and complexion, because of their order to the intrinsic health in man does not hold between God and creatures. For the perfection predicated must be proper and intrinsic to both God and creature.

But even in the case of perfections that are proper to each analogate, we find two sorts of analogy. And one cannot apply to God and creatures. This is the case where each analogate is like the other because they are both ordered to some third thing. For example, the perfection signified by the name *being* can be predicated intrinsically of both quantity and quality, but only because the being of both is order to a third thing, namely, the being of the substance. Quantity and quality are like each other because each has its proper relation to substance. Now God and the creature are not alike in this sense, for this would mean that some third thing is prior to God, to which he and the creature are ordered and because of which they possess analogous perfections. Nothing can be prior to God.

In the second type of proper analogy two things are like each other, not because each is proportioned to some third thing, but because one is proportioned or ordered to the other. For example, an accident is ordered to its substance, and so I can predicate being of both the substance and accident because the being of the accident is ordered to the being of the substance, and not because each is ordered to some third thing. The reason for this ordering is that the being of the substance is the cause of the being of the accident.

This is the kind of analogy that can exist between the creature and God. For the creature is ordered to God as to its principle and cause in whom pre-exists in an infinitely excellent manner all the perfections found in creatures. Therefore, we can predicate the perfections of being found in the creature analogously of the creature and of God. [21]

But besides this direct analogy of proper proportion between the creature and God, there also exists between them an analogy of proper proportionality, or a proportion of proportions. And this is based on the real distinction in creatures between their essence and existence and the distinction of reason in God between his essence and existence. For example, just as man has his wisdom, so does God have his wisdom. And so there is a proportionality between the wisdom of man and the wisdom of God. This analogy is called proper, for the wisdom in both cases is intrinsic to the analogate. [22] And this is called proportionality, for it is based upon the proportion between man and his wisdom and between God and his wisdom.

23. Answering the Objections

Let us try to answer the rather serious objections advanced against the possibility of any proportion or proportionality between the creature and God. What St. Thomas denied in the *De Veritate* was a determinate or measurable distance between the creature and God, some order or relation between them that would lessen the infinite distance in their being. In this sense, there can be no proportion between the creature and God. But if God's Being is in no way affected by the fact that the creature is ordered to it, then there can exist a proportion between the creature and God.

Now when God causes something, he does not become really

[21] See *S.T.*, I, 13, 5.

[22] An example of *improper* proportionality would be metaphor. For example, in the predication, "The meadow is smiling," the perfection "smiling" is not intrinsic to the meadow, but only to the man. But the meadow is called "smiling" because of a proportionality: just as a smile lights up the face of man, so does the sun light up the meadow.

related or ordered to what he causes. God's causal action is one with his divine substance. Hence when he produces an effect, his substance undergoes no change. The whole change is in the effect. As a result of divine causality the creature is really ordered to the creator, but the creator is not really ordered to the creature. The divine causality leaves the divine Being unchanged, and thus leaves unchanged the infinite distance between God and the creature.

We have an example of this even among creatures. When a thing really causes the knowledge we have of it, that thing in no way is changed or affected by this causality. Hence, while our knowledge is really related to the thing as effect to cause, the thing known (although a cause) is not really related or ordered to our knowledge. Our knowledge depends upon things, but things do not depend upon our knowledge. Thus we can answer the first objection by means of a simple distinction. When one thing is proportioned to another, the distance between the two is diminished if there results a relation between them that is mutually real. But this is not true in the case of God, because of the nature of the divine causality.

Our second objection, which denied proportionality between God and the creature because there is no proportion within God's Being, is solved as follows. We deny that two *really* distinct terms within each analogate are essential to the nature of the analogy of proper proportionality. It may be essential to the proportionality among finite beings, and it may also be essential to all mathematical proportionalities. But it is not essential to the notion of the analogy of proportionality itself. What is essential is that each being *because of its ontological status as being* is analogous to every other being.

In creatures, this ontological status is due to the unique relation within each analogate of its essence to its act of existing. In God, the peculiar ontological status of the divine Being, that which makes God be God, is the absolute identity between essence and existence. Because of this identity, God is the Being he is; just as the creature because of its composition is the being it is. Because

God is what he is and the creature what it is, there is constituted a proportionality or indirect likeness between the creature and God. The foundation for this proportionality is constituted by the way each exercises its act of existing.

Moreover, since we come to know God through creatures, the intelligibility of essence in God is rationally distinct from the intelligibility of his act of existing. We could not even affirm that essence and existence are absolutely identical in God, unless we first understood them as rationally distinct, or distinct in our knowledge of God. The rational distinction in our knowledge between God's essence and existence grounds our *knowledge* of the proper proportionality between his Being and the being of creatures. Whereas the absolute identity of the two in God makes God the kind of Being he is. [23]

Thus we can conclude that while it may be essential to our *knowledge* of the analogy of proper proportionality that two rationally distinct terms be considered in God, it is by no means essential to the *existence* of an analogy of proportionality between creatures or God. All that is required for such an analogy to exist is that each analogate exercise in a unique way its existential act.

An even greater mistake would be to confuse mathematical proportionality with metaphysical proportionality or the analogy of being. Mathematical proportionality is a likeness not between beings as being, but beings as quantified. Here the proportion between the proportions is itself univocal, and obviously two dis-

---

[23] Consider the following quotation from St. Thomas where this idea is clearly indicated. "A thing is said to be proportionate to another in two ways. In one way, a proportion is noted between the two things. For example, we say that four is proportioned to two since its proportion to two is double. In the second way, they are proportioned as by a proportionality. For example, we say that six and eight are proportionate because, just as six is the double of three, so eight is the double of four; for proportionality is a similarity of proportions. When things are said to be proportionate by way of proportionality, their relation to each other is not considered. All that is considered is the similarity of the relation of two things to two other things. Thus, nothing prevents an infinite from being proportionate to an infinite; for, just as a particular finite is equal to a certain finite, so an infinite is equal to another infinite." *De Verit.*, qu. 2, a. 3, ad 4m. That is, just as a particular finite essence is to its act of existing, so God's infinite essence is to its infinite act of existing.

tinct terms are needed, for we are dealing with discrete quantity.

Finally, both in the case of the analogy of proportion between the creature and God, and the analogy of proportionality between the creature and God, each analogy, while mutual, is not mutually real. The analogy or order is real from the side of the creature; it is merely of reason from the side of God. The creature has a real proportion to God, because the creature is really caused by God. God, however, has no real proportion to the creature, since his Being is in no way really affected by the existence of the creature. We merely *consider* the divine Being as ordered to the creature. And the creature has a real proportionality to God, since the really distinct terms of essence and existence are caused by God. God, however, has no real proportionality to the creature, since the way he exercises his existence depends in no way upon the manner in which the creature exercises its existence. There is a real proportion within the creature and a real proportionality between the being of the creature and the Being of God. But there is only a proportion of reason within God and only a proportionality of reason between God and the creature.

24. Conclusion

To summarize: (1) Names signifying perfections of being as being, are said of creatures and of God analogously, because of the order of causality that the creature has to God, in whom preexists in an infinitely excellent manner all the perfections of being caused in the creature. Thus there is an analogy of proper proportion between creatures and God. (2) This ordering of the creature to God in no way determines or limits the Being of God since, because of the nature of divine causality, the relation is not in God but only in the creature. Since in God "to act" is one with "to be," and this latter is absolutely immutable, the divine action in no way affects the divine existence. (3) Furthermore, since the perfections predicated of God and of creatures are perfections of being, the analogy or likeness that obtains between these perfections, and thus also between the names signifying these perfections, is an analogy in being. And because the being of each analogate depends upon the manner in which it exercises its act of existing (for the act of existing is the act of being as being), this analogy of being is one of proportionality. Here we have not a direct and immediate likeness of one being to the other, but a likeness between the proportions. (4) Finally, since finite beings are proportionate to the divine Being because they descend from that Being and imitate it, they are also proportionate to one another because of the different ways they are ordered to and imitate their same first principle. God is the prime analogate in the analogy of being, each creature participating in a different way the divine Being. From this point of view, we can say that creatures are like God by an analogy of participation, the nature and degree of the participation being determined by the relationship that each essence has to its proper act of existing.

25. Summary of the Chapter

"The name that most aptly designates God is *Who Is*. Moreover, other names signifying perfections of being as being are said properly of God, and of creatures and God according to an analogy of proper proportion and of proper proportionality."

a. State of the question

Having considered the way God can be known by us, in this chapter we considered the way God can be named by us. For a thing is named according to the way it is understood. Now God is known by us through creatures, according to the way of causality, excellence and removal. Thus God can also be named by us. This chapter, therefore, treated of the divine names, and answered these questions: How can we apply our knowledge to the divine essence? And more precisely, how do we predicate names signifying the divine perfections?

b. Explanation of terms

1) ". . . *name* . . . "—any spoken word (or words), which immediately signifies the concept we have of a thing, and through

this concept the thing thus conceived. As St. Thomas writes: "Words are the signs of concepts and concepts are the likenesses of things. And thus it is clear that words signify things through the concepts of the intellect. Therefore, according to the way a thing can be known by us, so it can be named by us." (*S.T.*, I, 13, 1)

2) ". . . *most aptly* . . ." A name signifies some meaning or intelligibility, to which there corresponds in the thing some likeness, which likeness is the cause of this meaning or intelligibility. The name that signifies the perfect intelligibility of a thing is its definition. And because the name "Who Is" signifies the quasi-essence of God, and therefore his quasi-definition, it is said to designate God most aptly.

3) ". . . *Who Is* . . ."—subsistent Being itself. Unreceived, and therefore subsistent, Existence.

4) ". . . *perfection of being as being* . . ."—because the act of being is "to be" (the act of existing), a perfection of being as being is one that follows the act of existing as such, rather than its reception in some potency (essence). And because the act of existing is simply act, and is in no way ordered to any other act, a perfection of being as being includes in its signification no imperfection.

5) ". . . *properly* . . ."—this is opposed to metaphorically. What is said properly of a thing is intrinsic to a thing, and does not merely have some extrinsic relationship (cause, sign, and so forth) to it. Thus, for example, heat is said properly of fire.

6) ". . . *analogy* . . ."—a proportion or likeness of one thing to another. "Analogy" is the proportion or likeness itself between two (or more) things. The "analogates" are the things that possess the likeness. The "principal analogate" is the thing that primarily and most perfectly possesses the analogous perfection. There are different kinds of analogy:

(*a*) *analogy of attribution:* this is had when the analogous perfection is intrinsic to only one of the analogates, but is attributed to the others because of some order which these have to the intrinsic perfection in the one analogate. For example, the perfection of health, which is intrinsic and proper to man, is attributed to medicine inasmuch as it *produces* health in man, to the diet insofar as it *conserves* this health, etc.

(*b*) *proper analogy:* this is had when the analogous perfection is intrinsic to each of the analogates. Proper analogy can be of two kinds:

i. *proper proportion:* the direct order or likeness of two things to each other. Thus an effect is directly proportioned to its cause.

ii. *proper proportionality:* the likeness of two proportions to each other. Thus the analogy between the analogates is not direct, since it is between the proportions. Each analogate has within itself some order or proportion, and because of this there is between the two analogates some proportionality, or proportion of proportions. For example, between four and a hundred there is a proportionality, since just as four is twice two, so a hundred is twice fifty. (See *De Verit.*, qu. 2, a. 11c; ad 4m; qu. 2, a. 3, ad 4m.) The likeness is not directly between the numbers, but between the proportions.

(*c*) *The analogy of being:* the order or likeness that obtains between beings as being, or between two things insofar as they exercise their act of existing and those perfections that follow this act of existing. The analogy of being is an analogy of proper proportionality, based on the proportion within each being of its essence to its act of existing.

c. *The proof*

1) *The name that most aptly designates God is "Who Is."* (*a*) Because "Who Is" signifies no form, but only act: the act of existing. And it signifies this act as a proper name. Therefore, since names are imposed on things to designate their very essence or nature, and since the divine essence is its act of existing, it is clear that the name "Who Is" most aptly designates God.

(*b*) Because "Who Is" designates God as in no way limited or determined. All other names, such as wisdom, love, the good (God), the truth, imply some composition or determination. And while such names as the One, the True, the Good, are convertible with Being, they nonetheless add to Being a relation of reason. And

so the name "Who Is" as signifying something altogether simple
and indetermined, most aptly designates God.

(*c*) Because "Who Is" implies existence in the present. And in
the case of God this is most befitting, since "his Being knows neither past nor future," as St. Augustine writes in his *De Trinitate*
(Book V). (See *S.T.*, I, 13, 11)

2) *Names signifying perfections of being as being are said prop-*
erly of God. Any name is said properly of a thing if *what is*
signified by the name is found really and intrinsically in the thing
signified. But perfections of being as being (or *what is signified* by
such names) are found really and intrinsically in God. Therefore,
names signifying perfections of being as being are said properly of
God.

Proof of the major: To have something properly is to have it as
one's property or proper possession (that is, really and intrinsically), and not merely metaphorically or by way of extrinsic denomination.

Proof of the minor: God, as Subsistent Being and Pure Act, possesses all perfections in whose signification there is contained no
imperfection. Otherwise God would not be the Perfect Being.
Moreover, God, as the cause of these perfections in creatures, must
act according to his nature. Hence, creatures are really like God
because of these perfections. Therefore, *what is signified* through
the names of such perfections is properly said of God. It is clear,
however, that *the way* such names signify these perfections is in
no way said of God. Finally, whatever there is of imperfection in
the creature, such as limitation and potency, is not in the creature
because it has been produced by God, but because it has been produced by God *from nothing*.

St. Thomas puts this last point clearly:

There are certain things in creatures according to which they are like
God, namely, things in whose signification there is no imperfection,
such as life, being, understanding, etc. And these are said properly of
God; in fact, they are said more properly and eminently of God than
of creatures. But there are other things in creatures according to which
they differ from God, and are consequent upon creatures' production

from nothingness, such as potentiality, privation, motion, etc., and these are not in God. All those names in whose signification fall such conditions (like potency, etc.), are said of God only metaphorically, such as lion, stone, etc., since they contain matter in their definition. These words are said metaphorically of God because of some likeness of effect.[24]

By "likeness of effect," St. Thomas means that God sometimes acts in his effects like a lion, a fire, a fortress, and so forth. For example, God can metaphorically be called "an angry fire" because of the severity of his punishments.

3) *Names signifying perfections of being as being are said of creatures and God by an analogy of proper proportion and proper proportionality.* (*a*) *of proper proportion:* Every effect is directly ordered to and properly like its cause. But creatures are the effects of God, who is their first efficient, exemplary and final cause. Therefore, *etc.*

(*b*) *of proper proportionality:* Proportionality is the proportion of two proportions to each other, or a likeness of proportions. But the likeness which obtains between created and divine perfections is a likeness of proportions. Therefore, *etc.* The *major* is the definition of proportionality, which has been explained above.

Proof of the minor: Among all beings there is present some real likeness: every being, as being, is like every other being. (I could not say: this creature is a being, God is a Being, unless the creature and God were like each other as beings.) Hence, the reason for this likeness must be found in the being itself of God and the creature. As we know from metaphysics, each thing holds its grade and perfection of being from its order or relation to its act of existing. According to the different ways beings exercise their act of existing is due the differences among things, and according to a like exercise of the act of existing is due the analogy or proportion among things.

Now God is the Being he is because he *is* his own act of existing, and creatures are the beings they are because they *have* (more or less perfectly) their acts of existing. It is clear, therefore, that between creatures and God there is some proportionality, because

[24] From *De Pot.*, qu. 7, a. 5, ad 8m.

just as the creature is the being it is because of its relation to its act of existing, so God is the Being he is because of his identity with his act of existing.

Suggested Readings

1. St. Thomas, *Summa Theologiae,* in *Basic Writings of St. Thomas,* by A. Pegis (New York, Random House, 1945), pp. 112–134.
2. G. B. Phelan, *Saint Thomas and Analogy* (Milwaukee, Marquette University Press, 1941).
3. J. F. Anderson, *The Bond of Being* (St. Louis, B. Herder Book Company, 1949), Chapter XXII, "The Essence of Metaphysical Analogy," pp. 295–313.

CHAPTER 7

The Perfections of God

*Since God is subsisting Being itself, nothing
of the perfection of being can be wanting to
him. Now all the perfections of all things
pertain to the perfection of being; for things
are perfect precisely so far as they have being in some fashion. It follows therefore that
the perfection of no thing is wanting to God.*
—St. Thomas, *Summa Theologiae*,
qu. 4, a. 2, resp.

Prenote

Thus far in our study of the nature of God we have discussed the
following points: (1) how we can know God from creatures and
grow in this knowledge by a growth in our understanding of the
relationships that creatures have to God; (2) how names signifying
perfections found in creatures are used when said of these perfections as existing in God. Now we are ready to go a step further and
ask ourselves this question: How do these perfections found in
creatures and predicated of God actually exist in God? Are all perfections found in creatures also found in God? and if so, how are
they so found?

In this chapter we shall divide our study of the divine perfections into four parts. In the first part we shall discuss the problem of
how the divine essence, although absolutely simple or uncomposed, nevertheless possesses all perfection. Secondly, we shall investigate how perfections found in creatures pre-exist in God.

228

Thirdly, since God possesses all perfections, we shall discuss the nature of his divine infinity, and this study of God as infinitely perfect will lead us to consider him as the supreme and absolute good. Fourthly, the chapter will end with a discussion of how the divine perfections are distinct from the divine essence and from each other.

A. DIVISIONS OF THE DIVINE PERFECTIONS

Our study of the divine perfections becomes clearer and easier once we have grasped the meaning of the terms involved. A large part of our study, then, will be devoted to the understanding of these terms.

a. God

From now on, since we are engaged in a scientific investigation of God, the name God is simply a serviceable substitute for that name which most aptly signifies the divine being, namely, "Who Is," or "Subsistent Being itself." "God" therefore equals "Subsistent Being," the divine essence as known by us and from which flow as from their ontological source the other perfections of God.

b. A divine attribute

A divine attribute is any perfection that I can say of God, any predicate I can make of my subject, subsistent Being. Traditionally, the divine attributes have been divided in various ways.

1) (a) *entitative:* that attribute which flows from the divine being considered in itself rather than in its operation, for example, simplicity, infinity, eternity, and so forth.

(b) *operative:* an attribute that implies some divine action, for example, love, wisdom, justice, mercy, and so forth. Also considered here are those attributes that are the direct sources of these activities, namely, intellect and will.

2) (a) *positive:* any divine attribute that is conceived by a positive concept or expressed by a positive term. By positive is meant the placing of something, rather than its removal, for example, love, mercy, wisdom, and so forth.

(*b*) *negative:* any attribute conceived after the manner of a negation and expressed by a negative word. By a negative term is meant a term that removes something from God rather than posits it. But here we should note that while the manner of conceiving the perfection and the word used to express it may be negative, what the word signifies is in itself something positive. For example, the word *infinity* denies limitation, but limitation is itself a denial of perfection. Thus infinity is really a negation of a negation, and two negatives make a positive. And this is true of all the so-called negative perfections of God, like infinity, immutability, immateriality, and so forth.

3) (*a*) *absolute:* a perfection that belongs to God necessarily and independently of any hypothesis or contingency, for example, independently of the contingent fact that creatures exist. Thus, the perfections of infinity, simplicity, knowledge, eternity, and so on.

(*b*) *relative:* some perfection that is said of God because of the actual existence of creatures, for example, creator, lord, provider, ruler.

4) (*a*) *incommunicable:* a perfection in God that cannot be shared by the creature since it signifies a removal of an imperfection that is necessarily connected with created perfection. Thus all the negative perfections of God are incommunicable perfections, for example, immutability, infinity, and so forth.

(*b*) *communicable:* an attribute that can be shared by the creature in a finite way. Thus God's positive perfections like wisdom, goodness, or love.

Two things should be noted about these divisions. First, they are not mutually exclusive. For example, infinity is an absolute, negative, incommunicable and entitative perfection. In fact, any perfection of God would fall under one of the two sets of the different divisions. Secondly, these divisions have come down to us chiefly from such men as Moses Maimonides and Suarez [1] and not from St. Thomas. But as traditional divisions they should be known by the student.

[1] See *Deus Dominus,* pp. 329–330.

1. The Divine Perfection of Simplicity

A being is simple insofar as it lacks composition. Hence there will be varying degrees of simplicity within a being according to the different orders within that being in which it is not composed. A composed being is one that possesses parts or principles, but parts so ordered to each other as to effect a unity, a composed unit. The actual union of these parts into a unified whole we call composition. Thus matter and form are parts of a material essence, but they are so ordered to each other as to effect a unity, namely, the composed essence. Thus that thing is simple which is not made up of parts and excludes composition.

There are two kinds of parts and thus two kinds of composition. First, there are physical parts, like matter and form, essence and the act of existing, substance and accidents. And these parts enter into physical or real composition, a composition within the actual existing being. Secondly, there are logical parts, like genus and specific difference. These enter into logical composition to form a definition. Thus *animal* and *rational* form the definition of man. That being is absolutely simple which is made up of no parts, either physical or logical. Composition in every order of being is excluded.

2. God Is Absolutely Simple

St. Thomas urges two objections against God's absolute simplicity, which we shall give here by way of setting the problem. Every agent acts according to its nature. But every effect of God's action is a being that is composed. Hence the agent, God, must himself be composed. Secondly, composed things are more noble and perfect than simple things. For example, the composite man is more perfect than his separated soul; a compound is more perfect than an element. And since God is the most noble and perfect of all beings, he must be composed.

3. Solution

Perhaps the best way to prove that God is absolutely simple is to show that he is not composed in any of the orders of being. This is the way St. Thomas proceeds in his question in the *Summa Theologiae* on divine simplicity. [2] Simplicity is in itself a positive attribute, for it denies composition, which is an imperfection. Whatever is composed possesses some potency in its being, since any two parts in order to form a unity must be related to each other as potency to act. Moreover, a composed being needs an extrinsic agent to effect its composition. In denying that the divine Being is composed, we attribute a positive perfection to that Being. Here is our proof that God cannot be composed in any order of being.

1) God is not a body, and so possesses no quantitative parts. Every body is potentially divisible and moves only insofar as it is moved by another, as, for example, our human body is moved by our soul. But as we have seen in the five ways, God is pure act and the first unmoved mover. And so he cannot be a body.

2) There is no matter in God, and so he possesses no essential parts. For matter is pure potency, and God is pure act.

3) In God, essence and the act of existing are the same, and so God is not composed in the order of being. If in God these were different, two contradictions would follow. Since essence would have to be ordered to the act of existing as potency to act (for from two acts in the order of being, two beings would result), it would follow that there is potency in God, which is impossible. Secondly, these two principles of being, if different, would need an extrinsic agent to bring them together in composition. But God is completely uncaused. Therefore in God essence and the act of existing are absolutely the same.

4) In God there are no accidents, and so he is not composed of substance and accidents, that is, he is not composed in the order of activity. Substance is in potency to its accidents, for it receives them and is perfected by them. But in God there is no potency; thus there can be no accidents.

5) Finally, the perfection of God's essence cannot be classified according to genus and specific difference, as can, for example, the essence of man, which is rational animality. For the essence of God is one with his act of existing—his essence is identified with his Be-

2 S.T., I, 3, aa. 1 to 8.

ing. And being, as we know, transcends all species and genera. Thus the divine essence has no logical parts.

4. General Proof

We place here by way of summary two general proofs of God's complete simplicity:

1) Every composite being must have a cause. For what of themselves are different, do not come together to form a unity unless they be brought together by some cause uniting them. But God as first cause is absolutely uncaused. Therefore, he is also absolutely uncomposed or simple.

2) In every composite there is act and potency. In order to form a unit, one part must be related to the other as potency to act, because two acts cannot make one act. But in God there is absolutely no potency, for he is pure act. Hence in God there is absolutely no composition.

5. Answering the Objections

The first objection against God's simplicity was as follows. Every agent acts according to its nature. But every effect of God is composed. Therefore, God as agent must be composed. We answer that it is of the nature of a caused being that it be composed, at least of essence and existence. It is of the very nature of uncaused being that it be uncomposed, even of essence and existence. Every agent acts according to its nature insofar as this is possible. God can communicate his perfections to others, but only as participated, and hence as composed. The objection simply applies a principle in a fallacious sense.

As regards the second objection, we say that among us composite beings are more perfect than some that are less composed, because a finite being reaches its perfection through many acts and not simply by existing. Thus man has more parts and is more perfect than an electron. But this is not true in God whose activity is one with his existence.

To conclude this discussion of God's simplicity, we should add that God cannot enter into composition with any other being. He is also simple in the sense that he cannot enter into composition with another as a part. St. Thomas mentions three errors in this regard. [3] Some have said that God is the World-Soul (Animistic Pantheism). Others have said that the divine substance was the formal principle of all things. Finally, David of Dinant held the rather odd doctrine that God is the same as prime matter, since there is no way to differentiate between the two. [4] David of Dinant was a logician, not a metaphysician, and he was the victim of a bad syllogism: God is pure potency; prime matter is pure potency. Therefore God and prime matter are the same.

It is obviously impossible for God to be either the formal or material cause of the world or of anything else. For these causes, as the very intrinsic constituents of the being, are numerically one with the being. But God is the efficient cause of all being, and an efficient cause can never be numerically one with its effect, for it is extrinsic to the effect. Thus God could not be the material or formal cause of any thing.

6. God Is Completely Perfect

When we say that God is perfect, we mean that God possesses that act or actuality proper to him as God. Hence, within this context, to say that God is *completely* perfect, means that God is completely in act. We mention this point at the outset so that we will not confuse the problem of the perfection of God with the infinity of God. The two problems are very closely related, but they are not exactly the same, as we shall see.

Etymologically, a thing is perfect that has been *per factum*, totally made or accomplished. And since what is made is reduced from potency to act, the word *perfect* has been transposed to mean *anything in act, insofar as it is in act*. Thus, man is perfect at the level of essence, but he is imperfect, or perfectible, at the level of accident. Each being is perfect in its substantial "to be," but imperfect, or perfectible, in its other modes of being. We say that God

---

[3] See *S.T.*, I, 3, 8.
[4] See Etiènne Gilson, *History of Christian Philosophy in the Middle Ages* (New York, Random House, 1955), pp. 241–43.

is completely perfect, since he is completely in act in the order of being; nothing is wanting or lacking to the Being of God. [5]

7. Proof

Each thing is perfect insofar as it is in act. Now every agent, as agent, is in act. But we have seen that not only is God an agent, but the first agent. Thus as first agent, as uncaused efficient cause, God is completely in act and hence completely perfect in Being.

B. HOW THE PERFECTIONS OF CREATURES PRE-EXIST IN GOD

1. Prenote

In this second part of our study we wish to do two things. First, to establish the fact that any perfection found in a creature must also in some way pre-exist in God. Secondly, and more importantly, to show *how* these perfections can be said to pre-exist in the divine Being.

It would seem that not all perfections that exist in creatures pre-exist in God. For some of these perfections are contraries, like hot and cold, black and white, which can hardly be in the same subject at the same time. Moreover, the essence or nature of God is subsistent Being. But *to live* is more perfect than merely *to be;* and *to be wise* is more perfect than merely *to live.* Thus if God's essence is a subsistent "To be," how can he be said to possess the further perfections of life and wisdom?

2. Solution

In God are the perfections of all things. The reason is that God is the first efficient cause of all things. An effect must pre-exist in some way in the power or virtue of its efficient cause. If not, there would be no reason why the cause could produce it. Moreover, the effect must pre-exist in the power of the cause according to the being of the cause. And since God's Being is completely in act and completely perfect, these effects must exist in God according to a com-

[5] See *C.G.*, Bk. I, Ch. 28. For some objections against the divine perfection, read *S.T.*, I, qu. 4.

pletely perfect manner of being. Moreover, each perfection in the creature is a perfection only to the degree that it has being. "The perfections of all things," writes St. Thomas, "pertain to the perfection of being; for things are perfect because in some way they have being." [6] And since God is *subsistent Being*, no perfection of any thing is lacking to him.

It remains to be seen *how* the perfections found in creatures can be said to be in God. Once more we must have an exact understanding of the terminology involved. We have already seen that perfections can be of two kinds. First, those perfections in whose very notion there is contained imperfection, like reasoning, animality, etc. These are called *mixed* perfections, for of their very nature they involve imperfection. Secondly, there are those perfections in which there is no imperfection, like to be, to live, to know, and so forth. These are called *simple* perfections, or perfections of being as being.

We can make the following statements about these two kinds of perfections: (1) both are found in God virtually and eminently; (2) simple perfections are also found in God properly. Let us see precisely what the terms virtually, eminently, and properly mean.

1) *virtually:* one thing is contained, or pre-exists, in another virtually, if the latter has the power or virtue to be the efficient cause of the former. For example, the perfection of a painting exists virtually in the art of the painter. Another term closely associated with virtually is equivalently. One thing possesses another equivalently, if it can produce effects of the same nature as something in which these effects exist formally. For example, the human soul can be said to be equivalently an animal and vegetative soul. For although formally only rational, the human soul is the source of man's sensitive and vegetative functions. The word virtually refers more to efficient causality, equivalently more to formal causality.

2) *eminently:* one thing is contained in another eminently if it is contained in that other according to a higher mode of being than it has in itself. For example, wisdom is in man according to an accidental mode of being, but wisdom is in God as identified with

[6] *S.T.*, I, 4, 2.

the divine substance. Thus we say wisdom is more eminently in God than in man.

3) *properly:* a perfection is properly in another when the actuality that is the perfection belongs to it intrinsically and by reason of the very perfection itself. Thus, humanity belongs properly to Paul, and goodness belongs properly to God.

3. Second Solution

1) *Every perfection* found in creatures pre-exists in God both virtually and eminently.

(*a*) *virtually:* every thing in the creature is a perfection insofar as it has being or is ordered to being. But everything insofar as it has being or is ordered to being comes from God as from its first cause. Thus every perfection pre-exists virtually in God.

(*b*) *eminently:* whatever is in God, is God, for God's Being is absolutely simple. Hence, as in God, these perfections are identified with the divine Being, and so exist in God in a higher and more perfect way than they do in creatures.

2) *Simple perfections* are also in God properly. To show what we mean, let us take an example of two different perfections, analyze them, and see in what sense each may be said to be in God.

(*a*) *"to sense"* (*the perfection of sensation*): this is an act by which a sense faculty grasps cognitively a sense object—by seeing it, hearing it, tasting it, etc. The thing to be noted about such an act is this: it includes within itself sensible matter. Sensation is the act of a sense organ, and so cannot exist except as affected by the conditions of matter. Hence this perfection, according to what it signifies, necessarily includes imperfection due to matter.

In what sense can such a perfection be said of God? If I say, "God hears me," this predication must be by way of metaphor, for God has no sense faculties and so cannot *properly* be said to hear.

But I can say that sensation is *virtually* in God, for God has the power to produce beings who can properly sense. This is all that virtual presence means in an efficient cause. It simply states a fact that must be true; namely, since God does possess the power or virtue to produce them, these mixed perfections can be said to exist in this power as in their cause.

Secondly, I can also make this statement about mixed perfections: Since they do exist in the power of God as in their first efficient cause, and since the power of God is one with the Being of God, mixed perfections are in God *eminently*. Just as virtual presence refers to the power that can produce the perfection, so eminent presence refers to the mode of being of this power. Sensation is in an animal properly, since it is there by reason of the perfection itself. But sensation is in God only virtually, since God has the power to produce this perfection in animals. But since this perfection is present in God's power, and since this power is one with God's Being, we must also conclude that the perfection of sensation is eminently in God, for it is present there according to a higher mode of being than in the creature. And this is all we mean when we say a mixed perfection, like sensation, can be said to be in God virtually and eminently. What this two fold presence in God is opposed to is the presence the perfection has in the creature. For sensation exists in the effect (the animal) formally, properly, and according to the mode of being of the thing in which it is.

(b) *"to understand"* (*the perfection of understanding*): this also is an act. It is that act by which an intellect grasps cognitively an intelligible object, that is, by understanding it. If we analyze what this perfection is in itself, we do not discover any imperfection. This perfection does not depend upon matter, nor upon any of those conditions that follow dependence on matter, like motion, time, place, etc. Like sensation, understanding is an act; but unlike sensation, understanding is not dependent upon matter in order to be, and hence it is simply act.

With this in mind, in what sense can I say "God understands?" Obviously, I can say God has understanding in the sense that he can produce beings who can understand. In this sense understanding is virtually in God. The understanding that I find in creatures exists in God as in its first efficient cause. Further, since the power by which God causes is his own divine substance, the perfection of understanding also exists in God eminently.

Finally, the perfection of understanding, unlike that of sensing, exists in God *properly*. That is, this perfection belongs to the Being of God by reason of the very perfection itself. It is there intrinsically and in its own right, and not, for example, merely because God can cause it. Just as a perfection like rationality is proper and intrinsic to the being of man, so all simple or unmixed perfections are proper and intrinsic to the Being of God. The perfection itself that is signified is in God, and is God. In relation to the existence that these simple perfections have in creatures, they are said to be in God eminently or according to a more perfect way of being; but the perfection itself is also the proper possession of God. And the reason for this is that such perfections involve no imperfection, and so as in God they can exist according to the fullness and completeness of pure act.

We have made the statement that since the perfection of understanding involves no matter, it was simply act. Why then would it not follow that the perfection of an angelic essence, which possesses no matter, is simply act and thus properly in God? This should be noted about such a perfection of essence. While act in the order of essence, it is potency in the order of being (where act is "to be"), for it is ordered to the act of existing as potency to act. Therefore God, who is pure act in the order of being, cannot possess such a perfection properly. It is possessed properly only by the angel whose essence it is, and by God virtually and eminently. In a word, the perfection of an angelic essence is not a perfection of being as being, it does not flow from the act of existing; it is the essence itself.

Most authors use the word "formally" where we have used the word "properly." They say that simple perfections are formally in God. There is an advantage and a disadvantage in using this word. The disadvantage is this: the word tends to formalize or essentialize the actuality of simple perfections. These perfections are not forms. They cannot be abstracted by the intellect as forms are abstracted from matter. The abstract terms *wisdom* or *life* are not conceptual abstractions like *man* or *animal*, and do not have the same intentional relation to the existent as do these latter terms. *Formally*, then, has the disadvantage of formalizing these perfections in God. But the word does bring out this fact: simple perfections constitute the very essence of God. God has these perfections essentially; whereas no simple perfection ever constitutes the essence of a creature. Creatures possess these perfections only by participation. In this sense they are not *formally* in creatures, whereas they are in creatures *properly*.

By way of summing up this teaching of how the different perfections that exist in creatures exist also in God, let us analyze a simple example and apply it, by way of an analogy, to our problem. We know that every agent acts according to its own nature. We know also that effects that proceed from a non-univocal cause, such as God, are less perfect than their cause, both as to the nature of the perfection and its manner of being. For example, what is simple and one in the cause is composite and many in the effect. Thus, one agent through a single causal power can produce a diversity of effects. For example, fire can heat, burn, blacken, or liquefy. So, too, God by the single power of his Being can produce a multitude of different creatures. [7]

Let us analyze this example of fire a little further, for it will throw much light on the problem of the pre-existence of perfections in the divine Being. In every effect, whether it proceeds from a univocal or an analogous cause, there is something that is like the cause and something that is unlike the cause. The likeness comes from the form that is educed and the unlikeness from the matter from which the form is educed. Consider the case of a brick being hardened by fire. Insofar as it is heated by the fire, the brick is like the fire. Both are hot. But insofar as what is heated becomes hard and solid, it is unlike the fire. These last two effects are due to the matter that is being heated. If that in which the brick is like the fire be predicated of the fire, it will be predicated properly of the fire. For heat is properly both in the fire and in the brick. Indeed heat will be predicated primarily and more perfectly of the fire, since

[7] See *De Pot.*, qu. 7, a. 1, ad 1m.

heat exists more perfectly in fire than in a hot brick. Fire is naturally hot, while a brick is hot only if heated.

On the other hand, if that in which the brick differs from the fire is said of the fire, the predication would be false. It is simply false to say that fire is hard and solid. But fire is *virtually* hard and solid because it can produce these qualities in the brick.

Now let us apply this example to divine causality. There are certain things in the creature that are like God, and these are those perfections that connote no imperfection in what they signify, perfections like being, life, and understanding. These perfections are properly said of God. Indeed they are said primarily of God and more eminently of God than of creatures. Just as heat was said properly of the brick and the fire, but primarily and more eminently of the fire, so being, life and so forth, are said properly of God and of creatures, but primarily and more eminently of God than of creatures. God is Being and life essentially, while a creature is, or is living, only by participation.

On the other hand, there are things in creatures by which they are unlike God, just as in the case of the brick and the fire. And these things belong to the creature insofar as it is produced from nothing, just as these other things were in the brick because of its matter. Because the creature is "from nothing," it possesses potency, motion, privations, and so forth. And these things are false when said of God. Therefore, those names in whose meaning the conditions of created being are included, cannot be said properly of God. Of course, as we have already seen in the section on the divine names, such perfections, and even privations, can be said metaphorically of God. I can say, "God is deaf to my cries," or that he is a strong fortress, a purging fire. For in some of his effects God may act like a purging fire, and so on.

4. Answering the Objections

Our first objection was this: not all perfections can be in God, for some, like black and white, hot and cold, are contraries, and can hardly be in the same subject at the same time. The answer is clear. Perfections that have contraries are mixed perfections, and are not properly in God, but only virtually and eminently. It would be the proper possession of these contraries that would constitute a contradiction.

The second objection stated that life says more than being and wisdom says more than life. But if God is subsistent Being, then he does not have the further perfections of life and wisdom, for these are not included in the notion of being. If they were, all beings would be living and wise. Here we must distinguish between being and the Being of God. It is quite true that something can participate in being, that is to say, in simple existence, and not participate in life or wisdom, which are higher ways of being. But the Being of God is subsistent Being, and subsistent Being includes all the perfections and modes of being. [8]

In a word, this objection is based on a faulty notion of the act of existing. For the act of existing is much more than simply that by which a being is outside nothing. Rather, it is the actuation of everything within a being. The act of existing is not perfected by life or understanding in living and intelligent beings; rather, it is the very actuation of living and intelligent beings. In different beings, the act of existing is more or less perfect because it is more or less limited by the essence. And so in God, where essence is the act of existing, the Being of God is subsistent and all-perfect.

C. GOD IS INFINITE AND SUPREMELY GOOD

1. Prenote

Since the Being of God is completely in act, he is completely perfect; absolutely nothing is lacking to his Being. Therefore, we say that God is also infinite; there is no limit or term to his Being. To be perfect and to be infinite are not the same thing. The former posits in God the complete actuality of being and all the perfections of being; the latter removes or denies any term or limit to this being.

[8] *S.T.*, I, 4, 2, ad 3m.

But infinity flows from perfection: since God's Being is completely in act, there can be nothing potential or limiting within it.

2. Is the Being of God Really Infinite or Without Limit?

It would seem not. What has some limit or term is finite. For example, a being which is in this place is limited or terminated by this place, so that it cannot also exist in some other place at the same time. Such a being, we say, is finite according to place. In like manner, a being that is this being, so that it cannot be another, is limited or finite in its being. But God is God and nothing else. He is not the world nor any part of the world. Therefore, God is not infinite in his Being.

3. Solution

A thing is called infinite that in some way is not terminated. Literally, it is not finished. In a material being, matter is finished or terminated by form, and form by matter. Matter is terminated by form in the sense that before it received a certain form it was in potency to it and to many others; but having received the form, this particular potency of matter is terminated or finished by the form. Form, in its turn, is terminated or finished through matter, because considered in itself and apart from matter, form is common to many; but as in matter, it is the form of this thing only.

However, there is a great difference between the infinity or indeterminateness of matter without form and of form without matter. Matter is made perfect by the form that determines it. Thus material infinity, or uninformed matter, implies imperfection. Of course, matter does not exist without form, except as potency. All infinity based upon the potency of matter implies imperfection, for it considers the material being as not terminated by form. An example of such infinity would be the infinite divisibility of quantity and its potency to be infinitely added to.

Formal infinity, on the other hand, involves no imperfection. Form is not made perfect by matter, but rather contracted and limited by it. Thus form not determined by matter has the characteristic of that which is perfect. [9] Now that which is most "formal" in a thing is its act of existing. Not in the sense that "to be" is a form, but in the sense that everything in a being is related to the act of existing as potency to act, and that existence itself cannot receive anything. Existence says simply act and in no sense potency. Now the "To Be" of God is not received in anything. God is subsistent Being. And unreceived Being is simply infinite. God is infinite in his Being, without limit or term of any kind.

Furthermore, only God is simply infinite, for only his Being is unreceived. An angel is infinite in the order of essence, for its essence is not received in matter. But its act of existing is received and limited by the essence. And since "to be" is the act of being, the being of an angel is limited or finite. Infinity in Being is the peculiar and incommunicable attribute of God.

4. Answering the Objections

It was objected above that since the Being of God does not include the being of the creature, God is not infinite but finite. Indeed the fact that God is subsistent Being whose act of existing is not received in anything, distinguishes God from all other beings and removes all these beings from God. God is by his very essence, creatures are by participation. But to answer the objection, we say that whatever of being is possessed by the creature God also possesses in an infinitely more perfect way. Thus the fact that there are beings other than God does not mean that God is not infinite in his Being. Moreover, if the Being of God included the participated being of the creatures, God would be finite, material, and so on, which is absurd.

Finally, while the fact that infinite Being co-exists with finite beings gives us more beings than the infinite Being alone, it does not give us more being (*plura entia sed non plus entis*). For example, after a teacher communicates his knowledge to many students we have many more who know (*plures scientes*), but we do not have any more knowledge (*plus scientiae*). So, too, after the crea-

[9] See *S.T.*, I, qu. 7; *C.G.*, Bk. I, ch. 43.

tive act of God, by which he communicates being to creatures, there are more beings, but not more being.

5. Is God Supremely Good?

Let us see where we have thus far arrived in our consideration of the divine Being. We established, after the proofs for his existence, that the essence of God as known by us is most properly grasped under the aspect of subsistent Being. All the properties or attributes of the divine Being are what they are because of this fact. As subsistent Being, God must be pure act. Because God is completely in act, God is absolutely perfect. Because God is absolutely perfect, he has no limit or term, and so is infinite. And now we want to show that an infinitely perfect Being is also supremely good.

What precisely is *good?* Aristotle says the good is that which all desire. A thing is good insofar as it is desirable. The good is being as desirable. But what makes being desirable? It is that which is most perfect and best in being. For example, we say this is a good play, or this is a good basketball game, because each has a certain excellence or perfection about it. A thing is good according as it is perfect. Being as good is being as in some sense perfect. Good and being are the same in the thing; but good adds to being the notion of desirability, which being as such does not expressly include. And so we say that good and being are different according to what they connote.

Let us consider more in detail this difference between good and being, so that on the one hand we will be better able to understand how in God the attribute of goodness differs from the divine Being, and on the other hand, how divine goodness is seen to flow from and depend upon the divine Being.

Since being and good differ in their notion, a thing is not said to be simply being and simply good in the same sense. A thing is said to be insofar as it is in act. [10] Now act has an order to potency.

[10] See *S.T.*, I, 5, 1, ad 1m.

Therefore something is simply being according as it is first distinguished from that which is only in potency. That by which a being is first distinguishable from what is only in potency is its substantial "to be." Thus each thing is simply being because of its substantial "to be." Because of subsequent and superadded acts, a thing is called being not simply, but "in a certain sense." For example, *being white* is not simply to be, but to be in a certain way. To be white does not remove simple potency, since it accrues to a being already existing in act.

Things are just the reverse as regards the notion of good. Good adds to being the notion of desirability, and hence is said of a thing according to that which is perfect and ultimate in it. Thus it is according to its ultimate perfection that a thing is said to be simply good. Consequently, that thing which does not have the ultimate perfection that it should have, although it does possess some perfection insofar as it is in act, is not simply perfect, and therefore not simply good. It is good only "in a certain sense."

Hence, according to its substantial being a thing is simply being but not simply good. And according to its ultimate perfection of being, a thing is simply good but not simply being. So when we speak of God as good, we are considering the divine Being precisely as ultimately and completely perfect, which is not explicit in the consideration of God simply as Being. The goodness of God, however, flows from and depends upon the Being of God. Since God is perfect Being, he is completely in act and good. Nor does the attribute of good add anything to the Being of God. It is simply the divine Being as more expressly considered; namely, considered precisely as the *fullness* of being.

God is not only good, but the highest good. And he is not only the highest good, but he is good by his very essence. That he is good goes without saying, for he is the cause of those perfections in things which we desire. These perfections are nothing more than participated likenesses of the divine goodness, so that in seeking them we are really seeking the goodness of God. St. Thomas puts this in a striking manner.

All things in seeking their own perfection are seeking God himself, inasmuch as the perfections of all things are certain likenesses of the divine Being. And so of those that seek God, some know him according to himself. And this is proper to the rational creature. Others know certain participations of his goodness, and such knowledge extends even to sensible cognition. Others, finally, have a natural seeking of God without any knowledge, and this is insofar as these things have been inclined towards their ends by some higher knower. [11]

That God is the highest good is also easy to see. Things are good because they participate in the goodness of God. Good therefore pre-exists in God as in the first cause of all things. As we have seen, God is not a univocal cause but an analogous one. Hence, good exists in God according to a manner of being infinitely more excellent than that which it has in creatures. And in this sense God is called the highest good. [12]

Finally, we say that God is good by his essence, which is not true of any other being. Let us see why this must be so. A thing is said to be good insofar as it is perfect; for good is being as desirable, and hence according to its fullness or perfection of being. Now the perfection of a thing is threefold. First, insofar as it has substantial being; secondly, insofar as it has added to it certain accidents necessary to act in a perfect manner; and, lastly, insofar as it reaches its end, which is the final perfection of a being. For example, the perfection of man consists, first of all, in the being that he has through his substantial form; secondly, in possessing such accidents as intellect and will by which he can act perfectly as a man; and, thirdly, in attaining the end of being a man.

Now no one but God holds this triple perfection by reason of his very essence. The essence of God is one with his Being, and that which is said by way of accidents of others, is said essentially of God, for God has no accidents. Finally, God is ordered to no end, but all other things are ordered to him as their final end. It is clear, therefore, that only God possesses all manner of perfection by his very essence. Thus he alone is good through his essence.

11 S.T., I, 6, 1, ad 2m.
12 Ibid., a. 2.

D. HOW THE DIVINE PERFECTIONS ARE DISTINCT FROM THE DIVINE ESSENCE AND FROM EACH OTHER

The divine Being is absolutely simple, and so absolutely one and uncomposed. Independently of our knowledge of God, his essence is not different from his perfections. Nor are these perfections different from one another. God and the perfections of God are one and the same in God. The difference is in our knowledge of these perfections. There is no plurality in God, only in our knowledge of God. This much is clear. But there is another and more difficult question we want to answer here. Is this plurality only and wholly in our intellect? Is the difference between the essence of God and his attributes, and the difference among the attributes themselves, due entirely to the operation of our intellect in knowing God?

To this question we answer no. At the outset, a simple distinction will be of help. The plurality and distinction between God's essence and his attributes and among the attributes themselves, is in our intellect as in its subject. But this plurality and distinction is also "in" God as in its source and foundation. In more technical terminology, we say that there is no real distinction between God's essence and his attributes nor among the different attributes themselves. There is only a distinction of reason. But this distinction of reason is not due merely to the one reasoning. It is also due to the very thing reasoned about, namely, God and the perfections of God. Thus, the difference between God's goodness and his truth is not the same, for example, as that between man and rational animal, where the whole reason for the distinction is due to the act of the one knowing. Rather, the distinction between God's Being and his perfections and among the perfections themselves is like the distinction between being and its transcendentals and among the transcendentals themselves.

And the reason for the distinction in both cases is fundamentally the same. Just as our intellect cannot exhaust in a single concept the fullness of being, but must exploit this fullness by more and more express and explicit concepts—like one, true, good, and so forth, so neither can our intellect exhaust in one concept the full-ness of God's Being as knowable through creatures, but must ex-press that fullness in many and distinct concepts. These distinct concepts, therefore, are due not merely to the intellect that knows God, but also to the fullness and transcendence of the divine Be-ing. And just as our concepts like one, true and good signify being itself, but under different aspects, so all our concepts of the divine perfections signify God himself, but under different aspects. These perfections are not distinct in the thing (God), but only in my knowledge of the thing. Hence no real distinction is involved here, but only a distinction of reason. But it is not a mere distinction of reason, since the *foundation* for the distinction is not merely in the intellect but also in God.

So far these are so many statements of facts. Now let us exam-ine their proof. And since the proof throws much light on the whole question of our knowledge of God, it will be worth our while to go here into some detail. We will put the problem in the form of a question, urge two objections against our answer, and then try to disengage and understand the elements of a solution.

1. Question: Does the Plurality of Meanings That The Divine Attributes Have Exist Only in Our Intellect or Also in God?

It would seem that in no way can this plurality of meanings exist in God. Whatever is in God, is God. Thus, if the meanings accord-ing to which these attributes differ are in God, they are God him-self. But God is one and simple. Therefore, as existing in God, these meanings cannot be many.

Furthermore, that which in itself is absolutely one cannot be the *foundation* for any plurality or distinction. But we have seen that the divine essence is absolutely simple, excluding all physical and logical composition. Therefore this divine essence cannot be the foundation for any plurality or distinction. Hence the plurality of meanings that the divine perfections have seem in no way rooted in the divine essence, but only and solely in our intellect knowing that essence.

2. Solution

In our solution to this problem we maintain that all the divine perfections, like wisdom and goodness, are entirely one and the same thing in God, but they are different in their meanings. We also say that this difference in meaning is not due merely to the intellect knowing God, but also to the very nature of God himself.

To grasp this important teaching, four questions must be answered. First, what is this meaning according to which the divine attributes differ? Secondly, how is meaning said to be or not be in a thing? Thirdly, are the different meanings of the attributes in God or not? Fourthly, is the plurality of these meanings due only to our intellect or are they also in some way due to God?

We answer the first question as follows. Meaning is that which is signified by a word; or meaning is that which the intellect understands when it grasps the representational value of a word. In the case of those things which are capable of a strict definition, the perfect meaning would be this definition. But things can have a meaning even though they cannot be defined, for example, such things as quantity or quality. The meaning of quantity is that which is signified by the word "quantity." And this is simply that by which quantity is quantity. It makes no difference, therefore, whether that which is said to have a meaning is or is not capable of being defined. Thus, for example, divine wisdom is not capable of being defined by the human intellect, since it does not know this perfection according to the infinite mode of being it has in God. Yet our intellect does have a notion or idea of divine wisdom, namely, that which the intellect knows when it understands the meaning of the phrase "divine wisdom."

We are now in a position to answer our second question. How can meaning be said to be in the thing known? Obviously, meaning itself is not in the thing. Nor is the way a meaning is grasped by the mind in the thing. For both meaning and its mode of being are in the mind as in their subject. Rather, meaning is said to be in the thing known insofar as in the thing known there does correspond something to what the mind has conceived. For example, when I say *John is lazy*, the meaning of laziness is not in John; but what laziness signifies has its correspondent in John, for example, those different acts or lack of acts that fulfill this meaning.

Meaning contained in a concept can correspond to the thing existing outside the mind in three different ways. Sometimes what the intellect conceives is the *likeness* of the thing existing outside the mind. This happens, for example, when the intellect conceives the intelligible content of a word like *man*. Such a conception of the intellect has its proximate foundation in the thing, insofar as the thing itself, because of its conformity to the intellect, produces the very truth of the intellect, and is the cause why the name signifying this concept is said of the thing.

Sometimes, however, that which a name signifies is not a *likeness* of the thing existing outside the mind, but is something that results from the way the thing outside the mind is understood. These are meanings or notions that our intellect in some way constructs. For example, that which is signified by the word *genus* is not the likeness of any thing existing outside the mind. Rather, from the fact that the intellect understands that the perfection *animal* can be in different kinds of animals, the intellect attributes to animal the notion or meaning of genus. Obviously, what corresponds to the meaning of genus is not something existing outside the mind. With meanings of this kind, the proximate foundation is not in the thing but in the intellect. For it is the intellect which sees that animal can be predicated of many species and thus attributes to it the notion of genus. However, the *remote* foundation is the thing itself. Because the perfection of animal in the thing is of such a nature that it can be found in many kinds of animals, the intellect can attribute to it the notion of genus. And so the intellect is not false or in error when it constructs these meanings.

Sometimes, finally, that which is signified by a name has *no foundation* in the thing, either proximate or remote. For example, the notion of a Chimera—a fire-breathing monster that is part lion, part goat, and part dragon—is a concept that is neither the likeness of anything that exists outside the mind, nor does it result from the way the mind understands some thing outside the mind.

And so such a concept is false if said of anything existing outside the mind. Thus the answer to our second point is clear. A notion or meaning is said to be in the thing insofar as what is signified by the meaning is in the thing.

We are now ready to answer our third question. Are the meanings that the mind conceives of the divine attributes in God? According to St. Thomas, there were two main opinions in his day concerning this question. One was that of Avicenna and Maimonides, and the other that of the Pseudo-Denis and Saint Anselm of Canterbury. [13] Both these opinions deserve careful study, since almost any position we take regarding our knowledge of God's perfections is reducible to one of them.

3. The Opinion of Avicenna and Maimonides

According to St. Thomas, Avicenna and Maimonides taught that God, as existing outside our mind, is a subsistent Being (*esse*), and nothing else. There is nothing else in God except Being (*esse*). [14] Thus they taught that God was Being without essence. Whatever other perfections we attribute to God are true only by way of negation and causality. For instance, it is true that God is wise in the sense that such attribution removes from him that defect found in things that lack wisdom. Or a given negation may *result* in something that is true of God. When, for example, I say God is undivided, this negation tells me that he is one. Or when I say God is immaterial, I know that he is intelligent. Thus, according to Avicenna and Maimonides, all such names are used by us to remove something from God rather than to put anything in God.

Knowledge by way of causality is also true of God in a twofold sense: either because God produces the perfection found in the creature, or because God conducts himself, so to speak, after the manner of a creature. Thus, for example, I can say God is wise in the sense that he is the cause of wisdom in creatures, or that in producing certain of his effects he acts as a wise man acts.

[13] *In I Sent.*, d. 2, q. 1, a. 3, *solutio.*
[14] Thomas's references to the works of Avicenna and Maimonides, upon which he bases his interpretation, are found in the text cited above.

Let us look for a moment at this doctrine. The first thing that strikes us is that while the doctrine is true in what it says, it does not go far enough. It errs in saying this is all names tell us about God. Moreover, the interpretation Maimonides gives to his doctrine is really agnostic. For he expressly says two things: First, that all the names used of God are used equivocally; and, secondly, that no likeness of the creature to its creator results from the fact that the creature is good or wise or possesses any other perfection whatsoever it may be. According to Maimonides, that which our intellect conceives when it understands an attribute like wisdom or goodness does not refer to God as a likeness of something that is in God. There is nothing in God that corresponds to our notion of the divine attributes. Whence it follows that the meaning of these names are not in God as in their proximate foundation, but only as in their remote foundation. They are just like those relative names that are predicated of God because of time—words like creator and lord. For these relations are not in God, but follow merely from our way of understanding God, just as we have seen above as regards the notions of genus and species.

Thus, according to the opinion of Avicenna and Maimonides, the notions of the divine attributes are only in our intellect and not in the thing—not in God. Rather, the intellect constructs these notions from a consideration of creatures by way of negation and causality. In a moment we will see what is true and what is false about this doctrine. But before we do so, let us turn our attention to the second doctrine, that of Denis and Anselm. [15]

4. The Opinion of the Pseudo-Denis and St. Anselm

These two men taught that the perfections existing in creatures exist in God, but in a pre-eminent way. And this pre-eminence is threefold. First, it is a pre-eminence of *universality:* for in God all perfections are found joined together, while in creatures they are dispersed and scattered. Secondly, it is a pre-eminence of *plenitude:* for God's perfections are without defect, whereas this is not

[15] The teaching of Denis is found in Chapter Twelve of his *Divine Names,* and that of Anselm in Chapter Three of his *Monologion.*

true of perfections in creatures. Thirdly, it is a pre-eminence of *unity:* in creatures these perfections are many and diverse; in God they are all one and the same. Not only are these perfections joined together in God, they are all identified with God. In this one Being all things pre-exist, and so by it all things are caused, all things are known, and to it all things are similar, according to a likeness of analogy.

In this opinion, therefore, the notions or meanings that the intellect understands when it knows these attributes, are truly likenesses of that Being which is God, although they are only partial and deficient likenesses. Such notions do not exist merely in our intellect but have their *proximate* foundation in God. That is to say, what proximately corresponds to our notion of (for example) divine wisdom is God himself (and not any creature), but not God *in himself,* but as manifested through creatures. Thus this opinion concludes that what belongs to wisdom as such, rightly and properly belongs to God.

5. Reconciliation of These Opinions

St. Thomas attempts a reconciliation of these two teachings. He begins by pointing out that their apparent difference and opposition flow from the two different sources from which they have arisen. Avicenna and Maimonides have considered principally the created things themselves because of which the different names of the attributes were first given or imposed. For example, the name *wisdom* is given to a certain quality in man, and the name *essence* is said of things that are not subsistent being. And since such things as qualities and non-subsistence have nothing to do with God, this opinion teaches that wisdom is not in God, and that God is Being without essence.

On the other hand, Denis and Anselm have considered not the creatures themselves that possess these perfections, but the very perfections as such. And since God according to one act of Being is perfect by all the modes of perfection which these names imply, these men have said that such names belong positively to God. One opinion does not deny what the other affirms. The first does not deny that any mode of perfection is lacking to God, nor does the second affirm that God possesses qualities or is non-subsistent.

With this rather detailed explanation, the answer to our third question becomes clear. Are the meanings that the mind conceives of the divine attributes in God? The notions or meanings of the divine attributes are truly in God, for the meaning of a name is derived more from the reason the name is given than from the thing to which it is given. For example, the name "wisdom" is given because of the operation of ordering things to an end; but it is imposed upon something that is a quality. Thus its meaning is concerned more with the perfection of ordering than with the quality. This perfection of ordering belongs to God and is in God, but no quality is in God.

We come now to our fourth and last question which concerns the plurality of these notions. We have seen that these *notions* are truly in God. Can we also say that the *plurality* of these notions is also in God or only in our intellect?

First of all, this very plurality of notions comes from the fact that the thing known, namely God, exceeds our intellect. Our intellect cannot receive in one concept all the different modes of divine perfection. And this for two reasons. First, because the intellect receives this knowledge from creatures, in whom there exist different modes of perfection according to different forms or natures; and, secondly, because that which in God is one and simple is multiplied in our intellect. This multiplication flows from the very nature of caused knowledge, just as multitude and difference flow from the very nature of caused things.

To sum up: Since God according to one and the same thing, his divine essence, is perfect with all the modes of perfection, our intellect in one concept cannot integrally grasp his perfection nor, consequently, give this perfection one name. To know God we must have many and different concepts conveying many and different meanings. And so we must have many and different names for these meanings. These names are not synonyms, because they signify different notions or meanings. To the plurality of these notions there does correspond something in the thing, but there does not correspond a plurality of the thing. To the plurality of notions there corresponds the fullness of perfection of the thing, so that all these different names and notions are aptly applied to it. If our intellect were able to see God in himself, it could give to this understanding of God one single name. And this name would not signify merely goodness or wisdom, and so forth, but would include the signification of all these things. [16]

When Avicenna and Maimonides said that this plurality is only on the side of our intellect and the effects in creatures, they were in a certain sense right and in a certain sense wrong. If they refer to the cause of the multiplication, then what they say is true, for this cause is our intellect and the effects in creatures, since our intellect cannot conceive the divine perfection in one concept but needs many. If, however, these men are referring to the manner in which these notions are attributed to God, then their position is false. For God is not good because he makes good things or because he acts after the manner of something that is good. Rather, because God is good, he makes good things; and these good things,

---

[16] But it should be mentioned that although in heaven we shall all see the divine essence and therefore shall know God as he is in himself, we shall not comprehend God. The vision we have of his essence will not be a comprehensive vision, it will not exhaust the intelligibility of God. As the theologians put it, "the whole God shall be seen by us, but he shall not be wholly seen." God is infinitely knowable and our intellects remain finite in heaven. God will exceed our intellects even in the beatific vision, and from this point of view St. Thomas says that there will be *even in this vision* of God a plurality of names. Here is his explanation: "But nevertheless, if the intellect seeing God through his essence should give a name to the thing which he sees, and should name this thing through the understanding which he has of this thing, the intellect would still have to use many names. Because it is impossible that the conception of a created intellect should represent the whole perfection of the divine essence. Therefore, for the one thing seen, it would form different conceptions and would use different names, for God is not seen by the intellect with a comprehending vision. But that conception which perfectly represents God is the Uncreated Word, and thus this Word is one only. Therefore it is clear that the plurality of names comes from this fact, that God himself exceeds our intellect. And that God should exceed our intellect is due to God himself (because of the plenitude of his perfection), and to our intellect (which is unable to comprehend God). And therefore also the plurality of notions is not merely because of our intellect but also because of God himself, insofar as his perfection exceeds any conception whatsoever that our intellect can form of it." *In I Sent.,* d. 2, qu. 1, a. 3, *solutio.* Words in parentheses added.

because they participate in his goodness, can act after a manner
that is like the goodness of God. If God had never created, he still
would be such that he could be considered according to all those
notions that our intellect now possesses when it considers him.
The plurality of these names is not merely on the side of the intellect forming them, but also on the side of God himself, insofar as
something in God corresponds to all these concepts, namely, the
fullness and completeness of God's perfection. Each name signifying these notions is said of God truly and properly. But no diversity or multiplicity is placed in God by reason of these diverse
and multiple attributes.

6. Answering the Difficulties

We can now answer the two objections that stated the plurality
of meanings exists only in our intellect and in no way in God. The
first objection was this: Whatever is in God, is God. But God is
absolutely one and completely simple. Therefore the plurality of
notions can exist only in our intellect. We answer this difficulty
by saying that just as the meaning of the word "man" is not something in the existing man, but is in the intellect as in its subject
and in the existing man as in the source of its truth, so in like manner the meaning of the words "divine goodness" is in the human
intellect as in its subject, but in God as in that which corresponds
by some likeness to this meaning, giving this meaning its truth.

Our second objection was this: That which is absolutely one
cannot be the root or foundation for any plurality. But this is the
case with the divine essence; therefore the plurality of meanings
is in no way rooted in the divine essence, but only and solely in our
intellect knowing that essence. We answer this objection as follows: Something can be said to be rooted or fixed in another if it
has from this other a certain stability or firmness. Now intellectual
meanings possess a twofold "firmness"—that of their existence,
and that of their truth. The first kind of stability a meaning has
from the intellect in which it inheres, just as any other accident
derives its existence from its subject. But a meaning has the stability of its truth from the thing to which it is conformed. The way

a thing is or is not determines our understanding of it. The meanings, therefore, of the divine attributes are fixed or rooted in the human intellect as regards the stability of their existence, since our intellect is their subject; but they are rooted in the divine essence as regards the stability of their truth. And this "rooting" in God, since it is not as in a subject, in no way compromises the divine simplicity.

7. Summary of the Chapter

"God is absolutely uncomposed (simple), and yet a completely perfect Being. For in him pre-exist virtually and eminently all perfections found in creatures. Perfections of being as being also exist properly in God. He is, therefore, absolutely infinite and supremely good."

a. State of the question

Having seen in Chapter 6 how names signifying perfections first found in creatures can be said of God by way of analogy, in this chapter we discuss how these perfections themselves, signified by these names, are contained in the divine essence.

b. Explanation of terms

1) ". . . simple . . ."—lacking parts or composition. Simplicity is really a positive perfection, since it denies composition, which implies potency and hence limitation.

2) ". . . absolutely . . ." God is not composed in any order of being (essence, existence, activity, logical order, and so forth). This is true only of God, since every creature is at least composed in the order of existence.

3) ". . . completely perfect Being . . ." A thing is perfect (per factum) insofar as it is in act. God, as completely in act, is completely perfect.

4) ". . . perfection . . ." A perfection is anything that has existence, or is ordered to existence. As we have seen, a thing is called perfect insofar as it is in act; hence, perfection is denominated from the act, or order to the act, of existing.

5) "... *virtually* ..." To be present in a thing virtually is to be in the causal power of that thing.

6) "... *eminently* ..." To be present in a thing eminently, is to be there in a more perfect manner (than in something else).

7) "... *properly* ..." To be present in a thing properly is to be there as the intrinsic property and possession of that thing. Moreover, to possess a perfection properly is to possess it by reason of the perfection itself.

8) "... *perfections of being as being* ..."—perfections in whose notion there is contained no imperfection.

9) "... *infinite* ..."—without limit or boundary. A thing is absolutely infinite if it has no limit or term whatsoever to its being. Only God is absolutely infinite, since all creatures are limited in their being by their essence.

10) "... *good* ..."—being as desirable; hence, being considered according to its ultimate perfection, since a thing is desirable insofar as it is perfect. The supreme good would be the most perfect Being. This is God.

c. The proof

1) *God is absolutely simple.* (*a*) What is composed must have an efficient cause of its composition, since diverse parts cannot form a unity unless they are brought together by some cause uniting them. But God has no cause. Therefore, *etc.*

(*b*) In every composite there is act and potency; for from two acts we cannot have one act, or unity. But in God there is no potency. Therefore, *etc.*

2) *All perfections found in creatures are virtually present in God.* Nothing gives (causes) what it does not have. But God is the first cause of all perfections found in creatures. Hence, all perfections found in creatures pre-exist in the causal power of God. But this is to be virtually present in God. Therefore, *etc.*

3) *All perfections found in creatures are also eminently in God.* The causal power of God is one with the essence of God, since, as we have already proved, God is absolutely simple. Hence, perfections that pre-exist in this power, pre-exist as identified with

the divine essence. But this is to exist according to a higher mode of being than these perfections have in creatures. Hence, all perfections found in creatures are eminently present in God.

4) *But only perfections of being as being exist properly in God.* (*a*) Mixed perfections, as including within their very signification some imperfection, cannot exist in God by reason of themselves, but only in the sense that God can cause them (virtual presence), and cause them with a power that is one with his divine essence (eminent presence). God, as Pure Act, can contain no imperfection.

(*b*) But simple perfections, as including within their signification no imperfection, can exist in God by reason of themselves, since, as simply act, they can exist in God according to their complete fullness and perfection of act.

5) *God is absolutely infinite.* A being is absolutely infinite if there is no term or limit to its act of existing. But God's act of existing is not limited by, or received into, any potency or essence. Therefore, the Being of God is absolutely infinite.

6) *God is supremely good.* Good is being considered according to its ultimate perfection. Hence, that being which is completely perfect, and in no sense perfectible, is the supreme good. But God, as completely in act and absolutely infinite in being, is completely perfect. Therefore, God is supremely good.

Suggested Readings

1. St. Thomas, *Summa Theologiae,* in *Basic Writings of St. Thomas,* by A. Pegis (New York, Random House, 1945), Vol. 1, pp. 25–62. *On the Power of God (De Potentia),* translated by English Dominican Fathers (Westminister, Newman Press, 1952), three books in one volume, Book III, pp. 1–46.

CHAPTER 8

The Omnipresence, Immutability, and Eternity of God

> *God is entirely outside the order of time, housed, so to speak, in the tower of eternity. This eternity is all at once, and to its single, simple glance is present the whole flow of time. And so by one glance, God sees whatever is done in any part of time.*
>
> —St. Thomas, *In Perihermeneias*, Book 1, lect. 14

Since there is absolutely no limit or term to the divine Being, that Being must be present everywhere. Thus from the discussion of God's infinity, which we have just completed, we are led logically to the study of his omnipresence. Concerning this attribute, we want to answer three questions. First, in what sense can it be said that God is present in all existing things? Secondly, in what sense can God be said to be present everywhere, that is, in all *places?* Finally, is this presence in all places something peculiar to the divine Being, or can it be said also of other things?

1. Is God Present in All Existing Things?

It would seem that God cannot be present in all things. For what is in a thing is contained by that thing. But God cannot be contained by a thing but rather contains it. As Saint Augustine writes:

"All things are in Him, rather than that He is in any thing." [1] Therefore God is not in all existing things.

Solution. The solution to this problem is quite simple. God is said to be present in all things, not as part of their essence or as an accident is present in a subject, but as an agent is present where it is acting. Every agent is immediately joined by its power to the effect it is causing. Now God causes by his very essence, and all created being is his proper effect. And not only does he cause the being of all things but conserves that being. Therefore God is continually present by his essence in all things. And since being is that which is most intimate and profound in a thing, God is intimately and profoundly present in all things. Put in a simple syllogism our proof runs as follows: Wherever a thing operates, there it is present. But God operates in all existing things causing and conserving their being. Therefore, God is present in all things. [2]

How do we answer the objection that what is in a thing is contained by that thing? We must distinguish here between the presence of bodies and the presence of spiritual beings. Bodies are contained by the thing they are in, but spiritual beings contain the thing in which they operate. For an incorporeal substance virtually—that is, by its power—contains the thing with which it comes into contact, and is not contained by it. Thus for example, our human soul is in our body as containing it, not as contained by it. For the whole body is dependent upon the power of the soul. Now God is pure spirit. But as Saint Thomas points out, by a certain analogy with bodies, we can say that God is in all things inasmuch as he contains all things. [3]

2. Is God Present Everywhere—in All Places?

To be everywhere (ubiquitous) means to be in every existing *place.* We have just seen how God is omnipresent, that is, how he is in every existing *thing.* To be in all places is not the same as

---

[1] *Octogenta trium Quaestiones,* qu. 20 (PL 40, col. 15).
[2] See *S.T.,* I, 8, 1.
[3] *Ibid.,* ad 2m.

to be in all things. For example, God is present in the angels, but he is not present there as in a place, since there exists no place to be in; for the angels themselves, being spiritual, are not in any place. So our question here is: Is God present in all places, wherever there are bodies? It would seem not. For if the entire thing is in one place, nothing of that thing is in any other place. But if God is in one place, his entire Being is in that place. Therefore God cannot be in all places, or everywhere.

Solution. Again, our solution is a simple one. Since place is a reality, and God is in all reality, God must be in all places. But how is God in all places? He is in a place, as giving it whatever being and local function it possesses. Is God also present in a place as a body is, namely, by filling the place and displacing any other thing that is there? Yes and no. That is, God fills the place, but not as a body does—by displacing another body. God's presence in the place does not exclude other bodies' being there. Rather, God is said to fill a place, and all places, insofar as he gives being to all bodies that fill all places. [4]

But how answer the objection given above? If God's whole Being is in one place, how can it also be in all other places? The word "whole" is a relative word, and has meaning only in relation to "parts." Parts can be of two kinds: parts of the essence of a thing, as matter and form are parts of the composite; and parts of quantity, that is, parts into which a given quantity may be divided, like a quantity of fudge or a quantity of pizza pie. And if there are two kinds of parts, essential and quantitative, there are two kinds of wholes: a whole or totality of essence and a whole or totality of quantity.

With this distinction in mind we can answer our objection. That which is a whole by a totality of quantity cannot be outside the place in which it is, since its quantity is commensurate with the quantity of the place. But a totality of essence is not measured by the totality of the place. And, therefore, if by the totality of its essence the entire thing is in a place, it can also be elsewhere. Consider, for example, those accidental forms which have quantity

---

[4] See St. Thomas, *S.T.*, I, 8, 2; also, *C.G.*, Bk. III, Ch. 68.

not of themselves but only by reason of something else. Whiteness is not quantified because it is whiteness, but because it is in a surface. Now the whole of whiteness is in each part of the surface by the totality of its essence, because the same perfection of whiteness is found in each part of the surface. But if one considers the totality of the whiteness according to the quantity it has because of the surface it is in, then it is not "total" in each part of the surface. In the case of incorporeal substances, no quantity at all is present; hence there is no totality of quantity, but only of essence. Thus, for example, the soul of man is whole and entire in each part of the body, and God is whole and entire in each and every place. [5]

3. Only God Is Present Everywhere

Our final consideration concerning God's omnipresence is this: it is proper to God alone to be in all places. There are many objections that could be brought against this statement. For example, the universe can be considered as a certain perfect and whole body. But the whole universe must be present everywhere, since no place exists outside it. Or if there were only one body and that body were infinite, it, too, would be everywhere, for there would be no place outside it. Again, since the whole soul is in each part of the body, if there were only one animal in the world, its soul would be everywhere. Hence it seems that this property of being present everywhere is not something that is peculiar to God.

Solution. Only God, according to his whole essence and under any hypothesis, is present everywhere. If something were present everywhere inasmuch as its different parts were present in differ-

[5] According to traditional theology, as found for example in St. Gregory the Great (*Moralium Libri,* Bk. 2, Ch. 12 (PL 75, 565) and brought into the scholastic tradition by Peter Lombard (*Sent.,* Bk. 1, dist. 37, Ch. 1), God is said to be everywhere and in all things in three ways: by his power, his presence and his essence. These are simply three different ways of considering the same divine presence. God is said to be in all things by his power, inasmuch as all things are subject to his power; he is said to be in all things by his presence, inasmuch as all things are open and transparent to his divine gaze or knowledge; and God is said to be in all things by his essence, inasmuch as that essence, which is one with his existence, is in all things as the cause of their being. See. St. Thomas, *S.T.,* I, 8, 3.

ent places, that thing would not be present everywhere according to its whole essence. Different parts of the body would be present in different places, but the whole essence of the body would not be in all the places. Or on the supposition that only one body existed (for example, one grain of wheat), that body would be everywhere, but only if we make this supposition. Whereas no matter what the supposition, God would still be present everywhere. For if an infinite number of places is granted, God would be in all of them, since nothing can exist except through him. And he would be present in all these places according to his whole essence and not by reason of any part. And in this sense we say that only God is present everywhere. [6]

The answers to the objections thus become clear. The whole universe is present everywhere only according to its parts. The whole universe is not in every place, but different parts are in different places. And an infinite body would indeed be present everywhere, but only according to its parts. Finally, if there were only one animal in the world, its soul would indeed be present everywhere, and according to its whole essence. But it is present everywhere only under this hypothesis. Given another animal, the soul of the first would no longer be present everywhere.

4. Is the Divine Being Entirely Immutable?

Concerning God's perfection of immutability, we wish to do two things: first, to show how the divine Being is entirely unchangeable; and secondly, to prove that only the divine Being is entirely unchangeable. We have already seen that God is pure act, absolutely simple, and infinitely perfect. It follows, therefore, that he is entirely unchangeable. These three perfections are so many reasons why the divine Being cannot be changed or moved in any way.

Solution. First, God is pure act, and so there is in his Being no admixture of potency. But whatever is moved in any way, possesses some sort of potency for that movement. And since God possesses

[6] *S.T.*, I, 8, 4.

no potency whatsoever, it is impossible that he be moved or changed in any way whatsoever.

Secondly, in any thing that is moved, there must be something that remains the same and something that changes. For example, what is moved from white to black, remains the same in substance, but changes in quality. Hence, in any thing that is moved, there is present some composition. But we have seen that the divine Being is absolutely simple. Therefore God cannot be changed in any way.

Thirdly, any thing that is moved acquires by this movement something it did not have before. But, as we have seen, God is infinite in his Being, comprehending in himself the fullness of perfection. Whence it follows that God can neither acquire anything nor extend his Being to anything that he does not already possess. Therefore, God is entirely unchangeable.

5. Only God Is Entirely Unchangeable

Is absolute immutability a perfection proper to God alone? It would seem not. For example, Aristotle teaches [7] that in all beings that undergo change matter is present. But there is no matter present in the human soul nor in the nature of an angel. So these beings must be unchangeable. Furthermore, since change or motion always gains some term or end, those beings which have reached their final end should no longer be able to change. Thus the blessed in heaven should be unchangeable. It does not seem, therefore, that immutability is a perfection proper to God alone.

Solution. Every creature is in some way changeable. To understand why this is so, we should consider that a thing is changeable in two ways: either because of some passive potency for change that is in it, or because of some active potency or power that exists in another. All creatures before they existed were possible because of the divine power or active potency that could bring these creatures into existence. But if creatures depend upon the divine power for their coming into being, they must also depend upon it for their remaining in being. If God were to withdraw

[7] *Metaphysics,* Book a (II), Ch. 2 (994b26).

this divine influx, all creatures would be reduced to nothingness. Therefore, we can conclude that just as it was in the power of the creator that things could be before they were, so it is still in his power that things should cease to be after they are. Hence, according to an active potency that is in another, namely in God, all creatures are changeable, insofar as God has been able to produce them from nothing and insofar as he is able to reduce them to nothing.

If we consider a thing as changeable because of some passive potency that exists within it, it is also true that every creature is in some way changeable. In every creature there exists some passive potency by which it is able to reach its perfection both in being and in attaining its end.

If we consider the passive potency that a creature has for its substantial being or perfection, not every creature is changeable as regards this perfection, but only material beings. Only in material substances is possibility for non-being intrinsically compatible with possibility for being. The reason for this we saw when discussing the third way of Saint Thomas for demonstrating God's existence. Because of the principle of matter within these beings, they are able to lose their substantial forms, and in this sense are in potency for non-being. Material creatures, then, are changeable even as regards their substantial being, which is given through their substantial form, for they are able to lose this form, and this by reason of the passive potency of matter within them. Material things are also changeable in their accidental being, according as they lose or gain new accidental forms and perfections.

The possibility of change is different in the case of those things in whose essence there is no matter, for example, the human soul and angelic substances. While it is true that these spiritual forms are related to their act of existing as potency to act, they nevertheless cannot suffer the privation of this act of existing. For existence (*esse*) comes through the form, so that nothing can lose its act of existing unless it loses its form. And since a form cannot "lose itself," angels and human souls are naturally incorruptible. There is within them no passive potency for non-being. Thus these creatures are unchangeable according to their substantial being. [8]

However, there still remains in immaterial substances a twofold mutability. First, as regards their end, for they can go from the election of good to that of evil. Secondly, there is within them a mutability according to place; that is, these spiritual substances can apply their power to various and different places. But this is not true of God who because of his infinity fills all places, as we have seen. But do not spiritual substances change also according to their acts of knowledge and love? As mentioned before, these are not the acts of a being in potency, but the acts of a being in act. However, as Thomas points out in his *Commentary on the Sentences*, if we take change in the broadest sense, as Plato did (according to whom every reception was a certain "to be moved"), then any being which is not simply perfect also changes in this sense. [9]

Thus we can sum up as follows. In every creature there exists a potency for change, either according to their substantial being, as in the case of corruptible bodies, or according to their order to their end and the application of their power to different places, as in the case of the angels. And this is due to a potency within the nature of these things. Secondly, all creatures are mutable because of an active potency or power that is in God, in whose power is their being and their non-being. And since the Being of God is not changeable in any of these ways, it is proper only to him to be entirely unchangeable.

The answer to our objections may add whatever light is needed to understand this divine immutability. Aristotle has said, "Whatever is changeable possesses matter." But the angels and human souls possess no matter; therefore, the angels and human souls are unchangeable. Aristotle is talking here about things that are changeable according to their substantial being, and we have seen that this is true only of material substances. Immaterial substances are still changeable in their election of the end.

[8] See *S.T.*, I, 9, 2.
[9] *In I Sent.*, d. 8, qu. 3, a. 2.

But what about the angels and the blessed who have reached their final end in the beatific vision? We answer that in this case, to the immutability of their substantial being, which they possess by reason of their very nature, there is now added an immutability of choice of their final end, which is not had by reason of their nature, but because of the divine power, [10] just as man after the resurrection will be incorruptible, not by reason of his nature (for he shall still be composed of body and soul and hence naturally corruptible), but by reason of the divine power. Of course, the angels and saints in heaven are still mutable according to place and according to the active potency that is in God.

6. God Is Eternal

From a consideration of the divine immutability one is logically led to a discussion of his eternity; for a being that can in no way undergo change must be eternal. Here we will consider three points concerning the attribute of eternity. First, what is eternity? Secondly, is God eternal? Thirdly, is only God eternal?

Since the human intellect is enmeshed in time and matter, the only way at its disposal to an understanding of the non-temporal and immaterial is by way of an analogy with the temporal and material. We gain such knowledge by removing whatever imperfections are due precisely to a thing as in time, or as in matter. For example, we learn of the nature of simple things through a consideration of composite beings. And so in like manner we must learn about the nature of eternity by a consideration of the nature of time.

Aristotle defines time in his *Physics* [11] as the "number of movement in respect of the before and after." Time is motion considered as successive. Since every body that moves has one part coming after another through the place where it is moving, the mind grasps the notion of time insofar as it observes ("numbers") the succession of a thing in motion. In a thing that does not move but which always has itself in the same manner, there is not present this part

[10] S.T., I, 9, 2, ad 2m.
[11] Bk. 4, Ch. 11 (220a25).

following part. There is no before and after, no succession. There-fore, just as the notion of time consists in the numbering or ob-serving of what is before and after, or of what is successive in motion, so in like manner the notion of eternity consists in the apprehension of the uniformity of that which is entirely without motion.

In another place, [12] Aristotle writes that "those things are said to be measured by time which have their beginning and end in time." In everything that is moved, the mind can consider a begin-ning and an end. So just as that which is entirely unchangeable is without any succession whatsoever, so also is it without any beginning or end. From an understanding of time, then, the mind can come to understand what is meant by eternity. Materially, time consists of the physical motion of bodies; formally, it consists in the mind numbering or observing that motion according to its physical succession, according to its before and after, its begin-ning and end. St. Thomas puts this as follows:

. . . It is manifest that the material element of time is because of mo-tion, namely, "before and after," but the formal element of time is due to the operation of the mind. And this is why Aristotle says that if there were no mind there would be no time. [13]

Time, then, is a measure. And to this notion of time two things are essential: first, plurality (before and after, beginning and end), and secondly, some succession or continuation due to the con-tinuity of the motion. So by a denial of this plurality and succes-sion in the duration of God's Being, we come to some understand-ing of divine eternity. First, we see that eternity is a duration in being that is interminable (without beginning or end), and sec-ondly, it is existence that is given all at once (without any suc-cession).

a. The classic definition of eternity

Boethius, in his work *The Consolation of Philosophy*, has fur-nished scholastic philosophy with its classic definition of eternity.

[12] *Physics*, Bk. 4, Ch. 12 (221b28).
[13] *In I Sent.*, d. 19, qu. 2, a. 1, *solutio*.

"Eternity is the perfect and 'all at once' possession of unending life." [14] The two key words of the definition are "unending" and "all at once." While "unending" is negative in expression, it implies a perfection, for it denies an imperfection. It denies a beginning or end in duration of being. What might strike one as strange in this definition is the use of the perfection "life" instead of "being." Saint Thomas defends its use by saying that what is truly eternal is not only being, but living being; and *living* brings out what being does not, namely, the *activity* of what perdures. As he writes in the *Summa:* "The protraction of duration seems to be more according to operation than being; whence even time is the number of motion." [15] The full givenness of a thing's duration is considered more from the point of view of activity than simple existence; even what time measures is *motion* rather than simple existence. Saint Thomas has an interesting comment on the word "possession" in Boethius' definition. Why possession? Because what one possesses is had fixedly and in peace. So to emphasize how complete and unchanging is God's duration we use the word "possession."

b. The eternity of God

We have seen what eternity is. But is God really eternal? It would seem that he is not. Let us consider two simple objections, not so much for their intrinsic value, as to bring out more clearly the concepts involved in God's attribute of eternity. Eternity, like time, is a certain measure of duration in being. But God cannot be measured. Hence, God cannot be eternal. Moreover, in eternity there is no past or present or future. But words denoting past, present and future are often said of God in Holy Scripture. So it would seem that God is not eternal.

Solution. That God is eternal, or rather that God is eternity, is easy to understand. The notion of eternity follows upon unchangeableness, just as the notion of time follows upon motion or change. Since God is entirely unchangeable, he must also be eternal. Not only is God eternal, he is his own eternity, because he is his own

[14] *De Consol. Phil.*, Bk. 5, prose 6 (PL 63, 858).
[15] *S.T.*, I, 10, 1, ad 2m.

duration. This is not true of any other being. Finite beings *have* their duration, because they have their existence. But God, since he is his own Being, is his own duration. And God is his own Being *uniformly*, without any change or variation. Hence God is his own eternity.

What are we to say about the objection that eternity is a certain measure of duration, and God cannot be measured? In our understanding of eternity, it is considered as a certain measure of the divine Being. But when we say that God is eternal, we do not mean that he is measured by his eternity. For in God eternity is nothing else than God. As regards the second objection, it is true that Scripture uses words denoting time when speaking of God. It can do this insofar as God's eternity contains all time, just as his Being contains all being. But by these words Scripture does not mean that God's Being varies according to past or present or future.

7. Only God Is Eternal

Is God the only Being without beginning or end and possessed all at once? Consider this objection. What is necessary or cannot be other than it is, is unchangeable, and what is unchangeable is eternal. But many things are necessary. For example, the truth that two and two are four. Hence not only God is eternal.

Only God is truly eternal. A thing is eternal insofar as it is unchangeable. But since only God is entirely unchangeable, only God is strictly and completely eternal. Thus to the degree that a being participates in the immutability of God, to that degree it also shares in his eternity. And to the degree that a being is changeable, to that degree it is not eternal. Angels and human souls are unchangeable in their substantial being; and thus, while they were brought into being, and so had a beginning, they can never of themselves cease to be. Their being is everlasting, and in this sense, eternal. Even corruptible beings, because of the great length of their duration, are sometimes said to be eternal. For example, we speak of the eternal mountains and the everlasting hills. Finally, those who possess the beatific vision of God are immutable in this operation of seeing God and other things in God; and so they possess in and through this vision eternal life. They share in eternity, but they are not eternity. Only God, as completely unchangeable, is strictly eternal.

How do we answer our objection about necessary truths? Are not these strictly eternal? Just as good and evil are in things, truth and falsity are in the intellect. Hence truths are necessary and eternal according as they are in an eternal intellect. As only the divine Being is strictly eternal, so also only the divine intellect is strictly eternal. And since these truths are eternal because they are in the intellect of God, it does not follow that there is anything eternal outside God.

8. Summary of the Chapter

"Only the Being of God is everywhere, entirely unchangeable and eternal."

a. State of the question

Having considered the simplicity, perfection, goodness and infinity of the divine Being, we are logically led to a consideration of his omnipresence. For what is infinite has no limit, and so God as infinite in his Being would seem to be everywhere. In this chapter, then, we consider the omnipresence and immutability of God, and the eternity what flows from such immutability.

b. Explanation of terms

1) ". . . *is everywhere* . . ." can mean two things: to be in all *things* (omnipresent) or to be in all *places* (ubiquitous). To be in all places and in all things is true only of the Being of God. A body is in a place *circumscriptively*, that is, by the contact of its quantity with the quantity of the surrounding bodies. A spirit is in a place *virtually*, that is, by the contact of its power (*virtus*) with the body it is affecting. A spirit is where it acts. Thus the human soul is in every part of the body, since it actively informs the whole body and all its parts. Moreover, the whole *essence* of a spirit is present in each part of the place where it acts. Having

no quantity, and hence no extension, a spirit can be wholly present (that is, according to its whole essence) in each part where it acts. Thus the soul is present according to its whole essence in each part of the body, and God is present according to his whole essence in all things and in all places.

2) "... *entirely unchangeable* ..." To change is to become other, that is, to lose or gain some perfection. That being is entirely unchangeable which can in no way become other than it is.

3) "... *eternal* ..."—to be without beginning or end or any succession whatsoever in one's duration of being. Put positively, this means the totally simultaneous and perfect possession of one's being.

c. The proof

1) *Only God is everywhere*—in all things and in all places. (*a*) An agent is present where it acts. But God acts in all things, causing and conserving their being. Therefore, etc.

(*b*) A place is a certain reality, namely, a body insofar as it is commensurate with or contains other bodies. Hence, God is in all places insofar as he gives being to all places.

2) *Only God is entirely unchangeable.* That which is pure act, absolutely simple, and infinitely perfect is entirely unchangeable. But this is true only of God. Therefore, only God is entirely unchangeable.

(*a*) Whatever is changed possesses some potency or capacity for the change. But God, *as pure act*, is entirely without potency. Hence, he is entirely unchangeable. Every creature, as possessing some potency, is changeable.

(*b*) Whatever is changed becomes other than it is, and thus possesses something that remains the same and something that changes. Hence, a changeable being is a composed being. But God is *absolutely uncomposed* (which is not true of any creature). Therefore, God alone is entirely unchangeable.

(*c*) Whatever is changed loses or gains some perfection. But God, *as infinitely perfect,* can neither lose or gain any perfection (which is not true of any creature, for a creature can always gain some new accidental perfections). Therefore, only God is entirely unchangeable.

3) *Only God is eternal.* A thing is eternal insofar as it is unchangeable. But only God, as we have seen, is entirely unchangeable. Hence, only God is eternal in the strict sense. For to change is to undergo some succession in one's being. And to be eternal is to possess one's being without any succession or variation whatsoever.

Suggested Readings

1. St. Thomas, *Summa Theologiae,* in *Basic Writings of St. Thomas,* by A. Pegis (New York, Random House, 1945), Vol. 1, pp. 63–84. *On the Truth of the Catholic Faith* (*Summa Contra Gentiles*), translated by A. Pegis (New York, Hanover House, 1955), Book One, pp. 158–170.

CHAPTER 9

God's Knowledge of Himself and Other Things

Oh, the heights of the riches of the wisdom and knowledge of God!
—St. Paul, *Letter to the Romans*,
Ch. 11, verse 33

Having seen something about the perfections of the divine Being as these can be known by us, we are ready now to take up a new problem in natural theology. In this chapter we wish to discuss the operations of the divine Being as these can be known by us through the operations of creatures. The transition from the study of the divine Being to that of its operations is a logical one, since a being operates according to the way it is. Operations are of two kinds: those that remain in a being and perfect it, like operations of knowledge and will; and those that proceed from a being and perfect some external effect. Thus our order will be the following. First, we shall study God's knowledge of himself and of things distinct from himself. Then we shall study God's love of himself and of things distinct from himself. Next we shall study the divine operation as a principle of an external effect in the creative act. This will lead us to a study of God's providence over these external effects. [1]

[1] In order to understand the difficult doctrine of God's knowledge of himself and of things distinct from himself, the student is urged to read the entire fourteenth question in the First Part of the *Summa*. It is one of the best questions in the whole of the *Summa*. Along with this the student should also read the Second Question of the *De Veritate*.

The present chapter will be divided into two sections: (1) God's knowledge of himself; (2) his knowledge of other things. In the first section we shall discuss these four questions: (1) Whether there is understanding or knowledge in God; (2) whether God understands himself; (3) whether he comprehends himself; (4) whether his act of understanding is identical with his divine Being. We shall end the section with a discussion of whether the divine Being is subsistent truth and the cause of the truth of all things.

A. GOD'S KNOWLEDGE OF HIMSELF

1. Is There Knowledge in God?

It would seem that God cannot know anything, even himself. For knowledge is union. It is the intentional union of the knower with the known. It is a union, moreover, with the known precisely as other, precisely as distinct from the knower. Even in self-knowledge, to *be* oneself and to *know* oneself are not the same. And since the divine Being is absolutely simple and cannot enter into union with any object, even intentionally, it would seem that God cannot know anything. But to know is to know something. Hence, it seems, there can be no knowledge in God.

Solution. Not only is there knowledge in God, but God possesses the most perfect kind of knowledge possible. To understand how this must be so, let us consider the difference between a being that knows and a being that has no knowledge. A being that has no knowledge, say a stone or a statue, possesses its own form only; whereas a being that knows has a nature that is capable of possessing not only its own form, but also the forms of other things as well. For the form of the thing known is in the knower.

Let us use a simple example to illustrate this remarkable phenomenon of knowledge. If some day you should visit the Church of St. Peter in Chains in Rome, you will see there the magnificent statue of Michelangelo's *Moses*. This piece of sculptured marble has the form and figure of Moses, and it has it to a high perfection. Yet while the statue possesses the form of Moses, it does not know

Moses through that form. But as you stand there gazing upon this masterpiece, you will possess the form of that statue, and by that form you will know the statue.

Why is it that the statue has the form, but knows nothing through it, while you have the form and by it know the statue? The reason is that the marble possesses the form subjectively, as *matter* possesses form. But you possess the form objectively, as *form* possesses form. And because the latter reception is objective (since the form is received precisely as object), you receive that form in its *otherness;* you receive the form as other than you. Beings that do not know are able to receive *other forms,* but not the forms of other things; whereas beings that know are able to receive the forms of other things. [2]

This is not the place to go into the difference between subjective and objective union with form, which is the proper study of psychology. We simply mention this difference to show how the nature of a being that does not know, like the marble statue, is more limited and less expansive than the nature of a being that knows. This latter has a greater amplitude and extension. We who know are monarchs of all we survey, whereas the statue of Moses looks out upon the world with sightless eyes.

Because of this amplitude and extension of being effected through knowledge, Aristotle says that the human soul is in a way all things. [3] The limiting or contracting of a form is due to the matter in which it is received, so that the more a form is removed from matter the more it approaches a certain infinity. "Whence it follows," says St. Thomas, "that the immateriality of a thing is the very reason why it can know." [4]

To say that immateriality is the root of cognition is not the same as to say that form is the root of cognition. Every finite being possesses a form, but not every finite being possesses knowledge. Rather, when we speak here of immateriality, we refer to a *mode of being* that a form has. Some forms, like the forms of elements

[2] See S.T., I, 14, 1; 80, 1.
[3] *On the Soul,* Bk. 3, Ch. 8 (431b21).
[4] S.T., I, 14, 1.

and inanimate substances, have a completely material mode of being, since they are completely enmeshed in matter. Other forms, like those of plants, are a little less confined by their matter, for while they cannot know other things, they can produce other plants. Plants have a certain immanent activity, which while not cognoscitive is reproductive, and to that extent expansive. The form of brute animals is still more removed from matter and hence has a more immaterial mode of being—to the extent that it has sense knowledge.

A form which possessed an absolutely immaterial mode of being would be a form identified with complete actuality. Such a form would not only be removed from all matter, but also from all potency. This form would be one with its being and would be Being. Immateriality would be one with actuality, and not merely a share in actuality. God is immaterial but has no form, and so is immateriality itself. Other beings share in immateriality. Immateriality is a perfection of being as being, and hence is on the side of the act of existing rather than of form. [5]

This insistence that the immateriality which is the root of cognition is a simple perfection of being and not of essence, is made in order to avoid a difficulty that may arise in the student's mind. Having learned about knowledge in a context of psychology rather than metaphysics—where it is always a question of a certain kind of knowledge, and not a study of knowledge as knowledge—the following difficulty could present itself. If immateriality is the root of cognition, then the substance of an angel, which is completely immaterial, must be completely intellectual. In this context it is hard to see how the nature of God could be any more intellectual than the nature of an angel, or how God's knowledge could be any more perfect than an angel's.

The difficulty is in considering immateriality as a predicamental perfection, whereas it is not. Immateriality is a perfection of being. St. Thomas, after he had said that immateriality is the reason why a thing is cognoscitive, goes on to say: "according to a thing's degree of immateriality will be its degree or perfection of knowl-

[5] See *C.G.*, Bk. 4, Ch. 11.

edge." [6] Aristotle says that plants cannot know because of the materiality of their being. Brutes can have sense knowledge because they can receive the forms of sensible things without having to receive the actual physical matter of sensible things. [7] Intellectual beings like men can have an even higher degree of knowledge, for they can abstract from the individual sensible matter of existing things. And God, as absolutely immaterial and devoid of all potency, has knowledge that is perfect.

To sum up then, we say that the act of existing (*esse*), which is the act of being, is more immaterial than either form (such as a brute soul or human soul) or essence (such as an angelic essence). For while primary matter is pure potency in the order of essence, form and essence are themselves pure potency in the order of being. Hence, in this order, form and essence are themselves "material"—that is to say, limiting and receptive—as regards the act of existing. And so it follows that God, who is his own act of existing, is more immaterial than a creature whose form and essence limit as a material cause their act of existing. It is this immateriality or actuality of the act of existing that is the root of cognition, and not form taken as a principle of limitation of this act.

God must know, then, for his Being is perfect immateriality. It is removed not only from all matter, as is true in the case of the human soul and the substance of an angel, but is without potency of any kind. But if God has knowledge, how do we answer the objection given above that knowledge is an intentional union between subject and object? Even in self-knowledge, the subject as knowing must in some way be other than the subject as known.

---

[6] S.T., I, 14, 1.

[7] The phenomenon of sense knowledge brings out in a striking way the difference between subjective and objective union with a form. Consider this simple example. A person with a ring on his finger places his hand on a warm radiator. Both his hand and the ring become physically warm. There is a subjective union between his hand and the heat, just as there is also a subjective union between the ring and the heat. But whereas the man knows or senses that his hand is warm, the ring he wears does not sense that it is warm. There is also an *objective* union between his hand and the heat because of which the heat is known (sensed) as other, as heat. But there is no such objective union between the matter of the ring and the form of the heat received into it; and so there is no knowledge on the part of the ring.

But in God there is no composition, and hence no subject-object composition.

This objection should remind us that divine knowledge, like the divine Being with which it is identical, is cloaked in mystery. But in mystery, not in contradiction. The composition in God that would involve a contradiction would be that between act and potency. The union from whence knowledge flows is a union of act with act. But in God there cannot be two acts. Of course not, at least not two ontological acts, for then we would have two Gods. But there is no contradiction in having a Being that is also an act of knowledge.

This becomes a bit clearer when we recall that God does not possess his Being subjectively, that is, his act of existing is not received into any essence or potency. He is that act. Hence God possesses his Being non-subjectively or trans-subjectively. The subjective can never be one with the objective, and knowledge is a union with the object as object. But it is not a contradiction to say that the non-subjective can be identified with the objective. In our knowledge of God there is always a distinction between his "to be" and his "to know," for they constitute two distinct notions and are not synonyms. But as in God they are the same non-subjective-objective act. [8]

2. Does God Know Himself?

Having established the general truth that God does have knowledge, we now wish to study the specific objects of this knowledge. We begin by asking this question: Does God have knowledge of himself?

Solution. When we say that something knows itself, we mean that it is both knower and known. Hence to understand how God knows himself we must see why it is that he can become knower and known. We shall do this by examining once more the perfection of knowing.

[8] The revealed doctrine of the Blessed Trinity, of three distinct Persons in one Divine Nature, throws some light on the mystery of Divine Knowledge (and Divine Love), where knowledge is seen as constituting a Divine Person, the Word of God, which is a subsistent relation.

A thing possesses perfection in two ways. First, by possessing the perfection of its own being, which each thing has according to its proper substantial form. According to this perfection, the being of one thing is distinct from the being of another, and it lacks or does not have the perfection of anything else. According to the perfection it has because of its substantial form, a being is not simply perfect, since it lacks the perfection of other and more perfect beings. Its proper perfection is only part of the totality of the perfection of other distinct beings. In this sense the total perfection of the universe is made up of the different perfections of the different distinct beings.

As a certain remedy against this ontological "aloneness," we find in created things another mode of perfection, according to which the perfection which is the proper possession of one thing is found in another. This is the perfection of a knowing being precisely as knowing. For something is known by another insofar as the thing is present in the knower. Once more we recall Aristotle's remark that the soul is in some way all things, for by its nature it can know all things. [9] According to this second mode of perfection, the perfection of knowledge, it is possible that in one thing there can exist the perfection of the whole universe.

The perfection of one thing cannot be in another according to the determined and limited being it has in itself, for by this it is itself and nothing else. If we are to consider this perfection as it is able to be in another, we must consider it as lacking those things which determine and limit it. What is it that determines and limits perfections? It is matter. Thus each perfection as knowable or as able to be in another, must be separated from matter. Moreover, not only is separation from matter necessary to the thing knowable, but also to the one knowing. For if the knower were completely material, it would receive the perfection according to a completely determined and limited being. Perfection would not be in the knower as something knowable, as something which, existing as the perfection of one thing, is also able to be in another.

[9] See also St. Thomas, *De Veritate*, qu. 2, a. 2.

Forms are not received in the intellect the same way they are received in matter. The intellect is immaterial, so a form must be received into it immaterially. Thus according to the immateriality of a being will be its perfection of knowledge. Plants, and beings below plants, can receive nothing immaterially, and so they are deprived of all knowledge. Sense powers can receive sensible forms without their physical matter, but not without the conditions of matter, [10] since they are the powers of sense organs. The intellect, on the other hand, can receive forms without the conditions of matter, since the intellect is not the power of any organ.

Just as what knows must in some degree be immaterial, so also must be the thing known. Material existing things are not intelligible unless our intellect makes them intelligible. Of themselves they are intelligible only in potency. They are made actually intelligible through the light of our agent intellect, just as colors are made actually visible through the light of the sun. On the other hand, immaterial things are intelligible of themselves. Of themselves they are more knowable than material things, although for us, because our intellect is the power of a form that is in matter, they are less knowable than material things.

Let us apply to God this twofold immateriality required in the knower and in the thing known. God's separation from matter and from all potentiality is absolute. Therefore his nature is at one and the same time perfectly knowing and perfectly knowable. Since God is his own act of existing, his nature is one with his Being; and since that nature is at one and the same time perfectly knowing and perfectly knowable, God as knower and known is one with his Being. For God, to be, to be knowing, and to be known, are one and the same. "And therefore God is the understander and comprehender of himself because his absolutely trans-

---

[10] By the "conditions of matter" we mean those characteristics of a form that follow upon its being in individual sensible matter. Since the sense power is the act of a bodily organ, and since a bodily organ (such as the eye, ear, etc.) is composed of individual sensible matter, sensible forms received into such organs are affected by the conditions of matter; they are in time, place, and so forth.

parent nature is that thing which is God himself. And so we see that God must know himself." [11]

Notice what has happened here in our analysis of God's knowledge of himself. When we know or understand something, our intellect must be informed and actuated by the intelligible species of that thing. Knowledge, as an immanent operation, has its term in the knower. The way the term is present in the knower determines the way the knower is in act. Recall here the important observation of Aristotle: [12] the intelligible in act is the intellect in act. As non-informed by the intelligible species, our possible intellect is in potency; and as not present in our intellect, the intelligible is in potency. And this is the only way they differ. "The intellect is distinct from the intelligible only insofar as both are in potency." [13] But the intelligible in act is the possible intellect in act. The intellect *is* what it knows. By this knowledge it is assimilated to the thing known and conformed to it. [14]

Since God is pure act, there is in him absolutely no potency. Hence we cannot distinguish between his intellect in potency and his intellect in act, as we can with our intellect. Moreover, on the side of the thing known (his divine essence), we cannot distinguish between that essence as potentially intelligible and as actually intelligible, as we can with the things we know. We need an intelligible species since our intellect is in potency; and this intelligible species is other than the substance of our intellect, even when we are actually understanding. But in knowing himself, God's essence is the intelligible species; and so God knows himself through himself.

3. Does God Comprehend Himself?

To comprehend something means to understand it perfectly, to understand it to the degree that it is understandable. In comprehensive knowledge there is an absolute equation between the

[11] St. Thomas, *De Verit.*, qu. 2, a. 2.
[12] *De Anima*, Bk. 3, Ch. 4 (430a3).
[13] *S.T.*, I, 14, 2.
[14] *Ibid.*

knowledge that the knower has of the thing and the knowability of that thing.

As we have seen, the divine essence is without any potency whatsoever, and thus supreme in its power as knower and perfect in its intelligibliity as knowable. It follows, therefore, that God not only understands his divine essence, but that he understands that essence perfectly, or comprehends it. To say that God comprehends himself means there is nothing hidden or unknown in his knowledge of himself.

Solution. The better to understand how this must be so, let us recall that something is knowable insofar as it is in act. A thing acts insofar as it is in act, and not insofar as it is in potency. Now the knowable must act upon the knower if it is to be known. God as pure actuality is absolutely knowable. On the other hand, the divine essence as separated from all matter and from all potency is an infinite power for knowing. Thus it is clear that God knows himself insofar as he is knowable, that he comprehends himself. [15]

But does not this comprehensive knowledge involve a contradiction? If God comprehends himself, his Being must be finite. What we comprehend, we somehow circumscribe and contain. But God is infinite. Therefore, he cannot be comprehended, not even by himself. This difficulty arises from our way of knowing God. Comprehension includes all knowledge of a thing and thus excludes all ignorance of it. To remove this ignorance, we say God comprehends himself. But we do not mean by this that God's Being is measured by his understanding, as though his understanding were different from his Being as the measurer from the measurable. Since God's knowledge and Being are one, nothing of his Being escapes his knowledge.

Comprehension is predicated of God's knowledge by way of proportionality. Just as a finite being does not exceed finite knowledge, so God's Being does not exceed his knowledge. But we do not mean that God knows himself as something finite. God knows himself, understands himself, comprehends himself, and is infinite. God is infinite, not as matter is infinite, but as an unreceived act

[15] *S.T.*, I, 14, 3.

of existing is infinite. If there were no "end" to God's Being in the sense that there is no end to matter as deprived of form, where part can be added to part indefinitely, God could not comprehend himself, for he would never come to the end of the parts. [16] But there is no end or limit to God's Being in the sense that it is not received into any subject or potency. It is infinite act, and it is infinitely known as infinite act.

Only God can comprehend himself. Since every created intellect is a received intellect, its power of knowing is finite. Thus it is absolutely impossible for any created intellect, even as elevated by the light of glory in the beatific vision, to comprehend the essence of God. In heaven, we will know God as he is in himself, but we will not comprehend him as he comprehends himself. Only the divine intellect is infinite in the same way the divine essence is infinite; God alone can comprehend himself. Not in the sense that through this comprehension there is some end or term to his act of knowledge, but in the sense that there is nothing lacking in this knowledge of himself.

4. God's Act of Knowledge and Act of Being Are the Same

That the divine substance is one with the divine knowledge is clearly implied in the foregoing considerations. If there were any difference between the two, the divine substance would be in potency for this knowledge, for to know is the act and perfection of the knower. St. Thomas gives a simple consideration to make clear this identity between God's knowledge and his Being. [17] To know is the act and perfection of a being as knowing, just as to be is the act and perfection of a being as existing. Furthermore, just as the act of existing follows upon the presence of the substantial form, so the act of knowing follows upon the presence of an intelligible form. Now in God there is no distinction between form and existence, since his essence is identical with his existence. Moreover, this essence is the intelligible form by which God knows. No other form distinct from the divine essence could represent that

[16] See *De Veritate*, qu. 2, a. 2, ad 5m.
[17] *S. T.*, I, 14, 4.

essence as it is in itself, for no other intelligible form is its own to be, and God's essence is its own to be. Since in God the intelligible form is one with the divine essence and the divine essence is one with the divine Being, God's act of knowledge is the same as his act of Being. In God, the intellect by which he understands, what he understands by the intellect, and the intelligible form through which he understands, are all one and the same thing. Thus the conclusion of St. Thomas: "When, therefore, we say that God is intelligent, we place no multiplicity within his substance." [18]

5. The Essence of God Is Subsistent Truth

Since the divine essence is pure actuality, we can say that God is subsistent Being; and since the divine essence is completely perfect, we can say that God is subsistent good. Can we say also that God is subsistent truth, and if so, why?

The divine essence is subsistent truth because of the very nature of truth. Truth is the conformity of intellect and thing. Thus truth is found in an intellect insofar as it understands a thing as it is; and truth is found in things insofar as things are conformable to an intellect. Whether we look upon truth from the side of its presence in an intellect or from the side of its presence in things, the divine essence is truth itself. For not only is this essence conformed to the divine intellect, but is the divine intellect. Here there is not only conformity between intellect and object, but identity.

Moreover, we cannot distinguish in God between his intellect in potency and his intellect in act. God's intellect is one with his act of knowing. Nor can we distinguish between the divine essence (which is the object of God's knowledge) as potentially knowable and as actually known. Thus there is an actual and absolute conformity between God's knowledge and Being. Moreover, this conformity—or rather identity—is not merely on the side of form. For example, when we say that the intelligible in act is the intellect in act, we mean that the intellect and the intelligible species are one in form. And because of this oneness in form the intellect is conformed to the thing. Since being (*esse*) follows upon the pres-

[18] *Ibid.* See also *C.G.*, Bk. I, Chs. 45 and 46.

ence of form, we actually are, with an intentional being (*esse*), the things we know. Now in God there is no distinction between his form and his Being, and no distinction between his form as intelligible and as essence. Therefore, there is no place in God for any distinction between intentional being and real being. Whence it follows that God's intellect and God's Being are not only conformed to each other by an identity that is on the side of form (or intentional), but also by an identity that is on the side of act (or ontological).

God is subsistent truth because he is, if we may so express it, subsistent conformity, a conformity that is an identity between his intellect and his Being. And this is an identity not only as regards intentional being, but real being. In God, not only do we have a unity of intellect and Being, but a unity of intentionality and actuality. And because in God intentionality is one with actuality, creatures, while retaining their actual being, can become other things by intentional being. Unless these two kinds of being were one in God, a creature could never become something else by knowledge. The two modes of perfection possessed by a knowing creature are one super-eminent mode of perfection in the creator.

6. Is the Truth of God the Cause of the Truth of Things?

Because God is subsistent Being, he is the first and proper cause of the being of other things; and because he is subsistent good, he is the first and proper cause of the good of things. Thus, since God is subsistent truth, he must be the first and proper cause of the truth of things. Everything that is true must ultimately be so by the truth that is God. But this seems impossible. For example, the statement, "Mary Magdalene committed adultery," is true. But if the cause of its truth is ultimately from God, then her sin, which makes this statement true, must also be ultimately from God, and this is impossible. It would seem, then, that God cannot be called subsistent truth in the same way he can be called subsistent Being or good.

How answer this objection? Everything that limits or makes a being less perfect—like matter, privation, change, motion—are present in that being not insofar as it comes from God and imitates God, but insofar as it comes from nothing and does not imitate God. Now sin as such is a privation of being, and so does not possess of itself any truth. It is false, therefore, to say that its truth comes from God, since it has no truth. But while a privation has no truth of itself, since it has no being of itself, yet it does have some truth in our knowledge of it. The truth of blindness, for example, consists in my apprehension of a subject that lacks a perfection that should be there. Now all apprehension or knowledge comes from God. Whence it follows that whatever truth is in this statement, "Mary Magdalene committed adultery," is from God. But if we were to argue that therefore the *adultery* is from God, we would be guilty of a fallacy. It is the action of adultery that is the sin and privation, since it is this action that lacks proper order. And this lack is due only to Mary Magdalene.

7. Summary

Truth is the adequation of the intellect with the thing. When, therefore, we say that God is truth we mean to assert that the divine intellect is conformed to the divine essence. Because the divine intellect first of all understands the divine esssence, and through this essence (as we shall see) all other things, when we say that God is truth we principally imply this adequation of his intellect with his essence. But, secondarily, we imply the adequation of his intellect and created things.

Finally, the divine intellect is not conformed to the divine essence as that which measures is conformed to the thing measured. The divine intellect is not the principle of the divine essence; one *is* the other. The subsistent truth that results from this equality in no way implies the notion of a principle, whether we consider that truth that results from the side of the divine essence or from the side of the divine intellect. Just as in God the one knowing and the thing known are the same, so the truth of the essence and the truth of the intellect are the same. That is to say, in God ontological and logical truth are identical, with neither of them having the notion of a principle, with neither of them being the cause or measure of the other.

If, however, we understand the truth of the divine intellect as it is conformed to created things, while it is still the same truth (God knows both himself and creatures through himself), there is now added to our understanding of the divine truth the notion of principle or relationship to creatures. The divine intellect is compared to the creature as measurer to thing measured. This relation, of course, is one of reason only.

B. GOD'S KNOWLEDGE OF OTHER THINGS

This consideration of the conformity between the divine intellect and created things brings us to the second part of our chapter and presents us with an entirely new and different problem: God's knowledge of things that are distinct from himself. This problem we shall divide into three questions: First, does God know anything other than himself? Secondly, how does God know these other things? Thirdly, does he know these things in themselves, according to their own proper and individual natures? In the final part of the chapter we shall say something about the unchangeableness of God's knowledge in face of the changeableness of its objects.

1. Does God Know Anything Other Than Himself?

At first glance it would seem quite impossible for God to know anything outside himself. Two simple considerations will make clear this seeming impossibility. First, the thing known is the act and perfection of the one knowing it. Thus, if God knows something other than himself, this something would be the act and perfection of God. And this is impossible, for in God there is no potency for any further perfection. Secondly, whatever God knows he must know from all eternity, for his knowledge cannot change. But creatures have not existed from all eternity. Thus God cannot know creatures.

Solution. St. Thomas in his different writings gives many reasons why God must know things other than himself. In the *De Veri-*

tate [19] alone he gives eleven. We will examine three of the more important ones.

We have seen that God not only understands himself, but understands himself perfectly, or comprehends himself. This perfect understanding of the divine essence must include the perfect understanding of the power of that essence. And the perfect understanding of the power of that essence must include those things to which this power extends. Now the divine power extends itself to other things, for as we demonstrated in the second way of St. Thomas, God is the first efficient cause of all beings. Hence we conclude that God must know all these beings to which the power of his essence extends.

Our second proof is drawn from the fact of finality. Whatever of its very nature tends toward something must be directed toward it by another. If not, a thing would be either its own end (and would not tend toward anything), or it would direct itself to its end, and so possess knowledge. But many natural things that have no knowledge tend towards other things. Hence they are directed toward them by another. We must conclude, therefore, that above all natural things there exists some intellect who has ordered these things to their ends, giving to their nature this inclination or appetite. But nothing can be ordered to an end unless it and the end to which it is ordered are known. In the fifth way we demonstrated that it is from the divine intellect that natures and the ordering of natures have their origin. Hence in this divine intellect there is a knowledge of natural beings. The Jewish philosopher, Moses Maimonides, commenting upon the words of the Psalmist, "He who has made the eye, does he not consider?" says this could mean: He who has made the eye proportioned to its end, which is to see, has he not considered, that is, understood, the nature of the eye? [20]

Our third proof is based upon the identity in God between his Being and his knowledge. It becomes evident that God must know things other than himself if we consider that the divine Being,

[19] Qu. 2, a. 3.
[20] See St. Thomas, *ibid.*

which is the first efficient cause of all things, is the divine knowledge. Since every effect must pre-exist in God as in its first cause, it follows that every effect must pre-exist in God as in an act of knowledge. And since a thing is in another according to the manner of this other, these effects must pre-exist in God's understanding according to an intelligible mode of being. They must pre-exist in God's understanding precisely as known. [21]

Let us clarify this reasoning a little further. We know that every agent acts insofar as it is in act. Therefore, that which is effected through the agent must somehow be in the agent, which is the reason why every agent produces something similar to itself. Now, as we just stated, everything that is in another is there according to the manner of the one in which it is. If the efficient cause or active principle is a material being, its effect will be present in it materially, because it will be there as in a certain material power. If, on the other hand, it is a question of an immaterial cause, its effect must be present in it immaterially. Now something knows another according as it receives that other immaterially. Whence it follows that material causes do not know the things they effect, because these effects do not pre-exist in them as knowable. But in the case of immaterial causes, their effects pre-exist in them as knowable, since they are in them immaterially. So every immaterial cause knows its effects. And since God is the immaterial cause of all things, it follows that he possesses the knowledge of these things.

Answering the objections. The first objection against the possibility of God's knowing anything outside himself was this: The thing known is the act and perfection of the one knowing it. But God cannot be actuated or perfected by anything outside himself.

The answer to this objection is very important, and prepares us for the question of *how* God knows things other than himself. We begin our answer by introducing an important distinction. The thing known is not the act or the perfection of the one knowing it according to the thing *that is understood.* For what is understood is outside the one knowing it. Rather, the thing known is the act and perfection of the one knowing it according to the likeness or

[21] See *S.T.,* I, 14, 5.

species *by which* it is understood. A perfection must be in the one having the perfection, and what is known is not in the intellect, but only the likeness of what is known. For example, the stone we know is not in the intellect, but only the form by which we know it. It is this form or likeness that is the act and perfection of the intellect.

With this distinction in mind we can now make a further distinction. The likeness of the thing known can be in an intellect in two ways: As something other than the intellect that knows, or as the very substance of the intellect. For example, when my intellect understands itself, it also understands other human intellects, insofar as my own intellect is similar to these. So I can say that other intellects are in my knowledge according to the very substance of my intellect. [22]

But the likeness or form of a stone existing in my intellect is not the substance of that intellect, since it has been received into it. Turning our attention now to this form that is other than the intellect, we see that it is sometimes related to the thing whose form it is as the effect of this thing, and sometimes as its cause. In the case of our speculative intellect, which simply understands and considers things, the likenesses or forms in our minds are the effects of things. What we know is the cause of the form by which we know it. Whereas in the case of the practical intellect, or the intellect considered as making or doing things, this form or likeness is a cause. For example, the form of a house in the mind of an architect is the cause of the form of the house he builds.

With these considerations in mind, we can make a final distinction which will answer our original objection. When the intellect understands something through a form that is not the substance of the intellect, then the intellect is perfected and actuated by something other than itself. Moreover, if this form is the cause of the thing, as in the case of the practical intellect, then the intellect is actuated and perfected only by this form, and in no way by the thing whose form it is. For example, the architect is not perfected by the house, but rather the house by the architect. If, on the other

22 See *De Veritate*, qu. 2, a. 3, ad 1m.

hand, the form or likeness is an effect of the thing, then this thing itself in some way perfects and actuates the intellect, insofar as it is the cause of the form received into the intellect. If, however, the form of the thing known is the very substance of the knower, the knower is not perfected by any thing other than himself. And since God's knowledge of things is not caused by these things, and since the form by which he knows them is his very substance, it follows that although God knows things other than himself, he is in no way actuated or perfected by these other things.

Our second objection was this: If God knows creatures, he must know them from all eternity, since his knowledge cannot change or vary. But creatures have not existed from all eternity. Therefore, God cannot know creatures. We answer that God knows creatures from all eternity, even though no creature has existed from all eternity. It is not necessary that a creature must be existing in its own proper nature when it is known. Just as we can know distant places like China and New Zealand, so we can know distant times or past events that no longer exist. So there is no reason why God cannot know from eternity non-eternal things. [23]

Moreover, it is not the existence of things that causes God's knowledge of them, but rather God's knowledge that causes the existence of things. Things do not have to exist in order for God to know them. From all eternity God knows each thing in its own proper nature, because he will cause each thing in its own proper nature. God's eternity embraces all times and all things in time, for it is one with his Being which causes all times and all things in time. Hence, as St. Thomas teaches in the *Summa Contra Gentiles* (Book One, chapter 66, paragraph 7), while time is not already present in eternity, yet all the successive moments of time possess in eternity the same presence that each one of them has in time.

2. How Does God Know Things Other Than Himself?

By what medium of cognition, or by what intelligible form, does God know things other than himself? Just as God knows himself

[23] See *De Veritate*, qu. 3, a. 3 ad 12m.

through his divine essence, so God knows all other things through that same essence. The intelligible species by which God knows creatures is his own essence. God knows other things in themselves, but he knows them through himself. Why he knows them in their own proper nature we will discuss in our next question. Our present concern is to understand how he knows them through himself.

But is it possible for God to know through his essence things that are not his essence? Here we will consider three objections against this possibility. These objections will manifest the nature and difficulty of our problem. Our first objection is this: If God knows creatures through his essence, then God knows one thing (the creature) through another (the knowledge he has of his essence). But every intellect that knows one thing through another is discursive and reasoning, and this involves motion and imperfection, which can have no place in the divine intellect. Thus God cannot know creatures through his essence.

Our second objection is a more serious one. The medium through which a thing is known must be proportioned to that thing. But the divine essence is infinite, and so is not proportioned to the creature which is finite. Therefore, by knowing his essence, God cannot know the creature.

Finally, if God knows the creature through his essence, he can hardly know that creature as distinct from his essence. For as in God the creature is one with God. But if God knows the creature through his essence, he knows that creature as in his essence, and hence not as distinct from him and in its own proper nature.

Solution. The problem of *how* God knows other things is one of the most difficult in all of natural theology. At the outset we should warn the student that the way God knows things and the way we know things are entirely different. The problem is made all the more difficult since comparisons taken from human knowledge tend to lead us into error, rather than give us any insight into what it means for God to know things. But the only kind of knowledge we have to analyze is human knowledge. Our problem is to leave to one side whatever is essential to human knowledge and keep only what is essential to knowing as such. With this warning in mind, let us see what we can learn about God's knowledge of things other than himself.

We begin by recalling that a thing can be known in two ways. It can be known either because of itself, or because of something else. A thing is known because of itself when it is known through a form that is derived from the thing. For example, when the eye sees a stone through the sensible form of that stone, the stone is seen of itself; or when the intellect understands the nature of a stone through the intelligible form abstracted from the phantasm, the stone, once more, is known because of itself. It is seen or understood because of its own proper form, a form or species that is directly derived from the thing known.

On the other hand, a thing is known because of something else, and not because of itself, when it is seen through a form or species that in some manner or other contains it. Let us consider a few examples of this.

When I know a whole, I know also the parts contained in the whole. The part is seen in the whole through the species of the whole. Or consider this example: A man looks at himself in a mirror. He sees himself. But he sees himself through the image or reflection in the mirror. Television can furnish us with still another example. Those in the studio audience watching Perry Como see him because of himself. They see him because of a form or species produced directly by Perry Como. But those who are watching their television screens, while they do indeed see the selfsame Perry Como, see him not because of himself, but because of his image on their screens.

These are so many different ways that things can be seen or understood because their form or species is contained in some other thing which, when known, gives knowledge of these things. Let us remember, however, that they are only examples to illustrate a point of doctrine, namely, that a thing can be known through something that contains its species. They are by no means perfect examples. For instance, Perry Como is the cause of his image by which he is seen on television, and the man who sees himself in

the mirror is the cause of his reflection in the mirror. Whereas the
creature in no way is the cause of the species of itself that is contained in God's essence.

A thing seen in another is, nevertheless, seen in itself. By "in
itself" we mean in "its own proper nature." John sees *himself* in the
mirror. His image need not first be known before, and independently of, the thing whose image it is, and then only consequent to
this lead him to a knowledge of himself. No, the image in the mirror is a form in which or by which the man standing before the
mirror is directly and immediately seen. This cognition of the other
is immediate. The man does not reason from his image to himself.
This knowledge is immediate, but it is in another.

God knows himself through himself, for he knows himself
through his own essence. But God does not know things distinct
from himself through themselves, as we know a stone through the
form of the stone. Rather, God knows these things in himself, insofar as his essence contains the forms of these things.

How does God's essence contain the form or likeness of creatures? God must know creatures according to the way they are in
him. An effect that exists in its efficient cause is not other than this
cause if we consider it precisely as cause. God, of course, is much
more than a cause. But an effect existing in a cause is not different
from the latter considered precisely as cause. For example, the
house that the architect builds, as existing in the art or practical
knowledge of the architect, is in no way different from this art or
practical knowledge. Of course, this practical knowledge is different from the architect as man, but not as architect, not as the
actual cause of houses. The house to be made pre-exists in the
architect as one with his art or practical knowledge. The reason
is easy to see. That by which the architect acts is his art; thus that
by which the real house is assimilated to the architect is his art.
Hence the effect, the house, is in the agent as identified with the
art or practical knowledge of the agent.

If, therefore, an agent would act through its form alone, it would
follow that the effect would pre-exist in the agent insofar as the

latter possessed this form. The effect as in the agent would not differ from this form. [24]

Applying these principles to God, we see that because God acts through his essence, he acts through form alone, and through a form that is his own essence. Hence, effects in him are not distinct from this essence, but are one with it. Therefore, that by which God knows creatures is nothing else than his own essence. [25]

Answering the objections. Is it true, as the first objection stated, that because God knows creatures by knowing his essence, there is some discursive movement or reasoning in God's knowledge of creatures? The intellect is said to reason from one thing to another, only when it knows each thing by a different act of understanding. There are two different and diverse apprehensions involved in going from one apprehended thing to another apprehended thing. For example, when our intellect goes from the knowledge of an effect to the knowledge of its cause, it is by one act that it understands the effect and by another and different act that it understands the cause. And so the intellect is said to reason from effect to cause.

But when by one and the same act the intellect knows the medium by which it understands and the thing understood by the medium, there is no reasoning in its knowledge. For example, when we know the stone through the species of the stone existing in us, or when we know the thing in the mirror through the mirror, we do not reason to the thing. In these cases, it is by one and the same act that we know the medium and the thing by the medium. It is by one and the same act that we know the image in the mirror and the thing whose image it is. As St. Thomas writes, in cognition it is the same thing to tend to the likeness of the thing and to the thing known by this likeness. [26] Each is known immediately.

And this is so because a medium such as a mirror or a sensible or intelligible species is *formally* a medium: Its whole *raison d'être* or function is to lead to the knowledge of something else. Whereas

---

[24] See *De Veritate*, qu. 2, a. 3, ad 3m.
[25] *Ibid.*
[26] *Ibid.*

in the case of reasoning, or the discursive movements of the mind, the first truth is only *materially* a medium: it is first known for itself and in its own right. And then, because of some further relationship that it implies, it is formally seen as leading to the knowledge of something else.

Let us apply this to God's knowledge. God knows his effects through his essence as a thing is known through its formal likeness. Thus, by one and the same act of cognition, God knows himself and other things. And so there is no reasoning in the divine intellect. God knows himself and creatures *by one act,* and this is the act by which he knows his essence. In knowing his essence he knows also the things of which that essence is the likeness.

The answer to our second objection may shed new light on God's knowledge of creatures. The objection had argued that there must be a proportion between the species and the thing known through the species. But the species, God's essence, is infinite, and what is known through that species, the creature, is finite. Hence, God cannot know creatures through his essence.

We answer that one thing may be proportioned to another in two ways. First, when there exists between the two things a direct proportion; for example, as four is directly proportioned to two, because four is twice two. Secondly, when there exists between the two things a proportionality, as six is proportioned to eight, because just as six is twice three, so eight is twice four; for proportionality is a likeness of proportions. One proportion is similar to the other proportion: twice three is similar to twice four, and so six and eight are proportional. Now since in a proportion the likeness between the two things is due to some determined or definite excess of one over the other, it is impossible for the infinite to be like the finite by such a direct proportion. [27]

But in those things which are like each other by proportionality, the likeness is not between two things, but between two proportions. In this sense, nothing forbids the infinite from being proportional to the finite. Just as a finite thing is equal to another finite

---

[27] See *De Veritate,* qu. 2, a. 3, ad 4.

thing, so the infinite is equal to another infinite. [28] For example, God's infinite power of knowing is equal to the infinite intelligibility of his essence. Here the medium is directly proportioned to the one knowing through the medium. And because of this proportion, nothing prevents there being a proportionality between the medium (God's infinite essence) and the things known through that medium (finite creatures). And because of this proportionality, nothing prevents God from knowing the creature through his essence.

The student should recall here what was said earlier concerning the proportionality in being that exists between the creature and God. All we are adding is this consideration: Since God's Being is the very medium or likeness by which he knows things other than himself, there is a proportionality between this medium and the finite beings known through it.

But does it not seem a little strange that proportionality in *being* between the creature and God makes the creature very little like God, for the ontological difference between them remains infinite; whereas because of this proportionality of *medium*, the creature can be known perfectly and completely by God? Our difficulty disappears if we remember that the first proportionality is one of being, and the second one of being *as represented*. The two are by no means the same. In fact, we sometimes see that the less the likeness in nature between knower and the thing known, the more perfectly is the thing known. For example, both the intellect and the senses can know a stone. In nature and mode of being, there is a greater likeness between the stone and its form in the senses, than between the stone and its form in the intellect. For the form of the stone in the intellect is more removed from matter. And yet St. Thomas will not hesitate to say that our intellect knows the stone more perfectly and with more perspicacity than do our senses. [29] A likeness of nature is not required between the knower and thing known, but there is required a likeness in the order of representation. And so while there exists an infinite difference be-

28 *Ibid.*
29 See *De Veritate,* qu. 2, a. 3, ad 9m.

tween the nature of God and the nature of the creature, there is
the greatest likeness of the creature to God, in the sense that the
nature of God perfectly *represents* the creature. Thus the divine
intellect knows creatures perfectly.

There remains only our final objection. If God knows the creature through his essence, he knows the creature as in his essence.
But as in his essence, the creature is not distinct from God. Thus
if God knows the creature through his essence, he cannot know
the creature as distinct from himself.

We answer by saying that God does not know others as they
are *in him*, if this phrase, "as they are in God," refers to his cognition of *the thing known*. God knows things not only according to
the being they have in him, where they are one with him, but also
according to the being they have outside him, where they are different and distinct from him. But if the phrase, "as they are in
God," refers to his *way of knowing*, then it is quite true that God
does not know a thing except as it is in him. For he knows it by a
likeness that is one in being with himself.

If we look at the *way* God knows, then God knows both himself
and creatures in the same way. We have the same knower, the
same act of cognition, and the same medium of knowing. If, however, we look at the things known, then God does not know himself and other things in the same way. There is not the same relation of himself and of others to the medium by which he knows.
He is one with that medium (his essence) through identity,
whereas other things are one with it only through assimilation.
And therefore God knows himself through his essence; whereas
he knows other things through a likeness. It is true that that which
is his essence is also that which is the likeness of other things. Yet
as medium by which he knows himself, it is properly called essence, since it it known as his own very Being. But as a medium
by which he knows other things, his essence is properly called a
likeness, for it is known as the species of other things.

In point of fact, this distinction of viewpoints furnishes us a basis
for answering many difficulties concerning the divine knowledge.
From the side of God knowing, and from the side of the medium

by which God knows, the divine knowledge is simple and indivisible. But from the side of what is known this is not the case. Furthermore, we have seen that the divine essence itself is a twofold medium of cognition for God. It is the medium by which God knows himself, and by which he knows objects other than himself. Considered as that by which he knows himself, this medium is correctly designated as essence, and is the same as the object known. But considered as that by which God knows other things, this medium is more properly called a likeness, and it is different from the objects known, which objects are the creatures existing outside God.

But this last truth provides us with a new difficulty. Is not the divine essence, considered as a likeness by which God knows creatures outside himself, a multiple and diversified likeness, since it gives God a knowledge of many and diversified objects? If God's essence represents a multitude of creatures, why is there not some multiplicity within that essence? The reason is that what is multiple in its power to represent need not be composed in its being. God's essence can represent many creatures because many creatures can imitate his divine essence. Hence the multiplicity in the representational value of the divine essence is on the side of the creatures represented. Insofar as the divine essence is known by God as variously imitable by creatures, we say that the divine essence contains many ideas. But God knows his essence as thus imitable by one simple, undivided act of knowledge, and so his essence is absolutely one and simple in its Being. It is multiple in its power to represent, but this multiplicity means that many things can imitate this essence, and since these things are distinct from God they put no multiplicity in God's act of knowing. For it is by one and the same act of knowledge that God knows himself through his essence and creatures through a likeness that is that same essence.

3. Does God Know Creatures in Their Own Proper Natures?

What does it mean to know something in its own proper nature? It means that whatever belongs to the thing as its peculiar property and perfection is understood by the one knowing it. It is opposed to a mere partial knowledge of the thing, or a general knowledge of the thing. To know a thing in its proper nature means a complete and particular knowledge of the thing.

Let us consider some examples that would constitute only a partial or a general knowledge of an object. Fire causes heat in a piece of wood and a piece of iron. On the supposition that this fire could know itself, it would know the nature of fire; and knowing the nature of fire, it would also know the wood and the iron insofar as they are hot, insofar as they participate in the nature of fire. This would be a general and partial knowledge of the wood and the iron. It would not be a knowledge of these things in their own proper nature, that is to say, as wood or iron.

But this example itself seems to prove that God cannot know things in their proper natures. The nature of God is Being. So God in knowing his nature, knows all things only insofar as they are beings, and not as they are *this* or *that kind* of being. Hence God does not know each being in its own proper nature.

Solution. The fact that God must know things in their own proper natures is very easy to prove. We shall give two simple proofs, one drawn from the perfection of God's knowledge, the other from the notion of finality.

To know something only in a general and universal way is to know it imperfectly. For example, if I know Paul only according to those perfections that he has in common with other men, my knowledge of Paul is general and imperfect. I know Paul perfectly when I know everything that pertains to him *as Paul.* Thus if God knows an object only in regards to the things it has in common with other objects, his knowledge is imperfect. But if God's knowledge is imperfect, so is his Being. For his knowledge is one with his Being. We must conclude, then, that God knows each thing distinctly, completely, and perfectly.

Again, we have seen that God orders each thing to its proper end. Therefore he must have a proper knowledge of each thing and of each end. For each thing has a determined order to its end.

We have seen, then, that God must know each thing in its own proper nature. Now let us consider two reasons why he can so know them. First, whatever perfection is in the creature pre-exists in God according to a more excellent mode of being. Not only do those things which all creatures possess in common pertain to their perfection, but also those by which one creature is distinguished from another. There pre-exists in the essence of God every perfection an individual possesses, both those he holds in common with others and those by which he is different from every other individual. The essence of God is compared to the essences of creatures not as that which is common to that which is proper, but rather as that which is perfect to that which is imperfect. [30]

Secondly, the proper nature of each thing consists in some participation in the divine perfection. God would not know his essence perfectly unless he knew how it was imitable by other beings. Thus through a knowledge of his divine essence God knows each thing that is by a perfect, complete, and proper knowledge. Although the divine essence excels and transcends all creatures, yet it is the proper likeness of each creature, insofar as this transcendent essence is differently imitated and participated by creatures.

Some simple examples will illustrate the truth that God knows other things in their own proper natures. If you see a stone because of its species that is in your eye, you see that stone in its own proper nature, in the way possible to sense cognition. If you see that same stone through its image in a mirror, you still see the stone as before, namely, in its proper nature. The fact that the species by which you see the stone is a species contained in a mirror, does not preclude you from seeing the stone in itself, in its own proper nature. So, too, the fact that God knows creatures through his essence does not prevent him from knowing them in their own proper natures.

Answering the objections. But how do we answer the objection that since the nature of God is Being, and God knows other things in knowing his own nature, he knows these things only insofar as they are beings, and not as they are this or that proper kind of be-

[30] See *S.T.*, I, 14, 6.

ing? This objection, once more, is based on a false understanding of being. "To be," or the act of existing, is not some minimum perfection that all things have in common, and which is further perfected and actuated by the proper perfections of each thing. The act of existing is the source of all the perfections within the individual existent. All other principles in the existent are limitations, in one way or another, upon this act. In fact, these principles of limitation have whatever reality they possess as limiting principles because of their order to the act of existing. Hence God, in knowing his nature, which is subsistent or unlimited existing, knows every perfection within the existent, not merely those the existent has in common with others but also those perfections properly and peculiarly its own.

4. Some Clarifying Examples

Before we discuss the immutability of God's act of knowledge, let us consider a few examples which may clarify somewhat what it means for God to know other things. The student should remember that these are only examples and analogies; they are not meant to explain the doctrine, but to illustrate it. And they illustrate it only imperfectly.

When you see a clock on the wall, you see it because of an image that the clock has produced in your eye. Now suppose this image of the clock was not merely in your eye, but was the very substance of your eye; and suppose that instead of being produced by the clock, this image produced the clock. Then your eye would see the clock on the wall by its own substance which has produced it. This is the way God knows things.

Or consider this example. Suppose a hundred objects were lined up in front of a mirror. They are all seen in the mirror. Now let us suppose that this mirror has the power to know. Moreover, let us suppose that it knows itself perfectly. In knowing itself, it would know itself as mirror, and hence know whatever images it contains and thus the things whose images they are. Finally, if the mirror were the very cause of the things whose images it contains, it would know everything outside itself because of itself. So we could say that God is the perfect and subsistent mirror of being, knowing all things in themselves because he has caused all things in themselves, and knowing them by the likeness of his own essence.

5. God's Knowledge Is Immutable

Can there be any change in God's knowledge? Since the act of God's knowledge is one with his divine substance, his knowledge is as absolutely unchangeable as his substance. Things may change and vary, but God's knowledge of them remains unchanging.

Let us consider this truth by way of some obvious objections. Knowledge is a relationship between the knower and the known. But creatures that are known by God vary and change. Therefore, God's knowledge of them, if it is to be true knowledge, must vary and change.

We answer that the relationship between God's knowledge and creatures is according as these creatures are in God. A knower is constituted as knower, as actually knowing, according as the thing known is in his intellect. Created things are in God's intellect as invariable and unchanging. It is only in themselves that they vary and change. Knowledge is an immanent act, the whole reality and perfection of which is in the knower. God may know changing things, and he may know the changes of things, but he knows all this by an act that is absolutely unchanging.

Let us bring this out better by another objection. God knew that Christ would be born, but he no longer knows that Christ will be born, since now Christ will not be born. Hence God's knowledge has changed.

We answer that God's knowledge has not changed. What has changed is the truth of the proposition. Without any change in his knowledge, God knows that the proposition, "Christ will be born," was once true and is now no longer true. If God thought this proposition were still true, then of course his knowledge would change, for from true knowledge it would become false. Our knowledge changes with the changing of things, for things cause our knowledge. But things do not cause the knowledge God has of them. And so he knows that things are, or have been, or will be, or could be. And he knows all this by one single unchanging glance of his unchanging essence, which essence is the cause of what is, will be, could be, or has been, and the cause of the very changing of things. God, in knowing his essence which contains the likeness of all that exists or could exist, knows all things that exist or could exist by an act that is perfect, complete, and unchanging. [31]

C. THE LIFE OF GOD

Since life belongs to beings that possess understanding, from a consideration of the knowledge of God we are led to the question of his divine life. Here we shall answer briefly two questions: first, what does it mean to live? And, secondly, in what sense is there life in God?

1. What Does it Mean to Live?

By examining those things which men say are alive, we can come to know what things have life and what do not. Animals are said by all to be alive. Hence, that because of which animals have life can be used as a criterion to distinguish living things from non-living. This will be that by which life is first manifested and which is last to remain in a living thing.

Now we first say that an animal is living when it begins to move itself, and we judge that it is alive as long as such self-movement is present. But once an animal can no longer move itself, but is only moved by another, we say the animal is dead, that it no longer has life in it.

Hence it is clear that those things are living that can move themselves according to some kind of motion, whether it be strict motion (the act of a being in potency, for example, local motion, increase or decrease in quantity) or motion in the broad sense (the act of a being in act, for example, to sense, to know). A living be-

---

[31] See *S.T.*, I, 14, 15, and the answers to the objections. The student is urged to read articles eight and thirteen of this same fourteenth question, where St. Thomas explains these two important points: in what sense God's knowledge is the cause of things, and how God knows future contingent events.

ing is one that can move itself to some sort of motion or operation. And a non-living being is one that cannot so move itself. If the latter is found in motion, it has been put in motion by something other than itself. [32]

But is life, properly so called, the vital operation of the living being, or is it the living being itself? The answer to this question becomes clear once we recall the process by which names are given to things. All human knowledge begins with the senses, whose proper objects are the external accidents of things. It is from such external accidents that we arrive at a knowledge of the essence. As we have seen, a thing is named the way it is known. Thus names are usually given to the essence because of its external properties. What occasions the name is some external act or accident; but what the name is meant to signify is the essence itself.

So it is with the name "life." It is occasioned by an external phenomenon, namely, self-motion. But it signifies primarily not this self-motion, but the nature that has this self-motion. Thus "to live" is nothing else than the "to be" of certain natures. Life is the very being of living things. And "life" is simply the abstract word for "to live," just as existence is the abstract word for "to be." Hence, "to live" is the substantial act of a living thing and is one with its act of being. It is a perfection of being as being and not of essence. [33]

2. Is There Life in God?

Let us approach an answer by way of two simple objections. A thing has life if it can move itself. But God, as pure act, cannot be moved, not even by himself. Therefore, there is no life in God. Secondly, in all living things there is a principle of life, for example, the human soul in man. But God, as absolutely simple, can have no principle. Hence, there can be no life in God.

Solution. Not only does God have life, he is life. A thing is said to be living insofar as it can produce some operation of itself, and

[32] See *S.T.*, I, 18, 1.
[33] See *S.T.*, I, 18, 2.

not as moved by another. The more this is true of a thing, the more perfectly does it have life. Now in things that move and are moved, we can distinguish three principles of motion. First, there is the end that "moves" (attracts) the agent to its act. Secondly, there is the principal agent that acts through the power of its own form. And, thirdly, there is the instrumental agent that does not act through the power of its own form, but through the power of the principal agent. The instrument merely executes the act. The saw cuts the wood, but it does so through the power of the carpenter.

Let us apply these three principles of motion to living things and see why it is that God is life itself. There are certain living things that move themselves only as regards the *execution* of their motion, but are moved by another both as regards their end and the form by which they act. The end for which they act and the form by which they act are determined for them by the author of their nature. Plants are such living things. For example, they move themselves to an increase or decrease of their quantity.

Next, there are those living beings which move themselves not only as regards the execution of their motion, but also as regards the form which is the principle of this motion, insofar as they acquire this form of themselves. And these are animals, whose principle of motion is a form that is not in them by nature but is received through the senses. But although animals receive the form that is the cause of their motion, they do not establish for themselves the end of their motion. This end is determined for them by their nature. Instinctively they act for this end, but they do so through a form that is apprehended by their senses.

And so above animals are those living beings that move themselves even as regards the end of their motion, which end they establish for themselves. They establish this end through reason and understanding, to which it belongs to recognize the relation between the end and that which is ordered to the end, and to relate the one to the other. Thus, since they move themselves more perfectly, beings that have an intellect possess a higher form of life than those that have no intellect. For intellectual beings not only execute their operations and do so through a form they acquire through cognition, but also set up for themselves the end for which they operate. Man is such a living being.

But although man establishes for himself some of the ends for which he operates, there are others that are determined for him by his nature. For example, his intellect is naturally determined to the truth and his will to the good. As regards these ends, man does not move himself, but is moved to them by the author of his nature. Now we are ready for our final conclusion. That being who is not determined by anything else, and whose very nature it is to know, must have life most perfectly. Such is God. For God is his own end and his own act of understanding. Subsistent Being is subsistent understanding and subsistent life. [34]

Answering the objections. Our first objection stated that life is self-movement, and since God cannot be moved, even by himself, there is no life in God. First of all, in God a vital act is an immanent act, not a transient act. That is to say, it remains in the agent and perfects the agent; whereas a transient act proceeds from the agent, is in the patient and perfects the patient. Now God's vital act, which is his very substance, does not perfect God in the sense that by it he acquires any perfection. Rather it "perfects God" in the sense that it is the perfection that is God. It is God considered as self-perfection and as completely self-sufficient in his Being and immanent operation.

In answer to the second objection, we agree that God has no principle or cause of his life. Just as he is his own Being and his own knowledge, so he is his own life.

D. SUMMARY OF THE CHAPTER

"God understands and comprehends himself through his divine essence. Hence his knowledge and his Being are one, and his divine essence is subsistent truth. Moreover, through his same divine essence God knows things other than himself, and he knows these things in themselves with a proper, perfect and immutable knowledge."

[34] See S.T., I, 18, 3.

a. State of the question

Having considered in Chapter 8 some perfections that pertain to the divine Being, in this chapter we begin our consideration of those perfections that pertain to the divine operations. Operations are of two kinds, those that remain within and perfect the subject acting, and those that proceed from the subject and perfect some external matter. We begin our study of the first kind of divine operations. And since knowledge is such an immanent operation, upon which depends all subsequent immanent and transient operations of the divine Being, in this chapter we treat of God's knowledge of himself and of other things.

b. Explanation of terms

1) ". . . *understands* . . ."—an act of intentional identity between subject and object, in which the subject becomes aware of the object in a strictly immaterial fashion.

2) ". . . *comprehends* . . ."—to understand perfectly, that is, to know an object to the degree that it is knowable.

3) ". . . *his divine essence* . . ."—that intrinsic and infinite act by which God is God: the divine Being itself in itself.

4) ". . . *Truth* . . ."—the conformity of the intellect and the thing. Finite intellects share or participate in truth insofar as they receive the forms of other things. God's intellect is subsistent truth insofar as it is identified with his Being that contains the forms of all things.

5) ". . . *things other than himself* . . ."—anything that can imitate God or be caused by God. Hence God knows all possible and actual beings.

6) ". . . *in themselves* . . ."—that is, God knows each thing that is distinct from him according to its own individual and proper nature.

7) ". . . *proper* . . . *knowledge* . . ." Here proper knowledge of a thing means knowledge of each and every perfection within the individual.

8) ". . . *perfect* . . . *knowledge* . . ."—a comprehensive or exhaustive knowledge of the thing.

9) *". . . immutable knowledge . . ."*—an act of knowledge
that is incapable of any change whatsoever. By one and the same
unchanging act God knows changeable things and the changes
of things, since this act is the very cause of things and the changes
of things.

c. *The proof*

1) *God understands himself.* A thing is knowable insofar as
it is removed from matter and potency, and a thing can know insofar as it is removed from matter and potency. Hence, the Being
of God, as supremely immaterial and completely in act, is perfectly knowable and perfectly knowing. And so the divine Being,
as absolutely transparent to itself, knows itself.

2) *God comprehends himself.* As completely without potency,
God's Being is infinitely knowable: there is nothing within it that
is impervious to knowledge. And as completely in act, God's power
of knowing is infinite: nothing escapes his act of knowledge.
Hence, God not only knows himself, but comprehends himself;
that is, he knows himself to the degree that he is knowable.

3) *God knows and comprehends himself through himself.* God's
Being is absolutely simple and uncomposed, as we have proved
in a previous chapter. Hence, in God there is no real distinction
between what God knows and the form by which he knows. But
what God knows and comprehends is himself. Thus he knows and
comprehends himself through himself, and not through some su-
per-added form or intelligible species.

4) *God's knowledge and Being are one.* Just as the "to be" of a
thing follows upon the presence of a physical form, so "to know"
follows upon the presence of an intentional form. But we have seen
that the divine essence (by which God is) is one with the intelligible form by which God knows. Hence, since God is and knows
by one and the same act (his divine essence), it follows that God's
Being and God's knowledge are one and the same.

5) *The divine essence is subsistent truth.* Truth is the conformity of the intellect with the thing. But God's intellect is conformed with the thing (the divine essence). In fact, it is identified

with it. As conformed through identity with the essence, this divine intellect is true, and since this essence is subsistent Being, the divine intellect, as identified with this essence, is subsistent truth. Moreover, just as logical truth is the conformity of the intellect with the thing, so ontological truth is the conformity of the thing with an intellect. And since the divine essence is identified with the divine intellect, in God logical and ontological truth are the same subsistent truth.

6) *God knows things other than himself.* (*a*) In knowing himself perfectly, God knows his divine power perfectly; and in knowing his divine power perfectly, God knows the things to which that power extends. But that power extends to all things. Hence, God knows things other than himself.

(*b*) God's act of knowledge and Being are one. Now every effect must pre-exist in its cause, for no cause gives what it does not have. Thus all things must pre-exist in the divine Being (and hence in the divine knowledge). Thus God must know things other than himself.

7) *God knows things other than himself through himself.* Here we prove that the divine essence is the intelligible species by which God knows things other than himself. Because God knows his essence perfectly, he must know that essence as imitable. But in knowing that essence as imitable, God must, by that very fact, know whatever imitates or can imitate that essence. Just as one who knows an image knows by that very fact the thing whose image it is, so God, in knowing himself as imitable, knows all other things. Moreover, God by one and the same act knows himself and all other things through himself. For it is the same simple and uncomposed essence by which he knows himself and things distinct from himself. Multiplicity and composition are on the side of the different things that imitate God, and these things are outside God. By an infinitely perfect image (his essence as the cause of things), God can know perfectly a multiplicity of finite objects.

8) *God knows other things in themselves.* God knows whatever is proper to each individual existent. For as a subsistent act

of existing, God possesses whatever finite perfections are shared in by each individual existent.

9) *God's knowledge of other things is perfect.* In comprehending his own Being, God must likewise comprehend (know perfectly) all other things which share in his Being.

10) *God's knowledge is immutable.* The act by which God knows himself and all other things is one and the same act. And this act is one with the divine Being, which is absolutely unchangeable. Hence God knows all things by an absolutely unchangeable act of knowledge. By this unchanging act, God knows changing things and the changes of things. For God's knowledge is the cause of all things, and hence of changing things and their changes.

Suggested Readings

1. St. Thomas, *Summa Theologiae,* in *Basic Writings of St. Thomas,* by A. Pegis (New York, Random House, 1945), Vol. 1, pp. 135–161. These pages cover the all-important Fourteenth Question of the First Part of the *Summa.* The student should read at least articles 5, 6, 9, 13, and 15.

   Truth (De Veritate), translated from the definitive Leonine text by R. W. Mulligan, S.J. (Chicago, Henry Regnery Company, 1952), Vol. 1, pp. 59–76. These pages cover the two very important articles of God's knowledge of himself and other things.

2. Etiènne Gilson, *The Christian Philosophy of St. Thomas Aquinas,* (New York, Random House, 1956), pp. 110–114.

CHAPTER 10

The Perfection of Will in God

> *The divine will is so efficacious that not only does it bring about the things that God wishes to be, but it also brings them about in the way God wishes them to be. Now some things God wishes to take place necessarily, and some things to take place contingently. And therefore for some effects God prepares necessary causes, which cannot fail and from which the effect proceeds necessarily; while for other effects God prepares contingent causes, which can fail and from which the effect proceeds contingently.*
> —St. Thomas, *Summa Theologiae,*
> I, qu. 19, a. 8

Having considered God's knowledge both of himself and of other things, we now want to consider that perfection which follows upon knowledge, namely, the perfection of willing. This is the act by which God is said to be inclined to his own divine goodness and the goodness of other things. We want to consider, therefore, how God wills and loves himself and creatures. This problem we will divide into three sections: first, how God wills and loves himself and creatures; secondly, in what sense there is free choice in the divine will; and thirdly, how this free choice is reconciled with the immutability of God. We will then say a word about a very difficult and mysterious problem: the reconciliation of God's unchanging will with man's free choice.

A. HOW GOD WILLS AND LOVES HIMSELF AND CREATURES

In this first section, we will discuss God's willing and loving of himself and his willing and loving of creatures. And here we will ask ourselves three questions: Is there a will in God? Does God will himself necessarily and creatures freely? Does God love himself necessarily and creatures freely?

1. Is There a Will in God?

This question is easy to grasp once we understand the nature and function of form. The function of form is twofold, existential and intentional. Through its form a thing receives its act of existing, insofar as the form limits this act to this particular being. Here form is considered as a certain quiescent perfection of the thing. But by this same form a thing is also inclined toward its end, so that it can act according to its proper nature. As inclining a thing toward something else, form is considered as a dynamic perfection of a thing, and in creatures is considered together with the active potencies which immediately particularize this inclination or ordering. [1]

That which we call knowing and that which we call willing are two different ways of being inclined or ordered toward things. By knowledge we are ordered to a thing according as it can have a certain presence within us; not, therefore, according to its own proper being, but according to a certain likeness of that being. By willing we are inclined towards a thing according as that thing exists in itself, as it possesses its own proper nature and act of existing. [2] We have said above that the presence of form always gives rise to inclination or intention. The presence of a natural form gives rise to a natural or ontological inclination. The presence in

[1] See S.T., I, 19, 1.

[2] That is why St. Thomas teaches that in things below man, it is better for man to know them than to love them; but in things that are above man, it is better for him to love them than merely to know them. For the things that we know we invest with our own being. But the things that we love invest us with their being. See S.T., I, 82, 3.

the divine will, is God's own goodness. It is because of this goodness that God wills whatever else he wills. God wills creatures because of his own goodness; namely, God wills that his own goodness, which cannot be multiplied according to its essence, be diffused to many, at least according to a certain participation of likeness. Thus creatures are the secondary objects of God's will. The divine will is necessitated to will the divine goodness. Not, however, by a necessity of coercion, but by a necessity of natural ordering which is not repugnant to divine liberty. God is not able to wish that he be not good, nor intelligent, nor powerful, nor any other of those things that belong to the notion of his Being. Hence, God necessarily wills himself.

But as regards no other object is God's will necessitated. Let us see why this is so. The reason for willing those things which are ordered to the end is the end itself. If my end or goal is to cross the river, the reason for wanting a boat is to cross the river. Thus what is ordered to the end is compared to the end the same way it is compared to the will. So that, for example, if the boat is the only way to cross the river, then the boat is a necessary object of the will and thus is willed of necessity. If that which is ordered to the end is so ordered that the end cannot be attained without it, then whoever necessarily wills the end, also necessarily wills this thing so ordered to the end. One, for example, who wills to stay alive, wills by that very reason the eating of food by which life is preserved and without which it cannot be preserved. But if what is ordered to the end is ordered in such a way that the end can be achieved without it, then the will, in willing the end, does not necessarily will this means to the end. If it does will it, it wills it freely.

Let us apply these considerations to the divine will. Just as no effect equals the power of the divine cause, so nothing that is ordered to God as to its end equals that end. No creature is perfectly like God. So no matter how much a creature is ordered to God or is like God, it is still possible for some other creature to be ordered more perfectly to God and more perfectly represent the divine goodness.

It becomes clear, then, that because of the love God has for his divine goodness there is no necessity for him to will this or that creature. There is no necessity to will any creature or all creatures. The divine goodness is perfect in itself, even if no creature existed. God has no need of the good that is in us. Moreover, the divine goodness is not an end that is attained through those things that are ordered to it, as, for example, the crossing of the river is attained through the use of the boat, and the conservation of life through the use of food. Rather, the divine goodness is an end by which those things which are ordered to it, namely creatures, are effected and perfected. That is why Avicenna says in the VIII book of his *Metaphysics*, which St. Thomas is fond of repeating, [5] that only the action of God is completely generous. For God gains nothing from the things that he wills and does for creatures. Even our most seemingly selfless acts gain for us something, at least some sort of increase in virtue. But God's action for us gains him literally nothing.

We conclude, therefore, that whatever God wills concerning himself, he wills necessarily; but whatever God wills concerning creatures, he wills contingently, or freely.

4. Answering Some Objections

At the beginning of our analysis, the statement was made that from the side of God's act of willing there is necessity. From all eternity, by one and the same act of willing, God wills both himself and all other things. But these creatures so willed from eternity are in themselves contingent and temporal. How explain this seeming contradiction?

The explanation becomes clear once we realize that a thing can be necessary in two ways. Absolutely necessary, and necessary by supposition. A thing is said to be absolutely necessary because of a necessary relationship between it and something else. For example, man is necessarily an animal, since the intelligibility of animal belongs to the intelligibility of man. Or the whole is greater than its part by an absolute necessity, since the intelligibility of

[5] See *De Veritate,* qu. 23, a. 4.

"greater than part" belongs to the intelligibility of "whole." On the other hand, something is necessary by supposition when it is necessary not of itself, but only because of something that is supposed. For example, that Socrates should run is not absolutely necessary, since running does not belong to the intelligibility of Socrates. But on the supposition that Socrates is running, it is necessary that he run, and it is impossible for him while running not to run.

In like manner, when God wills some creature, for example, that Paul should exist, this willing is not absolutely necessary, since the divine will has no necessary relation to any creature. But on the supposition that God wills this creature, or wills something concerning this creature, it is impossible for him not to will it, since the divine will is unchangeable. This act of God's will is necessary by supposition. God necessarily, and from all eternity, wills whatever he wills concerning creatures, but only on the supposition that he wills it.

That what God wills concerning creatures is not absolutely necessary is due to the creature. No creature is necessary to God, and so no creature enters into the intelligibility of God's will-act, except on the supposition that God wills the creature; and then it necessarily enters.

One final objection may help for further clarification. Just as the will of God implies order toward the creature, so does the power of God and the knowledge of God. But it is absolutely necessary that God be able to do what he does, and to know what he knows. So, in like manner, it would seem absolutely necessary that God wills what he wills.

We answer that the first two cases are not the same as the third. While the power of God and the knowledge of God imply a respect or order to creatures, they imply this order inasmuch as creatures pertain to the very perfection of the divine essence itself, in which essence everything is absolutely necessary. One is said to know, insofar as what is known is in the knower; and one is said to be able to do something insofar as he is in complete act as regards what can be done. A man has the power to move his hand, even though he never raises a finger. Now whatever is in God is there by absolute necessity. And whatever God is in act, he must necessarily be in act. On the other hand, when I say God wills something, I do not mean that *what* he wills is in God. All that is implied here is the order of God to the making of this thing in its proper nature. And from this point of view there is lacking the condition of absolute necessity.

5. God Loves Himself Necessarily and Creatures Freely

Something is necessary which cannot be other than it is. God wills himself with absolute necessity. Under no condition could he not will his divine goodness. God wills creatures freely. He is able not to will them, or he could have willed others than those he has. But God freely wills creatures with hypothetical necessity. On the hypothesis or supposition that God wills them, he necessarily wills them.

But what is the difference between willing something and loving it? Every act of the will is a willing of something, just as every operation of the intellect is a knowing of something. But just as there are different kinds of knowing, for example, understanding, and reasoning, so there are different kinds of willing, different kinds of inclinations toward an object, for example, desire, hope, and love. Thus while every act of love is an act of the will, not every act of the will is an act of love.

What constitutes an act of love? To love is to wish good to another; to love something is to wish it good. The act of love, therefore, tends toward two things: the good that is wanted or willed, and the one for whom it is wanted or willed. When we want the good for ourselves, we love ourselves; when we want the good for another, we love that other. Natural love, which is present in all things, even non-cognoscitive beings, is simply the natural inclination that each thing has for its own proper good, for that good which constitutes its proper end and perfection. Love of concupiscence is love of a thing because of the good I can get from that thing. Love of friendship is love of a person to whom I wish good things. For example, I love food and drink with a love of concupiscence. But I love my friends with the love of friendship.

God loves himself with the love of complacency, because he enjoys and takes delight in the divine goodness. And he loves himself necessarily because he necessarily delights in his goodness. But God also loves other things, for he wishes good to other things, insofar as he wants other beings to participate in his divine goodness. He freely or contingently loves other things, for the good that God wants the creature to have is not a good that God needs in order to attain his end. Just as God freely wills creatures, so he freely loves them. God, however, does not love creatures in the same way that we do. Our will is not the cause of the good in things, but rather the good that is in creatures moves and attracts our love. By this love we wish these creatures to keep the good they already possess, or to have other goods added to them. And out of our love we act to achieve this end. But God's love is creative; it causes the good in the creature. [6]

B. WHETHER THERE IS FREE CHOICE IN GOD

This second section of our problem concerning God's will is simply a corollary to the first. If God freely wills creatures, it follows that he freely chooses creatures, and therefore is endowed with the prerogative of free choice. But since free choice seems to imply mutability, and hence imperfection on the part of God's will, in this second section we want to see exactly what free choice means as in God.

We can best set our problem by putting forth two simple objections against the possibility of God's having free choice. St. Augustine defines free choice as the power to choose between good and evil. But God cannot choose evil; therefore, God does not have the power of free choice. Secondly, free choice is the power to

[6] With what kind of love does God love creatures? Since the love of friendship is usually explained as being between two equals, and since the nature of man is infinitely below the nature of God, God is said to love man, not with the love of friendship, but rather with a love of benevolence, or well-wishing. However, in the supernatural order, where man shares in the divine nature itself, God loves us with a love of friendship. Here we are no longer servants, but friends. See *St. John*, ch. 15, vs. 15.

choose between opposites, to choose this or that, or to choose rather than not to choose. But God's will is unchangeable, and so cannot have this power of indifference toward opposites.

Solution. We say that there is free choice in God. [7] But the perfection of free choice is predicated analogously of God, of the angels, and of man. That God has free choice is evident from what we have already seen. There is an end or object of his will toward which God naturally tends, namely, his divine goodness. All other things he wills as ordered to this end. These other things he does not will necessarily, but only by a necessity of supposition. Absolutely speaking, God wills these things freely, for his divine goodness has no need of these things that are ordered to this goodness, except for its manifestation. And since this goodness can be manifested in many different ways, God has free choice to will this creature rather than that, just as we are free to want this thing rather than that.

But there are differences between free choice as in God, in angels, and in man. The power of free choice presupposes two things: a nature and a knowing power. Now both nature and the knowing power are present differently in God, in angels, and in men. The divine nature or essence is its own existence and its own goodness. And so in God there can be no defection or change either in his Being or his goodness. But the being of an angel and of a man is from nothing; and hence, of itself, it is possible for such a nature to change and to fail in its willing of the good. That is to say, God's free choice is only toward different goods, but the free choice of an angel or of a man can be toward evil. Since the nature of an angel or a man is not its own end (its end is God), these beings can defect from their end (by choosing themselves, as their end rather than God). This is "to choose evil," for although the nature of a man or angel is good, such a choice lacks the proper order that it should have, and hence is an evil choice. Men and angels, then, because of their very natures, can choose between good and evil. God can choose only between good and good.

As regards the power of knowing, this, too, is found differently

[7] See *S.T.*, I, 19, 10; *De Ver.*, qu. 24, a. 3.

in man, in the angel, and in God. Man has a weak and, as St. Thomas puts it, [8] shadowy sort of knowledge, and he arrives at the knowledge of truth through reasoning. So man finds himself confronted by doubts and difficulties in making his judgments and in discerning what is good. But in the angels and in God there is a simple grasping of the truth without any discursive process or without any investigation. Thus God and the angels make a prompt and immediate election of their free choices, whereas man has difficulty in choosing because of his doubts and incertitude.

Answering the objections. The answers to our objections are relatively easy. We admit that God does not have the power to choose evil. But the power to choose evil does not belong to the essence or perfection of free choice. Rather, it is essential only to that kind of free choice that is present in a created, and hence defectible, nature. Moreover, to be able to choose evil belongs to the imperfection of free choice, for it is in the creature insofar as the creature is from nothing and not insofar as the creature is from God. Since the creature is not its own end, it follows that by its very nature it can decline from its true end, which is God.

Our second objection stated that since the will-act of God is immutable, it cannot have itself indifferently or equally to two goods, or to will rather than not to will. We answer that what would be repugnant to the immutability of God's act of will would be for God to will something and then afterwards not to will it. For this would constitute a true change in his act of will. But to be able to will this or that, or to will or not to will, does not go against the immutability of God's act of willing. Since on the supposition that God wills or does not will something, he necessarily wills or does not will it.

C. HOW RECONCILE FREE CHOICE IN GOD AND HIS IMMUTABILITY?

This brings us to our third problem, which to a large extent we have already solved. Why does not the presence of free choice in the will of God militate against the absolute immutability of that

---

[8] See *De Ver., loc. cit.*

will? Let us consider the divine will a little more carefully from this point of view.

An important distinction should be kept in mind when considering the absolute immutability of God's will in the face of his many and different free choices concerning creatures. It is one thing for God to change his will, and quite another for him to will the change of things. It is the latter that he does, not the former. The former would introduce change into his will and hence into his Being. But God can and does will changing things and the change of things. In point of fact even we, without any change in our wills, can, for example, wish today to see a ball game, and tomorrow to stay home and watch it on television, and the next day not to watch it at all. But if this morning I decide to go to the ball game and at noon decide not to go, then I have changed my will. This is what God cannot do.

When a person changes his will, this is due either to a change in his knowledge or in the disposition or attitude of his will itself. Since the object of the will is the good, one can begin to will or want something anew for two reasons. First, because the thing he wills now begins to be good for him, whereas before it was not. For example, when summer comes it is good for us to lie on the ground, whereas in winter it was not. And in this case there is a change in the very disposition or attitude of our will. Secondly, we can will anew because of new knowledge. We now want something, whereas before because of our ignorance we did not. Now in God there is no room for either such "newness"—a newness in what is good or a newness in knowledge. The infinite goodness of God's essence, and the infinite knowledge of that essence, are absolutely unchangeable. Hence God's will must be also absolutely unchangeable. But through an unchangeable will he effects changeable things and changes in things.

D. HOW RECONCILE GOD'S IMMUTABILITY WITH MAN'S FREE CHOICE?

With these considerations in mind, let us turn our attention to one final problem concerning God's will. Just as free choice in

God does not contradict the immutability of his will, so neither does the immutability of his will contradict free choice in man. This is not only a very important problem, but also a profound and mysterious one. Let us state the problem as clearly and precisely as we can. If whatever God wills always and necessarily takes place, then whatever happens in the universe necessarily happens. No event could be other than it is. But if this is true, then there is no room in the universe for a truly free will. What are we to say in this matter?

Solution. We answer that whatever God wills takes place. But not every thing that God wills takes place necessarily. Some of the things he wills take place freely, and this is because God wills that they should take place freely. Let us see whether we can grasp the metaphysics behind these statements.

Every effect is like its cause. And the more powerful the cause, the more perfect will be the likeness between effect and cause. For example, the more perfect the power within the seed of the father, the more perfectly will the son resemble his father, not only in the specific perfection of being a man, but in many accidental features of face, form and gesture. [9] Now the divine will is the most powerful of all causes. And thus what it effects can be assimilated to it in all the ways possible. God's will, therefore, can bring it about that not only should that happen which he wants, but that it should also happen in the way God wants it to happen. That *what* God wills should take place is like a father having a son: an assimilation according to the same species. But that this thing should take place *in the way God wants it to take place* is like a father having a son that walks and talks and acts like himself: an assimilation according to the accidents of the son. Now

[9] This example, and the whole doctrine here reported, is taken from St. Thomas. See *De Veritate*, qu. 23, a. 5. Whether the biology of the example is true is not the point. The example is used merely to illustrate a philosophical doctrine; namely, the more powerful the cause, the more like itself it can make its effects. The student is also urged to read on this problem of the transcendent power of God's will and the freedom of man, the following texts from St. Thomas: *S.T.*, I, 19, 8; 22, 4; *C.G.*, Bk. I, Ch. 85, Bk. II, Ch. 30; *De Malo*, qu. 16, a. 7; *In I Perihermeneias*, Bk. I, lect. 14. This last text is especially enlightening.

God wills that certain things should happen, and at the same time wills that they should happen in a certain way. For example, that they should happen necessarily or freely, quickly or slowly. And here we have an assimilation to the divine will not only in *what* is willed, but also in *the way* it is willed.

According to the way God wills an event to take place will depend the kind of secondary causes he selects or adapts for the fulfillment of this event. If God wishes something to take place necessarily, then he selects or prepares necessary causes, causes which cannot act other than they do and from which the effect proceeds of necessity. But if God wishes something to take place freely, he adapts or prepares contingent or free causes, causes which are defectible and fallible and from which the effect flows freely. "And therefore," says St. Thomas, "things willed by God do not happen contingently because their proximate causes are contingent, but rather because God wills them to happen contingently, he prepares for them contingent causes." [10]

Hence we see that the immutability of God's will-act places no necessity upon man's free choices. For God wills, and wills immutably, that man should have the power of free choice, a contingent and free cause from which the effect (the act of free choice) flows freely and not of necessity. And when God moves this power to its act, he moves it according to the nature of this power, that is, he moves it freely. [11] We shall see this more in detail when discussing divine providence. But perhaps the following observation will make more clear the metaphysical foundations of why the human will remains free under the movement of God, the first cause of the free act.

A free human act, precisely as free, is related not only to its proximate cause, which is man's will, but also to its first free cause, which is God. A free act as such, that is to say, as free, is a simple perfection of being as being. Therefore, such an act is found intrinsically and properly in God. God is free through his essence;

[10] See S.T., I, 19, 8.
[11] See S.T., I, 83, 1, ad 3m.

man is free through a participation in the freedom of God. And just as, for example, all created wisdom includes an order of dependence to uncreated wisdom, so in like manner every free choice of man includes an order of dependence to the first free Being. In an analogy of proper proportionality, in which the perfection signified is found properly and intrinsically in both analogates, the participated perfection has an intrinsic order of dependence to the unparticipated perfection which is its first cause. Just as God's wisdom makes us wise, so God's freedom makes us free.

Since this is so, when our free will is being moved by the free will of God, far from this fact removing freedom from us, it is rather that which makes us freely operate. Our free will is not the *first* free cause of its act, since it is intrinsically dependent upon another free cause, God, in whose freedom the will participates and by which it is actually moved. Hence, when our free will is moved from potency to act, it is actually achieving itself and its participation in God, where there is only act.

All this is clearly summed up by St. Thomas as follows:

Free choice is the cause of its own movement, because by his free choice man moves himself to act. But it does not of necessity belong to liberty that what is free should be the first cause of itself, as neither for one thing to be the cause of another need it be the first cause. God, therefore, is the first cause, who moves both natural and voluntary causes. And just as by moving natural causes he does not prevent their actions from being natural, so by moving voluntary causes he does not prevent their actions from being voluntary. Rather, he is the cause of this in them, for he operates in each thing according to its nature.[12]

It is also here in this question of God's immutability and man's free will that we must distinguish between God's willing something absolutely and willing something conditionally. For example, God wants all men to be saved, not absolutely, for then they would be saved in spite of themselves; but conditionally—on the condition that they keep his commandments, co-operate with his grace, and so forth.

[12] *Ibid.*

E. SUMMARY OF THE CHAPTER

"God wills and loves himself necessarily and things distinct from himself freely. There is present, therefore, in the divine will the perfection of free choice. This free choice in no way contradicts the immutability of God's Being, nor does this immutability contradict free choice in man."

a. State of the question

Having seen that God knows himself and other things, we now want to see in what sense he wills himself and other things. Beings endowed with intelligence are also necessarily endowed with a will or rational appetite. For the good is that which all desire. And since beings endowed with intelligence can understand something as good, they can want or will such good. Thus they are endowed with a rational appetite or will—an inclination toward intellected good.

b. Explanation of terms

1) ". . . will . . ."—the power or faculty by which a being is inclined toward a thing seen by the intellect as good, that is, as perfect in itself and perfective of the one knowing it. Any act (actual inclination) of this power is called an act of willing. In God, this act and power are identified with the divine Being. Moreover, the good that God knows and wills necessarily is this same divine Being. Hence, in willing himself God is not *inclined* toward something that perfects him, but rather delights in and enjoys the infinite perfection that he is.

2) ". . . love . . ."—an act of the will in which good is wanted for oneself or another. There are different kinds of love, for example:

(a) *Love of concupiscence:* an act in which we love something for the good we can derive from it.

(b) *Love of benevolence:* an act in which we love another for the good that he has or that we wish him to have. If this love is between equals it is called the *love of friendship.*

(c) *Love of complacence:* an act in which one delights in and enjoys the good of another or of himself. God loves himself with a love of complacence, and things other than himself with a love of benevolence.

3) *". . . to will or love necessarily . . ."*—to be inclined by the necessity of one's nature toward the known good. Thus God cannot not will and love his infinite goodness. Such a necessary act is *voluntary* in the sense that it is not forced upon God from without, but flows from the inner nature of his will (*voluntas*).

4) *". . . to will or love . . . freely . . ."*—to exercise an act of choice. A known good is chosen freely in the sense that it need not be chosen. An act of choice is of means, not of the end. And an act of choice is free when there are more than one means to the end, or if the means are not necessary for the end.

5) *". . . the perfection of free choice . . ."*—the power or faculty of willing, insofar as it can direct itself indifferently toward different known goods. Hence, the essence of free choice does not consist in being able to choose between good and evil, but between good and good. Such an act of choice is a perfection of being as being, since it contains no imperfection. In God, this act is one with his essence.

6) *". . . the immutability of God's Being . . ."* Since God's act of free choice is one with his Being, and since his Being is absolutely unchangeable, God's act of free choice is absolutely unchangeable. This does not contradict the notion of free choice, which consists not in the ability to change our choices (this is due to the imperfection of the one choosing), but in the ability to will indifferently different goods. God immutably, but freely, chooses whatever creatures he wills, and he does so by an act that is one with his essence.

c. The proof

1) *God wills and loves himself necessarily.* That act of the will is necessary when the known good, toward which it is inclined, cannot not be wanted. But God cannot not want his own infinite goodness, since it is one with his Being and will. Hence, God wills

and loves himself by a necessity of his nature. And since God is not necessitated to this act by any thing outside himself, he enjoys supreme *liberty of being,* for he is absolutely free from all coercion. Insofar as the divine goodness is one with his act of will, we say that God *wills* himself necessarily, and insofar as this divine goodness is God's supreme and infinite perfection, we say that God *loves* himself necessarily.

2) *God wills and loves creatures freely.* That act of the will is free when the known good can indifferently be willed or not willed. Insofar as God knows things distinct from himself, he *can* will them. But insofar as these things are not necessary for the divine perfection, he *need not* will them. If God wills them, he wills them freely. That no creature whatsoever is necessary for the divine perfection is clear from the fact that God is completely perfect in himself, and whatever perfection there is in a creature has been derived from God. Hence, God freely, and not by any necessity of his nature, wills whatever creatures he wills.

3) *Therefore, God has the perfection of free choice.* Since God has chosen creatures freely, it follows that he possesses the power of free choice. And since this power to choose among different goods implies no imperfection, there is no reason on the side of the power why it cannot be in God. But several things should be noted here. First, God's power of free choice is one with his act of free choice, and this act is identified with his essence. Secondly, the fact that God actually wills himself necessarily and creatures freely, puts no composition within the pure act that is God. For just as God by one and the same act knows himself and creatures (in knowing himself as imitable), so by one and the same act God wills himself necessarily and creatures freely.

Nor does this *way* of willing creatures (freely) put any composition into God's will-act. For this way is due to the things willed (creatures) and not to the one willing. What *moves* God to will creatures is his divine essence as communicable, and this is one with God. Thirdly, and finally, the fact that God wills creatures from all eternity, and by an act identified with his Being, does not mean that he is not free to will or not will them. From all eternity

God freely wills that creatures should begin to be at different times (according to his will). When creatures begin to be, God in no way changes. The change is on the part of the creature. And even had God willed no creatures at all, he would still exercise from all eternity (and that by an act identified with his Being) his power of free choice; namely, in choosing not to will what he could will. In all this there is no change in his Being, since the only thing affected is the object of God's will, namely, the creature.

4) *Free choice in God does not contradict his immutability*. The act of free choice in God would contradict his immutability if God were to change a free choice once made. For this would be to change his *act* of free choice and hence his Being which is identified with that act. But this God cannot do. Hence, free choice in God does not contradict his immutable nature. Men change their mind about an object either because of new knowledge or because the attitude of their will toward the object changes. But there is no room in God for either any new knowledge or any new good; for both his knowledge and goodness are infinite. Thus while God is free to choose or not choose, or to choose this good rather than that, he cannot change his free choices. For this would be a sign of imperfection, either in his knowledge or goodness. Hence, on the supposition that God chooses some good, he immutably chooses it. He freely, but immutably, wills changing things and the changes of things.

5) *The immutability of God's choices does not destroy free choice in man*. God, as we have seen, is the first cause of every effect. Every effect, insofar as it shares in existential act, has God as the first and proper cause of this act. Thus man's acts of free choice, as existential, have God as their first cause. Now such acts would not be free if under the influence of God's causality they could not be other than they are. But this is not the case. First of all, the will of man, as a certain power of free choice, is a participation in God's perfection of free choice. Secondly, when the will places its free act (as secondary cause) under the influence of God (as first cause), the motion of God is in the will according to the nature of the will. That is, God freely moves the will. This "free

motion," is *in* the will but *from* God, as from the first free Being. And since whatever is received is received according to the nature of the one receiving, this motion moves the will freely, that is, in such a way that it is not necessitated to choose the good. Just as God immutably, but freely, chooses creatures, so God infallibly, but freely, moves creatures to their free choices. And just as God's immutable Being is in no way incompatible with his perfection of free choice, so neither is his infallible causality incompatible with the free choice of the creature. For the efficaciousness of the divine will is so transcendent that, as St. Thomas teaches, [13] not only do the things that God wills take place, but they take place in the way he *wills* them to take place, that is, freely or necessarily.

Suggested Readings

1. St. Thomas, *Summa Theologiae,* in *Basic Writings of St. Thomas,* by A. Pegis (New York, Random House, 1945), Vol. 1, pp. 195–211. These pages cover the important Nineteenth Question concerning God's will. The student should read at least articles 1, 2, 3, 7, 8, and 10.
   On the Truth of the Catholic Faith, translated by A. C. Pegis (New York, Hanover House, 1955), Vol. 1, pp. 239–271.
2. Etiènne Gilson, *The Christian Philosophy of St. Thomas Aquinas* (New York, Random House, 1956), pp. 114–120.

[13] See *S.T.,* I, 19, 8, and ad 2m.

CHAPTER 11

Creation

*From Him, through Him, and in Him are
all things.*

—St. Paul, *Letter to the Romans,*
Ch. 11, verse 36

THE MANNER IN WHICH THE WORLD
COMES FROM GOD

In our last chapter we saw that God freely wills creatures and
that therefore things are not caused by him through any necessity
of his nature. God's causality is free, and hence proceeds by way
of an act of his will. We know that whatever a cause produces is
in some way like this cause, and so in some way must pre-exist
within the cause. We have seen, moreover, that what is in another
is there after the manner of the thing in which it is. And since
God's Being is also an act of knowing, creatures pre-exist in God
as in an act of knowledge. Now whatever is in an intellect does
not proceed from it or is not produced outside it except through
the mediation of the will. The will is the executor of the intellect,
and it is the intelligible form that moves the will. Thus whatever
comes forth from God does so by way of his will. [1]

But this procession of creatures from God constitutes a problem
for the metaphysician. On the one hand, creatures must be produced by an action of God. But any action of God must be absolutely identical with the substance of God. And as the action

[1] See *De Pot.*, qu. 3, a. 15.

337

and perfection of God, it must be an immanent act. On the other hand, precisely because of this act, the creature is produced. The act posits an external effect. Hence at least the efficacy or power of this act must, so to speak, pass over to the creature. To this mysterious act we give the name "creation."

In this chapter on creation we will answer the following four questions: (1) In what manner has the world or visible universe been caused? (2) What is the nature of this act by which it has been caused? (3) Is creation anything real in the creature? (4) What is creation in the creature? We will end the chapter with a note on the divine ideas, according to which God knows and makes other things.

1. In What Manner Has the World Been Caused?

We will attempt to answer our first question by discussing these four points: (a) What creation is not; (b) What creation is; (c) Can God create? (d) Can only God create?

a. What creation is not

In order to purify our concepts from elements due to the imagination, let us work toward an understanding of creation by seeing what it is not. First of all, the act of creation is not motion. Motion takes place when there exists in act one common subject for both terms of the change. This is motion in the proper sense. Examples of such motion would be changes in quality and in quantity. Here the common subject is the substance in act. In all these motions, which are accidental changes, one and the same subject existing in act is changed from one opposite to another; for example, from small to large, non-red to red, and so forth.

Secondly, the act of creation is not a substantial change. In substantial change there is still one common subject for each of the two terms of the change. However, it is not the same subject in act, but only in potency. In every change there must be something common to each term of the change. If the opposite terms of the change had *nothing* in common, we could not talk about one thing becoming another. There would simply be no transition or change from one to another. Change means that something has itself differently now than it did before. Therefore, the terms of the change cannot both be in act at the same time. If they are, then they must refer to different subjects. One subject can be man and the other can be non-man. But one and the same subject cannot be actually man and actually non-man. The same subject can be actually man and potentially non-man, and so can undergo substantial change, namely, generation or corruption. In substantial change it is prime matter that is the common subject of both terms, namely, of the substantial form and of the privation. But prime matter is not being in act, but being in potency. So in a substantial change we do have the same subject for both terms of the change: for the privation, which is the term from which the change begins, and for the substantial form, which is the term at which it ends. But it is the same subject only in potency.

Thirdly, there is another sort of change, which we will call imaginary change, and which again is not creation. Here there is no common subject of the so-called change, neither a common subject in act nor in potency. The only common element present is the same continuous time, in the first part of which there is one opposite and in the second part the other opposite, so that we can say that the one comes from the other. For example, we say that morning becomes noon, or that winter turns into spring. Obviously this is not change in the proper sense, but only by way of metaphor. It is like change in this sense, that we have imagined time itself as the subject of those things which take place in time.

b. What creation is

The act that is creation, then, is none of these three things. For in creation there is absolutely nothing in common to the two "terms" that are involved: that is, non-being and being. There is no common subject existing in act, nor is there any common subject existing in potency. There is not even the same time, for here we are talking about the creation of the universe, before which there was no time. Before the world existed, there was no "before." There was only God. But in considering the act of creation our imagination, and our imagination alone, furnishes us with a sort of common subject, insofar as we imagine a time when there was no world, and then afterwards the world is brought into existence. Just as outside the world there is no real magnitude, and yet we are able to imagine a magnitude, so before the beginning of the world there was no time, although it is possible to imagine a time when there was no world. In itself the act of creation does not include the notion of change. It is included only in our imagination.

So we see what creation is not: it is not change in any sense of the word, since there is present no common subject of change, either in act or in potency. Put positively, we can define creation as the production of something from nothing, noting however that "nothing" is not to be understood here after the manner of a material cause, but rather as the denial of such a cause. To create is to bring something into existence, purely and simply. This is a very mysterious act, but we say that God can do it, and now we want to see why.

c. Can God create?

To produce something from nothing seems impossible. For from nothing, nothing can come. Something coming from nothing is a contradiction in terms, like God making the part greater than the whole. Even God cannot do the impossible. Another objection that one might urge against the possibility of creation is this: an infinite distance cannot be traversed; otherwise it is not infinite. But the ontological distance between non-being and being is infinite. That this distance is infinite is evident from the fact that the less a thing is disposed for a certain act, the further removed it is from that act. For example, a room full of air is further removed from the perfection of being a statue than a room full of marble. Therefore, if we take away all potency whatsoever, the distance from the act will be infinite. But in *nothing* there is no potency, and so between non-being and being there is an infinite distance. [2]

Solution. We say that God can and does produce things from nothing. To understand this fact, let us reflect that *every agent acts*

[2] See *De Pot.*, qu. 3, a. 1, obj. 1.

insofar as it is in act. Thus any action that an agent produces is ascribed to that agent according to the way that it is in act. For example, a certain particular thing, like a certain man or a certain chemical element, has only a particular act and so is in act in a particular way. This is true in two senses: first, in comparison with itself, for its whole substance is not act, since it is composed of matter and form. A natural material thing does not act according to its whole substance, but only according to its form, which is its principle of operation. Secondly, in comparison to other things that are in act. For in no natural agent is there included the acts and perfections of all those things that are in act. Each such agent has an act that is determined to one genus or to one species. Man can produce only another man. So no particular natural agent is productive of being as being, but only of some particular being that is in a determined species. Agents act like themselves, and so a particular, determined agent can only produce a particular, determined effect like itself.

Any agent, therefore, with a limited nature cannot produce simply being. It can only determine some already existing being to a certain species. Since it does determine some already existing thing, every such agent acts by moving. Thus matter is needed as the subject of this motion or change by which the agent determines some already existing being to a certain species. And since matter is required as the subject of this motion, no natural agent can produce something out of nothing. [3]

Now let us consider God as agent or efficient cause. God is totally act, complete act and completely in act, both in comparison with himself, for he is pure act without any admixture of potency, and in comparison with things that are in act, because in him is the origin of all being. Just as the origin of Paul as Paul is in his father, so the origin of all that is, insofar as it is, is in God, whose very nature is Being. Thus it follows that God, through his action, can produce the whole subsisting being, nothing whatsoever presupposed. God is the principle or beginning of the whole being,

3 *Ibid., resp.*

and according to its totality of being. Thus God can make something from nothing, and this action we call creation.

Answering the objections. What do we say to the objection that from nothing comes nothing? Aristotle has called this truth the common conviction of the mind and the opinion of all philosophers. [4] This indeed is very true. For being as understood by the philosophy of nature does not act except through motion, and so requires a subject of this motion. But in the metaphysics of creation this is not required, as we have just seen. In creation something comes from nothing, not in the sense that there is no efficient cause which produces it, but in the sense that there is no pre-existing material out of which it is formed. But how can the infinite distance between non-being and being be traversed? Let us answer this second objection by distinguishing the notion of "infinite distance." Is the ontological distance between non-being and being really infinite? Yes and no. The distance between non-being and the Being of God is truly infinite, since it is infinite from both sides, like the distance between infinite blackness and infinite whiteness. But the distance between non-being and finite being (as in the case of creation) is infinite from one side only, the side of non-being, like the distance between infinite blackness and finite whiteness. Now there can be no transition from non-being to infinite Being. But there can be a transition from non-being to finite being, insofar as the transition from non-being to finite being is terminated from one side, the side of finite being. However, this transition, which is effected by creation, is not a transition properly so called. A transition takes place through a continuous motion; and by such a transition nothing that is infinite, even from one side, can be crossed through. [5]

That the world could come forth from God only by way of an act of creation is not hard to see. By "world" here we mean all beings other than God, considered at the ontological moment they were produced by God. By supposition, there are three ways the world could have proceeded from God: by way of a strict emanation, by way of information, or by way of creation. The first

[4] See *Physics,* Bk. I, Ch. 4 (187a28).   [5] See *De Pot.,* qu. 3, a. 1, ad 3m.

two ways are impossible. In strict emanation the world would be of the same nature as God, thereby placing in the nature of God imperfection and potentiality. In production by information, forms are educed from matter, and thus matter is presupposed for the divine action. Therefore, we would have some being, namely matter, uncaused by God, which is impossible. So we see that the world must have come forth from God by way of creation. Even if the world has existed from all eternity, it still has received its being from all eternity by an act of creation. Finite being would be just as dependent upon infinite Being, whether its duration is measurable or immeasurable.

d. Can only God create?

It should be quite clear that only God can create. Nor can God communicate his power of creation to any finite agent, even instrumentally.

It would be heretical to say that an angel or any creature could create of itself, for this would be ascribing infinite power to a creature, since only a being with infinite power can make something from nothing. But some have held, like Peter the Lombard, [6] that God could communicate this power of creation to a creature as a principal cause communicates its motion to an instrumental cause. For example, we have seen that the divine nature which is its own to be, is the only proper and principal cause of the act of existing. But creatures, inasmuch as they participate in the act of existing, although it is not their very nature, can produce this act as instruments of the divine power. Can this also be true as regards the creation of being? Is the creative power of God communicable to a creature as to an instrumental cause?

If we reflect, we will see that such an instrumental communication is impossible. First of all, the action of anything, even of an instrument (which causes insofar as it is moved by the principal cause) must proceed from the power of the thing. Now the power by which the act of creation is produced must be infinite, whereas the power of any creature must, like its being, be finite. God can-

[6] In his *Sentences,* Bk. 4, dist. 5, Ch. 3 (Quaracchi ed., vol. 2, p. 575).

not communicate infinite power to a finite being, for as finite, the being would receive this power in a finite way. Hence it is impossible for a creature to create even as an instrumental cause.

Why does the act of creation require an infinite power? St. Thomas gives many reasons. [7] We will consider only one of them. Every accident must have its existence in a subject. The subject of an action is that thing which receives the action. Now the action of a creature is an accident, and so must be received into some matter. Action is in the patient. Hence every action of a creature presupposes existing matter and so cannot be a creative action. He alone, therefore, can make something without requiring any receiving matter whose action is not an accident, but is one with his very substance. But only the action of God is one with his substance. Therefore, only God can create.

This consideration brings out the unique nature of the creative act and vigorously contrasts it with every other kind of action. Our actions that produce things outside ourselves are accidents, and so have their reality, both actively and passively considered, in the patient, in the receiver of the action. But the action of God is the substance of God. And so his action is formally an immanent one. But because of the infinite power of the act, an effect is posited. Our actions that produce things outside ourselves are formally transient; they are not *in* us but *from* us. As action they are in the patient, as from the agent; as passion they are in the patient as of the patient. This consideration brings us to our next problem, the nature of the creative act.

2. What Is the Nature of the Act of Creation?

Creation is that act by which the whole substance of the effect, called the creature, is produced from nothing. Since it is God that produces the creature, the act by which the creature is produced is the act of God. But if creation is the act of God, it must be identical with the substance of God, for God is pure act and uncomposed. Creation, therefore, is the very essence of God. Thus according to its intrinsic and proper perfection, creation is truly

[7] See *De Pot.*, qu. 3, a. 4.

and formally immanent. It is truly immanent, since it is truly one with the divine substance, and it is formally immanent because it is one with the divine form that is God. Considered in itself, therefore, or in its reality as that act by which beings are caused from nothing, creation is the divine essence. But creation adds to the divine essence a relation of reason to the creature. [8] Just as the will of God is the divine essence with a relation of reason to the divine goodness and to the secondary objects of that will, so creation, considered as act, is the divine essence with a relation of reason to those things outside himself that God has made.

This same act of creation that is one with the substance of God and so formally immanent in God is at the same time a virtually transient act. Recall once more these two kinds of action: the one, that which is formally immanent, remains in the agent and is the perfection and act of the agent—like the act of knowledge or of will. The other, that which is formally transient, "goes forth" [9] to an external matter outside the agent and is the perfection and act of this external matter. When fire heats our hand, the action of the fire has "gone forth" into the external matter of our hand in the sense that the motion of heat has been educed from the potency of our hand by the activity of the fire. But this action by which our hand becomes hot, namely, the action of heat, is in our hand and is the act and perfection of our hand.

Now no action of God can be of this kind that is not in the agent. For God's action is his substance. Therefore, God does not act by that sort of action that is outside himself, as though proceeding from him and terminating in the creature—as the action of the fire is said to go forth from the fire since the fire produces heat in the patient. God acts and operates by thought and will, and so his creative act is not formally transient, but formally immanent.

But this creative act, while formally immanent in God, is vir-

[8] See *De Pot.*, qu. 3, a. 3.
[9] Speaking more precisely, no action goes forth from the agent into the patient, since no accident goes from one subject to another. Rather what happens is this: the agent, because of an exercise of act, educes an action (motion) from the potency of the patient, through which motion some new perfection is achieved in the patient.

tually transient. That is to say, this act which is God has the power or the virtue of producing an effect outside God, and in this sense has the property of an act that is formally transient. Thus we say that the act of creation, the divine action of the infinite power of God, is of such efficacy that it can place in existence external effects. From this aspect it is called a virtually transient act, for this act has the virtue or power to do what a formally transient act does, namely, produce external effects. But it does so without the help of any intermediary causes. And this is in no way repugnant to a formally immanent act.

3. Is Creation Anything Real in the Creature?

We have seen what creation is actively, or considered as the action of God whereby an external effect begins to be. Now we want to discuss a different problem. If by this act the creature begins to be, is creation anything real in the creature? What is creation from the point of view of the creature produced, considered, therefore, passively rather than actively? Is it anything real in the creature, and if so, what is it?

Let us set the problem by way of predication. When we say, "We are creatures of God," the perfection of creature must be something in us. Otherwise we could not identify ourselves with it. But we are creatures by creation. Therefore, in what sense is creation in us? At the very outset we should be clear on one point. The act of creation by which God creates is identified with the substance of God. So there is no question of this act being in the creature. But by this act the creature is produced, and because of it is called a creature. Our question then is: What is creation for a creature? Is it anything real in the creature?

We answer that creation is something real in the creature. It is a real relation or a real order that the creature has to its creator. It now remains to see what this means and why it must be so. The problem involved here is not easy, but it is important. Let us approach its solution by urging one objection that would seem to prove creation cannot be anything real in the creature, not even a real relation to the creator.

Everything that is, is either God or some creature. Now creation as in the creature cannot be the creator, for then the creature would have been from all eternity. But neither can creation be any creature. For if it were a creature, it would have been created by some creation; and this second creation, being a creature, would need to be created by another creation, and so on, *ad infinitum*. Thus it would seem that creation is nothing real in the creature.

Solution. When one thing depends upon another (as, for example, our knowledge depends upon things), but this other does not depend upon it (as things do not depend upon our knowledge of them), then the relation or order that these two things have to one another is real in the one really dependent, and only according to reason in the one not so dependent. My knowledge is really related to the things that cause it; but things are not really related to my knowledge, since my knowledge does not cause things.

Let us apply this to the relation that exists between the creator and creature. The name *creature* says a relation to a creator, and the name *creator* says a relation to creature. The creature really depends upon the creator, but the creator in no way depends upon the creature. Hence it follows that the relation by which the creature is ordered to the creator must be a real relation. But the relation implied in the name *creator,* by which God is ordered to the creature, is merely a relation of reason: we put a relation there in our knowledge of God, but it is nothing real in God.

Creation can be considered actively and passively. If creation is taken in the active sense it signifies the divine operation; which operation is the essence of God with a certain relation of reason to the creature. In this sense, creation is simply the divine substance, as we have already seen. Creation taken passively is that by which a creature is a creature. It is an accident, and a real accident, in the creature. Creation thus considered signifies a certain reality; namely, the order of having being from another. This order follows upon the divine operation that is creation considered actively.

Let us see why this must be so. In every true change and in

every true motion, there is involved a twofold process: (1) The process of transition from one term to another, like a man being changed from white to red, or from non-man to man; and (2) the process from agent to patient, from the maker to the thing made. These two processes are simultaneously present in every change. They are not the same, however, as regards the thing as changing and as in the term of its change. As changing, a thing recedes from one term and approaches the other, which is not true of it as in the term of the change. For example, in a man that is being changed from white to red, in the term of the change he no longer approaches red; rather, he begins to be red. Furthermore, while in the very act of being changed, the patient is being changed by the agent. But when the patient is in the term of the change, it is no longer changed by the agent. It is made, and as made there follows a certain relation to the agent. For what is made has its existence from the agent and is in some way like the agent. For example, in the term of the generation of a man, there necessarily follows the sonship of the one generated.

Conclusion. As we have seen, creation is not a change. Hence, whatever belongs to something as changing, that is, whatever belongs to it before it is in the term of its change, is not true of something that is created. In creation we must consider the thing simply as made. There is no motion involved, no approach or transition to being. Neither is there any changing of the thing by the creating agent. All there is in creation is simply a beginning in being and a relation to the creator from whom the thing has received this being. Creation as a reality is nothing else than a certain relation to God implying a newness of being.

Another way to see that creation is a relation is this: creation is not a motion or change, and so it takes place without motion or change. Now motion considered as from the agent is action. And this same motion considered in the patient is passion. Action and passion are motion plus a different relation. Thus if we remove motion from action and passion, all that remains is a relation. And since creation is without motion, all that it implies is a relation.

We conclude, therefore, that creation considered passively, that is to say, as in the creature, is nothing else than a certain relation to the creator as to the cause of its being. What is related to the creator is the creature, and that because of which it is related is its creation. But that by which something is related is a relation. Hence, creation is nothing else than the real relation of the creature to its creator, just as sonship is nothing else than the real relation of a son to his father.

Answering the objection. In answering our objection we shall see more clearly the nature of creation as in the creature. Our objection stated that creation, to be something real, must be either the creator or some creature. It is not the creator, for then the creature would be from eternity. Nor is it any creature. If so, it would have to be created by some creation, and this creation, being a creature, would have to be created by some creation, and so on *ad infinitum*. Hence creation can be nothing real.

In answering this difficulty, one must distinguish between creation considered actively and passively. Actively considered, creation signifies the divine action as understood with a certain relation of reason. And in this sense, creation is uncreated. But as considered passively, creation signifies a real relation, and signifies this relation by reason of the newness of being that is implied. This relation is indeed a creature, if by creature we mean anything that comes from God. Nor is there any regress into infinity in created creations, since the relation that is creation is not ordered to God by any other relation, but is ordered to God of itself.

One being is ordered to another being by a relation, but a relation is ordered of itself. A relation of its very nature is order. One relation can never be related by another relation, for then it would cease to be a relation. However, if we take creature in a more strict sense, as meaning *that which is*, then creation is not created but *concreated*. For, properly speaking, creation is not anything *that is* (it is not *a being*), but rather that *by which* something is in a certain way (it is, like all accidents, *of being*). It is that by which a being is a creature.

4. Is Creation in the Creature a Predicamental or Transcendental Relation?

Certainly the relation that exists between created being and its cause must be of the closest nature. The simultaneity of cause and effect and the order of dependence between them demand the most intimate of ontological relationships.

But what name should we give to this relation between the creature and its creator? Should we call it a transcendental relation? [10] Such a choice will have its difficulties in terminology. For ordinary transcendental relations, like that between matter and form, or essence and existence, always involve a composition of the things related, and are had only between principles of being and never between complete beings. Even if we intend to use the word only in an analogous sense, we are still faced with other difficulties. For suppose we consider the whole created being as ordered to God. And then suppose we were to call this ordering a "transcendental relation" which is identified with the whole created being itself, but only as dependent. When we have done this, we would still have to show that such a "relation" was not merely the effect of the predicamental relation that St. Thomas himself puts in the creature. St. Thomas has the whole creature related to its creator, but by a predicamental relation. And if, in opposition to this clear teaching of St. Thomas, one were to say that created being is *of itself* related to uncreated Being, then the creature itself would be a relation!

St. Thomas has considered with great care this problem of the precise relation that exists between the creature and its creator. We would do well to study carefully what he has to say on this point. First of all, creatures are really related to God, because they

[10] This is the position of Father A. Hayen, S.J. See *L'intentionnel dans la philosophie de saint Thomas* (Bruxelles, Museum Lessianum, 1942), pp. 277–278. See also John of St. Thomas, *Cursus Philosophicus*. Logica II, qu. 17, a. 2. Nova ed. by Father Beato Reiser, O.S.B. (Torina-Roma, Marietti, 1930), p. 578. Father Arnou follows this opinion in his book, *Theologia Naturalis* (Roma, Univ. Gregor., 1943), p. 207. Monsignor de Raeymaeker expressly likens this relation to that which exists between essence and existence, matter and form, substance and accidents. See his The *Philosophy of Being*, tr. by E. H. Ziegelmeyer, S.J. (St. Louis, B. Herder Book Co., 1954), p. 105, note 5.

have been really created by God. And if a creature is really related to God, then this relation must be something real in the creature. [11]

Why is not this relationship the creature itself? Why cannot the creature be a sort of substantial relation ordered by its very substance to God? If something becomes related to God because it has been caused by him, and the whole substance is caused by God, why should it not be by this substance, and not by an added relation, that the creature is related to its creator? [12]

St. Thomas's answer to this objection deserves careful consideration. The creature is ordered to God by its very substance, as the *cause* of this relationship. But the creature is formally ordered to God by the *relationship itself*. We can say that one thing is like another because of the quality that *causes* this likeness. For example, one man is like another because of the quality of humanity. Nevertheless, *speaking formally*, one thing is like another because of the likeness itself. [13] The substance, then, causes the very relation by which the substance is, in its turn, related to God. The formal effect of a relation is to relate. The created substance causes this predicamental relation in the same way that a substance causes all its proper accidents. And the immediate formal effect of this relation is to relate the very substance that has caused it. To be a creature is not, for example, the same thing as to be a man or to be a substance. To be a creature means one thing: to have a creator, and hence to have a relationship to a creator. And this relationship is something real in all created being. But as cause of the relation, there is nothing to prevent us from saying that the whole substance is related to God by itself, insofar as the substance is the very source of the relation by which it is formally related. But if we are to speak strictly and in a formal sense, we must say that everything in the creature, and the creature itself, is related to God by a relation really inhering in the creature. [14] And this is a predicamental relation.

[11] See *De Pot.*, qu. 7, a. 9, *sed contra* 2.
[12] *Ibid., obj.* 4.
[13] *Ibid.*, ad 4m.
[14] *Ibid., resp.*

Between the substance as cause of the relation, and the relation as formally relating the substance, there is an absolute simultaneity as regards time. As regards dependence, the substance is prior as cause of the relation, but the relation is prior as cause of the relating. The relation precedes the substance in the sense that it formally *relates* the substance to God.

By this predicamental relation the whole creature is intimately and completely ordered to its creator. Let us clarify this by an example. We know that substance is transcendentally related to activity. But in order to realize this activity, there must intervene a metaphysical requisite, namely, the active potency. So also a created being is profoundly, and with the proper qualifications, transcendentally related to its creator. But that this relationship be achieved, there must intervene a metaphysical requisite, namely, the relation itself. And just as a substance that acted of itself would be pure act, so a creature that was related of itself would be a pure relation. And in the last analysis, that is what these authors make of the creature who say that it is transcendentally related to its creator independently of the predicamental relation.

Finally, we should note that this predicamental relation touches being at its most profound point of dependence, its act of existing, and at the point where that act itself is considered as dependent, namely, in its newness. This relation focuses our attention on what is most radically true about a creature: its production from non-being. And this newness of being is always present in the creature, in the sense that the creature's need for the creative presence of God is just as real and just as great at each succeeding moment as it was at the first moment. [15] From this point of view, the doctrine of St. Thomas on the relation between created being

[15] But see S.T., I, 45, 3, ad 3m, where St. Thomas points out that creation, in formal philosophical terminology, should be limited to the first moment of the creature's existence. "Nor is it necessary to say that a creature is being created during its entire existence; for creation imports a relation of the creature to the creator with a certain newness or beginning." Thomas is speaking here of a creature in its most formal sense, that is, of a being that has been produced immediately by God according to its whole substance. But whether we consider strict creation, or any production of being, the principles governing the predicamental relation in the creature and the activity of God as the only universal and proper cause of being, remain essentially the same.

and its principle loses none of its profundity. As "transcendentally" related to Being, created being remains everywhere a dynamic movement toward its creator; but as related by a relation, created being retains its substantial completeness, its own absolute character as created being.

5. A Note on the Divine Ideas

We saw in Chapter 9 that God has a knowledge of things other than himself. And in this present chapter on creation, we have seen that he has caused the world through creation. Since the world proceeds from God not by any necessity of nature, but through knowledge and free will, there must be present in the mind of God the ideas or exemplars of all things. Students who are familiar with the history of philosophy know what great difficulties attended the efforts of speculation on the doctrine of divine ideas. If these ideas are really in God, then the simplicity of his essence seems impossible. But if they are not there, then God is not the creator of all things. Now faith teaches that God is both absolutely simple and the creator of all things. To understand the philosophical solution to this difficult problem we have placed here this note on the divine ideas.

In working out a solution, we shall ask ourselves these questions: first, are there ideas in God? Secondly, are there many ideas in God? Finally, does God have an idea of everything he knows?

a. Are there ideas in God?

Etymologically, the word "idea" comes from the Greek word meaning "form." Thus, by an idea is meant the form of a thing, existing outside the thing itself. This can happen in two ways: either as the exemplar of that whose form it is (as the form of a house is in the mind of the architect), or as a principle of knowledge (as a house is understood through the form we have of it). And according to both these ways ideas are found in God.

Our proof for this is as follows: In all things that are not generated by chance, the form is the end intended by the generation. For example, when a father generates a son, the end of the generation is the form of man. Because an agent acts through its form, it can produce things like itself. The form produced can pre-exist in the agent producing it in two ways: either according to its natural being, as is the case of those agents that act through a necessity of nature—for example, when man generates another man, or fire another fire. Or the form to be produced can pre-exist in the agent according to an intelligible mode of being, as is the case with those agents that act through their intellect—for example, when the likeness of the house pre-exists in the mind of the builder. Now this likeness can be called the idea of the house, since the builder intends to assimilate the house to the form that exists in his mind.

Our conclusion is obvious. This world is not the result of chance, but has been made by God through his intellect and free will. And so there must exist in the mind of God the forms of all creatures, according to whose likenesses they have been made. And such forms are ideas. It is necessary, therefore, to place ideas in the divine mind. [16]

Two clarifying statements should be made at this point. Although, as we have seen, God knows himself and other things through his essence, this essence is the cause of these other things, but not of himself. For God has no cause. And so his essence has the notion of "idea" as regards these other things, not, however, as regards himself. The second statement is this: Since the divine essence is the likeness of all things, an idea in God is nothing else than the divine essence. [17]

b. Are there many ideas in God?

This second question is much more difficult than the first, as is clear from the following objection. We have just said that an idea in God is his essence. But this essence is one. Therefore, there can be only one idea in God and not many. And if we should say that the ideas are multiplied according to aspects to different creatures we have solved nothing. There must be a plurality of ideas from all eternity. For from all eternity God knows and can produce a

[16] See S.T., I, 15, 1.
[17] Ibid., ad 2m and 3m.

plurality of creatures. But creatures are not from eternity. Therefore, if these different creatures are the cause why the ideas are many, we have something temporal causing something eternal, which is impossible. Let us urge this objection by way of a dilemma. This plurality of aspects to creatures is either in the creature only, or also in God. If in the creature only, then this plurality is not eternal, since creatures are not eternal. But if this plurality is really in God, then the divine essence, with which the ideas are identified, is many and not one. Therefore, it would seem that there can be only one idea in God. This is the dilemma that so many Christian minds before St. Thomas found insuperable.

Solution. It is necessary to place many ideas in the mind of God. What is properly intended by the principal agent is the ultimate end. For example, what is properly intended by the general of an army is the order of the whole army, and not merely of one of its parts. Thus God, as the creator of the whole universe, intends the good of the whole universe, and not merely of one of its parts. But if this order of the whole universe is created by God and properly intended by God, it is necessary that he has an idea of this order, just as a general must have an idea of the order of his army. But an idea of the whole cannot be had unless one has also an idea of that which constitutes the whole, namely, the parts. A builder cannot conceive an idea of a whole house unless he has an idea of its different parts. So God must have an idea of each creature that makes up his universe. Whence it follows that in the divine mind there are many ideas.

The problem is to see how this does not compromise the simplicity of the divine essence. A solution is possible if we consider that the idea of something to be produced is in the mind of the one producing it as a *form that is understood*, rather than as a *species by which* something is understood. For, strictly speaking, a species is that which actuates the intellect. Thus, the form of a house is in the mind of the builder as something understood by him, to whose likeness he fashions the materials of a house. It is not against the simplicity of the divine intellect that it knows many things;

whereas it would be against the simplicity of the divine intellect if it were actuated by many species.

Let us see why this is so. God knows his essence perfectly. Therefore, he knows himself in all the ways he is knowable. But God is knowable not only in himself, but as participatible according to some likeness by creatures. Now each creature has its proper essence insofar as it participates some likeness of the divine essence. Therefore, insofar as God knows himself as thus imitable by a creature, he knows his essence as the proper form or idea of that creature. Thus God knows many proper forms of many things. And these are many ideas. [18]

Answering the objection. But how can there be many ideas in one essence? First of all, a divine idea is not precisely God's essence as essence; rather it is God's essence as the likeness of this or that thing. And so insofar as there are many likenesses understood from the one essence, there are many ideas. The distinction is a simple but important one. The divine essence *is* one and simple, but it is *known* as many. Thus the different aspects to creatures, by which the ideas are multiplied, are not caused by things (which are temporal), but by the divine intellect comparing his essence to things. These aspects which multiply the divine ideas, are not in created things. They are in God. But they are not real aspects, but *understood aspects*—understood by the divine intellect. [19]

c. Does God have an idea of everything he knows?

It would seem not. God knows evil. But there is no idea of evil in God. For then evil would be in God, since the ideas are one with his essence. Secondly, God knows things that neither have been nor will be. But ideas are the exemplary cause of things that are. Hence God does not have an idea of everything he knows. Again, God knows prime matter. But there is no idea of prime matter, since it is completely without form. Finally, God knows not merely individuals, but species and genera, and accidents. But there are

[18] See S.T., I, 15, 2.
[19] *Ibid.*, ad 1m, 3m, and 4m.

no ideas for such things, since the only things that exist are individuals.

Solution. The solution to this question is quite simple if we remember that the word "idea" can have two meanings. Strictly speaking, an idea is a form or exemplar existing in the mind of the maker according to which something is made. But an idea can also have the more general meaning of a principle of cognition, a species by which something is known. Ideas in the mind of God can have both these meanings. Insofar as an idea is a principle of *making* it is called an exemplar, and pertains to God's practical knowledge. Insofar as an idea is a principle of *knowing* it is properly called a *ratio* (species) and pertains more to God's speculative knowledge. Insofar as the divine ideas are exemplars they are concerned only with the temporal things that God has made. But insofar as they are species or principles of cognition, they are concerned with all things that God knows, even though they may never be made. Furthermore, in this wide sense, God can be said to have an idea (species) of whatever he can know with speculative knowledge. [20]

Answering the objections. God knows evil, not through a proper notion, but through the notion of the good. There is, then, no idea of evil in God, either according to its meaning as exemplar or according to its meaning as simple notion or species.

Concerning those things that neither are, have been, nor will be, God does not have an actually practical knowledge, but only a virtually practical knowledge. That is to say, he could make these things (he has the *virtus* or power), but he never will. And so God has no idea of these things in the sense of exemplar-idea, but only a species or notion.

Prime matter *in itself* neither is nor is knowable. God, therefore, knows prime matter (because he has concreated it) through the idea of the *composite,* and not by any idea apart from that of the composite.

Our last objection, concerning God's knowledge of genera, species, and accidents, is important enough to deserve a fuller treat-

[20] See S.T., I, 15, 3.

ment. Using the word "idea" in its strict and proper sense of exemplary cause, we say that God has ideas only of those things that
have been, are, or will be. Outside the mind what exists is the individual. Species and genera as such exist only in the mind, in abstraction from the individual. Hence, God has no idea (exemplar)
of the species apart from the individual, or of the genus apart from
the species. Insofar as God has any knowledge of species or genera
apart from individuals, it is through a notion (idea in the broad
sense) and pertains to his speculative knowledge only.

Concerning God's knowledge of accidents, this can be said.
Those accidents that are inseparable from the individual (proper
accidents) God knows through his idea of the individual, and not
by any distinct idea. However, according to St. Thomas, [21] God
can have an idea of separable accidents that are distinct from his
idea of the individual. A separable accident is one that comes to
the individual from outside and is not necessary for its existence.
For example, Paul's intellect is an inseparable and necessary accident, whereas his knowledge of metaphysics is separable and not
necessary. St. Thomas uses the following example to show what
he means: by one and the same exemplar-idea a builder knows
whatever is necessary to a house. But separable things, like the pic-
tures on the walls, he knows by a distinct idea. Of course, God can
have a speculative knowledge—through a *ratio*-idea—of both
kinds of accidents in themselves and apart from substance. [22]

6. Summary of the Chapter

"The way in which the world has come forth from God is
through creation. Creation considered actively is a formally immanent but virtually transient act. Considered passively, creation
is nothing else than a relation to the creator as to a principle."

a. State of the question

Having considered how God knows and wills things other than
himself, we want to see how things have come forth from God,

---

[21] See *De Veritate*, qu. 3, a. 7, *resp.*
[22] *Ibid.*, ad 1m, 2m, 3m, and 4m.

their first principle. Since God freely wills things other than himself, we know that these have proceeded from him freely and not by any necessity of his nature. Moreover, the entire effect, nothing presupposed, has come from God. And so we say that things have come forth from God by a creative act.

b. Explanation of terms

1) "... *world* . . ."—all things other than God at the ontological moment that they came forth from God.

2) "... *creation* . . ."—the production of a thing according to its whole substance, nothing whatsoever presupposed. By a creative act, the matter, form, substance, accidents, and act of existing of a thing are all simultaneously produced.

3) "*Creation considered actively* . . ."—that is, considered as the act of the agent. In this sense, creation is a divine action that is identified with the substance of God.

4) "... *immanent* . . . *act* . . ."—an act that remains in, and is the perfection of, the agent acting.

"... *formally immanent* . . ."—an act that in its own intrinsic and proper nature remains in, and is the perfection of, the agent acting.

5) "... *transient act* . . ."—an act that proceeds from the agent but is in the patient and perfects the patient.

"... *virtually transient* . . ."—that act, while formally immanent, has the virtue or power to do what is done by a formally transient act, namely, to effect something outside the agent.

6) "... *creation considered passively* . . ."—the act of creation considered as in the creature. This will be that because of which a creature is a creature.

7) "... *relation* . . ."—some kind of order of one thing to another.

8) "... *principle* . . ."—that from which something proceeds in some way or other. Here "principle" is a synonym for efficient cause.

c. The proof

1) *The world has come forth from God through creation.* (*a*) By elimination: There are three possible ways the world could have come forth from God: (1) by strict emanation, (2) by strict formation, or (3) by creation. But the first two ways are impossible. In strict emanation (or by a necessary overflow of a nature), the thing produced is of the same nature as the one producing it. But God is infinite and pure act; whereas the world is finite and potential in its being. An act of strict formation (or an eduction of forms from matter) supposes pre-existing matter. But if matter were uncaused and eternal in its nature, it would be pure act, which is a contradiction, since matter is pure potency. Thus the world could not have come forth from God by either emanation or information.

(*b*) Positively: the world had to come forth from God according to its whole substance, nothing pre-supposed. But this is to be created. Therefore, the world was created. Moreover, God can create, since as infinite Being he has infinite power, and so can produce the total actuality of a being.

2) *Creation considered actively is a formally immanent but virtually transient act.* (*a*) Considered actively, creation is that act by which God produces the whole substance of the creature. But as the act of God, creation must be identified with the substance of God, since God is pure act and absolutely uncomposed. As identified with the divine substance, creation is the intrinsic and proper perfection of God. Therefore, it is formally an immanent act. What creation adds to the essence of God is a relation of reason to the creature.

(*b*) But this same act, while formally immanent, is virtually transient, since because of its power (*virtus*) some effect is placed outside God. Since the power of the act effects the creature, this act does what a formally transient act does. Hence, it is virtually (has the power of) a transient act.

3) *Considered passively, creation is a real relation in the creature.* Creation considered passively is creation as in the creature.

It is that because of which a creature is a creature. But a thing is a creature because of its total dependence upon God as upon its cause. Real dependence upon another is a real order or relation to that other. Hence, creation as in the creature is a real relation to the creator. Finally, this real relation is a predicamental accident. By it, the whole creature is wholly related to God. If this relation were identified with the substance of the creature, the creature would be a substantial relation. But the creature is not a relation but rather something that is related. Thus it is related by a relation that is distinct from its substance. Creation, then, as in the creature is an accident.

Suggested Readings

1. St. Thomas, *Summa Theologiae*, in *Basic Writings of St. Thomas*, by A. Pegis (New York, Random House, 1945), Vol. 1, pp. 433–442. *On the Power of God* (*De Potentia*), translated by the English Dominican Fathers (Westminster, Newman Press, 1952), Book I, pp. 78–123, especially pp. 91–96.
2. Etiènne Gilson, *The Christian Philosophy of St. Thomas Aquinas* (New York, Random House, 1956), pp. 120–129.
3. J. F. Anderson, *The Cause of Being* (St. Louis, B. Herder Book Company, 1952), Chapter II, "Creation, Active and Passive," pp. 31–50.

CHAPTER 12

Divine Providence and Divine Power

Thou dost map out the path I take, and the lot I inherit; Thou dost foresee all my journeyings, and my words yet unspoken.
—Psalm 138, verses 4 and 5

The transition from a consideration of creation to that of providence is a logical one. In our study of the divine operations we considered God's knowledge of himself and of things other than himself. Next we studied that operation which follows upon knowledge, namely, God's love of himself and of things other than himself. These acts are formally immanent in God and are concerned with his intellect and will. Next we discussed that divine action which concerns both God's intellect and will, namely, that act by which God makes things outside himself. This act we called creation. As the action or operation of God, it is the divine essence with a relation of reason to the creature. Thus actively considered, creation is a formally immanent act identical with the divine substance. But this same act is virtually transient since it causes external effects. As in the creature, we saw that creation is a relation, namely, an order of having existence from another.

Now in point of fact, creatures are not merely ordered to God as to their first beginning. They are also ordered to him as their ultimate end. And each creature is also ordered to its own immediate end. Creatures, furthermore, are ordered to each other, as becomes obvious from an analysis of their different operations. It is to the order of these creatures to their ends, proximate as

well as ultimate, that we now turn our attention. That this order
exists, we take for granted. The precise point we want to establish
is whether God knows this order. And since the knowledge of this
order constitutes providence, our questions become: (1) Does
God have a providence over his creatures? (2) Does he have a
providence over each and every one of his creatures? (3) Does
he have an immediate providence over everything? These three
questions will constitute the first section of this chapter. [1]

In the second section we shall try to show how the presence
of physical and moral evil in creatures in no way contradicts the
providence of God. In the third section, we shall pass from providence in God, namely, the existence in the divine mind of the
order of all things to their end, to the external execution of this
providence. Here we shall see that God achieves this execution
through the mediation of creatures. This execution of divine providence is called government. [2] In the fourth section we will say
a word about the utility and efficacy of the prayer of petition in
the face of the immutability of divine providence. In the fifth
and final section we will discuss the power of God.

A. THE EXISTENCE AND NATURE OF PROVIDENCE

1. Is There Providence in God?

Two reasons would lead one to think that there can be no providence in God. Providence, the ordering of things to their correct
and proper ends, demands prudence, and hence consultation and
investigation. But in God there can be no consultation or investigation. For in God there is no doubt or any reasoning process.
Secondly, whatever is in God is eternal. But providence is concerned with the ordering to their ends of existing things which
are not eternal. Hence, it would seem that the perfection of providence cannot be predicated of God.

Solution. It is easy to see that there must be providence in God.
For every good that is in things has been caused by God. Not only

[1] See St. Thomas, *S.T.*, I, qu. 22.
[2] See St. Thomas, *S.T.*, I, qu. 103 and qu. 104.

is a thing good insofar as it possesses a certain substantial perfection, but also insofar as it is ordered to its end, and especially its final end, which is the divine goodness. This good that a creature has insofar as it is ordered to its end is a *good of order*. And since this good of order exists in things, it is caused by God. And if it is caused by God, it is known by God. For as we have seen, God's intellect is the first exemplary cause of all things. Therefore, the idea of each of God's effects pre-exists in his intellect. Thus it follows that the knowledge of this order of things to their end pre-exists in the divine mind. And since this knowledge constitutes providence, providence must be placed in God. [3]

Why do we call this knowledge in God of the order of things to their ends providence? Because of our knowledge of providence in man. The provident man is one who knows how to take care of himself and those things committed to his care. St. Thomas, following Aristotle, [4] teaches that providence is the principal part of the virtue of prudence. There are two other parts of prudence which are ordered to providence as to the principal part. These are the memory of past situations and the understanding of present situations. Because of this memory and understanding, we can to a degree foresee and take care of the future; which care is the proper act of providence.

The prudent man, therefore, is one who remembering the past and considering the present can take care of the future by ordering things to their end. A prudent *man* orders well the actions of his own life to the proper end of that life. The prudent *father* does the same as regards his family; the prudent *ruler,* as regards his subjects, and so forth. So we can also speak of a prudent or provident God. For God is the final end of all things, and hence can order and dispose all things to their end. Boethius has defined divine providence as that knowledge existing in the supreme ruler by which he disposes all things concerning his subjects. [5]

Answering the objections. There is a sense in which we can say

---

[3] See *S.T.*, I, 22, 1.
[4] *Nicomachean Ethics*, Bk. VI, Ch. 12 (1144a8).
[5] See *De Consolatione Philosophiae,* Bk. IV, Prosa 6 (PL 63, col. 814).

that there is prudence and counsel in God: prudence, in the sense
that God does have the knowledge of the end of all things; and
counsel, not in the sense that God must investigate to arrive at
counsel, but in the sense that his knowledge is certain knowledge.
People take counsel to arrive at a sort of certitude. We answer the
second objection by saying that the care of things has two elements: first, the knowledge of the order, and this is properly
called providence; secondly, the carrying out or execution of this
order, and this is called governing. Of these two elements, the
first is eternal, the second is temporal.

2. Are All Things Subject to the Care or Providence of God?

It would certainly seem that not all events are subject to the
care and providence of God. For example, a chance event is one
which, by definition, is not foreseen. If these events were foreseen by God, there would be no chance or fortune in the world,
and this is against the common conviction of all men. Secondly,
necessary events do not require any providence or care. That is
why Aristotle calls the virtue of prudence, of which providence
is the principal part, the right reason of things that might be
otherwise. [6] And since many events in nature take place necessarily, many events are not subject to divine providence.

Solution. It is quite necessary that everything that is, to the
degree that it is, be subject to the providence of God. This is
clear both from the absolute universality of God's activity and
the absolute universality of his knowledge. Every agent that acts,
acts for an end. The degree of ordination that a thing has toward
its end depends, therefore, upon the degree or extent of the causality of the agent. For example, some actions of natural agents
do not reach their proper end because the effect is actually produced by a cause not intended by the natural agents. If a golfer
strokes his iron shot towards the green and then some sudden wind
takes the ball into the trap at the side of the green, the fact that
the ball ends in the trap was not intended or caused by the golfer.
But the causality of the first cause, God, extends to all effects and

[6] See *Nichomachean Ethics,* Bk. VI, Ch. 5 (1140a35).

to everything in the effect. Hence everything which has being, and to the degree that it has being, is ordered by God to its end. And since the providence of God is nothing else than the knowledge of the order that things have to their end, everything that is falls beneath this providence.

The universality of God's providence is also evident from the universality of his knowledge. God knows all things, and since his knowledge is compared to these things as the knowledge of an artist to his art, it follows that all things are subject to God's ordering, just as a work of art is subject to the ordering of the artist. [7]

Answering the objections. Our first objection stated that chance events, since they are by definition unexpected or unforeseen, do not fall under God's providence. An effect can be outside the order or beyond the intention of some particular cause, and so escape the attention or foreknowledge of that cause. But no effect can take place outside the order of the first cause. What withdraws the effect from the order of a particular cause is some other particular impeding cause. For example, fire is ordered to heat wood, but it may be impeded by the action of water that has soaked the wood.

As we saw when demonstrating God's existence, all particular causes are included under the one universal first cause, and thus it is impossible for any effect to escape the order of this cause. In our example, God's knowledge and activity extends as much to the fire as to the water. Now insofar as a certain effect escapes the order of a particular cause, it is called fortuitous and is said to take place by chance. But in respect to the first cause, whose knowledge nothing escapes, this same event or effect is intended and foreseen. For example, the meeting of two young lovers over a cup of coffee would be a chance meeting from their point of view, but it would be foreseen and intended by some matchmaking friend who sends them both to the same coffee shop.

The second objection concerned necessary events that cannot

[7] See S.T., I, 22, 2.

be other than they are. What is necessary hardly needs to be subject to any providence. This objection flows from our thinking of providence in terms of human providence only. For example, man is not the cause of the natures that exist around him. He simply uses them, either in what he makes or in what he does. So that, generally speaking, human providence does not extend itself to those things that necessarily proceed from a nature. But divine providence extends to all natures, since God is the author of all natures.

3. Are All Things Immediately Subject to God's Providence?

It would seem that all things are not *immediately* subject to God's providence. Providence orders things to their end. Now the end of each thing is its good and perfection. The end of the intellect, for example, is truth and of the will is good. It belongs to each particular cause to bring its effect to its appointed end. In this sense, each agent has providence over its effects. But if all effects are immediately subject to the providence of God, this would seem to make empty and meaningless the actions of secondary causes. Furthermore, there are things that it is better not to know than to know; for example, such trifles as the existence of worms or dust, or such evils as the sexual perversions of which man is capable. And since what is better must be attributed to God, these things are not known by him, and so do not immediately fall under his providence.

Solution. To understand our solution, let us recall that two things pertain to providence: the knowledge of the order that all things have to their ends, and the execution of this order which is the actual directing of these things to their end. As concerns the first, God immediately foresees or has providence over all things whatsoever. In the divine intellect is the knowledge of all things and the knowledge of the order and the end of all things. God foreordains causes and gives them the power of producing foreordained effects. Thus the order of these effects pre-exists in the knowledge of God. But as regards the second element of providence, the execution of this foreseen order in existing things, God uses the mediation of creatures. [8]

Answering the objections. The first objection stated that since it belongs to each particular cause to bring its effect to its proper end or proper good, if all things were immediately ordered to their end by God, the actions of secondary causes would be void and meaningless. This objection has confused the *knowledge* of the order of each thing to its end with the *execution* of that order, which latter is the actual ruling and governing of existing things. It is in the first sense only that we say God has an immediate providence over all things. And this providence, which is the knowledge of the order, does not exclude the actions of secondary causes, which are the executors of the order. For example, a provident king knows all those things that must be done concerning his subjects, but it belongs to his dignity and goodness to execute this knowledge through his ministers. And so it is with God.

What are we to say about the second objection, that it is better for God not to know useless trifles and evil or perverted actions? We say it is better for us not to clutter up our mind with useless trifles, since it keeps us from learning about more important things. We cannot know everything. But this is not true of God who sees all things by one simple intuition of his essence. Again, it is better for us not to know too much about evil things, because such knowledge can influence our wills to do evil. But God's will cannot be so perverted, and so this is not true of God. It is not the knowledge of evil things that is evil, but the doing of them.

B. THE PRESENCE OF EVIL IN CREATURES DOES NOT CONTRADICT THE PRESENCE OF PROVIDENCE IN GOD

Here we wish to consider three things: First, why it would seem that evil contradicts providence, and to show how it does not; secondly, why God's infallible providence does not contradict man's free will; thirdly, the different way in which sinners and the just are ruled by God's providence.

[8] See S.T., I, 22, 3.

1. Existence of Evil and Divine Providence Reconciled

It would seem that the presence of physical evil in the world contradicts divine providence. A truly provident person, like a good father or a good ruler, would, if he could, exclude all physical evil from those over whom he has charge. But God's creatures are plagued continually with a whole host of physical evils— murders, wars, disease, famine, floods, earthquakes, and so forth. Either God is not able to prevent these things, and so is not all powerful, or he does not care about his creatures, and so is not a truly good and provident God. Just as a father who would stand on the shore and watch his family drown before his eyes, even though he could save them, is hardly a good or provident father.

If physical evil, which is the lack or privation of some physical good, is hard to reconcile with God's providence, moral evil is a thousand times harder. Moral evil or sin, that is, the deliberate acts of men against reason and the will of God, is detestable in the sight of God. Certainly any wise person is going to prevent, if he can, what is displeasing to him. Again we are faced with our simple but gnawing dilemma: either God is powerless to prevent sin, and so is not really almighty, or he does not really care what happens to sinners, and so while he may be a provident God to the good, he is hardly such to the wicked. The wickedness of men contradicts the providence of God.

What are we to say to these two difficulties, one concerning the presence of physical evil in the world that God has made, the other the presence of moral evil or sin in human beings? In the face of evil God's ways become mysterious.

It is not too difficult to understand how the presence of physical evils in his creatures does not contradict the providence that God has over them. There is a difference between one who must take care of only a few particular things, and God, who has an immediate providence over the whole universe. A particular provider will eliminate as much as he can all defects from what is committed to his care. But the universal provider will permit a defect in some particular thing, lest the good of the whole suffer.

Defects that are contrary to certain particular natures take place for the good of the whole. Some things must corrupt if others are to be generated.

If all particular evils were removed, the universe would be deprived of many and greater goods. If we are to have living lions, we must tolerate some dead sheep. If we are to have the patience and heroism of the martyrs, we must tolerate the cruelty of a Nero or a Diocletian. If secondary causes are to retain their proper activity we must, from time to time, put up with a Johnstown flood or a Kansas tornado. For example, if those who have charge of this nation wanted to do away with the evils of death and mutilation due to automobile accidents, they could do so by simply eliminating the automobile. But this would remove a great good from a great number. And so the evil is allowed in order that the good remain.

Almighty God is the universal provider of all being, and so it belongs to his providence that he permit certain defects in certain beings lest the complete and perfect good of the whole universe suffer. These particular evils could be removed, but only at the expense of emptying God's creation of that which is best and perfect in it: self-activity, self-determination, liberty and freedom. St. Augustine writes in his *Enchirideon*, [9] "Almighty God would never allow any evil to take place in his works unless he were so powerful and so good that he can bring good even out of evil."

But why does God allow sin, which is so displeasing to him? For some greater good. The greater the good, the greater God loves that good. And so, as St. Thomas teaches, God prefers the presence of some greater good (for example, the heroism of the martyrs) to the absence of some lesser evil (for example, the cruelty of the persecutor). [10] In order that these greater goods be present in his universe, goods like the tears and humble love of the penitent sinner or the faith and heroism of the oppressed and persecuted, God allows some of his creatures to commit sin, abusing their free will, which abuse is very displeasing to him. But

[9] Ch. 11 (PL 40, col. 236).
[10] See *De Verit.*, qu. 5, a. 5, ad 3m.

he allows this for the greater good and perfection of his creation.

We are often scandalized at the wisdom and providence of God. That the good should suffer so much and the evil prosper seems to our finite intellects simple injustice. We do not know by what rule God is directing and caring for each one of his rational creatures. But of this there can be no doubt, that in all the good things and in all the evil things that befall the just and the wicked, there is some wise reason according to which God is ordering these things. It is because we are ignorant of this reason that these things appear to us as disordered or irrational. We say, "It doesn't make sense," meaning that it does not make sense to us. We act like a person who enters the workshop of a carpenter and seeing the many and different-shaped instruments, thinks that they are uselessly multiplied, for he does not understand the use that each one has. But if that person could have an insight into the virtue and skill of the artist, he would see that each instrument has its rational and special use. [11]

Conclusion. Thus we see that neither the presence of physical evil nor moral evil in the creature is contrary to the universal and immediate providence of God. Not physical evil, for a universal provider is one who must provide not only for the good of each particular part, but for the good of the whole. So to attain this greater good, God permits particular evils. God could eliminate them, but their elimination would result in the concomitant elimination of greater and more universal good. Sin, too, which is not only a moral evil in itself, but also the root of many physical evils in the life of man, is not contrary to God's providence. God allows this evil only for the greater good of the sinner or the greater good of the just, in some way or other. God writes straight with crooked lines.

But someone may ask: Could not God have made a free nature that could not have sinned? The answer is no. God cannot do the impossible. He cannot draw a square circle nor make a living horse of gold. Nor can he create a finite nature that is free and yet not able to sin. As finite, the creature is not its own end, and not being

[11] See St. Thomas, *ibid.,* ad 6m.

its own end, it can fail to attain its end. The power to sin is as much a metaphysical property of a finite free nature, as the power for non-being is of a corruptible nature.

But could we not urge this difficulty: Just as things that are of themselves corruptible, God can keep from ever corrupting by a preternatural gift of immortality, so through the supernatural gift of his grace God could keep men from ever sinning? The answer is that this is precisely what God does and must do. None of us could go for a long period of time without serious sin except for the grace of God. But if this is so, why could not God give each man sufficient grace to save his soul? He does, but some men freely reject this grace.

But could not God select for each man efficacious graces that would so inflame his heart and move his will that each man would freely co-operate with these graces? Then there would be no sin because of grace and all would be saved, and freely saved.

There seems to be no reason why God could not do this if he wanted. But he does not want to do so. The reason is his own. But whatever it is, it is infinitely wise, for it is the reason of an infinitely wise and good God. Furthermore, we should always remember that grace is a gift, it is not owed or due to nature. We have no right to it. And so God is not unjust if he gives more grace to one than to another. We are only entitled to a sufficient amount to save our souls. And we are entitled to this because our natures have been elevated to a supernatural order. There is one very consoling fact in all this mysterious matter. The Church teaches that the gift of final perseverance, that is to say, the gift to die in the state of sanctifying grace, will be given to us if we pray for it as we should. [12]

2. An Infallible Providence Does Not Contradict Man's Free Acts

At first glance, the Christian position on divine providence is not without its difficulties. For if all things that happen in the world, even man's free acts, are subject to divine providence, then it

[12] See *The Church Teaches,* ed. by Gerald Van Ackeren, S.J. (St. Louis, B. Herder Book Co., 1955), p. 238.

would seem to follow that either divine providence is not certain, or that all things take place of necessity. For God's knowledge is the cause of things. And this knowledge is present to each event with the presence of eternity. God's knowledge is both certain and causal. Given God's knowledge of an event, that event must infallibly take place, for this knowledge is a cause of its taking place. What are we to say to this?

First, although God's providence is infallible, that is, although everything that God foresees will take place and will take place in the way that he foresees it will take place, it does not follow from this that all things foreseen by God necessarily take place. For some take place freely.

We have already discussed this difficult question in connection with the immutability of God's will. But the same principles hold true here as regards the infallibility of his providence. Divine providence imposes necessity upon some things, but not on all things. Let us see once more why this is so.

The ultimate final end of all existing things, an end that is separate from and outside the whole universe of created being, is God himself. Next to God, the relatively final end, and one that exists within created being, is the good or perfection of the universe considered as a whole. Now there can be no good of the whole universe unless there are particular goods ordered to this whole. And so we find different grades of being. It belongs to divine providence, therefore, to produce these different grades of being.

The created universe, then, is a certain whole made up of different and disparate parts. Among these different parts, the first distinction seems to be the contingent and the necessary. For all effects that take place in the universe do so either necessarily or contingently. We see that each particular agent tries, insofar as it can, to preserve its own natural disposition and being. Thus God intends that some of his effects proceed necessarily and others contingently. And so for some effects God prepares necessary causes in order that these effects will necessarily take place. For other effects, he prepares contingent causes, so that these events or effects will take place freely or contingently. But all effects take place in the way God foresees that they will take place, either necessarily or contingently.

Just as there is absolute immutability in God's will, so there is absolute certitude in his providence, both as to what will happen and the way it will happen. Necessity and contingency are modes of being of the effect. Therefore the mode of necessity and the mode of contingency fall beneath God's foreknowledge, since he is the universal provider of all being, although they do not fall beneath the knowledge of a particular providence or particular provider. [13]

Nor do the deficiencies of secondary causes, through which causes the effects of divine providence are produced, remove the certitude of this providence. For God is operating in all these causes, and operating there according to the decision of his own free will. And so it pertains to divine providence that contingent or defectible causes are sometimes allowed to act deficiently, and at other times are preserved from such defects.

3. Are Sinners and the Just Ruled by God's Providence in the Same Way?

Divine providence extends itself to human beings in two ways: first, insofar as they are watched over and taken care of by God; and, secondly, insofar as they take care of themselves and others and thus become sharers in divine providence. Insofar as men provide well for themselves and others, or insofar as they provide ill for themselves or others, they are good or evil men. Insofar as they are provided for by God, good or evil things are said to befall them. And according to the way men provide for themselves and others, will God provide for them.

Thus if men keep right order in their providence of themselves and of others over whom they have charge, God in his turn will care for them with a providence consonant with their human dignity. He will allow nothing to befall them that will not be for their good. All that happens to them will advance them in good and in

[13] See S.T., I, 22, 4, and ad 2m and 3m.

virtue. "To those who love God," says St. Paul, "all things work together unto good." [14]

Concerning God's providence over the wicked, St. Thomas makes a rather remarkable statement. [15] If the men who have a share in God's providence do not follow right reason and the norm of God's will, as befits a rational creature, but live their lives after the manner of brute animals, then divine providence will ordain things for them in a way that befits brute animals. That is to say, the good or evil things that happen to them will not be ordered to their own good, but rather to the good of others, just as the good of brute animals is ordered to the good of rational animals.

Thus it becomes evident that divine providence governs the just in a higher and more perfect manner than it does the wicked. For evil men, in removing themselves from one order of divine providence, namely, the order of doing God's will, fall into another order of God's providence, namely, the order in which God's will is fulfilled in them. But the just are correctly under God's providence in both these orders.

C. GOD GOVERNS CREATURES THROUGH THE MEDIATION OF OTHER CREATURES

Here we want to answer two simple questions. First, does God govern the world? And, secondly, does he govern it through creatures? That God does govern the universe is clear from a simple consideration. We know that the final perfection of each existing thing is the attaining or reaching of its end. God, whose goodness is infinite and whose power is perfect, would not give existence to things without also bringing them to their perfection, to their end. And this is to govern or rule. [16]

Does God rule the universe immediately or through creatures? Two simple objections would make one believe that God rules his universe through himself alone. It seems better that one agent

[14] See *Romans*, Ch. 8, verse 28.
[15] See *De Veritate*, qu. 5, a. 7, *resp.*
[16] See *S.T.*, I, 103, 1.

should bring about something, rather than have many agents bring it about. God can rule all things by himself. Therefore, it would seem that he does, since this is better. Secondly, God is in no way imperfect or deficient. But to rule through others seems to imply imperfection. The reason an earthly king does not rule everything immediately himself, is that he cannot do all the things that must be done, nor be in all the places where he would have to do them. This is not true of God, who is all powerful and present everywhere.

Solution. To understand our solution to this problem, let us recall that the divine goodness is the cause of the existence of things. God wills the perfection of his goodness according as it is possible to communicate it to a creature. This divine goodness has a twofold perfection: in itself (as it contains in a super-eminent way all perfection) and insofar as it is the cause of things and gives being to things. Now it is quite in keeping with the divine goodness that both these perfections should be communicated to the creature. A creature not only has from the divine goodness its being but also the power to give being to others. Just as the sun, through the diffusion of its rays, not only gives to bodies the perfection of *being* bright, but also enables them to communicate this received brightness to other bodies. The moon is not only bright with the light of the sun, it can also brighten the night. And there is a certain order observed here: the nearer a body is to the sun, the more intense is the light it can receive. So that this light is not only sufficient for itself, but can also be communicated to others. [17]

So too with the order of the universe. The creatures that are more perfect have received from the divine goodness such an influx of being that not only are they good in themselves, but they can be the cause of goodness in others. Among all God's creatures, those which are closest to him are rational creatures. These most of all imitate God in their being, life and understanding. And here St. Thomas makes an interesting observation. Because of this imitation, not only is it bestowed on them from the

[17] See *S.T.*, I, 103, 6; *De Veritate*, qu. 5, a. 8.

divine goodness that they should influence others, but that they should exercise this influence in the same way that God does, namely, through their will, and not through any necessity of nature. Hence, God governs his universe both through rational and irrational creatures, but with a difference. Irrational creatures bring things to their end by a necessity of nature. They are not themselves provident, but only active. Spiritual creatures, however, like man and the angels, are themselves provident; that is to say, they bring things to their end by an exercise of their intellect and will. [18]

Finally, to complete the picture, St. Thomas places an order within rational or spiritual creatures themselves. On the lowest rung of intellectual beings we find man, whose intellectual light in comparison with an angel's is a sort of darkness. Thus our knowledge is more limited and particular, so that our providence is limited to human affairs and to those things which we are able to put to use in our human living. Whereas the providence of the angels is more universal.

God, therefore, as principal cause uses other beings as instrumental causes in the government of his universe, that is, in bringing things to their proper ends. This government or rule is, as we have seen, the execution of divine providence; which providence is the knowledge God has of the order of each thing to its end. Thus providence is in God, but the execution of providence (or government) is in things. Government is the carrying out of the order established by God. And this government is achieved through the activity of secondary causes.

Answering the objections. But is it not better for God immediately to govern the world that he has made? Economy is desirable; and since God could govern the universe alone, why use creatures? This was our first objection. We reply that if God alone executed his providence, this would mean that creatures have no causal activity properly their own by which they attain their own end and direct others to the attaining of theirs. Hence it is more perfect to make use of creatures. Nor does God share his government

[18] See *De Veritate*, qu. 5, a. 8.

of the universe with creatures because of any imperfection or deficiency on his part, as the second objection stated. For even in the case of an earthly ruler, it pertains to his dignity that others execute his will. In fact, as St. Thomas points out, from the order and organization of his ministers, the power of the ruler is made manifest. [19]

D. DOES THE PRAYER OF PETITION TO GOD MAKE ANY SENSE?

There is one final problem connected with divine providence that should be treated here. Why pray to God, telling him of our needs and asking him to fulfill our desires? First of all, it seems unnecessary to tell God our needs, for he knows of them already. His knowledge is infinite. Secondly, we make our prayer in order that God will be moved by them to grant us what we ask. But the will of God is fixed and immovable, incapable of any change. Since prayer cannot change the unchangeable, it hardly makes sense to pray for what we want. Finally, it is more generous of a person to give a gift unasked, especially if he knows we want and need it, than to wait until asked and pleaded with. As the Roman philosopher Seneca once wrote, "Nothing is bought more dearly than what we have to plead for and beg." [20] But God is generosity itself. Hence it seems unnecessary to ask him for his gifts.

These are the common objections against praying to God for our needs. Concerning this prayer of petition there have been three erroneous positions among men. [21] Some have thought that the affairs of men are not directed by divine providence, and hence it is quite useless to pray to God. Others have thought that all the affairs of men take place of necessity, whether they reduce this necessity to the unchangeableness of divine providence or to the necessary physical laws of the universe. In either case, any prayer of petition to God is quite useless. Finally, a third error would be to think that the world is indeed ruled by divine providence, but

[19] See S.T., I, 103, 6, ad 3m.
[20] De Beneficiis, Bk. 2, Ch. 1.
[21] See St. Thomas, S.T., II-II, 83, 2.

by a providence that is changeable. And so the purpose of prayer would be to change the will and providence of God. Now all these opinions are false, either because they deny the existence of divine providence, or because they deny its unchangeableness. Our problem is to show that the prayer of petition is really useful and has meaning, and that although the divine plan is fixed and immutable, it does not follow that everything that happens in our lives does so of necessity.

To understand our solution, let us recall that God in his providence over us ordains not only what things shall happen to us in this life, but also the reasons why they will happen and the order in which they will happen. Now among the reasons or causes why things happen are our own human acts. We perform these human acts, therefore, not that through them we might change the divine plan, but rather that through them we might bring about certain effects according to the order that has been established by God. Let us explain what we mean from an example of our use of natural causes. If we want to eat our food, we must cook it. And if we want to cook it, we must use some kind of heat. Of course, God by a miracle could cook our food each time we needed it. But instead he has established these natural causes and through them he fulfills his plan for men.

The same thing holds true of our prayers. We do not pray that we will change the divine plan. Rather, we pray that what God has decreed to fulfill through out prayers will be so fulfilled. We pray that we might receive from God what he has decreed from all eternity to give us, provided we pray for it. [22]

With these principles in mind, the answers to our objections become clear. It is true that God knows all our needs before we pray, and so we offer him our prayers, not that he might know these needs, but rather that we ourselves might come to understand that in all our needs we must have recourse to God's help. Our second objection asked: If God's plan is unchangeable, why pray, for our prayers will not change that plan? We know now that our prayers are not ordered to the changing of God's plan, but

[22] *Ibid.*

that through them we might obtain what God has planned for our good. For many things in our own lives and in the lives of others actually depend on whether we pray to God for them or not. God knows in his eternity who will pray and who will not, and he knows what things will be given to us or withheld from us because of our prayers or our failure to pray.

The third objection concerned the generous man who gives without being asked. God is the most generous of fathers, and no doubt most of the gifts he sends come to us unasked. But his decision that some things will be given us only if we ask for them is a decision he has made for our own good. For by so praying to God, we learn to trust and confide in him and come to look upon him as the real source of the good things in our lives. As St. John Chrysostom so beautifully writes: "Consider what great happiness and glory is ours, that in our prayers we may talk to God as to a friend, and that we may converse with Christ, asking him for what we need and desire." [23]

E. THE POWER OF GOD

In studying the creative act, we saw by implication that God must be all powerful. For to create means to produce something from nothing. We have seen, furthermore, that God is all knowing. He knows whatever can be known, and to the degree that it can be known. We saw, finally, that the will of God is absolutely efficacious. Not only can God accomplish what he wants, but also in the way he wants—that is, necessarily, freely, and so on. What carries out the divine will is the divine power; what commands the divine power is the divine will; and what directs the divine will is the divine knowledge. All these things, of course, are one and the same in God. All are identified with his essence, which is itself identified with his act of existing. But they differ according to our way of understanding them. At this point we want to consider the divine power (as it can be known through creatures), and see what it can do and why it can do it. We shall ask ourselves three questions: (1) Is there power in God? (2) Is this power in-

[23] As quoted by St. Thomas, *ibid.,* ad 3m.

finite? (3) Can this power do all things? We shall end our discussion with the question of whether God could have made things better than he actually has. For example, could he have made this a better world?

1. Is There Power in God?

It would seem not. For we have seen that God's knowledge and will are the cause of things. Hence, there is no need to attribute any power to God, but only knowledge and will.

Solution. There are two kinds of potencies, passive and active. Passive potency is in no way in God, but active potency is there in the highest degree. Insofar as a thing is in act, it can be the active principle of something else. But God is pure act. Hence, he can be a perfect active principle of something else. But to be an active principle is to have power or active potency. Therefore, there is power in God. [24]

But if God causes all things by his knowledge and will, there seems no reason to put power in God. This was our objection. The answer should be obvious. In God, knowledge, will and power are one and the same. There is only a distinction of reason between them; that is to say, they differ only in the way we understand them. Because of the functions of knowledge, will and power in man, we say—by way of analogy—that it is God's knowledge that directs and it is his will that commands. And so it is his power that executes what his will commands and his knowledge directs. [25]

2. Is God's Power Infinite?

It would seem not. For a power is made manifest through what it can do. The power of a cause is measured by what it can effect. If, therefore, the power of God were infinite, it should be able to cause an infinite effect. But this is impossible. And so God's power would not seem to be infinite.

Solution. That God's power is infinite, or without any limit whatsoever, is quite clear. For among creatures we see that the more

[24] See *S.T.*, I, 25, 1.
[25] See *S.T.*, I, 25, 1, ad 4.

perfect something possesses the form through which it acts, the greater is its power in acting. For example, the more intensely something possesses the form of heat, the more power it has to heat other things. Now, as we have seen in our discussion of creation, the form by which God acts is his own divine essence. But this essence, as identified with his act of existing, is not limited by any receiving principle. And so his active power is also infinite. As completely in act, God is infinitely powerful.

But should not an infinite power be able to produce an infinite effect? God has power over being, not over non-being, which is nothing. An effect is something that is produced, but an infinite effect, by supposition, would be an infinite being. As caused, it would not be its own reason for existence, and hence composed of essence and existence; as infinite, it could not be so composed. In a word, an infinite effect is a contradiction of being, a simple impossibility. What God produces through his power will always be less than what that power can produce. And even had God produced no beings, his power would not be in vain. For that power is frustrated which is ordered to an end that it does not attain. But God is not ordered to his effects as to an end. Rather, God is the end to which all his effects are ordered. [26]

3. Can God's Power Do All Things?

It would seem not. For example, God cannot commit sin. And so he cannot do all things. We know that it is the common conviction of men that God is all powerful. But what precisely does it mean when we say that God can do all things? The answer is not as easy as one might think.

The Latin equivalent of the English word "able to" or "can" (*posse*) has the same root as the English word "possible." Power is related to the possible. What can be done is called possible. Thus, if we consider the matter carefully, we see that when we say that God can do all things, we really mean that God can do all possibles. And because of this he is called all powerful. There is a difference, then, between the question, Is God's power infinite?

[26] See S.T., I, 25, 2.

and, Can God do all things? The former places no limit upon the *active potency* by which God acts; the latter places no limit to the *effects* that he can produce.

But if we mean that God is all powerful because he can do whatever is possible, what do we mean by "possible?" The word "possible" can have two meanings. First, it can mean whatever falls beneath the active power of a certain thing. Thus, whatever man can do is said to be "possible" for man. Now if we use the word in this sense and say that God is all powerful because he can do whatever falls beneath his divine power, we are obviously involved in a vicious circle. For we are saying that God is all powerful because he can do all the things he can do. Hence we must find another meaning for the word "possible" if we are to get at the real roots of divine omnipotence.

The word has another meaning, which we shall call its *absolute* meaning. In this sense, a thing is said to be possible because of the compatibility of its "notes." For example, it is possible for Socrates to sit, since sitting is compatible with the nature of Socrates. But it is impossible for a man to be a mountain, since the nature of man is incompatible with that of a mountain.

Now since every agent acts through its form, those objects will be possible for that agent which are compatible with that form. For example, fire, which acts through its form of heat, can heat any object with whose nature heat is compatible. Thus it is possible for fire to heat material objects; it is absolutely impossible for fire to heat immaterial objects. Let us apply this to the power of God. The divine Being, the form through which God acts, is infinite. It is not limited to any kind of being, but pre-contains within itself the perfection of all being. And therefore any object that has the intelligibility of being is among those absolute possibles, in respect to which God is said to be omnipotent.

The only thing that is opposed to being is non-being. And so the only thing that is opposed to the absolute possible, over which God has power, is that which involves at one and the same time both being and non-being. God cannot produce an object that involves a contradiction in terms. And the reason for this is not any defect on the part of the power of God, but on the part of the object; for the object is not possible, is not makeable.

So we conclude: whatever does not imply a contradiction in being is contained among those possibles in respect to which God is called all powerful. And whatever involves a contradiction in being is not so contained, because it does not have the notion of possibility. Thus it is more correct to say that such a thing cannot be done than to say that God cannot do it. [27]

Answering the objection. We answer that God cannot sin precisely because he is all powerful. For sin is a defect in the act of an agent. To be able to sin, therefore, is to be able to fail in acting. And this is impossible for an all-powerful God.

Having seen that the power of God is infinite and that it can produce whatever is capable of existing, let us ask ourselves this final question: Could God have made better the things he has actually made? At first glance it would seem not. For whatever God has made, he has made by an act that is infinitely powerful and infinitely wise. But if God were to make things better than they are, they would be made more powerfully and more wisely, which is impossible. Hence it would seem that God could not have made things better than he has actually made them.

To understand our solution, let us recall that the perfection of any thing is twofold. One is its perfection of essence. In this sense, the perfection of a man is to be a rational animal. And as regards this perfection, God could not have made anything better than it is, although he could have made better things. Just as we cannot have a "better four," (for if it is better, it is no longer a four but some other number), so God could not make a better man, for then we would have not man, but some other kind of being.

The other perfection of a thing is its perfection of being as being. These perfections, as we have seen, God has through his essence, but creatures only by way of participation. Thus creatures can possess these perfections more or less perfectly. For example, a man can be wiser than he is. And according to these perfections

[27] See S.T., I, 25, 3.

God could have made the things he has made better than they actually are.

With this distinction in mind, the answer to our objection becomes clear. When it is said that God can make a thing better than it is, this is true if by "better" we have in mind the adjective. For God can make a thing better than it is, not in its perfection of essence, but in its other perfections. But if by "better" we have in mind the adverb, and refer to the way God has made it, then God cannot make anything better than he has; for he has made it by an act that is infinitely wise and good.

F. SUMMARY OF THE CHAPTER

"God has an immediate providence over all things, nor do the evils in the world contradict this providence. God governs creatures (executes his providence) through other creatures."

a. State of the question

Creatures come forth from God as their first principle and, as we shall see, are ordered to God as their last end. But creatures are also ordered to other more immediate and proximate ends. Does God know these ends, and does he order his creatures to them? Since this is nothing else than to have providence over his creatures, in this chapter we want to know: (1) Has God an immediate and universal providence over his creatures? (2) How is such providence compatible with evil in the world? (3) How does God execute this providence?

b. Explanation of terms

1) ". . . *providence* . . ."—the knowledge of things as ordered to their ends.

2) ". . . *immediate* . . ."—to possess this knowledge of oneself and not through another.

3) ". . . *evil* . . ."—a privation (or absence of a perfection that should be present).

(*a*) *Physical evil*—a privation of some physical good. Thus blindness is a physical evil for a man.

(*b*) *Moral evil*—sin; that is, an act of man's free will that lacks the proper order to its end. Thus, for example, lying is such a disordered act, since the end of communicable speech is the manifestation of the truth.

4) ". . . *governs* . . ."—the execution of providence, or the actual direction of things to their proper ends.

c. The proof

1) *God has immediate providence over all things. There is providence in God*, since God knows all creatures and the ends of all creatures. All natures act for an end, and so God in establishing these natures has pre-established their ends. And providence is nothing else than the knowledge of these natures as ordered to these ends.

This providence is immediate, since the knowledge of God is one with the essence of God. And so God has this knowledge of himself, and not through another.

This providence is universal, since divine knowledge is co-extensive with divine causality (God's knowledge is the cause of things), and all things have God as their first cause.

2) *Evil in the world does not contradict divine providence. Not physical evil*, since in a hierarchical universe, where there are many and diverse particular goods, God, as universal provider, allows the privation of a lesser good (evil) to achieve the presence of a greater good. For example, God allows the death of plants to achieve the growth and perfection of animals.

Not moral evil or sin, since God prefers the presence of some greater good to the absence of some lesser evil. And so, for example, God will allow the cruelty of the persecutor, which results in the heroism of the martyrs. Notice, God in no way causes this evil, but only tolerates it. The whole cause is within man's free will, with which God will not interfere—for then man would not be free—would not be man. Moreover, God would not tolerate evil, unless he were able to "draw from it" greater good. Finally, this greater good is not the reason (final cause) God tolerates evil (for evil has no final cause), but merely the occasion of his tolerating it.

3) *God governs creatures through other creatures.* Government, or the execution of God's providence, is the actual direction of things to their ends. But creatures achieve their ends through their activity. Hence creatures are active. But as active, creatures can cause other creatures and the operations of other creatures. Hence, creatures reach their ends through the causality (physical and moral) of other creatures. Thus while God knows immediately the ends of all creatures (providence), he mediately (through creatures) executes this providence.

Suggested Readings

1. St. Thomas, *Summa Theologiae,* in *Basic Writings of St. Thomas,* by A. Pegis, (New York, Random House, 1945), Vol. 1, pp. 229–237 (On the Providence of God); pp. 950–961 (On the Government of God); pp. 259–269 (On the Power of God).
Truth (De Veritate), translated from the definitive Leonine text by R. W. Mulligan, S.J. (Chicago, Henry Regnery Company, 1952), Vol. 1, pp. 220–251, especially 202–204; 209–210; 222–223; 232–234.
On the Power of God (De Potentia), translated by the English Dominican Fathers (Westminster, Newman Press, 1952), Book One, pp. 1–41.

CHAPTER 13

God as the End of Man

*I am Alpha, I am Omega, the beginning of
all things and their end.*
—*The Apocalypse*, Ch. 1, verse 8

We turn now to our final question in natural theology. In what sense is God the final term or goal of all created being? God is not only the first efficient cause of the universe, he is also its final end. But what do we mean by this?

1. Defining Some Terms

To understand our solution, let us begin by defining three different kinds of ends. First, there is the *finis operantis*. This is the end or goal of the *one performing* the action. Secondly, there is the *finis operis*. This is the end or goal of the action or *work performed*. Thirdly, there is the *finis quo*. This is not so much an end as a means. The *finis quo* is that by which the *finis operis* is attained, that by which the thing produced achieves its end.

Let us take a simple example to illustrate these three different ends. A man makes a watch. The *finis operantis* is the end or goal he had in making the watch. It is that which "moved" him in the order of finality to make the watch. Let us say it is to earn a living. But what is the *finis operis*, what is the end of the watch that he has made? This flows from the very nature of the watch. The end of a watch (*finis operis*) is to tell the time. Finally, what is the *finis quo*? How does the watch achieve its end, how does it tell the time? By moving its hands around its face.

2. Applying These Terms to God

Let us apply these terms to God and the creature. God has made the creature. Why? That is to say, what moved God in the order of finality to produce creatures? What is the *finis operantis*, the end of God creating? God is his own end, he cannot be moved by anything other than himself. The only end that could attract his will to the making of anything is himself. What moved God to produce creatures was his own infinite goodness, not, however, considered in itself, but considered as communicable to others. The *finis operantis*, the end of God creating, is the infinite goodness as communicable to creatures. Since this is so, once this goodness is actually communicated to creatures by way of participation, these multiplied and finite participations will automatically and necessarily mirror forth the uncreated goodness of God.

This is a simple but important truth. God is like an artist who paints a self-portrait. And God paints his own picture because he wants to communicate his likeness to the canvas. God wants to manifest himself by his painting. The painting, by the mere fact that it exists, mirrors forth the painter. And so creatures, by their very natures, manifest God. The *finis operis* of the self-portrait is the painter. And the *finis operis* of the creature is God. Notice what we are saying: that which the creature manifests is God. Hence God as *manifested* is what terminates (ends) the creature. The final end of the creature is not the *manifestation* of God; this is the *means* by which the end is attained. The manifestation is the *finis quo* by which the *finis operis* is achieved. The end of the creature is achieved by manifesting God; but God, who terminates the manifestation, is the end of the creature. God himself is the *finis operis* of every creature.

Let us make this idea more clear by a simple example drawn from the order of knowledge. What is the end, or *finis operis*, of a concept? It is to give us a knowledge of things. And how does the concept achieve this? What is its *finis quo*? A concept gives us a knowledge of a thing by representing it. We know the thing because of its representation by the concept. What I know is the thing, but I know it because of a representation. The end of the concept (*finis operis*) is the thing known.

Let us apply this example to God as our final end. There is, of course, only one perfect word, or exhaustive representation of God, and that is the Word, the Second Person of the Blessed Trinity. This is the internal and divine Word of God, consubstantial with his nature. But there are countless imperfect and deficient words of God, externally spoken by God and outside his nature. And all these words speak of, represent, his essence. Such words are the creatures of God.

What is their purpose? To manifest God. Creatures are so many finite words, created tongues, speaking the same thing, but speaking it in different words and with different sounds. All creatures, each in its own way, are talking about God. He is the term of their speech, that is to say, the end of their being. And how do they attain God? Simply by being what they are and doing what they should do. How does the self-portrait manifest the painter? By simply being what it is, a likeness of the painter. God has communicated his likeness to the creature, as the painter has communicated his likeness to the canvas. So all creatures necessarily manifest God. He himself is the end of his creation.

With this consideration we have come full circle in the order of finality. We know from metaphysics that the final cause is the first in the order of intention and the last in the order of execution. The *finis operantis,* or the end of God creating, is the first in the order of intention, for it is that which "moves" God to create. And what is this end? It is the infinite goodness of God as communicable to the creature. The *finis operis,* or the end of the thing created, is the last in the order of execution. And what is this end? It is this same infinite goodness of God, for it is this goodness that terminates the manifestation (*finis quo*) of the creature. Just as it was the divine goodness that was the end of God creating, so it is the divine goodness that is the end of the thing created. The *finis operantis* and the *finis operis* are one and the same: God as manifestable through creatures and (after creation) God as manifested through creatures.

But man is a special creature. Because of his intellect and free will, he does not merely manifest God by being what he is and doing what he should do, but he also can formally possess God. All creatures "materially" possess God, insofar as they necessarily and automatically manifest his goodness. But man through knowledge and love can formally possess God. He does so in this present life insofar as he knows and loves God in and through his creatures. On the natural level this is done through natural creatures; on the supernatural level, this knowledge and love is achieved through supernatural creatures, for example, divine faith and charity.

In heaven, God will be the end of our being in a very special manner. Here we will not merely manifest God, we will possess him; and we will not merely possess him through creatures, but through himself. For in heaven we will see God, not as mirrored by creatures (imperfectly) or by faith (darkly), but through the splendor of his own countenance. Here, once more, God himself is our end (*finis operis*), the Beatific Vision being the means (*finis quo*) of possessing him. God himself will terminate that vision, possessed now in a very special way. In this vision, which is called beatific, we will know God with the knowledge he has of himself, and we will love God with the love he has of himself. And this knowledge and this love will bring us perfect joy and happiness.

But, as should be obvious from what has been said, even those who go to hell still have God as the end of their being. For although they have lost the Beatific Vision, and hence the supernatural end for which they were created, they still manifest God, but especially now his justice.

3. Conclusion

With this discussion of God as the end of creatures, our study of natural theology comes to an end. Starting with creatures, we have mounted up to God, seeing him as the first principle and last end of all things. In seeing how all things are ordered to God as their final end, the work of wisdom is achieved. Achieved, that is, at a certain level of speculative knowledge, and according to a static contemplation of the truth. But the practical achievement of our end and the dynamic movement toward God must be the work of love. And this knowledge of itself can never give. But knowledge can make the work of love more enlightened and profound. And when the love of God enters the student's heart, he will not only be wise, but holy.

Suggested Readings

1. St. Thomas, *Summa Theologiae,* in *Basic Writings of St. Thomas,* by A. Pegis (New York, Random House, 1945), Vol. 1, pp. 431–432. *On the Truth of the Catholic Faith* (*Summa Contra Gentiles*), Book Three: *Providence;* translated, with an Introduction and Notes, by Vernon J. Bourke (New York, Hanover House, 1956), pp. 97–125.
2. Etiènne Gilson, *The Christian Philosophy of St. Thomas Aquinas* (New York, Random House, 1956), pp. 130–143.

APPENDIX A

Some Invalid Philosophical Proofs for the Existence of God

In our investigation of the existence of God, it is helpful to consider some of the more famous proofs used by philosophers to establish the existence of a supreme Being, but which seem lacking in real validity and conclusiveness. Understanding the weakness or fallacy of such proofs, the student is in a better position to see what a valid demonstration of God's existence entails.

We have already discussed St. Anselm's famous *ontological argument* for the existence of God, and St. Thomas's rejection of it. [1] Here we shall consider two other proofs, taken from the writings of modern philosophers, the first being that of René Descartes (1596–1650), the Father of modern philosophy.

1. The Experiment of Descartes

I will now close my eyes, I will stop my ears, I will turn away my senses from their objects, I will even efface from my consciousness all

[1] This argument is to be found in St. Anselm's *Proslogion seu Alloquium de Dei Existentia*, Migne, PL 158, col. 223–248. The proof itself is in col. 227–228. This little work can be read in English translation in A. Pegis's *The Wisdom of Catholicism*, pp. 202–228. The saint had already given us in his *Monologion* three perfectly valid *a posteriori* proofs, that is, proofs that proceed from perfections found in existing things to their necessary source in a first cause. These three proofs proceed from the fact of unequal degrees of good, being, and perfections in general, in the things of our experience. They may be found in *De Divinitatis Essentia Monologion*, Migne, PL 158, col. 145-146; 146-147; 148-150. For a good secondary source on all these arguments of St. Anselm for the existence of God, see Etiènne Gilson, *History of Christian Philosophy in the Middle Ages* (New York, Random House, 1955), pp. 130-134.

393

the images of corporeal things. . . . And thus holding converse only
with myself, and closely examining my nature, I will endeavor to obtain
by degrees a more intimate and familiar knowledge of myself. I am a
thinking (conscious) thing, that is, a being who doubts, affirms, denies,
knows a few objects, and is ignorant of many—who imagines likewise,
and perceives; for, as I before remarked, although the things which I
perceive or imagine are perhaps nothing at all apart from me (and in
themselves), I am nevertheless assured that those modes of consciousness which I call perceptions and imaginations, in as far only as they
are modes of consciousness, exist in me. And in the little I have said I
think I have summed up all that I really know, or at least all that up to
this time I was aware I knew.[2]

From this meager and precarious capital, Descartes sets out to
prove the existence of God. Our purpose here is to understand the
nature of this proof and see whether it is valid. First of all, how
does Descartes know that this knowledge that he has of himself
as a thinking thing is true knowledge? Because it is clearly and
distinctly perceived. ". . . It seems to me that I may now take as
a general rule, that all that is very clearly and distinctly apprehended (conceived) is true." [3] But how, from this little but true
knowledge that Descartes has of himself, can he proceed to establish a proof for the actual existence of God? First, by discovering
that there is within him an idea of God; secondly, by seeing that
he himself could not be the origin of this idea; thirdly, and finally,
by concluding that the only adequate source of the idea of an infinitely perfect being, that is to say, of our idea of God, is an actually existing infinitely perfect God.

Here is how Descartes himself describes these three steps:

But, among these my ideas, besides that which represents myself,
respecting which there can be no difficulty, there is one that represents
God; others that represent corporeal and inanimate things; others angels; others animals; and, finally, there are some that represent men like
myself. But with respect to the ideas that represent men, or animals, or
angels, I can easily suppose that they were formed by the mingling and

[2] René Descartes, *A Discourse on Method and Selected Writings,* Meditation III, "Of God, that He Exists." Translated by John Veitch (New York,
E. P. Dutton & Co., 1951), p. 104. The student should read the whole of this
Third Meditation.
[3] *Ibid.,* p. 105.

composition of the other ideas which I have of myself, of corporeal
things, and of God, although there were, apart from myself, neither
men, animals, nor angels. And with regard to the ideas of corporeal objects, I never discover in them anything so great or excellent which I
myself did not appear capable of originating. [4]

But what about my idea of God? Descartes continues:

There only remains, therefore, the idea of God, in which I must consider whether there is anything that cannot be supposed to originate
with myself. By the name God, I understand a substance infinite (eternal, immutable), independent, all-knowing, all-powerful, and by which
I myself, and every other thing that exists, if any such there be, were
created. But these properties are so great and excellent, that the more
attentively I consider them the less I feel persuaded that the idea I have
of them owes its origin to myself alone. And thus it is absolutely necessary to conclude, from all that I have before said, that God exists; for
though the idea of substance be in my mind owing to this, that I myself
am a substance, I should not, however, have the idea of an infinite substance, seeing I am a finite being, unless it were given me by some
substance in reality infinite. [5]

Now the very fact that I can reflect upon my own limitations
and imperfections, my doubts, and so on, leads me to discover
within myself the notion of the perfect, that is, the notion of God,
which although in me, is not due to me. Descartes continues:

I clearly perceive that there is more reality in the infinite substance than
in the finite, and therefore that in some way I possess the perception
(notion) of the infinite before that of the finite, that is, the perception
of God before that of myself, for how could I know that I doubt, desire,
or that something is wanting to me, and that I am not wholly perfect,
if I possessed no idea of a being more perfect than myself, by comparison of which I knew the deficiencies of my nature? [6]

The origin of this idea of God, then, cannot be myself. Nor can
this idea of God come from nothing.

And it cannot be said that this idea of God is perhaps materially false,
and consequently that it may have arisen from nothing (in other words,
that it may exist in me from my imperfection), . . . for as this idea

[4] *Ibid.*, p. 112.
[5] *Ibid.*, pp. 114-115.
[6] *Ibid.*, p. 115.

is very clear and distinct, and contains in itself more objective reality than any other, there can be no one of itself more true, or less open to the suspicion of falsity. [7]

By the objective reality here of the idea, Descartes means the content of the idea, what it represents, that by which one idea differs from another, for example, the idea of good from the idea of just. Each idea has a different objective reality; what all ideas have in common is this, that they are all modes of consciousness. What Descartes contrasts to the objective reality of the idea is the formal, or actual, reality of the thing. It is this formal or actual reality of God that puts within us from our very beginning at least the potential objective reality of his idea. I can actuate this potential presence by my reflection upon my own imperfection, and so forth. Here is Descartes' rather impressive conclusion of his argument:

There remains only the inquiry as to the way in which I received this idea from God; for I have not drawn it from the senses, nor is it even presented to me unexpectedly, as is usual with the ideas of sensible objects, when these are presented or appear to be presented to the external organs of the senses; it is not even a pure production or fiction of my mind, for it is not in my power to take from or add to it; and consequently there but remains the alternative that it is innate, in the same way as the idea of myself. And, in truth, it is not to be wondered at that God, at my creation, implanted this idea in me, that it might serve, as it were, for the mark of the workman impressed on his work; . . . but considering only that God is my creator, it is highly probable that he in some way fashioned me after his own image and likeness, and that I perceive this likeness, in which is contained the idea of God, by the same faculty by which I apprehend myself,—in other words, when I make myself the object of reflection, I not only find that I am an incomplete (imperfect) and dependent being, and one who unceasingly aspires after something better and greater than he is; but, at the same time, I am assured likewise that he upon whom I am dependent possesses in himself all the goods after which I aspire (and the ideas of which I find in my mind), and that not merely indefinitely and potentially, but infinitely and actually, and that he is thus God. And the whole force of the argument of which I have here availed myself to establish the existence of God, consists in this, that I perceive that I could not

[7] *Ibid.*, p. 115.

possibly be of such a nature as I am, and yet have in my mind the idea of a God, if God did not in reality exist—that is, a being who possesses all those lofty perfections, of which the mind may have some slight conception, without, however, being fully able to comprehend them,—and who is wholly superior to all defect and has nothing that marks imperfection. [8]

2. Rejection of the Argument of Descartes

This demonstration of the Father of modern philosophy can be rejected as we rejected the argument of St. Anselm, and for essentially the same two reasons. First of all, Descartes heartily takes for granted what must be proved; namely, that all men really have this innate idea of a supreme and infinitely perfect being that he attributes to them. The whole history of paganism and the false gods of the Gentiles deny its presence. So it can hardly be called a clear and distinct idea, about whose truth the thinking subject cannot doubt or even suspect. Descartes had this idea, it is true, but not so much because of his understanding as because of his memory. And here we recall the words of St. Thomas: [9] What we learn as children becomes for us a second nature, innate, as it were. All those lofty characteristics that Descartes gives to his notion of God are traits of the Christian God. Descartes, in finding this notion of a divine Being within him, was simply remembering his catechism. And so we could deny this part of his argument as contrary to the fact; namely, that all men have this idea of God.

But in a sense this is not yet to refute Descartes. For at this stage of his experiment, it is only his own existence of which Descartes is certain. What difference does it make to him if other men do not have his idea of God, since he does not even know whether there are such things as other men. In point of fact, he tries to establish God's existence as a guarantee against deception in this matter. For if God exists and is infinitely perfect and true, he would not let Descartes be deceived as to the existence of the world and other men. And so let us grant Descartes the knowledge of such an idea about God, an infinitely perfect being, and see whether

[8] *Ibid.*, p. 121.
[9] See *C.G.*, Bk. I, Ch. 11.

he is justified in going from this knowledge of God to God's actual existence.

We see that Descartes' starting point has made impossible any egress from the order of thought to the order of existence. For he begins with himself as a *thinking substance*. For Descartes, at the beginning, there is no distinction between he who *thinks* and he who *is;* there is no difference between thought and actual being. In his experiment, actual being *is* thought; and so there is no way that he can infer real existence. Any existence that Descartes could infer would be, according to his own principles, existence *as thought*. Descartes is inexorably entombed in the monolithic prison of his own thinking.

But one might say: Is this really the case? Has not Descartes found a way out by the mediation of the principle of causality? What is wrong with asserting that the only possible adequate cause for the conceptual content of an infinitely perfect Being must be a correspondingly infinitely perfect existing Being? To the objective reality of my concept there must correspond, as its cause, the actual existence of the thing known by the concept. To this we answer that such correspondence is by no means necessary. In Descartes' own argument, the potential presence of this innate idea is identified with the subject itself in its capacity as a thinking substance. What actuates this idea is the reflection upon the deficiencies and imperfections of this thinking substance. So that from the notion of imperfection, I understand perfection, or rather degrees of perfection; and so I can imagine the absolutely perfect, the supreme degree of perfection. I call this supreme degree of perfection God; thus I end up thinking about God. But that does not mean there is such a God existing outside my intellect.

What, then, has caused this notion I have of God? The processes of my own thinking. The mode of being of such an idea is, of course, finite, since it is simply a mode of my own *consciousness*. The content or objective reality of such an idea, namely, an infinitely perfect Being, has been furnished by my notion of degrees of perfection, and hence the ability to talk about or "think about" a highest degree. But I have no right to say that *therefore* there exists outside my mind an infinitely prefect Being. For example, I may think about my idea of heat, and how this notion is capable of degrees; that is to say, I can have a notion of something hotter, and, therefore, finally, of that which is hottest. But does that mean that *therefore* somewhere in reality there *exists* the absolutely hottest object *possible?* So neither can I conclude from the idea I have formed of an infinitely perfect Being that there exists in reality such a Being.

If the experiment of Descartes proves anything it is this: a thought can never be our point of departure for proving the actual existence of anything. If we are to demonstrate the real Being of God, we must at least begin with the real being of things. If there is any force or semblance of truth to the argument of Descartes it is precisely inasfar as he has surreptitiously introduced such real elements into this thinking. But this argument, taken as intended by Descartes, has no validity to prove the existence of God. [10]

[10] Descartes gives a slightly different proof in his V Meditation: "For as I have been accustomed in every other matter to distinguish between existence and essence, I easily believe that the existence can be separated from the essence of God, and that thus God may be conceived as not actually existing. But, nevertheless, when I think of it more attentively, it appears that the existence can no more be separated from the essence of God than the idea of a mountain from that of a valley, or the equality of its three angles to two right angles, from the essence of a (rectilinear) triangle; so that it is not less impossible to conceive a God, that is, a being supremely perfect, to whom existence is awanting, or who is devoid of a certain perfection, than to conceive a mountain without a valley." *Ibid.*, pp. 136–137. The argument is quite simple: since existence is a perfection and God possesses all perfection, God must possess existence. Hence, to think of a non-existing God is a contradiction in terms. The refutation is equally simple. Just as I cannot think of a mountain without *thinking* of a valley, so neither can I think of an all perfect Being without *thinking* that it exists. But it does not follow from this that therefore it *does* so exist. On the Cartesian experiment as regards God's existence, the student should read Etiènne Gilson, *God and Philosophy* (New Haven, Yale University Press, 1941), pp. 74-91. Maurice Blondel has seen in this argument of Descartes the very cornerstone of his philosophy. See his article, "La clef de voute du systeme cartesien," in *Cartesio nel terzo centenario del Discorso del Metodo*, Milan, 1938, pp. 69-77. Many modern thinkers have followed Descartes in this argument for the existence of God. They may at times state the argument a little differently, but it is essentially the same argument. This is true, for example, of Malebranche, Bossuet and Fenelon.

3. Leibniz's Argument from the Notion of a Necessary Being

Baron Gottfried Wilhelm Leibniz (1646–1716), German philosopher and mathematician, in his little work, *The Monadology*, has given us an *a priori* proof for the existence of God which, if nothing else, is remarkable for its ingenuity. As in the case of Descartes, let us first hear the proof in the words of its author, try to understand it, and then decide whether or not it has any validity.

First, we begin with Leibniz's notion of God. "We may hold that the supreme substance, which is unique, universal and necessay with nothing independent outside of it, which is further a pure sequence of possible being, must be incapable of limitation and must contain as much reality as possible." [11] The necessary Being is absolutely perfect and the source of all the perfections of other beings. "Whence it follows that God is absolutely perfect. . . . There where there are no limits, that is to say, in God, perfection is absolutely infinite." [12] "It follows also that created things derive their perfections through the influence of God, but their imperfections come from their own natures. . . ." [13] Moreover, God is not only the source of existences, but also of essences, of whatever is real in the possibility of things.

It is true, furthermore, that in God is found not only the source of existences, but also that of essences, in so far as they are real. In other words, he is the source of whatever there is real in the possible. This is because the Understanding of God is in the region of eternal truths or of the ideas upon which they depend, and because without him there *would be nothing real in the possibilities of things,* and not only would nothing be existent, *nothing would even be possible.* [14]

Leibniz then tells us why this last statement must be true. "For it must needs be that if there is a reality in essences or in possibilities or indeed in the eternal truths, this reality is based upon something existent and actual, and, consequently, in the existence of the nec-

---

[11] *Monadology,* n. 40. Translated by Dr. George R. Montgomery, in *Discourse on Metaphysics, Correspondence with Arnauld and Monadology,* 2nd ed. (Chicago, The Open Court Co., 1918), p. 259.

[12] *Ibid., Monad.,* n. 41, p. 260.

[13] *Ibid., Monad.,* n. 42, p. 260.

[14] *Ibid., Monad.,* n. 43, p. 260. Italics added.

essary Being, in whom essence includes existence or *in whom possibility is sufficient to produce actuality.* [15]

Notice this conclusion. Whatever is real in the possibility of things has its source in God. In God, divine essence includes existence. Whatever is real in his essence, whatever is possible in his being, is, for God, actual existence. That is, in the necessary Being, possibility is sufficient to produce actuality. So that, if God is possible, he must actually exist. And this is precisely what Leibniz now proceeds to say, and the statement is for him an *a priori* proof of God's existence.

Therefore God alone (or the Necessary Being) has this prerogative that if he be possible he must necessarily exist, and, as nothing is able to prevent the possibility of that which involves no bounds, no negation, no contradiction, this alone is sufficient to establish *a priori* his existence. [16]

Spinoza has pretty much the same argument in his *Ethics.* [17]

Here, then, is the way Leibniz has argued: A necessary Being, that is, one which has no imperfection whatsoever, is possible. But if a necessary Being is possible, it exists. For in a completely perfect Being, the reality of its possibility is one with the reality of its existence, since its essence includes that existence. Hence, the necessary Being necessarily exists.

Perhaps the argument of Leibniz will become even clearer if we ask ourselves two questions: first, is the essence or reality of man, a rational animal, possible? Yes, since no contradiction is involved in these notes. Can I conclude from the essence or reality of man that man actually exists? No, since the essence of man, not being infinite perfection, does not include necessary existence. Now let us ask our second question: is the essence or reality of God, an infinitely perfect Being, possible? Yes, since infinite perfection, a being without limits, is not a contradiction. Can I conclude from the possibility of such an essence to its actual exist-

[15] *Ibid., Monad.,* n. 44, p. 260. Italics added.
[16] *Ibid., Monad.,* n. 45, pp. 260-261.
[17] See *Ethics* and "De Intellectus Emendatione," ed. E. Rhys in Everyman's Library (New York, E. P. Dutton & Co., 1910), I, def. 1 and 6, prop. 11, pp. 7-10.

ence? Yes, since a being without limits includes within itself the perfection of actual existence. Since this necessary Being is possible, it must necessarily exist.

Notice we are asking these questions within the framework of Leibniz's own metaphysics, which is a pure essentialism, where not only is existence considered simply as another formal perfection, but where there is also a primacy of essence over existence. The act or source of the reality of a being was not for Leibniz its act of existence, but its essence. And that is why he could speak, which would be nonsense to a Thomist, about the "possibility of the being of God," apart from its existence, and of God as one "in whom possibility is sufficient to produce actuality."

4. Leibniz's Argument Rejected

What are we to say about this argument of Leibniz? First of all, insofar as Leibniz has found the source of the reality of contingent beings in the influence of the necessary Being, he claims to have given us an *a posteriori* proof for God's existence. "But a little while ago we also proved it (God's existence) *a posteriori*, because contingent beings exist which can have their ultimate and sufficient reason only in the necessary being, which, in turn, has the reason for existence in itself." [18] We have no quarrel with this proof. In point of fact, certain analyses of contingencies and series of contingencies that Leibniz has made immediately prior to his *a priori* proof, have furnished him with his notion of a necessary Being. Our quarrel is with the proof as Leibniz intended it: as a sufficient, self-contained *a priori* proof, that is to say, a proof independent of experience and of contingent existents, a proof that argues solely from the notion of the possibility of a necessary Being to its necessary existence.

But must we not admit that God's existence is possible? Yes, but only in the sense we have explained earlier; namely, considering the sensible and material beings of our experience and the fact that the intellect knows and understands being, there is no

[18] *Monad.*, n. 45, p. 261. Words in parentheses added.

reason why, if given the proper evidence, the intellect of man cannot conclude to the existence of some superior being. But this is not Leibniz's question. When he asks in his argument, is God possible? he is not talking about the possibility of proving the truth of the proposition, God exists; rather, he is asking about the possibility of the Being of God himself. And his answer is that since God is without *limits*, is necessary, not only is he possible, but this possibility of his Being includes the necessary existence of his Being. All of which begs the question. For until we have proved that there is a God, it is a fallacy to say that he is without limits, is necessary, infinitely perfect, and so on. The Being of God may be possible, but the only legitimate way the mind *comes to understand this* is by its knowledge of actually existing beings. [19] Because some things are, the mind knows that others could be, and that there may be a God or a supreme Being. Our rejection of Leibniz, Descartes, St. Anselm, and of every other philosopher whose argument for the existence of God closes its eyes to the existence of things, is always the same: if we are to know or talk about being, we must know and talk about the *existence* of things (and not about our notions); for the act of being is "to be." We cannot *begin* with a notion of God and then conclude to the existence of God; all we can conclude to is the existence of our *notion*.

5. Conclusion

The foregoing arguments of Descartes and Leibniz, with their variant forms in other essentialistic thinkers, have been given different names in the history of philosophy. They have been called, for example, the ontological argument, in the Wolffian and Kantian sense of ontological, namely, any cognition that is prior to and independent of experience. For much the same reasons they are also simply called *a priori* arguments. But strictly speaking, since a true *a priori* argument goes from cause to effect, and since God has no cause, some call such arguments *quasi a priori* or *a simul-*

---

[19] This is also the way Leibniz came to understand it, as is clear from what we have seen in nos. 42, 43, and 44 of *The Monadology*.

taneo; that is to say, they proceed from a consideration that is immediately and necessarily linked with the existence of God, which existence is thus simultaneously inferred. For example, from the notion of infinite perfection we infer actual existence as "part of" or linked to this perfection; in much the same way as from the immateriality of the human soul we can immediately infer its immortality.

Because of our critique of these invalid arguments for the existence of God, proofs that try to go from the existence of a concept to the reality of an existential act, or from existence as conceptualized to existence as exercised, we are in a position to see what a valid demonstration of God's existence must contain. First of all, it must begin with the existence of extra-mental beings, for we want to prove that God exists, not that we think he exists. Secondly, it must begin with beings other than God, for to begin with some statement about God or some perfection of God is to beg the whole question; when we ask whether God exists, we cannot begin with something that in the order of *knowledge* already presupposes that existence. Thus our demonstration of God's existence, to be valid, must begin with the material and sensible beings of our experience. Our whole proof is to show that such beings are, as a matter of fact, not just beings, but effects; effects of some one supreme Being who alone could be here and now the proper cause of their act of existence. Thus our demonstration is *a posteriori,* following and depending upon our experience of things, going from effect to the cause of the effect. So that any valid demonstration of God's existence has three steps: first, an existential fact; secondly, seeing this existential fact in a new light, namely, as an effect; thirdly, the concluding to, or inferring, of the existence of what alone could have produced such an effect, the first cause of being, which we call God.

Agnosticism

The problem of agnosticism is an important one and deserves some serious treatment. Understanding in some measure the positions and the arguments of these thinkers, we will be better disposed to appreciate the difficulties involved in any demonstration of the existence of God and the things we must ourselves guard against in establishing our own arguments. St. Thomas has said [1] that the demonstration of God's existence is the whole foundation of the science of sacred theology. And we might add that the whole of general metaphysics is the foundation for the demonstration of God's existence. It is against the background of this general Thomistic metaphysics that we will investigate the positions of the agnostics, seeing wherein they have erred. It would, however, be foolish to pretend that the discussion here of these positions is either exhaustive or their refutation completely critical. This is impossible in an introductory text to natural theology. We will simply state these positions and indicate how, from the standpoint of our own metaphysics, such positions are false.

Etymologically, the word "agnostic" (*a gignosco*) means one who professes ignorance or a lack of knowledge. Historically, it was the English biologist, Thomas Huxley, in the year 1869, who first proposed the use of this word in its modern sense.

"Having reached the estate of man, Huxley discovered one day that he was no longer a Christian, but a free-thinker. 'The majority of my contemporaries,' he said, 'thought that they had arrived at a certain gnosis and claimed to have solved the problem of exist-

[1] *C.G.*, Bk. I, Ch. 9, end.

ence. For my part, I was perfectly sure that I knew nothing about this subject, being well convinced that the problem is insoluble. And since I had Hume and Kant on my side, I did not believe myself presumptuous in holding to my opinion.' Huxley joined the Metaphysical Society, a club where each member professed some definite system. Wishing to show the difference between his own thought and the philosophical and theological views of those who pretended to know so many of the things of which he was ignorant, it seemed to him that the epithet 'The Agnostic' would be most suitable." [2]

Thus the word "agnosticism" has come to mean in modern times that doctrine which professes that the human intellect is incapable of reaching a knowledge of anything immaterial, and in particular, of God and divine things.

There is a twofold agnosticism, the Agnosticism of Unbelief and the Agnosticism of Belief. The former states that concerning God man can know absolutely nothing, not even whether he exists or does not exist. It is simply beyond the capacity of the human intellect to give any answer whatsoever to the question of whether or not there corresponds anything in reality to what we call God. Of course, there *may* exist some corresponding reality to this notion of ours, but we can never know it. Thus these men profess agnosticism, not atheism; but their agnosticism is one of unbelief in this sense, that they will not hold the existence of this unknowable reality on faith, or for any other extrinsic reason. Another name for this doctrine is *pure* agnosticism.

The Agnosticism of Belief, or *dogmatic* agnosticism, likewise professes to know nothing about God. But this doctrine maintains that to the idea men have of God there does exist some corresponding reality, but they maintain the existence of this reality on purely subjective or dogmatic grounds. No rational arguments can be given to prove this existence; for any such arguments must tell us something about the nature of God, whereas this nature is simply unknowable to human understanding. And yet these ag-

[2] Quoted from the article, "Agnosticisme," by Chossat, in the *Dict. Apol.*, col. 1.

nostics do blindly assert the existence of God for some non-rational motive: need, feeling, and so on. [3]

A. THE HISTORICAL PREDECESSORS
OF MODERN AGNOSTICISM

1. Moses Maimonides

There have always been agnostics in the history of thought. One of the most famous of these was Moses Maimonides, the "Plato of the Jews," who died in the year 1204. This theologian, philosopher and physician held as valid the classical *a posteriori* proofs for the existence of God; and so his agnosticism is not concerned with God's existence, but with our knowledge of his nature. Reacting against the literal interpretation of the Jews concerning the divine attributes that are mentioned in Holy Scripture and against the anthropomorphisms of the Talmud, Maimonides taught that the human mind can know absolutely nothing positive about the nature of God. Here all our knowledge is either simply negative or completely relative. For example, when I say that God is good, either I mean that he is not evil, or that the good that I find in things has been put there by God. But I know nothing positive about God himself; "good" is simply an extrinsic name that I can apply to God, since he is not evil and is the cause of good.

Maimonides' doctrine on our knowledge of God can be found in his book, *The Guide for the Perplexed.* Not all historians agree that this Jewish Rabbi was a real agnostic. Sertillanges, for example, in his book, *Agnosticisme ou Anthropomorphisme* (Paris, 1809), will not admit it. Chossat, on the other hand, in his article on agnosticism quoted above, maintains that all the arguments advanced by the modern agnostics can be found in the doctrine of Maimonides. The Dominican, Penido, in his important book, *Le Rôle de l'Analogie en Théologie dogmatique* (Paris, 1931, pp. 125-131), steers a middle course, saying that Maimonides was not an agnostic in intention, but only in his expressions. As we have seen, St. Thomas himself interpreted Maimonides in an or-

---

[3] See Gisquière, *Deus Dominus* (Paris, Beauchesne, 1950), p. 30.

thodox sense, where in an important article [4] he gives the philosophical foundations for Maimonides' point of view and shows how that point of view can be easily corrected according to Maimonides' own principles. But in any event, the arguments of this Jewish medieval philosopher are the same as those sometimes used by modern agnostics to bolster their own doctrine.

2. The Philosophy of Nominalism. William of Ockham

In the history of philosophy, the two men probably most responsible for the agnosticism of the modern mind are William of Ockham and Immanuel Kant. Before the introduction of the metaphysics of Aristotle into the Western world, logic or dialectics had been a sort of surrogate for philosophy, a simple instrument of understanding waiting for the day when it could give way to philosophy. But after the metaphysics of Aristotle (especially as interpreted by Averroes and the Averroists) was considered by the theologians to have failed as a philosophical light to aid in the understanding of faith, dialectics again reasserted itself. But now in the hands of Ockham (ca. 1300–1350), logic attains the status of a full-blown philosophical system. It was really Peter Abelard who, two centuries before (ca. 1070–1142), had set the stage for the eventual appearance of Ockham and the philosophy of Nominalism. For it was Abelard who reduced logic to nominalism, substituting a logic of words for a logic of the concept.

In Abelard, what corresponded to the universality of the concept was the meaning of a word, and not anything actually or virtually intelligible in the thing itself outside the mind. The step from the logical nominalism of Abelard to the philosophical nominalism of Ockham was an easy and natural one. And with William of Ockham and other thinkers in the latter part of the thirteenth century, we come to the *via moderna,* the modern way, the way of Nominalism in philosophy. And this *via moderna* will everywhere oppose itself to the *via antiqua* of Thomas Aquinas and Duns Scotus and the first part of the thirteenth century. By the *via antiqua* was meant the old way of philosophical realism. Ock-

[4] *In I Sent.,* d. 2, qu. 1, a. 3.

ham, with his razor, will play havoc not only with metaphysical reality but with metaphysical demonstration. And that is why his influence on the science of natural theology can hardly be exaggerated. Unfortunately, our treatment of his position here must be brief, but at least we should see enough of his position to understand what it entails for the science we are studying. [5]

The proposition that dominates Ockham's philosophy is the following: "Every positive thing existing outside the mind is by that very fact singular." Ockham was not the first to posit this proposition, but he was the first to carry out all its consequences to their logical conclusion. St. Thomas had said that whatever was in Socrates was individuated, and in this he was following Aristotle, who had taught that no universal *as such* could possibly exist outside the mind. But for St. Thomas, a material existent was not individuated in its own right, by the very fact that it existed, but by a *principle of individuation*. Ockham's proposition is: "whatever is in the singular, is singular"; which is a different position from St. Thomas's. That is to say, according to Ockham anything outside the intellect is individual precisely insofar as it is real, and not by any principle of individuation that it possesses. Now to be singular as real, to be individual as real, is to be irreducibly singular, irreducibly individual. Whence it follows that a universal has *absolutely no reality* outside the intellect. Ockham rejects both the common nature of Avicenna and Scotus and the potential universality of Aristotle and St. Thomas; no universality whatsoever exists in the thing. Let us see what the doctrine of Ockham is.

A singular is that which is one and not many. This singular may be a sign *pointing out* a plurality, but even then, in itself, it remains a singular. Insofar as there are such signs in the mind, I may call this sign a universal; but it is in no way universal in its being, but only in its signification. It is as singular in its existence in the mind as is any singular thing outside the mind.

Such signs are of two kinds, natural and arbitrary. To understand the philosophical nominalism of Ockham, we have only to

[5] The student is urged to read what Gilson has written on Ockham in his *History of Christian Philosophy in the Middle Ages, op. cit.*, pp. 487–497.

understand his notion of a natural sign. A natural sign is a concept, something that has been conceived or produced by the mind. It exists in the mind even before we utter it by the medium of a word. The proof that such signs are natural is that they are the same for all minds. Take a simple example. Different languages have different words to designate what in English we call a dog; for example, *Hund, canis, chien,* and so forth. Wherever dogs exist there is a name for them. The name we may give this notion "dog" differs from language to language, but no matter what the country or language, people form the same natural notion when they see a dog. Such a notion is a natural sign, since this notion or mental image can apply to all dogs. So we call these notions or natural signs *universals,* that is, one singular notion that can signify many different individuals. But when I designate this mental image, this universal sign, by a word, the *word* I use is arbitrary. Thus all words are arbitrary signs. And since language is arbitrary or conventional, we have a plurality of languages; but because the images they designate are facts of nature, these are the same for all people.

Now a universal has no other reality, no other being, than that of an act of the intellect. It is real because it exists in the mind, it is an accident of the mind, and more specifically, a quality. It is something made, produced; hence, I can call it a *fictum.* But it is not a *fictio,* for it is not arbitrary, but natural. Just as smoke is not an arbitrary but a natural sign for fire, so these concepts are natural signs of things. Groaning is a natural sign for pain, laughter is a natural sign for joy. So, too, our mental notions or images, naturally caused in us by the objects, are natural products of the intellect acting in a determined way in the presence of an object; consequently, they are apt to signify this object.

What Ockham has done here is to reduce the universal concept to an act of the understanding, [6] to which there corresponds noth-

[6] Hence in Ockham there is no distinction between the concept, which he calls a *nomen mentale* (hence, the name, *nominalism*), and the act of understanding, which he calls *actus intelligendi. Quodlibeta septem,* Paris, 1487, (Quodl. IV, 19). The student should be familiar with St. Thomas's distinction between the act of understanding and the concepts formed by that act.

ing of universality in the thing, not even virtual or potential universality. It is a singular act which naturally stands for some singular thing. Here are his words: "The intellection by which I understand man is the natural sign of man, just as groaning is the sign of sickness, of sadness, or of pain, and such a sign can stand for men in mental propositions, just as a word can stand for things in vocal propositions." (See Gilson, *op. cit.*, p. 492.) Scotus and Thomas Aquinas were both laboring under a common delusion. Scotus put distinct formalities in the thing, which formalities corresponded nicely to the universal concept I had of them. St. Thomas put some kind of virtual intelligibility in the thing, which by the operation of abstraction became formally universal; hence, there was some sort of intelligible correspondence between the *content* of my concept and the *reality* of the individual. Ockham will have none of this. He does not believe in "something common" that makes Socrates resemble Plato more than he resembles a monkey. Of course, Socrates *does* resemble Plato more than a monkey, but they do not resemble each other by a *resemblance*, by any common intelligibility in them, but simply by being what they are: *sufficit quod per seipsos plus conveniunt*.

In trying to find a reason why so many illustrious philosophers have been deluded into placing some common intelligibility in things, Ockham decides that it is due to a false notion of relation. Two existing men are seen to be alike, and so these philosophers put within them a real relation, a relation of likeness. But a relation is not something real in the things. If we reflect, says Ockham, we will discover that the relations that exists between individual men is simply the word *man* which we predicate of them.

The all-important conclusion of Ockham's philosophy of nominalism is this: every signification is about singulars. Real universality has been exterminated. Only the singular exists and only the singular is signified. But a singular can be signified in two ways, either confusedly or distinctly. And this because there are two ways a singular can be known, confusedly and distinctly. What is a confused concept of a thing? A confused concept is a mental image which does not allow us to distinguish its object from other similar objects. An example of such a confused concept or mental image is that which we designate by the word *man*. For this image does not represent distinctly the singular Socrates or the singular Plato.

What follows from this? That the concept designated by the word *man* has, of itself, no signification at all. When I think *man*, I am simply thinking of my own mental image, and that concept has no signification except the signification of itself. It points to no reality, since all reality is singular. But if I see Socrates, I form a distinct concept of him, and consequently the term that stands for what I see, really stands for a concept that signifies some *thing*. Since only singulars can be signified, when I predicate the general of the particular, for example, when I say *Socrates is a man*, I am simply predicating the singular confusedly known of the singular distinctly known. The predication *Socrates is a man* signifies that Socrates distinctly known is Socrates confusedly known.

Since there is no real universality in things, not even virtual universality, since the singular is simply a singular, no abstraction of universality is possible. Hence there is no such thing as an agent intellect in man. What we call the agent intellect is simply the soul as affected directly by the natural presence of the sense object. Universality as such is merely the knowledge of the singular as confused knowledge. That is to say, once I have had a direct intuition of a sense object, and that object is now absent, I can recall it only in a confused or universal fashion.

a. Conclusion

We have gone into some detail in presenting the position of Ockham, the Father of nominalism, because of the devastating consequences that this doctrine has for the science of natural theology, and in fact for all scientific knowledge. It is now time to see some of these consequences. Since we have no intuition of God in this world, we can have no abstract knowledge of him either. All knowledge of God is impossible. Nor is this all. Reason or demonstration can never get beyond the immediate evidence of sense experience; so reason cannot demonstrate with certitude the existence of God. This becomes all the more obvious if we realize that since there is nothing common in beings, nor any universality whatsoever in reality, if we remember that reality is made up of a number of irreducible singulars, there exists nothing *in things* by which the mind can make any *inference* from finite to infinite being. For example, the mind intuits existential events: fire burning a log, sun melting the snow, this rock crushing my foot. But it does not intuit any *principle of causality* in these events, any relationship between fire and burning log, sun and melting snow, rock and my crushed foot. And since for Ockham intuition is the only way we can grasp objective reality, the principle of causality is a mere subjective reality, a relation existing only in the mind, induced there by habit or custom.

Ockham will allow us the knowledge of the individual existent, which is the first step in our demonstration for God's existence. But his philosophy of nominalism precludes the second step: seeing that existent in a new light, as a real effect; that is to say, a being possessing in itself a real existential ordering, a real relation to some other being, because of which relation I can legitimately conclude to the existence of that other being. For if Ockham is right, if the reality of a relation is solely in the mind, then I cannot use it to infer anything about existing things. Descartes, by beginning with the postulate that only himself as a thinking substance existed, made all science of *things* impossible. Ockham, by postulating that a thing is singular has made all *science* of things impossible. For if the existing singular is in *no way* universal, there can be no scientific knowledge of that thing. For all scientific knowledge is both universal (it tells us what is common to many singulars) and a knowledge of things (it tells us something about the thing in itself). Descartes imprisoned himself in his own thinking; Ockham has imprisoned things in an unintelligible and impervious singularity.

The influence of William of Ockham on modern thought can hardly be exaggerated. Gilson calls him the sorcerer's apprentice. [7]

[7] *Op. cit.*, p. 498.

He released forces and ideas, that once released, he could not control. To him we owe agnosticism in theology, and empiricism and skepticism in philosophy. His indeed is the *via moderna,* the modern way. And the philosophical step from the irreducible singular of Ockham to the noumenon of Immanuel Kant will be a short and easy one.

3. The Pseudo-Mystics and the "Reformation"

The Nominalism of Ockham gave rise to an extreme skepticism in philosophy. Plagued by this skepticism and seeing no philosophical answer to it, many began to seek a knowledge of their creator in religious and mystical experiences. It may be perfectly true that genuine mystical union yields the soul an experiential knowledge of God that is higher and different from that knowledge gained through unaided reason meditating upon creatures. But such pseudo-mystics as Michael Molinos in Spain (1628–1696) and Jacob Boehme in Germany (1595–1624) taught that this was the *only kind* of valid knowledge of God that was accessible to man. All purely rational knowledge of God was to be rejected as invalid or merely subjective. God makes himself known to the soul only in mystical experience. The soul is the image of God. And God, working and operating in this image as in a mirror, is grasped in his divine operation. In understanding this term of the divine influence, this operation within the soul, man comes to some knowledge of God. All rational knowledge, based on our knowledge of creatures, is not a knowledge of God, but of something else: of our own ideas, of other creatures, and so forth. As we shall see, this teaching has had its influence on modern agnosticism.

Finally, before we take up the study of modern agnosticism itself, we should at least say a word about the influence of the Protestant Reformation on human reason in its relation to God. *Intellectum valde ama,* St. Augustine had pleaded. Love your intelligence with a great love. But the reformers, and especially Luther himself, taught us to despise and condemn reason. [8] In

[8] See Jacques Maritain, *Three Reformers* (London. Sheed & Ward, 1928), pp. 3-50.

their doctrine, original sin has made of human nature a depraved thing, and man's reason is no longer light, but unsavory darkness. Only through God's revelation, and the religious experience that accompanies it, can man have any knowledge of God. Protestantism, like nominalism, has made enormous inroads upon the human intelligence. One has only to read the writings of the contemporary Protestant theologian Karl Barth to understand that this fight against reason still goes on. Barth professes a total agnosticism as regards man's natural knowledge of God. Sin has made such knowledge impossible. Only through revelation, that is to say, through the intervention of God in the reading of the Scriptures, is knowledge of God possible. [9] This theologian calls the scholastic theory of an analogous knowledge of God through creatures the invention of the devil, and this was pretty much the sentiment of Martin Luther himself. [10]

B. THE MODERN AGNOSTICS

1. Pure Agnosticism

a. The Subjective Empiricism of David Hume

David Hume (1711–1776), the Scottish philosopher and historian, taught that all man's knowledge consists of perceptions, which fall into two classes: impressions and ideas. These have their origin in sensible experience, but while impressions are the first and vivid products of the mind, our ideas enjoy a derivitive or inferred character and can be manipulated and ordered among themselves by the imagination, according to the "law of association."

What we know are our *perceptions*, not external reality. What we know is a fact of *consciousness*, not something existing outside that consciousness. We are aware of our perceptions, not of things. And these are subjective modifications produced in us by sensible experience. The second thing to note is that there is no way we can infer the existence of things outside us. We cannot say, for ex-

[9] Barth, *La confession de foi de L'Église* (Neuchâtel-Paris, 1943), p. 12.
[10] See Gisquière, *Deus Dominus, op. cit.*, p. 33 and note 47.

ample, "Our perceptions have been produced or caused by things; therefore things exist." For we have no perception of a cause. All that we experience, all that we perceive, are *successive* sensations: we see (sense) the flame of the match, the cigarette moving into the flame, then the sensation of the burning cigarette; three successive sensations of flame, movement, and burning. And that is all. We don't experience any *intrinsic connection* between these sensations, nor any *necessity* for such a connection. What, then, is this principle of causality that so many philosophers think they *know*? It is a mere subjective product of habit. We have gotten so used to seeing things burn when placed in fire that we say the fire *causes* the burning. But since we do not sense this causing, causality is a figment of the imagination. Thus, for Hume, there is no way that we can admit there is anything real, or anything objectively existing outside the states of our consciousness. For him, the real existence of things was an hypothesis incapable of being verified, a postulate that can neither be proved nor disproved.

One obvious conclusion from all this is that it is impossible to prove the existence of God, for it is impossible to prove the existence of anything. The way of causality is precluded, since causality has no objective value. Why, then, do so many people have an idea of God? Well, why do they have an idea of causality? God, too, is a product of our imagination; something we have "made up" out of our many sense impressions. It has its psychological value and use, as do so many of the other things created by our imagination. But the real existence or non-existence of God is outside our power to know. Hume did not want to be an atheist. He recognized the utility of religious faith in our private and public lives. Of course, a supernatural religion was pure phantasy, and even "natural religion" had no experiential or rational foundation.

The refutation of Humean empiricism is properly and scientifically the task of epistemology. Here we can do no more than indicate his error. The existence of things is not an hypothesis or a postulate, that is to say, something that we *assume* since we cannot prove it. An hypothesis, or assumption, is something that here and now we can neither prove or disprove; for example, that Red

China will be in the United Nations by 1961. We can assume that she will be, but we cannot prove it. Nor can we prove that she will not. If in 1961, she is in the United Nations, then we are no longer dealing with an assumption, but with a *fait accompli*. Now the existents of our experience are *faits accomplis*. They are not assumed; they are given. Of course, they cannot be proved, because they need no proof; they are self-evident. We begin with things because things are there to begin with. And we judge that they exist, because they do exist.

Moreover, the knowing subject, the one who knows and judges things, is a *man*, a unified composite of intellect and sense, not a being who merely senses, but a being who simultaneously senses and understands. And the first judgment that man makes about the things he senses is that they exist. Existents force themselves upon man's senses, and in sensing them with his senses he judges them with his intellect. He judges that they are, that they exist. We agree with Hume that existence cannot be *sensed*, but we disagree with him that it cannot be known. For the existence of things is a fact, an intelligible fact. The senses carry a message of which they may be unaware, but which the intelligence of man knows and asserts: that the things which he senses *are*. Hume has simply closed his eyes to the actual function of the intellect.

b. The Positivism of Auguste Comte

"The present day position of the problem of God is wholly dominated by the thought of Immanuel Kant and Auguste Comte." [11] Positivism is one of those "weasel words" so dear to the heart of contemporary thinkers. There is logical positivism, empirical positivism, psychological positivism, sociological positivism, and just plain positivism. What is philosophical positivism, or positivistic philosophy? In general, it is that doctrine which teaches that man can know only sensible phenomena and the laws of these phenomena. He can know sensible material things, the laws that govern them and the connections that obtain among them. But no more. Man can know no object that is suprasensible, or spiritual.

[11] E. Gilson, *God and Philosophy, op. cit.,* p. 109.

And since sensible things are continually changing, man cannot know any absolute truth.

A positivist is not an atheist, but an agnostic. As the French positivist, Littré, once wrote: "Positive philosophy does not accept Atheism . . . Those who believe that positive philosophy either denies or affirms anything at all about first causes or final ends, are mistaken. Such philosophy neither affirms nor denies these things. For to deny them or to affirm them would be to say that one has some knowledge of the origin of things and of their end." [12] It is interesting to note, however, that while professing themselves to be agnostics, they nevertheless maintain that they can adequately explain the historical origin of all religion and belief in God without any appeal to a suprasensible object, as we shall see in a moment.

The father of positivism is Auguste Comte (1789–1857). Our only interest in discussing his doctrine here is to see its implications for the science of natural theology. Thus we shall trace briefly the law of his three stages, by which the positivistic temper of mind is achieved and all knowledge of God's existence or nature abolished. [13] At the beginning of his six volume work, *Cours de Philosophie*, Comte gives the reader his famous law of the three states or stages. This law can be stated briefly as follows: human knowledge, whether we trace its development in a single individual or in the human race taken as a whole, passes through three stages, the theological, metaphysical, and the positivistic, this last being the perfect and definitive state for human cognition.

In the first or primitive state of human knowledge (the theological state), man seeks to know the nature and causes of sensible phenomena but has no scientific method to help him know what these phenomena are in themselves. So he uses his imagination, projecting his own emotions and ideas into these phenomena, either vesting them with life and understanding, or at least re-

[12] *Paroles de philosophie positive,* pp. 31 ff.
[13] The student should confer, Etiènne Gilson, *Unity of Philosophical Experience* (New York, Charles Scribner's Sons, 1952), pp. 248–270; Gisquière, *Deus Dominus, op. cit.,* pp. 36–39.

ferring them to an extrinsic and transcendent cause that, like himself, has an intellect and will. This is the stage of the personal gods and spirits, the theological stage. At its most primitive, the theological stage is fetishism; at its best development it is monotheism, especially as found in the Christian religion.

In the second stage, where the child becomes the adolescent, man depersonalizes his gods and becomes a metaphysician. Gods now become causes, abstract essences, ontological beings, separate substances, or just Nature. In this intermediate stage, man is still using his imagination, but his explanation of phenomena is now natural rather than supernatural. Here the perfect development of metaphysical knowledge is pantheism, where all reality is synthesized in a single Being.

Forced by the very tensions and contradictions that he sees between the theological and metaphysical explanation of phenomena, man enters into the third stage of thinking. He sees that he must no longer ask himself questions about the ultimate causes of what he observes, but simply limit himself to what is observed. He now understands that the unobservable is the unknowable. He becomes of age. He is a Positivist. The solicitude for final answers is still there. But the positivist recognizes in this solicitude a carry over from the other stages. And so he dismisses it as the lingering of a bad dream, as a temptation of his youth.

Human knowledge is today in this positivist stage, the perfect and definitive stage for man, where he has learned to dismiss vain and speculative disputations and to stick to the observable facts. Of course, there is still theological and metaphysical thinking going on; the three stages have always some co-existence with each other. But the positivist spirit is in the ascendancy, and the other two stages are destined to become weaker and weaker and to disappear. Man must finally become just man, and thinking just scientific, that is, positive. Here the perfect science is sociology (a term coined by Comte), and the perfect religion the religion of humanity. For there is to be religion, and lots of it, in Comte's third state. Comte surrounded his Religion of Humanity with all the practices and ceremonies of organized religion: a priesthood, holy-days, rituals, and so forth.

Comte tried to prove that his law of the three states was verified in the actual history of the human race as also, more or less, in the individual history of every man. Children are easily satisfied with fantastic, that is, transcendental or "theological" explanations of reality, and youth is always asking the "why" of things and is en-cumbered with metaphysical illusions. Only the adult, having learned his lesson, prudently stays within the bounds of observa-ble phenomena and the laws of these phenomena, leaving use-less speculation to others.

c. Rejection of Comte's Three States

What are we to say about Comte's three states of human knowl-edge? The least we can say is that his theory is not good positivism, for it does little justice to the observable facts. For example, the religion of primitive man was vitiated by much superstition; but as man developed his intelligence, only the superstition was dropped, religion itself becoming more profound and purified. The two are, observably, not the same. Then, too, there have been profound philosophers who also had a passion for careful scien-tific investigation of observable phenomena, people like Aristotle and St. Albert the Great. History on many scores contradicts Comte, showing his theory of the three states to be arbitrary and *a priori*.

Furthermore, the normal development of a man is hardly the way Comte describes it. Little children delight in observable phe-nomena, but they are hardly inclined of themselves to give to these a religious explanation. Religious instruction and/or fairy tales must be furnished by the parents. And if callow youth has any metaphysical inclinations, it certainly succeeds in hiding them. Finally, even some excellent scientists become religiously devout in their declining years; and some men are known to have gone from the knowledge and love of science to the knowledge and love of philosophy. The historical horror of it is that since the day Comte proclaimed the advent of the third state, metaphysics has grown in stature. In point of fact, very few positivists today admit the validity of Comte's three states. What they do hold as valid is the positivist attitude of mind, the refusal to admit any knowledge that goes beyond observable phenomena and the laws that govern them. This position we will discuss now in the agnosticism of Immanuel Kant.

2. Dogmatic Agnosticism

a. The Transcendental Idealism of Kant

The system of Kant "is a fundamental sensism, mixed with an artificial conceptualism, surmounted by a pure idealism, and flanked by a moralism held on trust, with a religious postulate." [14]

Kant likened his bold departure from the traditional theory of knowledge to the Copernican revolution in astronomy. Copernicus turned astronomy upside down by showing that the sun and not the earth was the center of the universe. And Kant will try to show that the mind does not revolve around some object, copying this object and recording it in thought. Rather, the mind itself constitutes its object, determining and distinguishing it as it synthesizes within its consciousness the formless manifold of reality.

To understand what this means and why it must be so, let us place ourselves for a few moments in the Kantian universe and see how knowledge works. Obviously, reality is no object for us outside our consciousness. We can imagine reality in itself as a formless sea of undifferentiated sensuous data. Confronting this sea, which is content without form, is the mind of man. Now what does it mean to know, to have a "theoretical," that is, *de facto* knowledge of the world? It means not merely to receive this manifold, for as such it is meaningless, but to impose form upon it, so that it can become a real object of knowledge and understanding. Hence, the Kantian mind is at once a center of receptivity and of selective and distinguishing activity. The multiplicity of unformed sense impressions furnishes the mind with the raw material from which to construct its objects, which now become phenomena,

[14] Deschamps, *Le Génie des religions* (Paris, 1923), p. 173.

which now "appear" as *something* to be grasped in understanding. Reality, the "thing-in-itself" is trans-objective, a-spatial, a-temporal. It is the mind that objectifies reality, spatializes it and puts it in time.

And the mind can do this, for it has within itself organizing forms or principles of apprehension, that is to say, it has the ability to engage in an *a priori* synthesis whereby a unified and co-ordinated experience of phenomena is made possible. This synthesis is *a priori*, since it is necessary for the very possibility of an intelligible experience, and it is a synthesis, for it adds form to the raw material of reality. For example, we can experience an event simply as an event in time and space, or we can think of that same event as *caused*. In the latter case we have organized our object further, synthesized it with the *a priori* form of understanding called "effect."

There is no need here to go into detail as to the various ways the mind constitutes and organizes its objects. But one or two comments are necessary for our purpose. There are two *a priori* forms of sensibility: space and time. These forms apply to all our experience, since that experience is limited to our sensibility. The point to notice is that space and time have no reality apart from the sensibility of the thinking subject. The "thing-in-itself" *is* not in space or in time; rather, it is given to the mind as in space and time *because of* the natural and necessary function of our own sensibility.

The second thing to be noted is that the *a priori* forms of *understanding*, such as, for example, the categories of cause and effect, substance and attribute, whole and part, enable us to organize further the manifold of sense impressions. Because of these categories of understanding, which are simply the innate élan of the mind in its noetic activity, we can now give to the objects we have related in space and time a further relevance; a relevance that is trans-spatial and trans-temporal. We can understand the object now as caused, or as substance, or as part, or as whole, and so forth.

The student should begin to see why the noetic system of Kant is called transcendental idealism. Transcendental here is opposed to empiric; for we do not find our object of understanding ready made in reality, only awaiting our passive contemplation of it. Rather the object *transcends*, is other than and different from, the formless sea of manifold sense impressions which we can say constitutes reality. And Kant's noetic is an idealism, because what is added to reality, making it an object of thought, a phenomenon, is due to the activity of our own minds.

Kant is very careful to establish the necessity of his categories. That the mind is more than a mere passive spectator, that it has a spontaneity and activity that goes out after things and fashions them "for knowledge," he believes obvious from the way we formulate our questions about things. We ask questions in a way that can be answered. How often a teacher will say to a student, "The way you ask that question makes no sense, but if you put the matter this way. . . ." This, concludes Kant, indicates the *a priori* orientation of our mental activity, the presence of *a priori* categories of understanding. To eliminate the categories of understanding is to render impossible all noetic experience and all theoretical knowledge.

1) *Kant and Man's Knowledge of God.* It is not hard to see what happens in such a theory of knowledge to man's ability to know the existence or the nature of God. If all our experience is limited to what is in our sensibility, and if the categories of our understanding can operate only on the objects furnished our understanding in and through the forms of sensibility, then all theoretical knowledge of God is, *ipso facto,* rendered impossible. For God, by definition suprasensible, is not given in the manifold of sense impressions, and so in no way can become for the human mind an object of theoretical knowledge. Of course the mind can form a notion of God and ask many questions about God. And now we know why. The mind is built that way. Because of its categories of understanding (of cause, substance, and so forth), the mind can ask questions about a *first* cause, a *necessary* substance. [15] But no

---

[15] Kant will even allow the utility of our notion of God as a unifying principle of speculative knowledge.

answer can ever be forthcoming. For here the categories are working in a void. The categories can work only on content, and that content must come in and through the forms of sensibility. Just as content without form is unintelligible, so forms without content are empty.

Questions about God are empty questions, for it is impossible to give them an answer in terms of theoretical or speculative knowledge. We can speculate about, organize, co-relate through cause and effect, only objects of experience, and these are strictly limited, for theoretical knowledge, to the phenomena given to the understanding through the forms of sensibility. The mind may never cease trying to apply its *a priori* forms to the suprasensible, but each time it does so, it ends in a contradiction, an "antinomy," a reminder that it is trying the impossible.

Does all this mean that Kant rejects the existence of God? Yes and no. He rejects God's existence as an object of speculative reason, but he reinstates it as a postulate of practical reason. This is the moral flank of his system referred to above by Descamps. But why does Kant do this? That is the question we must now answer.

2) *Kant and Judgments of Feeling.* If one reads Kant's *Critique of Pure Reason* and then turns to his *Critique of Judgment,* one is aware of a deep and unresolved tension, a noetic dichotomy, in the thinking of this philosopher. In this latter work, Kant recognizes as valid two different kinds of awarenesses or assimilations of reality. One we have already discussed, and which we called theoretical or speculative knowledge. But there is also open to man another awareness of reality, a fleeting glimpse of things as a whole, seeing them in their meta-phenomenal unity, their ontological status. Such awareness allows us a momentary vision of the value or purpose or beauty of things. Here we have an esthetic enjoyment of the object, or an appreciation of its moral worth. By such knowledge, for example, we realize the value of the individual, his personal autonomy, and the moral respect we should have for him.

To help the student understand the difference between what

Kant meant by theoretical knowledge and a judgment of feeling, the following analogy may be useful. Suppose we sit down to read a poetic masterpiece, say the *Windhover* of Gerard Manley Hopkins. The words and rhythms and images of the poem may stand in relation to its total meaning and esthetic effect as a theoretical knowledge of an object stands in relation to an esthetic awareness of reality. We can consider the meaning of the different words apart from the meaning of the whole. We can consider the flow and movement of the rhythms apart from the meaning, the imagery apart from the rhythms. All these things are genuine objects of apprehension and knowledge, but none of them are knowledge of the poem itself. Organize or re-organize these elements as we may, the poem as a whole remains unintelligible. For the art-product in itself is an esthetic and meaningful *unit,* and must be grasped as such to be appreciated and enjoyed for what it is in itself. To a mathematician a whole may be equal to the sum of its parts, but to a poet or a philosopher this is never true. A poem, or some reality, is a fusion of parts into a unique whole. To lose its unity is to lose its being. And not to grasp the poem (or some reality) as a unit, is not to grasp it in itself. And so Kant would say that man appreciates beauty and realizes value by his esthetic intelligence; whereas he organizes and systematizes reality by his theoretical intelligence.

The importance of this distinction between these two kinds of knowledge now becomes clear. We grasp in a judgment of feeling, by a fleeting and unaccountable glimpse, our own moral worth and that of other persons. And because of this value judgment, the mind is led to *postulate* human freedom, moral obligation, and the existence of a Necessary Being. In this sense, esthetic intelligence has a certain "speculative" result, in that it prompts us to make these plausible hypotheses about which, however, we know nothing, not even if they are. God is not postulated by Kant as man's final end, or as his father or judge, or even as the principle of moral obligation; but rather as something practically necessary to the carrying out of our moral obligations, so that we may be happy in the doing of our duty. God is a postulate of man's practical reason, posited by man's will, and held on blind faith.

Did Kant, then, really believe in the existence of God? As we have seen, God could not exist for Kant as an object of speculative knowledge; nor, further, could Kant know God by his esthetic intelligence. God is for man neither a phenomenon nor a "thing in itself." Nor can God be inferred from our appreciation of moral value in any *causal sense*. For causal inference is valid only among phenomena. God is not *inferred* by the practical reason, he is *postulated*. He answers a need. So back to our question: Did Kant really believe that the Necessary Being which he postulated had objective existence in reality? How could he? for his faith was blind. Kant *said* there was a God, he might even had *thought* there was a God, but he could not *know* there was a God. Now knowledge through faith is possible, for real faith is an act of our *intellect* moved to assent by the authority of another. We know, for example, that Julius Caesar crossed the Rubicon. That is not a postulate or an hypothesis. It is an historical fact. But we know it only on faith. This is not Kant's faith in God. He postulates God by an act of the will, and so he does not know for sure whether there is a God or not. That is why Kant is a dogmatic agnostic.

3) *Conclusion*. We have no intention of refuting here the philosophical system of Immanuel Kant. [16] The errors of Kant become obvious when the student comes to understand the nature of an existential metaphysics and a realist theory of knowledge that flows from such a metaphysics. Again, the student should be aware by this time, especially from what was said in Chapter 1 about the nature of scientific investigation of sensible phenomena and the philosophical understanding of being, that Kant confused two different orders of knowledge. We agree with Kant that God is not an object of empirical knowledge, but we disagree that the existence of God is not subject to rational demonstration.

To ask the question, "Does God exist?" is to ask a question about

---

[16] For further discussion of Kant's thought, the student is urged to read pages 221 to 246 of Etiènne Gilson's *Unity of Philosophical Experience, op. cit.*, and the truly classic chapter four of *God and Philosophy*, "God and Contemporary thought," *op. cit.*, pp. 109-144.

existence, about being. And so the answer to this question can come only from metaphysics, the science of being. Because Kant's metaphysics was only a physics, it is no wonder that he had to reject the demonstration of God's existence as metaphysically impossible. In establishing our own rational demonstration for the existence of God, we saw that the mind grasps something more in being than "that which is sensible." Here we have explicitly Kant's trouble: namely, to adequate in our knowledge of reality the knowledge of being and the knowledge of what is sensible, or what can be derived from the sensible as such.

If the student does not see that what is at stake here is the very notion of being and the nature of the act of human understanding, he has missed at once both the message of Kant and the message of St. Thomas Aquinas. An actually existing thing is not only sensible, it is intelligible. It has a message not only for the senses of man, but for his intellect. And it is the very *being of things* that speaks this message to the intellect, that provides the evidence that is transparent to our understanding. All this is fundamental, but it is the evident possession of human experience. It is there to see for all those who do not bargain with their human powers, as Newman warned against, but who use them properly and with care.

"Today," writes Gilson, "our only choice is not Kant or Descartes; it is rather Kant or Thomas Aquinas. All other positions are but halfway houses on the roads which lead either to absolute religious agnosticism or to the natural theology of Christian metaphysics." [17] It is always wise to know where our true choices lie. But the really important thing is to know why we make the choices we do. And we should be grateful to Immanuel Kant that he has cleared the field of all lesser breeds. Largely because of him, we see now the importance of the act of existence and the intelligibility exercised by that act upon human knowledge. Kant has made compromise here impossible. As he would say, it is "this or nothing else."

[17] *God and Philosophy, op. cit.,* p. 114.

b. The Sentimentalists

"The heart has its reasons, which reason does not know. . . .
It is the heart which experiences God, and not the reason. This,
then, is faith: God felt by the heart, not by the reason." [18]

A sentimentalist, or one who professes the doctrine of sentimentalism, is a person who maintains that our knowledge of the existence of God, or at least the certitude of that knowledge, is not to
be looked for in some piece of evidence that is grasped and understood by the intellect, but rather in some affective principle or
subjective feeling or sentiment (hence the name *sentimentalism*);
which feeling, though subjective to man, is the objective reason
for holding the existence of God. Sentimentalism was the instinctive religious reply to, and defence against, the empiricism of
Hume and the agnosticism of Kant. There were many sentimentalists both in France and Germany during the last century. Here
we will briefly examine the position of two of these, Maine de
Biran (1766–1824) in France, and Schleiermacher (1768–1834)
in Germany. [19] After this we will make a few observations concerning this doctrine.

Maine de Biran was a fervent Catholic, a convert from atheism.
It seemed obvious to him that man leads a twofold life, and leads
it on two different levels. First of all, there is the lower life of man,
a life that is animal or merely human. Then there is the higher life,
or life of the spirit. It is on this higher level that man experiences
union with God and the effects of that union. This life of the spirit,
the life of the soul in union with God, constitutes man's religious
life, and this religious life constitutes an experience. For our purpose, the two points to be noted in this simple doctrine of Maine
de Biran are: First, the soul and God in this religious experience
are not the object of our intellect (things we know and understand), but objects of faith and love (a presence that we feel).

[18] Pascal, *Pensées*, translated by W. F. Trotter (New York, E. P. Dutton &
Co., 1932), p. 78.
[19] See Ortegat, *Philosophie de la Religion* (Bruxelles-Paris, 1938), pp.
387-392.

Secondly, it is because of this feeling we have toward God that we assert his existence, that we believe he is.

Schleiermacher, on his part, saw that the doctrine of Kant was, practically and logically, atheistic. To guard religion against the attacks of the Kantian reason, to make it safe from the inroads of rationalistic philosophy, Schleiermacher placed the essence of religion in the affective part of man, in his will and emotions which undergo a religious experience. It is true, of course, that religion, that is to say, the sum total of our relationships to God, embraces certain judgments of the intellect, judgments that are both speculative and practical, as well as experiences of an affective nature. But Kant had shown that the objective value of these judgments is at best hypothetical. And so such judgments can in no way be a foundation for any science of religion. But this is neither necessary nor to the point. For the true objects of religious knowledge are our own intimate religious *experiences*. These function as objects in religion, not as demanding some judgment of the intellect about an objective reality extrinsic to man (as Kant would have it), but simply as phenomena of our own internal religious life.

It belongs to theology to investigate these phenomena, to examine carefully their nature and origin, and their influence upon our activity. Theology is, therefore, not a science, but a phenomenology, the phenomenology of our religious consciousness. It is not a science constructed according to the laws of logic aimed at demonstrating and understanding objective truths about God, but a careful description of man's religious experience. Schleiermacher admitted that the traditional formulas of natural theology could be preserved, not, however, as having any rational value or meaning; but as subjective witnesses to the universality and necessity of our religious experience.

Applying these notions to the question of God's existence, Schleiermacher taught that human reason was incapable either of demonstrating God's existence or of understanding his nature. Man, by reason of his "religious sense," his "sense of the infinite," feels and experiences the presence of God and his complete dependence upon God, so that God's existence is held by him solely because of this affection and inclination of his heart and will. [20]

Some Observations. No one will deny, not even those who pride themselves on their "tough-mindedness" in philosophy, the hard core of truth in the doctrine of these men. One does not have to be a sentimentalist to be convinced of the important part played by the will and emotions in man's religious life. And these sentimentalists are splendid witnesses to the fact of the natural and spontaneous movement of man's heart towards God. For most of us, God is grasped, even at the beginning of our relationships with him, as a "presence confusedly felt" rather than a logical conclusion of some syllogistic demonstration.

We are also indebted to these men for their acute and often penetrating analyses of the psychological aspects of our religious experiences. Their error, and it is bad enough, is in exaggerating their case and in imagining that feelings could in some way be substituted for proofs. They yielded the field of natural theology to Kant, but tried to salvage religion and religious knowledge by establishing a new faculty, the "religious sense," as something separate from and independent of the intellect. But they did not get beyond Kant, and are really worse off than he was. Because for Kant God was at least a postulate of the practical reason. For the sentimentalists God still remains a postulate, but only of our affections.

c. *Religious Pragmatism. William James*

"The whole function of thought is to produce habits of action . . . we have simply to determine what habits it produces, for what a thing means is simply what habits it involves." [21]

With pragmatism, we come to the tough-minded philosophers. It is instructive to note that the man who coined the word "pragmatism" (C. S. Peirce) learned his philosophy out of Kant. In point of fact, the word "pragmatism" was suggested to Peirce by Kant's distinction between the *praktish* and the *pragmatisch*. In

---

[20] See Gisquière, *Deus Dominus, op. cit.*, pp. 50–52.
[21] Charles Sanders Peirce, *Collected Papers*, V, pp. 256-257.

the philosophy of Kant, when a belief is merely *contingent*, that is to say, affirmed with the consciousness that fuller and further knowledge may prove it wrong, and yet supplies us with a workable norm for the attaining of certain desirable ends, this belief is called *pragmatic*. A pragmatic belief is a mere workable hypothesis. On the other hand, our moral beliefs, for example our belief in the existence of human freedom or in the existence of God, is a *necessary* postulate of *practical* reason. It is a necessary and not a contingent postulate, since the need that gives rise to it is one that further knowledge or future experiences will not do away with; whereas the pragmatic is simply what will work, what is effective for present action.

Pragmatism, as a philosophy, finds in this norm the sole criterion of determining the truth or falsity of our ideas. This philosophy was made popular by the justly famous writings of William James. In its peculiar features it was born and bred in America and carries the stamp of American thinking, a business-like attitude toward reality. For the pragmatist, the whole function of man's intelligence is ordered to, and gets its meaning from, action. Knowledge has no other end than to furnish us with the rules for acting. Once the intelligence discovers what these rules are, it rests there. This repose of the intelligence is belief, that is, an immediate and necessary preparation for activity. The whole meaning of what we know is in the action that we perform, the whole value of knowledge is found there. Thought has neither value nor meaning except in its practical consequences.

Let us examine briefly the pragmatic criterion of truth, and the manner in which it was applied to our ideas concerning God. We must apply in our thinking about God the same careful and scientific experimentation that a scientist carries on in his laboratory when trying to determine what something is that he experiences. For example, take the case of light.

The most elementary examination of what light means in terms of direct experience shows that we never experience light itself, but our experience deals only with things lighted. This fundamental fact is never modified by the most complicated or refined physical experiments that have ever been devised; from the point of view of operation, light means nothing more than *things lighted.* [22]

Therefore, the *truth* of light consists in this, that it lights objects. A thing is what it does, for that is all I can know about it.

Now we all have a certain notion about God; namely, that he is. Is this notion true? Let us put it to the test. How do we do this? First of all, by asking ourselves if any contradiction would follow in our activity if God existed. Obviously not. Secondly, would any fruitful results follow for us personally and for society in general on the supposition that there is a God? Obviously, yes. Therefore, our belief in God's existence is true, since it has been seen to be pragmatically fruitful. For James, "God is not something that is known, something that is understood. He is something that is used." [23] Hence James speaks of "turning away from first things, principles, 'categories,' supposed necessities, and of turning towards last things, fruits, consequences, facts." [24]

False, then, is all our knowledge about God's nature, his attributes, and all those other metaphysical speculations concerning God that men have indulged in. And why? Because they fail the test. They have no practical utility for the individual and social life of man. God, then, for William James, was not some being whose existence could be scientifically demonstrated. Kant had once and for all made such demonstration impossible when he showed how our notions of causality and finality have no validity when applied to God. But God's existence can be reinstated from a pragmatic point of view. For no one will deny that faith in God has beneficial results for both the individual and society. God's existence and the existence of religion have been put to the test,

[22] Quoted from P. W. Bridgman, *The Logic of Modern Physics* (New York, 1927), p. 151.

[23] Quoted by James from Leuba, in *The Varieties of Religious Experience* (New York, The Modern Library), p. 497. These words aptly describe what may be called, if somewhat unkindly, the "American view" of Almighty God.

[24] *Pragmatism: A New Name for Some Old Ways of Thinking* (New York, 1906), pp. 54-55.

and seeing the good habits and effects they involve, we may hold these beliefs as true, that is, useful.

Conclusion. The refutation of the pragmatists' criterion of utility as a valid, and the only valid, norm for determining the truth of an idea belongs, of course, to epistemology. Our only interest here is to point out why these men are agnostics. In natural theology, their error was in thinking that the methods of science can be applied to the problems of existence. For them, to investigate reality meant not to achieve an understanding of being, but to experiment with our experience as a scientist experiments with his physical data. Thus they can never tell us why things are, or why they are *what* they are, but merely how they operate, or how they should operate to obtain useful results. For the pragmatists, God is not a Being with objective and independent existence. He is a workable hypothesis, an idea that gets things done.

Notice, finally, that the pragmatists, tough-minded as they are, are huddled themselves in a halfway house somewhere this side of Kant. Because for Kant, God was a *necessary* postulate of his practical reason. For the pragmatist, God is only a useful (that is, workable) hypothesis of pragmatic (and contingent) belief. If someday man and society could operate more fruitfully without God, he would then cease to have any meaning or truth, because he would cease to have any value.

d. The Philosophy of Immanence. Modernism

"The divine is within us. It is only in folding back upon itself and searching the conditions of its proper activity, that thought finds God." [25]

The ghost of Kant is still very much alive and will probably never be completely exorcised. Its influence is quite obvious in the philosophy of Immanence, which is another attempt by modern man to "get out" of Kantianism. In general, the philosophy of Immanence may be described as follows: agreeing with Kant that speculative reason has no objective validity in the suprasen-

[25] Piaget, *Deux types d'attitudes religieuses: Immanence et transcendance* (Geneva, 1928), p. 30 ff.

sible order, since this order lies outside the phenomena or objects
of speculative reason, man nevertheless is justified in holding to
the truths that transcend the phenomenal order, and this justification is found to be immanent in man, in the propensities and
affections of his own nature. In the formulation of this doctrine we
see at work Kant's teaching of the twofold knowledge of speculative reason and esthetic intelligence, and the sentamentalism of
Schleiermacher. Immanentism has taken many forms. We will
consider only two of these as regards our knowledge of God: modernism and the philosophy of Henri Bergson.

The student has probably often heard the word "modernism."
It is a heresy, or a conglomeration of heresies, that plagued the
Catholic Church at the beginning of this century. What do the
modernists teach concerning our knowledge of God's existence?
For them, the origin of man's knowledge of the existence of God
and the certitude he has of this existence is explained as follows:
Man has within his subconscious a certain religious sense or power.
This sense is actuated by man's *need of God,* a need that arises
from an inner anxiety of man when he confronts the problems of
life and the mysterious, unknown things of reality. This religious
sense, thus activated, breaks forth into consciousness, and in this
consciousness man perceives the reality of God and believes in
his existence. This act of faith is not an act elicited by man's intellect; rather, it is the simple perception of God's presence in man
as revealed by this religious sense.

The consciousness of God constitutes a religious *experience,*
and this experience is the only valid criterion man has for holding
the truths that he does about God. Possessed of this experience,
the intellect of man can now play its proper and Kantian function.
That is to say, it can think about this faith, it can reflect upon this
religious experience. And in this way the intellect generates in
man his idea of God. [26]

God, then, is impervious to reason. But he is attained and
grasped in this blind movement of the consciousness of man. The

[26] See Gisquière, *Deus Dominus, op. cit.,* pp. 58–59, and the encyclical of
Pope Pius X, "Pascendi dominici gregis," Denziger, 2074.

modernists themselves did not inquire into the nature of this movement, but Bergson, as we shall see, will reduce it to an intuition, a certain vital sympathy between the knower and the thing known. When man *formulates* his truths about God, it is his reason that is at work, and these formulas are simply the external symbols of his religious experience. As such, they have no intrinsic or objective validity, since God escapes our reason. Their functions as symbols are pragmatic; they systematize our religious experience and manifest it to others. Like all mere symbols, the formulations or "dogmas" of faith can change from age to age, as man finds new and better ways to express his consciousness of God.

Conclusion. This brief and inadequate explanation of the doctrine of modernism will suffice for our purpose. It is a doctrine that mixes up, in an almost inextricable manner, truth and falsity. For example, it is perfectly true that God is present and works within us. But he is present within us, or rather we are present within him, as an ontological reality, not as an object of pyschological perception. [27] It is a presence that is not perceived, but reasoned to, as we have seen. Again, a man's religious experiences may well be, when properly reflected upon, a certain confirmation of what he believes; or they may prepare the way for a man to come to the knowledge of the true God. But in tnemselves, subjective feelings can never be an adequate criterion for the truths we know about God or even for our faith in him. Independently of the judgments of reason, our religious experiences are simply a subjective state, a certain blind capital of affective experience which can "prove" nothing. Our emotions, that is to say, the products of our sense appetites and our will, are not a light that sees and judges, but blind inclinations and movements towards the possession of the good. And apart from knowledge and reason, not only are such emotions blind, they are impossible. [28]

Cardinal Mercier has written some wise words on this matter.

[27] See St. Thomas, *De Ver.*, qu. 10, a. 11, ad 8m.
[28] The student is urged to read the excellent treatment of Father Pinard de la Boullaye, in his article in the *DTC*, "*Expérience religieuse*," vol. 5, part 2, especially "L'expérience religieuses comme critère de connaissance," part V, col. 1828–1853.

To resolve the problems raised by our consciousness, reflecting reason must always have the last word. Feeling, of its very nature, is blind, and reason itself must show that such feeling is well-founded. Man is not obliged to admit that there is a God, unless he demonstrates his existence; nor are the acts of religion meritorious unless they are founded on reason and conviction. Reason alone is the instrument that can judge the truth or falsity of any position. Without an appeal to reason, feeling is unable to establish anything. [29]

e. The Philosophy of Henri Bergson

"(Mysticism) must furnish us the means of approaching, as it were experimentally, the problem of the existence and nature of God. Indeed we fail to see how philosophy could approach the problem in any other way." [30]

Three men stand out in the history of French philosophy—Descartes, Comte, and Bergson. And certainly the most brilliant and profound of the three is Bergson. Born in France of Jewish-Irish descent in the year 1859, this philosopher enjoyed enormous success up to his death in 1941. This success was due to many factors: the brilliant and magnificent literary quality of his style; the profound and penetrating insights that light up so much of his doctrine; his vigorous attack against the sanctuary of Kant, with its materialistic and deterministic foundation; his strong vindication of the spiritual side of man and the truths of the spirit. Father de Tonquedec, a severe enough critic of Bergson, called his thought the most powerful and promising that had appeared in the philosophical world for the last hundred years.

All we can do here is to state, as briefly as possible, some central ideas of Bergson and what they entail for our knowledge and proof of the existence of God. [31] Some pages ago we placed ourselves in the Kantian world to see how Kant's notion of knowledge functioned. Let us now confront the world as Bergson saw it, and see how the intelligence of man reacts to that world. Reality is

---

[29] *Traité élémentaire de Philosophie* (Louvain, 1911), p. 28.
[30] Bergson, *The Two Sources of Morality and Religion,* translated by R. A. Audra and C. Brereton (New York: Henry Holt and Co., 1935), p. 229. Word in parentheses added.
[31] See Gisquière, *Deus Dominus, op. cit.,* pp. 62–71.

an ever-flowing river of flux, a continuous motion that is an evolution, a creative evolution. The principle, the source, of this pure
duration is not to be found in any external efficient cause that
trancends the duration, but in an élan vital, an internal vital impulse, that resides within the flux itself. There are two sides to this
flow, the material, that ever tries to weigh it down and stop it, and
the spiritual, that lifts it up and moves it forward. Thus we have an
evolution, whose moving source is a vital spirit, the élan vital.

How does man grasp this reality as it is? By an intuitive act of
his intelligence. Bergson describes this intuition as a certain intellectual "sympathy" by which we can transport ourselves into the
interior of the object, a transport by which we coincide with the
object in a way that is unique and, therefore, inexpressable. [32] By
this concrete intuition we experience, we live reality, and this is
the only way we can attain it. The other function of our intelligence is conceptual and practical. Here the intellect fixes, immo-
bilizes, the experience of its consciousness, organizing and inter-
preting that experience for the uses of science and practical life.
"The immobility caught in the concept," writes Bergson, "is like
the surface of water that one isolates from the flow of the river." [33]
Such concepts neither contain nor express our intuitions. For
these concepts are immobile, separate, dissected; whereas reality
is living, continually in motion. And so it is radically impossible
to attain reality or know objective truth through the activity of
the speculative intellect.

But this should cause us no alarm. For whereas Kant thought
metaphysics was impossible because the speculative intellect
could not transcend phenomena, Bergson holds that speculative
knowledge is not the concern of the metaphysician at all. The activity proper to the metaphysician is the activity of intuition. Speculative knowledge is proper to the sciences and the needs of practical life and action. The whole task of philosophy consists in a
conscious and energetic effort to intuit or perceive the pure dura-

[32] See *Revue de Métaphy. et de Morale*, 1903, p. 3.
[33] *Ibid.*, p. 3.

tion of becoming, to glimpse the light at its source, and not as it has been refracted and broken into the myriad concepts of the intellect, useful enough to history, the natural sciences and practical living, but of no value in the grasping of reality as it is. Bergson calls such concepts "fabricated and useful rags."

What effect has this doctrine on our knowledge of God? This, at least: such universal principles of being as causality, finality, necessity, participation, and so forth, have no value in establishing the existence of God. Bergson taught that it is only by way of intuition, as he described that act, that God can be perceived. This is achieved when man, by an instinctive and powerful effort of intuition, perceives that God is the center and source of the creative evolution. In the ever-moving flux of reality, God is present, not as a certain distinct and separate substance, but as the very continuity and impulse of the motion itself.

When Father de Tonquedec pointed out that this seemed to jeopardize the transcendence and personality of God, Bergson replied in his famous letters to the Jesuit [34] that he meant his doctrine to imply a Creator-God, the Author of the evolution. And again, shortly before his death, he once more declared, this time to Father Sertillanges, that he had always considered his élan vital as an emanation from God, and a free emanation. [35] Hence it would be historically inaccurate to accuse Bergson of being, at least in intention, either an atheist or a pantheist.

Fortunately, Bergson lived long enough to write the much awaited book in which he had promised to deal explicitly with our knowledge of the existence of God. This book is his *Two Sources of Morality and Religion,* which he published in 1932. It is on the evidence of this work that we must make our final judgment of Bergson's attitude toward the problem of God's existence.

In this book Bergson changes none of his philosophical positions. On the contrary, he applies his twofold function of man's intelligence to the evolution of religion. [36] The two sources of re-

[34] *Etudes,* 20 Feb., 1912.
[35] See Gisquière, *Deus Dominus, op. cit.,* p. 65.
[36] And of morality, which we need not consider here.

ligion come from man's two powers of intuition and conception. Thus religion takes two forms, dynamic and static. Static religion, the result of man's conceptualizing intellect, yields no knowledge of God, but simply fulfills a need in man's social nature. Static forms of religion would be, for example, animism, magic, faith in gods, and so forth. Dynamic religion, which has its source in a vital intuition and experiential knowledge of God, alone gives us knowledge of God's existence. The only way God's existence can be known is by an intuition. Bergson is insistent on this point. ". . . We look upon an object as existing if it is perceived, or might be perceived. Such an object is therefore presented in actual or possible experience." [37]

But who has experienced God? Bergson's answer: the mystics. And how do we know? They have told us so. A metaphysician is one who has had an intuition into the very heart of reality, seeing it as a vital impulse of evolution and becoming. A mystic is one who has had a deeper intuition still, glimpsing and experiencing the very source of this impulse, which is God. Bergson's proof for the existence of God, then, is really quite simple. The mystics tell us that they have experienced the presence and the activity of God. Their experience, then, is a fact. And the mystics ought to be believed, and this for at least three reasons: first, because of the universal and operative charity they bear toward humanity, in which charity is mirrored the divine charity, which is God. For the mystics try to do what God does—push on humanity to what it should become. Secondly, they should be believed because the different experiences of the mystics manifest a marvelous agreement and unity among themselves, showing the truth and objectivity of the experience. And, finally, the mystics have achieved this knowledge of God through an intuition, the only valid way it could have been obtained.

Bergson admits that when all is said and done, this faith in the mystics gives us no philosophical certitude about God's existence, but only a high degree of probability which equates a sort of

[37] *The Two Sources of Morality and Religion, op. cit.,* p. 229.

practical certitude; enough to convince us, if not as philosophers, at least as simple human beings. For we see no reason to contest the validity of experiences so obvious and so frequent. [38]

Conclusion. If not in intention, at least in fact, the doctrine of Henri Bergson is philosophical agnosticism. He denies that human reason can demonstrate the existence of God through any evidence existing things yield to our intellects. In this, he is solidly Kantian. Moreover, in stating that the mystics perceive God in an immediate intuition, he goes to the opposite extreme, reducing God to a direct object of human understanding. We have seen how this is philosophically impossible. Finally, even admitting the objectivity of the mystics' experience, how do they know it is *God* or the activity of God they are experiencing, unless they have had some previous knowledge *that there is a God?* How do they know this is not the work of some higher, but finite being (an angel?) or even, as happens in many cases, the work of their own fervid and forceful imagination? And even at best, we have only a *probable argument* for God's existence, not a *scientific demonstration.*

The fundamental error in the philosophy of Bergson, as is also the case with so many other modern systems of thought, is the absence of a doctrine on the analogy of being. How could Bergson distinguish between the being of God and the being of creatures? For him, God was the creative impulse itself, but in its absolute purity; and creation was that same impulse, but in its progression. Now the source of the river and the current of the river are one and the same river. So that it is hard to see how this distinction saves the absolute transcendence of God, or how his thought can logically escape the charge that Penido, his most severe critic, made against it when he called it a "distended univocity." [39] In spite of its brilliance and many remarkable insights, the teaching of Bergson as regards man's knowledge of God, especially in what it denies to the speculative intelligence, is incompatible with Christian teaching and our metaphysics of being.

[38] See Sertillanges, *Avec Henri Bergson* (Paris, 1941), pp. 18 and ff.
[39] See *Dieu dans le Bergsonisme* (Paris, 1934), pp. 127-209.

f. *Logical Positivism. The Analysis of Language*

Logical Positivism (the term first appeared in 1930) is a contemporary attempt to establish the validity of what man knows by an analysis of what he says. After all, man's knowledge of reality is expressed in propositions, so that a linguistic analysis should reveal whether a given proposition is meaningful or simply verbal manipulation. All Logical Positivists agree on the following points: the Humean view of causality and empirical induction is the correct one; philosophy is logical analysis, that is, it consists in the clarification of the everyday language people speak; and, finally, such clarification leads to the rejection of "metaphysical propositions," statements about cause, substance, accidents, and so forth, for it shows that such statements are meaningless, at least in their original intent. [40]

Logical Positivism is probably the most popular philosophy in the United States at the present time, and that is the main reason for mentioning it here. Put in its simplest terms, a given proposition has meaning, and to that extent is "true," if the elements of the proposition, upon careful linguistic analysis, can be reduced, either directly or indirectly, to some sense experience or some sense data. If not, the proposition has no meaning, and in an ideal language could not even be stated.

To see how the Logical Positivist applies this analysis to propositions, let us take a simple example. People say: "chairs exist." What does this expression mean? First of all, there are no such things in reality as chairs. A "chair" is simply a verbal constant applied to what is actually an almost unlimited number of sense impressions and sense references, organized and brought into focus in the knowing subject. But there is no such thing in reality as a substance *"chair."* Secondly, since this is so, chairs do not *exist.* The existential word "exist" cannot conceivably be applied to "chairs," but only to the conglomeration of what we sense in the presence of what we "call" a chair. In an ideal language, the propo-

---

[40] See Gustav Bergmann, "Logical Positivism," in *Philosophical Systems* (New York, Philosophical Library, 1950), p. 472.

sition "chair exists," would read: "there is something such that this something is a chair." But does the expression "chairs exist," have any meaning? Yes, since such an expression can be directly reduced to sense data and sense experience.

In such an approach to reality, it is not hard to foresee what will become of the existence of God. To ask the question, "Does God exist?" is to ask whether the expression "God exists," has any meaning, whether it can be reduced, either directly or indirectly, to sense experience. Obviously, it cannot. For we have no experience of the verbal elements in any way. The proposition cannot be transcribed in terms of any known human experience. It is, therefore, meaningless; not true or false, just meaningless.

There is no need here to point out the errors of such an approach to reality. Logical Positivism, besides being vitiated by the different philosophical misconceptions of Humean empiricism, adds one of its own: the principle that "every meaningful proposition is verifiable in sense experience." The only trouble with such a principle is that it fails to pass its own test. This principle is somewhat analogous to the Protestant statement that "Unless a religious truth appears in the Bible, it is not to be believed." Which, if anything, means that one ought not to believe this statement about religious truth, since it does not appear in the Bible. "Every meaningful proposition is verifiable in sense experience." Well and good; but then, to have meaning, this proposition itself must be verifiable in sense experience. So we analyze it. What is meaning? What is the meaning of meaning? To what sense experience can the meaning of meaning be reduced? If the Logical Positivist should reply that his proposition simply stands for the total of all possible sense experiences and symbolizes those experiences, we are still left with something beyond all these actual and possible sense experiences. And that is *meaning itself*.

g. Conclusion

This ends our brief, and admittedly inadequate, survey of the different agnostic attitudes toward the existence of God. At this point the student may be wondering if there is any philosophical system or doctrine, outside our own metaphysics of being, which teaches that the human reason can demonstrate with absolute certitude, with conclusive and scientific arguments, the existence of God? And if he comes to realize that the answer is no, that within the context of Nominalism, Empiricism, Kantianism, Positivism, Pragmatism, Cartesian Idealism, Bergsonian Intuitionism, Logical Positivism, Extreme Existentialism (See Appendix D), and so on, such a demonstration is rendered impossible, he should not be disturbed. There are many ways we can be wrong about a thing, but only one way we can be right.

Error arises in our judgments from an insufficient consideration of the evidence of reality, or from not considering all the evidence, or misunderstanding or misinterpreting the evidence. The positions of these different agnostics are perfectly understandable once we see what they have done. Some have misunderstood the nature of man, seeing him (as did Descartes) as a mere thinking substance; or (as did the Empiricists) as a mere sentient subject. In either case some evidence was suppressed or misunderstood, and man was not seen for what he really is: a unique and unified composite of sense and intellect; who, therefore, has intelligible as well as sensible experiences in his cognitional life, and who can, as a result, judge about the being of things as well as about their sensible manifestations.

Others have misunderstood the nature of reality, the Nominalists seeing things as irreducibly singular, possessing within themselves neither actual intelligibility (as Scotus held), nor potential intelligibility (as St. Thomas taught), and hence incapable of producing in our understanding any knowledge of the principles of being, any knowledge of being as being. And all of them have misunderstood the knowledge process as exercised by man, a composite of sense and intellect. Man senses, abstracts, judges, in an immediate, unified and total cognitional experience of the existing thing. Unlike Bergson, we must refuse to man an immediate intellectual intuition of the existent. For this would demand actual, and not merely potential, intelligibility within the sensible existent (a contradiction in terms). But, against Kant, we defend for the intellect of man, an immediate abstractive knowledge of the real, accompanied by a perceptive judgment of existence, an activity that constitutes an ontological insight into the reality of the existent. But all of this we have seen in detail as we traced man's knowledge of God from his knowledge of things, as well as when we ascertained what kind of knowledge man can have and cannot have of God.

APPENDIX C

Some Invalid Proofs from Science for the Existence of God

The five ways of St. Thomas are valid philosophical demonstrations for God's existence. In Appendix A we discussed some philosophical proofs that are not valid. In general, a philosophical demonstration is one whose principles and procedures are based upon the being of things. But can we establish a valid proof for the existence of God upon premises and procedures that belong, not to the philosophical order, but to the order of positive science? Such a proof would be based not upon sensible being as existing (as being) but as observable or measurable in some way.

In this appendix we will do two things: first, we will examine two well-known proofs from positive science that some maintain do demonstrate God's existence, and see why they do not. Secondly, we shall show that it is intrinsically impossible for the positive sciences to establish the existence of God. [1]

1. Can God's Existence be Proved from the Law of the Transformation of Energy?

Let us begin our study of this proof with some definitions and presuppositions. The Law of the Transformation of Energy (also called the law of entropy) states that throughout changes in matter the quantity of energy remains constant. Another name for this law is the principle of the conservation of energy. Here energy means

[1] See Gisquière, *Deus Dominus, op. cit.*, pp. 249-262. Our treatment here is based on these pages.

the capacity to do work, in the strict physical sense of this word. Absolute energy is energy's remote capacity to do work. And this always remains constant. Actual energy is the energy involved in actual work. This energy is continually growing less and less.

Why is this so? Because all forms of energy are gradually transformed into the energy of heat, whereas the energy of heat is never totally changed back again into the other forms of energy. There always remains some part of the heat-energy that cannot be converted into the other forms of energy, and so can no longer be used in the production of work. That part of energy that is definitively changed into heat (so that it cannot be changed back into other forms of energy) is called entropy, from the Greek word meaning "inner conversion."

Thus the law of the lessening of energy (or the Principle of Clausius) can be stated as follows: "The entropy in the universe is continually increasing and tending toward a maximum, at which point the energy of heat will be equally diffused throughout the universe, and non-transformable into other forms of energy." When such equalization of heat energy is achieved, the whole process of change in the universe will come to an end, since in the production of change all forms of energy are gradually changed into heat, and the heat energy that is non-transformable cannot be used for change.

Now we are ready to see how some try to establish the existence of God from the law of entropy. The law tells us that all non-heat energy gradually changes into heat-energy; but this heat-energy does not wholly change back into dynamic energy, that is to say, into energy that can do work. And so little by little non-dynamic energy is equally diffused throughout the universe. Now obviously this lessening of energy has not been taking place from eternity. For then we would be faced with this dilemma: either (1) the quantity of dynamic energy was once infinite, and hence would have resided within an infinite quantity of matter—which is impossible; or (2) the quantity of dynamic energy was finite. But on the latter supposition we would (a) have either by now reached a state of quiescence, since the finite dynamic energy would have all changed into heat—but this is contrary to the fact; or (*b*) the universe, having reached a state of quiescence as regards its dynamic energy, has of itself started the process over again—which is also impossible, for it would not have the dynamic energy with which to start the process. So it is quite clear that a transformation of energy has not been going on from eternity.

But, on the other hand, it is equally impossible for such a process to have had a beginning. For if the process began together with matter, we must posit God as the creator of the matter subject to change. Or if the process began in pre-existing matter which did not have this change from the beginning, then we must posit God as the one who began the change, and as distinct from the matter. In either case, the existence of God as a principle distinct from the universe is required. This is the way some say God's existence can be demonstrated from an analysis of the law of entropy or the transformation of energy. [2]

2. Rejection of This Proof

What are we to say of the validity of this argument from positive science? And what should our judgment be about the law of entropy itself, upon which the proof is founded? Using science in the broad sense that includes both the philosophical and positive sciences, we say that the principles of each science have a certitude proper to the science whose principles they are. The law of entropy has a certitude, therefore, proper to a positive science. According to most contemporary scientists, a law or principle of a positive science is not absolutely certain, but has rather the force of a workable and useful hypothesis. In a word, the law of entropy as held today is not so certain that it was always held in the past, nor can we be sure that it will always be held by scientists in the future. Even today some scientists call the law into doubt. They

[2] Apparently the Jesuit astronomer Secchi was the first to use the law of entropy for purposes of apologetics: to prove the existence of God. Since him, the argument has been used and approved by such writers as Billot, Hontheim, Donat, Eymieu, etc. On the other side of the ledger, the following have denied the validity of the argument from entropy: Sertillanges, Descoqs, Pohl, Périer, etc. See Gisquière, *Deus Dominus, op. cit.,* pp. 249-253.

contend, for example, that the law of entropy is based upon our experience of integral bodies. It is not at all clear that it has the same value for atoms, and much less for the elements of atoms, which received their energy at the time of the formation of the matter of the stars. [3]

Finally, it is not at all certain that the law of entropy is valid for the whole universe, since our experience of the transformation of energy extends to only certain parts of the universe. Indeed, there are some scientists who say the law does not hold for bodies unaffected by gravity. It is absolutely absurd, therefore, to accept as a principle for demonstrating the existence of God a law that is only tentatively held by positive scientists. One does not use in his metaphysics the uncertain results of a positive science, and still less does one base any philosophical demonstration on a workable hypothesis borrowed therefrom.

But apart from our judgment about the law of entropy, what are we to say of the proof itself based on this law? A careful analysis shows that the proof does not eliminate other possibilities, nor are the disjunctions given in the argument themselves complete.

First of all, it is not an evident contradiction to say that the whole universe might be unlimited in its energy, or even in the quantity of its matter. Secondly, even if we grant a state of energy equilibrium (either before or after the entropological process), it is not evident that the universe could not begin a new entropological process, but this time due to a change of a higher and different order from that of entropy.

Is our universe a closed system, shut off from the influence of other unknown universes? We do not know. But we do know that there are many scientists who say that the hypothesis of a closed universe is fraught with many and serious difficulties. [4] And even granting the hypothesis of a closed universe, it is still possible for some principle intrinsic to the universe to give rise to a new impulse, so that the equilibrium of energy could break forth into

[3] See Gisquière, *op. cit.*, p. 250.
[4] See Alexandre Koyré's book, *From the Closed World to the Infinite Universe* (New York, Harper and Brothers, 1958).

new transformations. Such a theory cannot be rejected *a priori.* Perhaps heat can increase and decrease after the manner of the expansion and contraction of the heart.

Concerning this possibility of the contraction and expansion of heat energy, Father Sertillanges has a pertinent quotation in his book, *La Creation:*

> Is the system of the universe, supposed as closed and finite, universally and uniquely ruled by the law of the lessening of energy? Nothing is less certain. When the balance of energy is decreasing, then the scientist is calculating the law of entropy. And carrying the effects of this law to their absolute conclusion, he says: There will come a day when the equilibrium will be complete. But what this scientist is forgetting is that the thread of yarn is attached to the ball. That is to say, after the law of decrease, another law may assert itself. For who can say that there is not present in the world a law of decrease and a law of increase, a systole and a diastole, which is dependent upon a higher law which we do not know? Against such possibilities science has nothing to say. And since metaphysics permits them, the question remains. [5]

It is not at all impossible that the entropological process itself arose from another process of a different order not subject to the law of entropy. For it is not entirely certain that the law of entropy has been operative during the whole time in which the universe has existed. In other words, the entropological process could have had a beginning, but not an absolute one; that is to say, it need not have been begun by God. We conclude, then, that even though the process of entropy had a beginning, and this within a closed and finite universe, this beginning can still be explained without appealing to the immediate intervention of God. In brief, the argument from entropy has no validity as a demonstration for the existence of God.

3. Practical Use of This Argument

But has this argument any value at all? Here we can make four observations: first, it can be used as an *argumentum ad hominem* in

---

[5] *La Création,* Somme Theologique, I, Questions 44–49, 2ième ed. (Tournai: Desclée, 1948), p. 263. Author's translation.

the case of a man who is convinced of the absolute validity of the laws of positive science. Secondly, the argument has a certain suasive and probable force for the non-philosophic mind. The ordinary man seems convinced that the universe is neither infinite nor eternal, nor subjected to generically different kinds of cosmic processes. Thirdly, no matter how used, we must always remember that the argument from entropy never has the certitude of a metaphysical proof for the existence of God. Fourthly, and finally, the existential fact of entropy can be used as a point of departure for a metaphysical demonstration of God's existence. Entropy, as a continual change, or as a contingent process, or as manifesting order or finality, can be used as a starting point for one of the five ways: the way of change, or contingency, or finality. But the law of entropy in itself and of itself cannot constitute a distinct argument for the existence of God. Maritain explains this point as follows:

> To conclude from that [the principle of entropy] to a divine intervention at the origin of the world would be for science to go beyond the sphere of its competence. . . . To establish such a philosophical conclusion, it is necessary to proceed philosophically. This supposes the bringing into play of philosophically elucidated notions (which the physicist as such does not know) such as ontological causality, analogy of being, potency and act, order, finality, etc. and that the notion of entropy itself had taken on a philosophical as well as a physico-mathematical sense. [6]

4. Can God's Existence Be Proved from the Origin of Life?

A second argument, drawn from positive science, that is sometimes used as a proof for the existence of God is the *biological argument*. Let us see how the argument proceeds and whether it has any validity.

The argument usually takes the following form: Life did not always exist upon the earth, but only appeared after a certain fixed time. But the only adequate cause that can account for the origin of life is God. Therefore, God exists.

[6] *The Degrees of Knowledge,* translated under the supervision of Gerald B. Phelan (London, Geoffrey Bles, 1959), p. 187, note 3. Words in brackets added.

The major premise is proved and confirmed by positive science. There was a time when the earth was in a condition of extreme heat and consisted only of incandescent gases. This condition made any kind of life impossible. And geologists, from their analysis of rock strata, talk about an azoic or agnotozoic period, that is, a period when there was not the least trace of life upon the earth.

The minor premise, namely, that only a supermundane being can adequately account for the origin of life, is usually proved by elimination. There seems to be only three possible hypotheses to explain the origin of life: (1) panspermia; (2) abiogenesis; (3) the intervention of a supreme Being. But the first two are quite impossible. Therefore, a supreme Being exists.

The theory of panspermia consists in this: This world, from its origin, was filled with tiny living germs or sperms; or at least such germs descended to the earth from the stars. For the life synthesis found apt conditions in astral matter while such conditions were still lacking upon the earth. This theory of the origin of life has been seriously proposed by such men as Richter, Van Tieghem, and Svante Arrhenius. [7]

But, the argument continues, the theory of panspermia must be rejected for the following reasons: since the stars themselves seem to have been formed, or are being formed, in the same way as our world, they too had, or have azoic periods, in which all life would be impossible. So we cannot get our germs from the stars. Moreover, even if such germs existed they would have perished in interplanetary space. And this, not because of the tremendous cold in such space, but because of its great dryness and its cathode rays. For unless such rays are tempered by an atmosphere, they destroy all life.

But what about the theory of *abiogenesis?* This theory teaches that life arises from non-living matter, from the complicated interaction of non-living energies contained in matter. But modern science, especially through the experiments of Van Beneden and Pasteur, reject this idea of spontaneous generation, and say that

[7] See Gisquière, *op. cit.*, pp. 253–260.

every organism is from some egg, and every cell from some other cell.

This leaves us, the argument concludes, with only our third hypothesis—the intervention of some supermundane cause, whose operation produces life in non-living matter. And since such a cause possesses equivalently the power to create, it must be a supreme Being, or God.

5. Rejection of the Biological Argument

Is such an argument valid? The major premise seems incontestable. It is not based upon some theory, as was the proof from entropy, but upon the actual findings of geology and astronomy. At one time there was no life upon the earth. Then it appeared. This is historical truth, and no one doubts it. But what about the minor premise? It is here that the biological argument loses its validity.

Concerning the minor, this much can be said: We are probably justified in eliminating panspermia as the source of life upon the earth. It is a highly unlikely theory, and this for the reasons given in the argument. But are we justified in eliminating abiogenesis (or spontaneous generation, as it is sometimes called) as a hypothesis to account for the origin of life? It is true that some scientists think that the experiments of Redi, Swammerdam, Van Beneden, and Pasteur have demonstrated the impossibility of producing living cells from non-living matter. But the question is by no means definitively settled. All these experiments show is that in the present condition of the world, life always comes from life, and that so far we know of no other way to produce it. They prove nothing about the possibility of achieving life from non-living matter in other conditions of the cosmos, conditions that might have obtained once upon a time on the earth. Indeed, some scientists have not despaired of producing life artificially in the laboratory. And some day success may attend their efforts. No argument from science, philosophy or theology precludes the possibility.

And so we must conclude that the biological argument, as it is usually proposed, is at best only suasive and probable. In no sense is it a strict and certain demonstration for the existence of God.

6. Can the Biological Argument Be Made Valid?

There are some who say that "the argument from life" can be used as a valid demonstration for the existence of God, provided we take our stand at the level of philosophy and not of positive science. In other words, there are those who contend that abiogenesis or spontaneous generation is philosophically impossible. There is, they maintain, an essential and qualitative difference between inorganic and living beings. And so non-living matter could never give rise to living beings. Nothing gives what it does not have, nor can there be more perfection in the effect than in the cause from which it came. And so they conclude that philosophy itself demands a necessary appeal to a Creator-God to account for the origin of living beings.

Now this matter is not quite so clear and easy as these thinkers would have it. It is worth our time to examine the situation more closely. Certainly no one denies that there is a great difference between evidently non-living things and things with a high form of animal life, between, for example, a rock and a rhinoceros. But the difference between a non-living substance and one having a very low form of life, is so small that it can be detected only by those skilled in the positive sciences. But this, of course, is really not to the point. The point is this: Is there really an essential difference between a non-living substance and a substance possessing the lowest form of life possible? Not merely in the sense that the two substances have different essences (man has a different essence from a dog—but both are living, and there may be different essences among non-living substances), but in the sense that a non-living substance is incapable of any immanent operation.

I think we can all admit that there is such a difference between the operations of such chemical and physical forces as oxidation, magnetism, and electricity, and such vital operations as love, sense, and intellectual knowledge. The student has already studied in the philosophy of man the reasons for the difference: the unity of the living being, its inner development, the subordination of part to whole, the multiple and complex co-ordination of its acts for the good of the whole (acts which flow from a single internal principle of operation), and so forth. Here the student concluded that vital activity and the principle it presupposes are of a higher order than mere physico-chemical forces. That is why he rejected material mechanism, which teaches that life can evolve and arise from such forces alone, when correctly joined and ordered.

But is this the whole story? Is it not possible for non-living things to possess the forces of life, not actually, but virtually? Why can not the higher and more complex non-living substances contain virtually the forces of the lower and simpler forms of life? If so, then given the necessary conjunction of causes, life could arise from the natural action of non-living things, without any special intervention on the part of God. And if such is the case, then one can hardly argue philosophically from the origin of life to the existence of God.

To repeat: Such an origin of life from the virtual presence of life forces within actually non-living substances does not seem metaphysically impossible; because in this doctrine, unlike that of material mechanism, inorganic matter is not entirely outside the order of life, since such matter virtually contains life. And by virtual presence we mean the virtue or power in such matter to produce, given the proper conditions, living germs. Here we might quote a pertinent statement from Halleux:

The appearance of life upon the earth at a given moment does not necessarily prove an intervention of a creative power. For we simply do not know enough about the nature of matter to have any right to affirm that at a determined stage of its development it does not have the power to engender living germs. [8]

So there is no reason, as far as principles of philosophy are concerned, why the production of life artificially in laboratories is impossible. Many of the best scientists, however, agree that the difficulties involved are great, if not insuperable. [9] Regarding abio-

[8] See the *Revue Néoscolastique de Philosophie* (Louvain, 1909), p. 433.
[9] For some Catholics who hold the theoretical possibility of such a production, see Beysens, *Cosmology,* (Amsterdam, 1910), pp. 227-235.

genesis, therefore, we can make the following statements: (1) It is not held as impossible in the circles of positive science,[10] although more scientists reject it than accept it. (2) Nor can the impossibility of abiogenesis be demonstrated philosophically. In any event, it cannot be ruled out as a possible hypothesis to account for the origin of life upon the earth.

What, then, is our final judgment on the validity of the biological argument as a proof for the existense of God? We say that in itself and of itself it has no demonstrative value. The existence of God is not proved by this argument, since an actual intervention of God is neither discernible nor needed to explain the origin of life upon the earth. Of course, the argument can furnish us with data that can be used as a point of departure to demonstrate God's existence by the usual ways of causality, finality, degrees of perfection, and so on. The point is, the origin of life upon the earth of itself and in itself is not sufficient to establish the existence of God as a distinct proof. We cannot conclude from that fact *as such* to the existence of a Subsistent, all-perfect Being.

7. Observations Regarding Proofs Taken from Positive Science

We have gone into some detail in our analysis of the so-called entropological and biological arguments for the existence of God. They are called "scientific" arguments, as opposed to philosophical arguments. Because of its formal subject and method of procedure, a positive science as such is intrinsically and necessarily incapable of demonstrating God's existence. Physics, for example, is no more capable of proving the existence of a suprasensible being than mathematics is of proving the existence of a non-quantified being. To do this, they would have to change their essence, for they would have to go beyond their proper subject and proper method; and then they would no longer be positive sciences. The student should remember this, so that he will not, for example, be guilty

[10] The problem has renewed interest because of recent studies of viruses. See, for example, the article, "Are Viruses Alive?" by Sister Adrian Marie, O.P., in *The New Scholasticism* (July, 1957), pp. 297-316.

of making statements like the following, which is quoted from a book called *The Catholic Faith before Reason and Science:*

These modern arguments (like the two we have seen) are very clear and possess a solidity entirely tested. Basically they are reducible to the arguments of St. Thomas, but with this difference, that thanks to the actual evidence of positive science, we can now even prove the temporal origin of the world, which is a truth of capital importance (in proving the existence of God). [11]

What are we to say about *any* argument taken from positive science as regards the existence of God? The following five truths should be kept in mind concerning them:

1) Since such arguments are based upon the laws and theories of positive science, the arguments themselves can never achieve greater certitude than that of these laws and theories. And as we have seen, the scientists dispute among themselves as to the relative truth or value of their laws and theories.

2) Since the laws and theories of positive science are based upon sensible phenomena as in some way physically observable and measurable, they can never be used to transcend the phenomenal order. But God, as a term to be demonstrated, entirely transcends the phenomenal order. Thus any proof that is strictly and merely from positive science can never demonstrate his existence.

3) Even if we were to grant that positive science could establish the existence of some supermundane principle, it could never go on to prove that this principle is God; namely, a Necessary Being and Pure Act. To reach such a term (that is, to reach God) one would always have to resort to principles that are truly metaphysical.

4) Although no argument from positive science is of itself conclusive, it may still have a certain apologetic or *ad hominem* value for those who have absolute and exclusive faith in the laws of positive science and consider them as entirely proved and certain. Such arguments have also a suasive force for ordinary people.

[11] Joossens, *La Foi Catholique devant la Raison et la Science* (Louvain, 1938), p. 27. Words in parentheses added. Author's translation.

5) Finally, as should be obvious, no objection based on positive science has any value in disproving the existence of God. Since positive science functions in an entirely different order from philosophy, it is as equally incapable of disproving there is a God as of proving it. [12]

[12] See Gisquière, *op. cit.*, pp. 261–262.

APPENDIX D

God and Existentialism

1. Prenote

The most important movement by far in philosophy today is that of existentialism. The word itself has its difficulties. First, because it covers several and even contradictory approaches to existence. Secondly, existentialism implies a system, while most existentialists are against all systems. Furthermore, some of the most famous of them, as, for example, Heidegger, refuse to be called existentialists. Finally, as regards the problem of God, some of the existentialists are theists and Christians, such as Kierkegaard and Marcel; others are atheists, such as Heidegger and Sartre. To confuse matters even more, the existentialism of Kierkegaard is not even philosophical; it is religious. And that of Karl Barth is biblical. Some types of moderate existentialism are compatible with Christian metaphysics, and exploit what is richest and most profound in this metaphysics. Other types, such as Heidegger's and Sartre's, are irreducibly anti-metaphysical.

The movement comprises a bewildering variety of thought, particularly in regard to its theological implications. It ranges from determined atheism to Protestant Biblicism and Catholic theism. In the maze of contradictory theorems the mere name of Existentialism is no sufficient guide. For it is claimed by some who are hardly entitled to it, and it is disclaimed by others whom we consider prominent representatives of the movement. [1]

[1] Helmut Kuhn, "Existentialism," in the book *A History of Philosophical Systems,* edited by Virgilius Ferm (New York, Philosophical Library, 1950), p. 406.

In this appendix we shall try to do three things: first, explain as best we can the meaning of existentialism; secondly, trace some of its main features in the leading existentialists; and, thirdly, show how radical existentialism negates the existence of God. All we can do is throw some little light on a philosophical movement that is still very incomplete, and which contains, even within a single existentialist, ambiguities and contradictions. Our treatment here is necessarily inadequate and oversimplified.

2. What Is Existentialism?

In general, existentialism may be described as an attitude toward reality. It is an attitude that is almost exclusively preoccupied with the existence of things, and more especially with the existence of man. Moreover, it is not man as existing, but rather as an existent that interests the existentialist. It is the human individual as such (in its self-hood: unique, subjective, irreducible, incommunicable and communicable) that is important. The student is familiar with the distinction between essence and existence. Essence denotes *what* a thing is, existence *that* it is. Essence corresponds to the definition of the thing, existence to its ontological giveness. Hence, we can explain, analyze, and classify essences. But existence, in the sense given here, is incapable of any of this. To give a rational meaning to existence is to define its essence which is impossible, since it has none. To define existence is to essentialize it, to absorb it into essence. And this is to negate existence.

However, existentialism is the sense of a modern movement that began with Kierkegaard and is still going on, means something more than merely a preoccupation with existence over essence. Thomism, for example, places the act of existing at the core of being, and traces to it whatever reality and intelligibility is in the existent. And yet Thomism is not an existentialism in this modern, radical sense. For a radical existentialist, "to exist" is not the same as "to be." For them existence is not the mere objective giveness that things have in common. It is not something grasped in thought, but discovered in "encounter." This encounter with existence usually takes place in the anguish of crisis, or in the inter-communication of persons. Things are. Persons *exist*. And human persons begin to "exist" only when they "go out" (*exire*) from the undifferentiated and common reality they share with things, only when they shoulder their destiny and assert themselves as free, responsible, committed persons. In this act of self-commitment, of active surrender to destiny, a person encounters existence.

3. Some Radical Existentialists

Hardly any two radical existentialists are alike, even in important points. In examining a few of the features of the main ones, the student should get an idea of what they are trying to do, and what their doctrine means for Christian metaphysics and the science of natural theology.

a. Sören Kierkegaard (1813–1855)

Among modern philosophers, it was Kant who emphasized the fact that we can never go from essence to existence. No amount of analysis of essence ever discovers the fact of existence. For Kant existence becomes not perfection, but position, a giveness that is affirmed. This point has had its influence upon existentialists, as have other points in Kant, as we shall see.

It was Hegel who tried to bridge this ontological gulf between essence and existence. This he achieved by a Becoming, a passage from non-existence to existence, effected through a dialectic of mind. In Hegel, existence is absorbed into essence, the part into the whole, the individual into the absolute. While Becoming is most important in Hegel, it is a Becoming realized through reason—universal reason. It was against this abstract Idealism that Sören Kierkegaard rebelled. "One might say," he wrote, "that I am a moment of individuality, but I refuse to be a paragraph in a system." Perhaps one of the best ways to understand Kierkegaard is to see him in contrast to Hegel.

To Hegel, man was a specific epoch in the evolution of the universal Idea, a part of a whole. To Kierkegaard, man is a unique and individual existent. To Hegel's objective unfolding of reality as an absolute Idea, Kierkegaard opposed man's subjective and free commitment to real existence. Hegel's system absorbed and negated man; Kierkegaard disengages him to fulfill his destiny as an existent.

How does man achieve his authentic existence? By becoming a Christian. And how does he become a Christian? By a passionate commitment through free choice to the Incarnate God. The genesis of this commitment can be described briefly as follows: Man finds himself athirst for real existence. But through his intellect he is unable to transcend the sphere of essences and encounter trans-essential existence. This fills him with a sort of despair which puts him in a state of crisis. Set adrift by his intelligence amid his possibilities, man is filled with a dread or anguish. It is the dread of nothingness, the nothingness that faces the finite in the presence of infinite possibilities. But in this very experience man becomes aware of his freedom. For if everything is possible, then nothing is determined or certain. In his anguish, in his freedom, he must choose. His commitment is effected not by an act of intellect (which is the despair and scandal of man) but by a passionate intensity of feeling. The leap is effected by blind faith. In choosing Christ and the Christian life, man gains his authentic being, he begins to exist.

Obviously, this doctrine of Kierkegaard is not a philosophy at all. It is an irrational faith in Christ. God is not proved to exist by reason. He is encountered, in the crisis of anguish, by a passionate and free choice. But in the writings of Kierkegaard most of the existentialist themes are pre-figured. He is rightly called the father of radical existentialism.

b. Karl Jaspers (1883–   )

"The second major event in the history of the philosophy of existence occured when two German philosophers, Jaspers and Heidegger, translated the reflections of Kierkegaard into more intellectual terms. We may consider the philosophy of Jaspers as a sort of secularization and generalization of the philosophy of Kierkegaard." [2] Central to the philosophy of Jaspers are two notions, one traceable to Kant, the other to Kierkegaard. The student is familiar with the distinction in Kant between the noumenon (thing-in-itself) and phenomenon (thing-in-its-appearance). This idea recurs in Jaspers in his "background of being" or "All-encompassing" (*das Umgreifende*) and his "limited perspective" or "fragmentary grasp" of being. The second notion central to Jasper's doctrine is that of Kierkegaardian crisis.

To "exist" for Jaspers is to establish contact with the "All-encompassing," the hidden background of being from which we derive our reality. Such contact is effected in moments of crisis or "limit situations" (*Grenzsituation*) and can be described briefly as follows: In his search for knowledge and truth, man finds that he is up against an ineluctable limit. His is only a partial, limited aspect (or perspect) of being. This fact induces in him a sort of intellectual despair. Intelligence is powerless to transcend this human perspective. However, in moments of great crises, when man experiences his own helplessness and defeat, he senses something other than himself, something that transcends or exceeds him. This is a fleeting glimpse of the all-embracing, the absolute, from which he derives his being.

This encounter is described by Jaspers as a "rise into transcendence" (*Aufschwung in die Transzendenz*). It results in no knowledge of the absolute but in a symbolic equivalent of knowledge, in a "decodification" (*Entziffern*) of rationally unintelligible "signs" (*Chiffern*). The student may recognize in the difference between the way man understands limited perspectives of things and the way he glimpses the whole or absolute in moments of crisis a parallel between the speculative knowledge of Kant and his esthetic judgment.

Karl Jaspers is at least agnostic, if not atheistic. We do not know whether the "All-encompassing" is God. We have no intel-

---

[2] Jean Wahl, *A Short History of Existentialism* (New York, Philosophical Library, 1949), p. 9.

lectual knowledge of it at all. And whatever it is, it is not reached by any rational demonstration, but by an irrational and momentary glimpse.

c. Martin Heidegger (1889–   )

Heidegger maintains that he is not a philosopher of existence, but a philosopher of Being. He tells us that there are many different kinds or forms of Being. For example, there is "the being of things seen," or scenes, which manifest themselves to man; there is the being of tools and instruments, which are used and disposed of by man; there is the being of mathematical forms, which subsist, and the being of animals, which live. And there is the being of man, who alone among all these other beings truly exists. And it is through the existence of man, the only being with which we are really in contact, that we arrive at Being. Hence, for Heidegger, the problem of human existence is only part of, and an introduction to, the larger problem of Being.

Heidegger never tells us definitively or satisfactorily what Being is. He does, however, try to describe the general conditions of human existence, and show how man, in order truly to exist, must leave the realm of inauthentic existence and realize himself and his destiny. The inauthentic man lives in the everyday world, submerged in the ordinary, a part of an undifferentiated whole, unconscious of his own existence. He is an impersonal thing (*das Man*) rather than a person and personalizing "I." Let us see how man detaches himself from the inauthentic sphere and begins "to exist."

In certain human experiences, especially that of anguish, man is revealed to himself. He sees himself as a being flung forth into the world, from where he does not know, and into circumstances and conditions he has not chosen. He sees no reason for his being; that is to say, man is an existent without essence. He sees his existence in this world as essentially limited, finite. The essential limit of his existence is death. His existence is a "being for death." Man sees his possibilities, but he also sees death as the end of all possibilities. Death is the impossibility of possibility. This fact of his limited and destined-to-be-destroyed existence fills man with anxiety and gives to his anxiety a tragic character.

But man is not to remain in this state of anguish. He must shoulder his responsibility and assert his destiny. He does so by an act of "Resolute Decision," which is a free and active surrender to his condition. With this decision, man begins his movement of transcendence, of "passing toward." In the philosophy of Heidegger, man engages in five such transcendences.

First of all, there is his movement or transcendence toward the world. Man is an in-the-world being; he is an essential part of it. In this sense, he is outside himself, essentially open to and orientated toward the world. In this sense, too, man's existence is an egress, a going out of himself (hence, man has existence—*existere*). Man expands his being in communication with the world.

Secondly, there is a transcendence toward other men, other existents. Like his transcendence toward the world, this second movement is normal and natural for man. He is never entirely alone or separated from others. For "without others" is another mode of being "with others."

Besides moving beyond himself toward the world and toward other individuals, man is constantly moving beyond himself toward the future. This is one of the most fruitful and intriguing of the Heideggerian themes. Man seems to live in the future. He is constantly concerned about what he is going to do, about what is going to happen to him. He is always putting himself out in front of himself, projecting himself into the future. The limits and possibilities of the future are measured and controlled by the conditions and situations of the past. Man is part of a world with a history, including his own. And so the present moment, in which man realizes his existence, is the product of the juncture of his past and his future. For Heidegger, this extension of man toward the future is characterized chiefly by anxiety and care. As thus seized by man, Being is care and temporality.

This brings us to our last two movements, which are two sides of the same coin: a movement away from Nothingness and a movement toward Being.

Not only does Heideggerian anguish lead man to discover his possibilities, which as we have seen are relative and limited, but it brings him into contact with a sense of Nothingness, with Nothingness itself. From this Nothingness everything seems to erupt and into it everything as each moment threatens to dissolve. It is the background or *substratum* from which man seems to have been thrown into the world and into which he is destined to return. But what is it? "Naturally, this Nothingness is difficult to characterize. We cannot even say that it *is*, and Heidegger has invented a word, *Nichten* ("naughten"), to characterize its action. Nothingness "naughtens" itself and everything else. It is an active Nothingness which causes the world which erupts from it to tremble to the foundations. One might say that it is the negative foundation of Being, from which Being detaches itself by a sort of rupture. Let us remark parenthetically that in a postscript to the tract in which Heidegger discloses his theory of Nothingness, he tells us that this Nothingness, differing from each and every particular thing which *is*, can be none other, at bottom, than Being itself—for, he argues, what is there different from each thing that *is*, if not Being?" [3]

Man, in realizing his existence, moves away from Nothingness (sensed in his anguished and forlorn condition of flung-in-the-world) toward Being, toward the assertion and achievement of his destiny. What this Being is, other than the realization of our possibilities, and what Possibility is, other than the expansion of our being through the world and other persons, is difficult to determine. At any rate, man's various transcendences always remain immanent to the world. "We surpass ourselves, but always in the circle of the intermundane." [4]

In the ontology of Heidegger there is no place for God. Limited by Nothingness, Being, in its positive side, is historical temporality. It is possible for man to exist and to die, to freely accept his destiny (although what this always entails in practice is not very clear) or to reject it (to remain "inauthentic"). Man can go from

[3] Jean Wahl, *op. cit.*, p. 13.
[4] *Ibid.*, p. 17.

existence to Being; he cannot go from existence to God, or from Being to God. For in Heidegger there is no God. Moreover, since man is existence without essence, there is no intelligible structure or foundation within being by which he could rationally argue to a first cause of being. As possessed by the existent, existence can only be experienced; as possessed by others, it can only be described. In no case does it become a source of intelligibility for the rational inference of other beings, let alone a Supreme Being. The philosophy of Heidegger, if we can call it a philosophy, is metaphysically atheistic.

d. *Jean-Paul Sartre* (*1905–*)

Many of the themes of Heidegger are repeated and systematized in the writings of Sartre. Perhaps the notion most essential to his ontology is his distinction within Being of Being-in-itself (*l'en soi*) and Being for-itself (*le pour soi*). The former is simple self-identity. It is Being as massive, stable, undifferentiated, just itself, and nothing more: it is what it is. Being for-itself is perhaps best described as a negating or nullification of Being in-itself—a "hole" in the density of Being.

Man, for Sartre, is existence without essence. He *is not* (only Being in-itself is) but rather *has to be;* that is to say, in the perpetual act of escaping from undifferentiated Being in-itself, man exists. Since this is achieved by the complete freedom of man (there is nothing within or without man that can determine his activity), Sartre is an idealist. Existence is a subjective complement (or, as Sartre would have it, nullification), through man's thought and action, of Being in-itself. In Sartre, existence is identified with human existence, and man is made the measurer of all things. His philosophy is atheistic humanism.

There are many contradictions within the thought of Jean-Paul Sartre which need not detain us here. Since Being in-itself is absolutely independent of thought (Sartre wants to be something of a realist) and opposed to human consciousness, it hardly makes sense to describe it in intelligible terms, that is, as something massive, stable, uniquely itself, and so on. The simply unknowable is simply unknowable—Sartre has no right even to call it Being.

e. Conclusion

The student may be puzzled at the strange ambiguities, paradoxes, and contradictions in the thought of the radical existentialists. Most of them flow from a single source: the dislocation of the nature of being. There is a delicate balance and composition within being of existence and essence. The one is not the other. And to remove either is to doom metaphysics. Being without existence is Idealism, and we owe much to the existentialists for asserting the primacy of existence over essence. But being without essence is unintelligible continuity that can be described (and often brilliantly so) phenomenologically but which is impervious to our intelligence.

But if we remove essence from being why do we destroy its intelligibility since, even for St. Thomas, the root of intelligibility is the act of existing? The answer to this important question is found in the Thomistic notion of being. The Absolute for St. Thomas is God, a subsistent Act of Existing. In this Pure Act creatures share. Hence, creatures *have* being. Their existence is received in essence, and so their being is limited and composed. What we know, therefore, whether we know ourselves or other beings, is structured and composed. *What* we understand is *being*, not essence or existence, but the composite of the two.

But we know being because it is intelligible *in and through* its act of existing. *What* we know is being; *that by which* we know it is the act of existing. A thing is intelligible in the same way that it is. Now what is or exists is being, not the act of existing, although being exists by reason of this act. And so what is intelligible is being, not the act of existing, although being is intelligible through its act of existing. To remove essence is to destroy what exists: being. And this is to destroy what is intelligible.

Being without essence (which becomes existence without essence), is like light without anything lit, or sound without anything sounding, or like thinking without anything thought, or like motion without anything that moves. It is a metaphysical and (consequently) an epistemological contradiction. Radical existentialism, therefore, is not really a philosophy at all. It is not and cannot be a science of *being*. It is a phenomenology. That is to say, it touches through description, often brilliant and profound, the phenomena of an existent. But it does not understand its being. And only being is intelligible. And it is only with the reinsertion of essence that being can be regained for metaphysics. Then being becomes what it is—a finite participation in the Subsistent Existent that is God, a participation effected in the only way possible: by an act of existing being received in an essence.

APPENDIX E

Atheism

We will divide this discussion into three parts. In the first part we will clarify certain preliminary notions; in the second, we will give a brief history of atheism; and, finally, we will try to solve the problem of whether it is possible to be an atheist and what culpability is involved in being one. [1]

1. Some Preliminary Notions

In general, an atheist is one who says that there is no God. There are many different kinds of atheists. The practical atheist is one who lives and acts as though God did not exist, neither worshipping him nor paying any attention to his moral law. Unfortunately, there are in existence many practical atheists. But for them atheism is a way of life and not a philosophical position, and so they do not enter into our discussion here.

A theoretical atheist, on the other hand, is one who does have a philosophical position concerning God: he does not hold his existence. A theoretical atheist can be of two kinds: negative or positive. A negative atheist does not hold the existence of God, either because the thought of God has never entered his mind, and so he is simply ignorant of him; or if such a person has heard about a superior being, he has not deliberately or consciously reflected on what he has heard. A positive atheist, on the other hand, is one who denies the existence of God, having given deliberate reflection and attention to the matter. A practical atheist, therefore, is one

[1] See Gisquière, *Deus Dominus, op. cit.,* pp. 19–29. The treatment that follows is based on these pages.

who neglects God, a negative theoretical atheist is one who does not know God, and a positive theoretical atheist is one who denies God.

Positive theoretical atheism is opposed to deism and theism. While both deism and theism come from words meaning "God" (the Latin "*Deus*" and the Greek "*Theos*"), these two words have different meanings in English. A *deist* is one who believes in the existence of a personal God, and in this sense his position is opposed not only to atheism but also to pantheism. But a deist denies that God exercises providence over the world or that he has made any supernatural revelation to man. A deist, then, is one who believes in a circumscribed or limited sort of personal God. Some famous deists have been Rousseau and Voltaire in France, Hume in England, Lessing in Germany. A *theist*, on the other hand, usually means one who admits not only a personal God, but a God who has created the world, governs it, and who could make to man supernatural revelations.

2. A Brief History of Atheism

There have been atheists in the world from time immemorial. The early Greek materialists, men like Epicurus, Lucretius, Democritus, and Leucippus, in limiting all reality to material atoms, were really atheistic. But they rather ignored God than openly denied him. God was denied, however, by the poet-philosopher Diagoras, who seems to have been a disciple of Democritus. The atheism of this Greek arose from the consideration that in this world the innocent suffer while the wicked often go unpunished. Because of his teaching he was forced to flee from Athens. Protagoras, who made man the measure of all things and denied that there was any universal objective norm either for truth or for moral goodness, questioned the existence of God. Hence he was rather an agnostic than a true atheist. He, too, was forced to flee into exile and his works were publicly burned.

Theoretical atheism was rare in the Middle Ages. But starting with the sixteenth century it began to appear more frequently, especially with the advent of the literary Renaissance and the Reformation. The Renaissance abetted atheism indirectly, inasmuch as men neglected the study of theology and turned to purely philosophical and literary works. The influence of the Protestant Reformation on the progress of atheism was more direct, inasmuch as many of the Reformers vindicated for man a complete liberty in religious opinions. The myriad quarrels among the sects helped generate in some a rationalistic approach to religion and an atheistic frame of mind.

Among our contemporaries atheism takes different forms. Its most explicit and common form is the atheism of dialectic materialism as diffused in the philosophy of Communism. [2] The humanistic existentialism of Sartre, where man once more has become the measure of all things, is also atheistic. [3] The modern philosophical systems of idealism tend rather to be pantheistic than strictly atheistic.

3. On the Actual Existence of Atheists and Their Culpability

First of all, let us consider the problem of the negative atheist. A negative atheist is a man who, while enjoying the full use of reason and having attained to intellectual maturity, is nonetheless destitute of any conscious or deliberate knowledge of a being superior to man, and upon whom man somehow depends. We maintain that such a person cannot for a long period of time remain in such ignorance, at least not for his whole life.

After a person has reached the full use of his reason, he may perhaps for some time remain in ignorance concerning a being superior to himself, but he cannot persevere in this ignorance for a long time. We say this for two obvious reasons. First, if it is question of an adult living in the society of other adults, he will soon come to hear about God. For history proves that all people, even those we refer to as uncivilized, have some notion of a superior being. If, on the other hand, we imagine an adult who is cut off

[2] See *Acta Apostolicae Sedis*, 1932, pp. 177 ff.
[3] Jean-Paul Sartre, *Existentialism* (New York, Philosophical Library, 1947), pp. 18 ff.

from the intercourse of society, we maintain that the normal function of his own intellect will lead him to the knowledge of a superior being. The existence of the beings of his experience will lead his intellect naturally and spontaneously to suspect the existence of some superior being as the author of nature.

Now let us widen our discussion and ask ourselves this question: Is it possible for *any man* to pass his whole life in ignorance of the existence of God? And by "God" here we mean a being superior to man to whom man is related in the sense that he owes such a being obedience, and by whom he will be rewarded or punished for his actions. Experience seems to demand that we answer this question in the affirmative. Furthermore, if we ask ourselves whether it is also possible for some men who have been exposed to the idea of a true God, as understood in the sense just explained, not to make any explicit or conscious judgment concerning his real existence, we must again answer in the affirmative. Such ignorance of the true God is possible among men if we are to believe the evidence of history.

Now is such ignorance of God, which seems to be a fact, always able to be overcome? Is such ignorance always culpable? This is a very difficult and disputed question. The opinion among Christian writers up to the start of the present century was practically unanimous in denying the possibility that there could be such a thing as invincible and therefore inculpable ignorance in such a matter. No adult for a long period of time could inexcusably be in ignorance about the existence of the true God. However, in the last forty years writers of note have begun to question this opinion. [4]

The Jesuit Cardinal Billot, in a famous series of articles that he wrote for *Etudes* between the years 1919–1920, has gone further and stated that it is possible to have, and in fact there are, adults whose intellectual development never reaches the point where they possess a sufficient knowledge of their moral obligation, and who therefore are invincibly ignorant of the true God. Cardinal

[4] For example, Van Noort, in his *Tractatus de Deo Uno et Trino* (Amsterdam, 1907), p. 11.

Billot maintains the following: on the one hand, no one is capable of sin unless he knows the first principles of the moral order; and on the other, a knowledge of moral obligation includes an explicit knowledge of the existence of the true God. Hence, the ignorance such men have of God will always remain invincible and therefore inculpable.

Billot admits that such men, who while chronologically adults are really moral infants, have some knowledge of a superior being, but that this knowledge is so vague and unreflective, that it is insufficient to ground real moral obligation. The actual number of such men Billot leaves undetermined. But he seems to think that many such existed in a pagan culture. In point of fact, he implies that due to the little influx that education had in such a culture, this invincible ignorance of the true God was the condition of the average man.

Some authors today follow this opinion of Cardinal Billot. A few [5] even go further and apply this condition of ignorance to those who live in a state that is fairly developed culturally but completely laicized in its education. In such a society children never learn about God, except to hear him denied and condemned. Such a positively atheistic education, they say, impedes the acquisition of a knowledge of God that would be necessary for moral obligation, and hence culpability.

However, the majority of modern authors in one point or another disagree with Cardinal Billot. [6] First of all, they repeat the traditional doctrine, with which Cardinal Billot would certainly concur: an adult enjoying the use of reason in normal conditions of society cannot for a long time (at least all his life) remain invincibly and therefore inculpably ignorant of the existence of the true God. To say otherwise would contradict divine providence and the revealed theological doctrine of the universal salvific will of God. God desires all men to be saved, [7] but no man can be saved without knowledge of the existence of the true God.

[5] See Gisquière, Deus Dominus, op. cit., p. 26, note 21.

[6] See Descoqs, Praelectiones Theologiae Naturalis, op. cit., Vol. 2, pp. 459–465.

[7] See I Tim., Ch. 2, vs. 4.

These writers are willing to make exceptions, but not as sweeping as those of Billot. Some few individuals, due to an exceptional social and educational environment, can indeed go their whole lives inculpably ignorant of the true God; for they never acquire the sense of moral obligation and the intellectual maturity sufficient to make a correct or deliberate judgment concerning the existence of God. Just as God permits the existence of some feeble-minded and idiots (mental infants), so there seems no reason why he should not permit a certain number who never arrive at the age of moral reason (moral infants). In the case of these men, their ignorance of the existence of the true God remains invincible and hence inculpable all their lives. But, as against Billot, these writers say that the number of such moral infants is small, and is in no wise the normal condition of the human race.

4. Conclusion

In this discussion, two questions should be kept separate which these writers (Billot included) seem to confuse. The first is the one we are trying to answer: whether or not a person, because of special circumstances of environment and education, can pass his whole life invincibly ignorant of the true God. To this question we answer, yes. The second question is whether or not such a person would be incapable of *any* responsible moral activity, and be destitute of *all* sense of moral obligation. A person might know that good must be done and evil avoided even though he had no knowledge of the true God, even though he were a pagan who believed in the existence of many equal finite gods. There may be persons who are *complete* moral infants with *no sense* of moral obligation. And there may be a second class who are moral infants only as concerns the existence of the true God. The two classes are not necessarily co-extensive.

A complete moral infant would be one with no sense of moral obligation. Such a person would not know that good must be done and evil avoided. And only those entirely devoid of the use of reason are in such a condition. In the second class would be those who know that good must be done and evil avoided, but who are ignorant, for one reason or another, of the existence of the true God. Such persons would be morally responsible for the evil they do and know they should avoid, but they would not be responsible for the fact that they are ignorant of the existence of the true God. In other words, according to the position we are espousing here, a knowledge of the existence of the true God is not required for the presence of moral obligation. All that is required is that one knows the distinction between good and evil, with the accompanying knowledge that good must be done. And all who have the use of reason have this knowledge. Finally, there is a third question, which again does not concern us here: How does a person, endowed with a general sense of moral obligation but invincibly ignorant of the existence of the true God, attain salvation?

5. The Problem of the Positive Atheist

A positive theoretical atheist is one who deliberately and consciously denies the existence of God. Here we can distinguish three kinds of such atheists. The first class are those who are absolutely convinced, without the shadow of a doubt, of the nonexistence of God. The second class deny the existence of God, but not without some doubt in the matter. The third class's denial is also accompanied by some doubt, and this doubt remains permanent and constant all their lives.

We say that it is impossible for the first class of positive atheists to exist without culpability on their part. For there is no objective evidence or rational argument for atheism that could give rise to such an absolute undoubting assent of the mind and preserve the certitude of such an assent once it has arisen. Take, for example, the argument for atheism drawn from the existence of evil in the world. Over against such an argument can be placed the possibility of condign punishment and reward based upon the philosophical truth of the immortality of the soul. Since the soul is immortal, the souls of the wicked could suffer and those of the good be rewarded after the death of the body. Thus the problem of evil is no convincing argument against the existence of God.

Furthermore, all the arguments usually given for the existence of God should at least make the atheist doubt about his own position. Some writers indeed do not believe that this first class is sincere in their undoubting profession of atheism. Seneca, for example, writes: "They lie who say that they know there is no God; for while they may affirm it to you during the day, at night and when alone, they doubt it." [8] Father Descoqs, however, believes that such an undoubting atheism can be attained to and even sincerely persevered in during one's whole lifetime. But in its beginning, in its causes, this atheism was culpable and mixed with doubt. For example, he writes:

> Experience shows that false arguments, continually accepted and unresolved, involving as they do on the part of man a constant rejection of the light and of the truth, can produce in a person a hardness of heart and a blindness of intellect. This hardness and blindness can psychologically expel all fear and render man inept for the further reception of truth, even up to death. [9]

How else are we to explain the case of certain atheists who seem completely at peace with their atheism and who are otherwise sincere and good men? Psychologically, error long persevered in can come to be accepted by some as undoubted truth. The guilt of these atheists consists in having allowed themselves to reach such a tragic and fearful condition.

Concerning the second class of positive atheists, those who for a time seriously doubt the existence of God, experience and reason itself indicate that such atheists can exist and exist without fault on their part. It is entirely possible that a person, educated in a false philosophy, can have presented to him, in a clear and forceful manner, serious objections against the traditional proofs for God's existence. On the other hand, the proofs themselves may be improperly understood and not grasped in their true scientific value. Such a person could seriously and without fault doubt about the existence of the true God.

As we have seen, the truth that God exists is not self-evident for

[8] See *De Ira,* Book 1.
[9] Descoqs, *op. cit.,* Vol. 2, p. 480.

man. He must reason to it through the mediation of objective evidence. And where such evidence is not correctly understood or evaluated, there always remains room for doubt. The traditional arguments from causality do conclude to the existence of a supreme Being with absolute scientific rigor, but only for a person who understands the metaphysics upon which such proofs are based. The objections against the traditional proofs, drawn from a Kantian or Nominalistic philosophy, can be put so strongly and clearly that a student who would have otherwise been convinced of the proofs if these objections had not been urged, will now be convinced of them only if he possesses a profound grasp of the *metaphysics of being* that they presuppose. There is nothing easier than to make a Kantian shambles (in the mind of the student) of the five ways of St. Thomas; and there is nothing harder than to generate (again, in the intellect of the student) a true metaphysic of being that can alone dispel the objections.

Thus a person, through no fault of his own, can be a positive atheist of the second class. That is, he can positively doubt about the existence of God for some period of time. But such a person cannot remain permanently in this state of doubt. The third class of positive atheists, the permanent doubter, is impossible without culpability. For one who has doubts in a matter of such importance is bound in conscience to settle his doubt. Just as, for example, a parent who doubts whether a gun is loaded or not, is conscience-bound to remove that doubt before he allows his child to play with the gun. Whether there is a God or not is of the utmost importance to the life of man. If he doubts about God's existence, he is conscience-bound to remove it. And this doubt can be removed in favor of God's existence. For while atheism cannot be demonstrated, the existence of God can. [10]

[10] On the problem of contemporary atheism, the student should read Jacques Maritain's essay, "The Meaning of Contemporary Atheism," in *The Range of Reason* (New York, Charles Scribner's Sons, 1952), pp. 103-117.

APPENDIX F

Man's Natural Desire for the Beatific Vision

We have seen that man in this life cannot naturally know the essence of God in itself, but only as it is manifested through creatures. To know the essence of God as it is in itself is to have the Beatific Vision. Hence, it is impossible for man in this life to have the Beatific Vision. But theologians often speak of a natural desire in man for the Beatific Vision, a desire to see God as he is in himself. Is this true? Is there such a desire in man, and if so, how is it to be understood? The literature on this subject is as vast at it is confusing. [1] In this Appendix we will do two things: first, explain a text in St. Thomas that seems to have given rise to most of the difficulties; and, secondly, briefly discuss the problem independently of any text.

1. The Text of St. Thomas

In the *Summa Theologiae*, first part, twelfth question, article one, St. Thomas asks himself this question: Can any created intellect see the essence of God? He answers that it can, and his third proof is as follows: "There is in man a natural desire to know the cause, when he understands the effect. It is in this way that wonder

---

[1] For two of the better contributions in English, see L. E. O'Mahony, *The Desire of God in the Philosophy of St. Thomas Aquinas* (London, 1929), and W. R. O'Connor, *The Eternal Quest* (New York, 1947). The latter work has a rather complete bibliography (pp. 276–285). Our treatment here follows the explanation of Bañes. See *Scholastica Commentaria*, Rome, 1583, pp. 237–241.

arises in man. And so, if the intellect of a rational creature could not attain to the first cause of things, this natural desire would be in vain. Therefore, we must concede that the blessed see the essence of God." [2]

The text itself is easy enough to explain. St. Thomas is here speaking as a sacred theologian. He is not trying to demonstrate through reason alone that there exists in man a natural desire to see the essence of God. Rather, as is clear from the context, he argues as follows: our faith tells us that the Beatific Vision is possible, since we know that the blessed do see God face to face. Now this vision is compatible with a created intellect. Then St. Thomas adduces a probable reason to show why it is: the desire men have to know causes once they know the effect. This is simply another instance where St. Thomas adduces probable reasons to show that the mysteries of our faith are compatible with our nature and do not contradict it.

He does the same thing, for example, in the *Summa contra Gentiles* (Book IV, chapter 79), where he shows how the resurrection from the dead is possible. The soul is the form of the body, and so is naturally inclined toward the body. And since in the resurrection from the dead, the soul revivifies the body, this act is compatible with human nature and is not impossible. The argument does not prove that the resurrection is a fact. It simply proves that once we know from revelation the fact of the resurrection, reason sees that it is possible and compatible with our nature.

Here, too, in our text on the natural desire, St. Thomas argues the same way. There is in the rational creature a certain wish or desire to see God. Therefore, reason concludes, it is probable that the vision of God is possible for man, lest this natural desire be in vain. Faith tells us such a vision is possible, since the blessed do have it. Reason tells us that such a vision is not repugnant to our nature but compatible with it. But reason tells us this only after the fact is known through revelation. This is all St. Thomas seems to be saying here.

[2] *S.T.*, I, 12, 1.

2. Man's Natural Desire for the Vision of God

But independently of the text, let us ask ourselves these two questions: Does man have a natural desire to see God as he is in himself? And is God, thus seen, the natural end of man? We will answer the questions by way of four conclusions.

a. The vision of God according to his essence is not the natural end of man.

A natural end is one that a thing can attain of itself, because of its very nature. Thus to burn is the natural end of fire. To know is the natural end of the intellect, and to love is the natural end of the will. But man, by his nature, cannot see the essence of God in itself. Such a vision is not connatural to man, and no theologian teaches that it is the natural end of man.

b. But man has a natural desire to see God.

This desire is distinct from and not identified with the nature of man. Hence, it is an act. But it is an act that is elicited by the natural powers of man. Hence, it is a natural desire. Finally, this elicited natural desire to see God is conditioned and inefficacious. Let us briefly explain each of these points.

When man sees some effect there arises in him a natural desire to know its cause. This desire, while natural, is elicited; that is to say, it is not identified with man's nature, as, for example, the natural desire of the intellect for truth is identified with the nature of the intellect. Rather, this desire to know the cause is an act produced by man's nature. Seeing the effect, man now *wants* to see the cause. It is a definite elicited act about a definite cause. From a knowledge of the effect there is naturally elicited in man a desire to know the cause.

All this is simple fact, easily confirmed by experience. Man naturally desires to understand that of which he knows he is ignorant. But man can naturally prove that God exists, and that he is Pure Act and Perfect Being. Man naturally desires to know what God is. And were we to ask a man who knows God whether he desires to see God, he would reply that he does. Such a desire is therefore present and man has elicited it. This is what we are saying in the first part of this second conclusion: man can, and often does, actually have this desire to see God, a desire that brute animals cannot have because they do not know God.

But in the second half of our conclusion we say that this actual, elicited, natural desire to see God is conditioned and inefficacious. First of all, it is conditioned, at least implicitly. For man does not know whether such a desire is possible of fulfillment through the forces of his own nature. Thus, at least implicitly, his desire is conditioned; that is, man desires to see God *if such a thing is possible*. A simple example will clarify our meaning. A man may desire to live forever, if this is possible. And even though this condition (if it be possible) is not explicitly in his mind, it is nonetheless contained implicitly in the very object of his desire. To live forever is a *good* object, and so man can *desire* it; but it is an object impossible of attainment, and so man's desire for it is inefficacious. When an object is seen simply as good, man can desire it; if it is seen further as possible, man can hope for it. But if he sees or is told that the object of his desire is impossible of attainment, man no longer hopes for it, although the desire may still remain. In this sense the desire is inefficacious. And so it is with the conditioned and inefficacious natural desire we have to see God.

But supposing a man thought that the vision of God were naturally possible? Would he not then desire it absolutely and not conditionally? We answer that such an absolute desire could be present, and that a man could even place those acts which he thought were naturally necessary to attain the vision of God. But this desire could no longer be called natural. For such a person would be in error. And a natural desire is one that is placed according to the natural light of reason, and does not go against that light. Because it is out of error and ignorance that such a man desires and acts, the desire is no longer according to nature (that is, reason) but contrary to it, and so it is not natural. Again, an example may help here. Suppose a man who was desirous of living forever were to prepare certain medicines that he thought could keep him alive forever. He would be going against reason, and so his desire would become unnatural.

Of course, it goes without saying that if a man thought it were possible to see God's essence through grace, he would have a true absolute desire. For now it is from grace, and not from the forces of his nature, that he knows that both the end and the means to the end are possible.

c. Man has no natural potency for the Beatific Vision.

Properly speaking, there is within man neither a natural *inclination* nor a natural *aptitude* to see God as he is in himself. In a word, there is no appetite or potency, identified with man's nature, for the Beatific Vision. This is made clear from the following consideration. Nature is the principle of operation. Whatever belongs to a thing because of its proper nature is able to be reduced to act by a natural agent. For example, matter has a natural inclination for material forms, since these can be educed through the efficiency of natural agents. [3] But as we know, man cannot attain to the Beatific Vision through his own nature or through all the forces of the whole of nature. Indeed, man cannot attain to this vision even through the power of God as the author of nature, but only through God as the author of grace. Since no natural power can actually give man the Beatific Vision, it follows that there is in man no natural potency or capacity for this vision.

In the third part of the *Summa* (*S.T.*, III, 4, 1.), St. Thomas gives another proof that man has no natural aptitude to see God in himself. Here the saint teaches that an aptitude that is according to a natural passive potency does not extend to what transcends nature. But the Beatific Vision of God transcends nature. Therefore, there is in man no natural passive potency for the Beatific Vision. A *fortiori* there is in man no natural active potency for this vision. This would mean that man could see God through the natural light of his intellect.

[3] See *S.T.*, I, 7, 2, ad 3m.

d. There is in man an obediential potency for the Beatific Vision

There is, however, in man a capacity of nature, called obediential, because of which he can be elevated by God to a vision of his essence. What is an obediential potency? It is a capacity within a nature, because of which that nature can be ordered to an agent that essentially transcends it. "Obediential potency" is an analogous term, and hence applied differently to different orders. For example, wood has a natural potency to burn, but an obediential potency to become a statue. Air, on the other hand, has no such obediential potency to become a statue. Again, a stone has no obediential potency for the Beatific Vision. Even God could not give a stone such an operation. For it would cease to be a stone, since it would become rational and intellectual. Nor could God raise any irrational animal to a vision of his essence.

But God, through his grace (the *lumen gloriae*), can raise man to the Beatific Vision. And so there is in man a natural but obediential capacity for this vision, for this elevation of nature through grace, a capacity not found in any irrational creature. The nature of man is not destroyed, but perfected, through this elevation. St. Thomas describes this obediential potency for the vision of God in the *Summa* (I-II, 113, 10.), where he says that the soul, insofar as it is made to the image of God, is naturally capable of grace.

St. Thomas sometimes asserts that the Beatific Vision of God is according to the nature of man by reason of this capacity. For example, he writes in the *Summa* (III, 9, 2, ad 3m) that this vision (the *scientia beata*) is *above* the nature of the rational soul inasmuch as it cannot attain to it by reason of its own proper power. But it is *according* to the nature of the soul inasmuch as it is made to the image and likeness of God.

Index